The Apocrypha

The Apocrypha

FORTRESS COMMENTARY ON THE BIBLE STUDY EDITION

Gale A. Yee
Hugh R. Page Jr.
Matthew J. M. Coomber
Editors

Fortress Press
Minneapolis

THE APOCRYPHA

Fortress Commentary on the Bible Study Edition

Excerpted from the *Fortress Commentary on the Bible: The Old Testament and Apocrypha*
(Minneapolis: Fortress Press, 2014); Gale A. Yee, Hugh R. Page Jr., and Matthew J. M. Coomber, volume editors.

Fortress Press Publication Staff:
Neil Elliott and Scott Tunseth, Project Editors
Marissa Wold, Production Manager
Laurie Ingram, Cover Design.

Copyeditor: Jeffrey A. Reimer

Typesetter: PerfecType, Nashville, TN

Proofreader: David Cottingham

Library of Congress Cataloging-in-Publication data is available

ISBN: 978-1-5064-1587-1

eISBN: 978-1-5064-1588

CONTENTS

PUBLISHER'S NOTE

About the Fortress Commentary on the Bible Study Editions

In 2014 Fortress Press released the two-volume *Fortress Commentary on the Bible*. See the Series Introduction (pp. 1–3) for a look inside the creation and design of the Old Testament/Apocrypha and New Testament volumes. While each comprehensive commentary volume can easily be used in classroom settings, we also recognized that dividing the larger commentaries into smaller volumes featuring key sections of Scripture may be especially helpful for use in corresponding biblical studies courses. To help facilitate such classroom use, we have broken the two-volume commentary into eight study editions.

Please note that in this study edition the page numbers match the page numbers of the larger Fortress Commentary on the Bible volume in which it first appeared. We have intentionally retained the same page numbering to facilitate use of the study editions and larger volumes side by side.

The Apocrypha was first published in Fortress Commentary on the Bible: The Old Testament and Apocrypha.

ABBREVIATIONS

General

AT	Alpha Text (of the Greek text of Esther)
BOI	Book of Isaiah
Chr	Chronicler
DH	Deuteronomistic History
DI	Deutero-Isaiah
Dtr	Deuteronomist
Gk.	Greek
H	Holiness Code
Heb.	Hebrew
JPS	Jewish Publication Society
LXX	The Septuagint
LXX B	Vaticanus Text of the Septuagint
MP	Mode of production
MT	Masoretic Text
NIV	New International Version
NRSV	New Revised Standard Version
OAN	Oracles against Nations (in Jeremiah)
P.	papyrus/papyri
P	Priestly source
PE	Pastoral Epistles
RSV	Revised Standard Version
TI	Trito-Isaiah

Books of the Bible (NT, OT, Apocrypha)

Old Testament/Hebrew Bible

Gen.	Genesis
Exod.	Exodus
Lev.	Leviticus
Num.	Numbers
Deut.	Deuteronomy

Josh.	Joshua
Judg.	Judges
Ruth	Ruth
1 Sam.	1 Samuel
2 Sam.	2 Samuel
1 Kgs.	1 Kings
2 Kgs.	2 Kings
1 Chron.	1 Chronicles
2 Chron.	2 Chronicles
Ezra	Ezra
Neh.	Nehemiah
Esther	Esther
Job	Job
Ps. (Pss.)	Psalms
Prov.	Proverbs
Eccles.	Ecclesiastes
Song.	Song of Songs
Isa.	Isaiah
Jer.	Jeremiah
Lam.	Lamentations
Ezek.	Ezekiel
Dan.	Daniel
Hosea	Hosea
Joel	Joel
Amos	Amos
Obad.	Obadiah
Jon.	Jonah
Mic.	Micah
Nah.	Nahum
Hab.	Habakkuk
Zeph.	Zephaniah
Hag.	Haggai
Zech.	Zechariah
Mal.	Malachi

Apocrypha

Tob.	Tobit
Jth.	Judith
Gk. Esther	Greek Additions to Esther
Sir.	Sirach (Ecclesiasticus)

Bar.	Baruch
Let. Jer.	Letter of Jeremiah
Add Dan.	Additions to Daniel
Pr. Azar.	Prayer of Azariah
Sg. Three.	Song of the Three Young Men (or Three Jews)
Sus.	Susanna
Bel	Bel and the Dragon
1 Macc.	1 Maccabees
2 Macc.	2 Maccabees
1 Esd.	1 Esdras
Pr. of Man.	Prayer of Manasseh
2 Esd.	2 Esdras
Wis.	Wisdom of Solomon
3 Macc.	3 Maccabees
4 Macc.	4 Maccabees

New Testament

Matt.	Matthew
Mark	Mark
Luke	Luke
John	John
Acts	Acts of the Apostles
Rom.	Romans
1 Cor.	1 Corinthians
2 Cor.	2 Corinthians
Gal.	Galatians
Eph.	Ephesians
Phil.	Philippians
Col.	Colossians
1 Thess.	1 Thessalonians
2 Thess.	2 Thessalonians
1 Tim.	1 Timothy
2 Tim.	2 Timothy
Titus	Titus
Philem.	Philemon
Heb.	Hebrews
James	James
1 Pet.	1 Peter
2 Pet.	2 Peter
1 John	1 John

2 John	2 John
3 John	3 John
Jude	Jude
Rev.	Revelation (Apocalypse)

Journals, Series, Reference Works

ABD	*Anchor Bible Dictionary*. Edited by David Noel Freedman. 6 vols. New York: Doubleday, 1992.
ACNT	Augsburg Commentaries on the New Testament
AJA	*American Journal of Archaeology*
AJT	*Asia Journal of Theology*
ANET	*Ancient Near Eastern Texts Relating to the Old Testament.* Edited by J. B. Pritchard. 3rd ed. Princeton: Princeton University Press, 1969.
ANF	*The Ante-Nicene Fathers.* Edited by Alexander Roberts and James Donaldson. 1885–1887. 10 vols. Repr., Peabody, MA: Hendrickson, 1994.
ANRW	*Aufstieg und Niedergang der römischen Welt: Geschichte und Kultur Roms im Spiegel der neueren Forschung.* Edited by Hildegard Temporini and Wolfgang Haase. Berlin: de Gruyter, 1972–.
ANTC	Abingdon New Testament Commentaries
AOAT	Alter Orient und Altes Testament
AbOTC	Abingdon Old Testament Commentary
AOTC	Apollos Old Testament Commentary
A(Y)B	Anchor (Yale) Bible
BA	*Biblical Archaeologist*
BAR	*Biblical Archaeology Review*
BDAG	Bauer, W., F. W. Danker, W. F. Arndt, and F. W. Gingrich. *Greek-English Lexicon of the New Testament and Other Early Christian Literature.* 3rd ed. Chicago: University of Chicago Press, 1999.
BEATAJ	Beiträge zur Erforschung des Alten Testaments und des Antiken Judentum
Bib	*Biblica*
BibInt	*Biblical Interpretation*
BJRL	*Bulletin of the John Rylands University Library of Manchester*
BJS	Brown Judaic Studies
BNTC	Black's New Testament Commentaries
BR	*Biblical Research*
BRev	*Bible Review*
BSac	*Bibliotheca sacra*
BTB	*Biblical Theology Bulletin*
BZAW	Beihefte zur Zeitschrift für die alttestamentliche Wissenschaft
CAT	Commentaire de l'Ancien Testament

CBC	Cambridge Bible Commentary
CBQMS	Catholic Biblical Quarterly Monograph Series
CC	Continental Commentaries
CH	*Church History*
CHJ	*Cambridge History of Judaism*. Edited by W. D. Davies and Louis Finkelstein. Cambridge: Cambridge University Press, 1984–.
ConBNT	Coniectanea biblica: New Testament Series
ConBOT	Coniectanea biblica: Old Testament Series
CS	Cistercian Studies
CTAED	*Canaanite Toponyms in Ancient Egyptian Documents*. S. Ahituv. Jerusalem: Magnes, 1984.
CTQ	*Concordia Theological Quarterly*
CurTM	*Currents in Theology and Mission*
ExpTim	*Expository Times*
ETL	*Ephemerides Theologicae Lovanienses*
ExAud	*Ex auditu*
FAT	Forschungen zum Alten Testament
FC	Fathers of the Church
FRLANT	Forschungen zur Religion und Literatur des Alten und Neuen Testaments
HAT	Handbuch zum Alten Testament
HBT	*Horizons in Biblical Theology*
HNTC	Harper's New Testament Commentaries
HR	*History of Religions*
HSM	Harvard Semitic Monographs
HTKAT	Herders Theologischer Kommentar zum Alten Testament
HTR	*Harvard Theological Review*
HTS	Harvard Theological Studies
HUCA	*Hebrew Union College Annual*
HUCM	Monographs of the Hebrew Union College
HUT	Hermeneutische Untersuchungen zur Theologie
IBC	Interpretation: A Bible Commentary for Teaching and Preaching
ICC	International Critical Commentary
Int	*Interpretation*
JAAR	*Journal of the American Academy of Religion*
JAOS	*Journal of the American Oriental Society*
JBL	*Journal of Biblical Literature*
JBQ	*Jewish Bible Quarterly*
JECS	*Journal of Early Christian Studies*
JJS	*Journal of Jewish Studies*
JNES	*Journal of Near Eastern Studies*

JNSL	*Journal of Northwest Semitic Languages*
JQR	*Jewish Quarterly Review*
JRS	*Journal of Roman Studies*
JSem	*Journal of Semitics*
JSJ	*Journal for the Study of Judaism in the Persian, Hellenistic, and Roman Periods*
JSNT	*Journal for the Study of the New Testament*
JSOT	*Journal for the Study of the Old Testament*
JSOTSup	Journal for the Study of the Old Testament Supplement Series
JSQ	*Jewish Studies Quarterly*
JSS	*Journal of Semitic Studies*
JTI	*Journal of Theological Interpretation*
JTS	*Journal of Theological Studies*
JTSA	*Journal of Theology for Southern Africa*
KTU	*Die keilalphabetischen Texte aus Ugarit.* Edited by M. Dietrich, O. Loretz, and J. Sanmartín. AOAT 24/1. Neukirchen-Vluyn: Neukirchener, 1976.
LCC	Loeb Classical Library
LEC	Library of Early Christianity
LHB/OTS	Library of the Hebrew Bible/Old Testament Studies
LW	*Luther's Works.* Edited by Jaroslav Pelikan and Helmut T. Lehmann. 55 vols. St. Louis: Concordia; Philadelphia: Fortress Press, 1958–1986.
NAC	New American Commentary
NCB	New Century Bible
NCBC	New Cambridge Bible Commentary
NedTT	*Nederlands theologisch tijdschrift*
Neot	*Neotestamentica*
NICNT	New International Commentary on the New Testament
NICOT	New International Commentary on the Old Testament
NIGTC	New International Greek Testament Commentary
NovT	*Novum Testamentum*
NPNF^{1}	*The Nicene and Post-Nicene Fathers*, Series 1. Edited by Philip Schaff. 14 vols. 1886–1889. Repr., Grand Rapids: Eerdmans, 1956.
NTL	New Testament Library
NTS	*New Testament Studies*
OBT	Overtures to Biblical Theology
OTE	*Old Testament Essays*
OTG	Old Testament Guides
OTL	Old Testament Library
OTM	Old Testament Message
PEQ	*Palestine Exploration Quarterly*
PG	Patrologia graeca [= Patrologiae cursus completus: Series graeca]. Edited by J.-P. Migne. 162 vols. Paris, 1857–1886.

PL	John Milton, *Paradise Lost*
PL	Patrologia latina [= Patrologiae cursus completus: Series latina]. Edited by J.-P. Migne. 217 vols. Paris, 1844–1864.
PRSt	*Perspectives in Religious Studies*
QR	*Quarterly Review*
RevExp	*Review and Expositor*
RevQ	*Revue de Qumran*
SBLABS	Society of Biblical Literature Archaeology and Biblical Studies
SBLAIL	Society of Biblical Literature Ancient Israel and Its Literature
SBLDS	Society of Biblical Literature Dissertation Series
SBLEJL	Society of Biblical Literature Early Judaism and Its Literature
SBLMS	Society of Biblical Literature Monograph Series
SBLRBS	Society of Biblical Literature Resources for Biblical Study
SBLSCS	Society of Biblical Literature Septuagint and Cognate Studies
SBLSP	*Society of Biblical Literature Seminar Papers*
SBLSymS	Society of Biblical Literature Symposium Series
SBLWAW	SBL Writings from the Ancient World
SemeiaSt	Semeia Studies
SJT	*Scottish Journal of Theology*
SNTSMS	Society for New Testament Studies Monograph Series
SO	Symbolae osloenses
SR	*Studies in Religion*
ST	*Studia Theologica*
StABH	Studies in American Biblical Hermeneutics
TD	*Theology Digest*
TAD	*Textbook of Aramaic Documents from Ancient Egypt.* Vol. 1: *Letters.* Bezalel Porten and Ada Yardeni. Winona Lake, IN: Eisenbrauns, 1986.
TDOT	*Theological Dictionary of the Old Testament.* 15 vols. Edited by G. Johannes Botterweck, Helmer Ringgren, and Heinz-Josef Fabry. Translated by David E. Green and Douglas W. Stott. Grand Rapids: Eerdmans, 1974–1995.
TJT	*Toronto Journal of Theology*
TNTC	Tyndale New Testament Commentaries
TOTC	Tyndale Old Testament Commentaries
TS	*Theological Studies*
TZ	*Theologische Zeitschrift*
VE	*Vox evangelica*
VT	*Vetus Testamentum*
VTSup	Supplements to Vetus Testamentum
WBC	Word Biblical Commentary
WSA	Works of St. Augustine: A Translation for the Twenty-First Century
WUANT	Wissenschaftliche Untersuchungen zum Alten und Neuen Testament

WUNT	Wissenschaftliche Untersuchungen zum Neuen Testament
WW	*Word and World*
ZAW	*Zeitschrift für die alttestamentliche Wissenschaft*
ZBK	Zürcher Bibelkommentare
ZNW	*Zeitschrift für die neutestamentliche Wissenschaft und die Kunde der älteren Kirche*

Ancient Authors and Texts

1 Clem.	*1 Clement*
2 Clem.	*2 Clement*
1 En.	*1 Enoch*
2 Bar.	*2 Baruch*
Abot R. Nat.	*Abot de Rabbi Nathan*
Ambrose	
Paen.	*De paenitentia*
Aristotle	
Ath. Pol.	*Athēnaīn politeia*
Nic. Eth.	*Nicomachean Ethics*
Pol.	*Politics*
Rhet.	*Rhetoric*
Augustine	
FC 79	*Tractates on the Gospel of John, 11–27.* Translated by John W. Rettig. Fathers of the Church 79. Washington, DC: Catholic University of America Press, 1988.
Tract. Ev. Jo.	*In Evangelium Johannis tractatus*
Bede, Venerable	
CS 117	*Commentary on the Acts of the Apostles.* Translated by Lawrence T. Martin. Cistercian Studies 117. Kalamazoo, MI: Cistercian Publications, 1989.
Barn.	*Barnabas*
CD	Cairo Genizah copy of the Damascus Document
Cicero	
De or.	*De oratore*
Tusc.	*Tusculanae disputationes*
Clement of Alexandria	
Paed.	*Paedogogus*
Strom.	*Stromata*
Cyril of Jerusalem	
Cat. Lect.	*Catechetical Lectures*
Dio Cassius	
Hist.	*Roman History*

Dio Chrysostom
Or. *Orations*
Diog. *Diognetus*
Dionysius of Halicarnassus
Thuc. *De Thucydide*
Epictetus
Diatr. *Diatribai (Dissertationes)*
Ench. *Enchiridion*
Epiphanius
Pan. *Panarion (Adversus Haereses)*
Eusebius of Caesarea
Hist. eccl. *Historia ecclesiastica*
Gos. Thom. *Gospel of Thomas*
Herodotus
Hist. *Historiae*
Hermas, *Shepherd*
Mand. *Mandates*
Sim. *Similitudes*
Homer
Il. *Iliad*
Od. *Odyssey*
Ignatius of Antioch
Eph. *To the Ephesians*
Smyr. *To the Smyrnaeans*
Irenaeus
Adv. haer. *Adversus haereses*
Jerome
Vir. ill. *De viris illustribus*
John Chrysostom
Hom. 1 Cor. *Homiliae in epistulam i ad Corinthios*
Hom. Act. *Homiliae in Acta apostolorum*
Hom. Heb. *Homiliae in epistulam ad Hebraeos*
Josephus
Ant. *Jewish Antiquities*
Ag. Ap. *Against Apion*
J.W. *Jewish War*
Jub. *Jubilees*
Justin Martyr
Dial. *Dialogue with Trypho*
1 Apol. *First Apology*

L.A.E.	*Life of Adam and Eve*
Liv. Pro.	*Lives of the Prophets*
Lucian	
Alex.	*Alexander (Pseudomantis)*
Phal.	*Phalaris*
Mart. Pol.	*Martyrdom of Polycarp*
Novatian	
Trin.	*De trinitate*
Origen	
C. Cels.	*Contra Celsum*
Comm. Jo.	*Commentarii in evangelium Joannis*
De princ.	*De principiis*
Hom. Exod.	*Homiliae in Exodum*
Hom. Jer.	*Homiliae in Jeremiam*
Hom. Josh.	*Homilies on Joshua*
Pausanias	
Descr.	*Description of Greece*
Philo	
Cher.	*De cherubim*
Decal.	*De decalogo*
Dreams	*On Dreams*
Embassy	*On the Embassy to Gaius (= Legat.)*
Fug.	*De fuga et inventione*
Leg.	*Legum allegoriae*
Legat.	*Legatio ad Gaium*
Migr.	*De migratione Abrahami*
Mos.	*De vita Mosis*
Opif.	*De opificio mundi*
Post.	*De posteritate Caini*
Prob.	*Quod omnis probus liber sit*
QE	*Quaestiones et solutiones in Exodum*
QG	*Quaestiones et solutiones in Genesin*
Spec. Laws	*On the Special Laws*
Plato	
Gorg.	*Gorgias*
Plutarch	
Mor.	*Moralia*
Mulier. virt.	*Mulierum virtutes*
Polycarp	
Phil.	*To the Philippians*

Ps.-Clem. Rec.	*Pseudo-Clementine Recognitions*
Pss. Sol.	*Psalms of Solomon*
Pseudo-Philo	
L.A.B.	*Liber antiquitatum biblicarum*
Seneca	
Ben.	*De beneficiis*
Strabo	
Geog.	*Geographica*
Tatian	
Ad gr.	*Oratio ad Graecos*
Tertullian	
Praescr.	*De praescriptione haereticorum*
Prax.	*Adversus Praxean*
Bapt.	*De baptismo*
De an.	*De anima*
Pud.	*De pudicitia*
Virg.	*De virginibus velandis*
Virgil	
Aen.	*Aeneid*
Xenophon	
Oec.	*Oeconomicus*

Mishnah, Talmud, Targum

b. B. Bat.	*Babylonian Talmudic tractate Baba Batra*
b. Ber.	*Babylonian Talmudic tractate Berakhot*
b Erub.	*Babylonian Talmudic tractate Erubim*
b. Ketub.	*Babylonian Talmudic tractate Ketubbot*
b. Mak.	*Babylonian Talmudic tractate Makkot*
b. Meg.	*Babylonian Talmudic tractate Megillah*
b. Ned.	*Babylonian Talmudic tractate Nedarim*
b. Naz.	*Babylonian Talmudic tractate Nazir*
b. Sanh.	*Babylonian Talmudic tractate Sanhedrin*
b. Shab.	*Babylonian Talmudic tractate Shabbat*
b. Sotah	*Babylonian Talmudic tractate Sotah*
b. Ta'an.	*Babylonian Talmudic tractate Ta'anit*
b. Yev.	*Babylonian Talmudic tractate Yevamot*
b. Yoma	*Babylonian Talmudic tractate Yoma*
Eccl. Rab.	*Ecclesiastes Rabbah*
Exod. Rab.	*Exodus Rabbah*
Gen. Rab.	*Genesis Rabbah*

Lam. Rab.	*Lamentations Rabbah*
Lev. R(ab).	*Leviticus Rabbah*
m. Abot	*Mishnah tractate Abot*
m. Bik.	*Mishnah tractate Bikkurim*
m. Demai	*Mishnah tractate Demai*
m. 'Ed.	*Mishnah tractate 'Eduyyot*
m. Git.	*Mishnah tractate Gittin*
m. Pesaḥ	*Mishnah tractate Pesaḥim*
m. Šeqal.	*Mishnah tractate Šeqalim (Shekalim)*
m. Shab.	*Mishnah tractate Shabbat*
m. Sotah	*Mishnah tractate Sotah*
m. Ta'an.	*Mishnah tractate Ta'anit*
m. Tamid	*Mishnah tractate Tamid*
m. Yad.	*Mishnah tractate Yadayim*
m. Yebam.	*Mishnah tractate Yebamot*
m. Yoma	*Mishnah tractate Yoma*
Num. Rab.	*Numbers Rabbah*
Pesiq. Rab.	*Pesiqta Rabbati*
Pesiq. Rab Kah.	*Pesiqta Rab Kahana*
S. 'Olam Rab.	*Seder 'Olam Rabbah*
Song Rab.	*Song of Songs Rabbah*
t. Hul.	*Tosefta tractate Hullin*
Tg. Onq.	*Targum Onqelos*
Tg. Jer.	*Targum Jeremiah*
y. Hag.	*Jerusalem Talmudic tractate Hagiga*
y. Pesaḥ	*Jerusalem Talmudic tractate Pesaḥim*
y. Sanh.	*Jerusalem Talmudic tractate Sanhedrin*

Dead Sea Scrolls

1QapGen	*Genesis apocryphon* (Excavated frags. from cave)
1QM	*War Scroll*
1QpHab	*Pesher Habakkuk*
1QS	*Rule of the Community*
1QSb	*Rule of the Blessings* (Appendix b to 1QS)
1Q21	*T. Levi*, aramaic
4Q184	Wiles of the Wicked Woman
4Q214	Levi[d] ar (*olim* part of Levi[b])
4Q214b	Levi[f] ar (*olim* part of Levi[b])
4Q226	psJub[b] (4Q *pseudo-Jubilees*)
4Q274	Tohorot A

4Q277	Tohorot B[b] (*olim* B[c])
4Q525	*Beatitudes*
4QMMT	*Miqṣat Maʿaśê ha-Torah*
4QpNah/4Q169	4Q Pesher Nahum
4Q82	*The Greek Minor Prophets Scroll*

Old Testament Pseudepigrapha

1 En.	*1 Enoch*
2 En.	*2 Enoch*
Odes Sol.	*Odes of Solomon*
Syr. Men.	*Sentences of the Syriac Menander*
T. Levi	*Testament of Levi*
T. Mos.	*Testament of Moses*
T. Sim.	*Testament of Simeon*

INTRODUCTION

The *Fortress Commentary on the Bible*, presented in two volumes, seeks to invite study and conversation about an ancient text that is both complex and compelling. As biblical scholars, we wish students of the Bible to gain a respect for the antiquity and cultural remoteness of the biblical texts and to grapple for themselves with the variety of their possible meanings; to fathom a long history of interpretation in which the Bible has been wielded for causes both beneficial and harmful; and to develop their own skills and voices as responsible interpreters, aware of their own social locations in relationships of privilege and power. With this in mind, the *Fortress Commentary on the Bible* offers general readers an informed and accessible resource for understanding the biblical writings in their ancient contexts; for recognizing how the texts have come down to us through the mediation of different interpretive traditions; and for engaging current discussion of the Bible's sometimes perplexing, sometimes ambivalent, but always influential legacy in the contemporary world. The commentary is designed not only to inform but also to invite and empower readers as active interpreters of the Bible in their own right.

The editors and contributors to these volumes are scholars and teachers who are committed to helping students engage the Bible in the classroom. Many also work as leaders, both lay and ordained, in religious communities, and wish this commentary to prove useful for informing congregational life in clear, meaningful, and respectful ways. We also understand the work of biblical interpretation as a responsibility far wider than the bounds of any religious community. In this regard, we participate in many and diverse identities and social locations, yet we all are conscious of reading, studying, and hearing the Bible today as citizens of a complex and interconnected world. We recognize in the Bible one of the most important legacies of human culture; its historical and literary interpretation is of profound interest to religious and nonreligious peoples alike.

Often, the academic interpretation of the Bible has moved from close study of the remote ancient world to the rarefied controversy of scholarly debate, with only occasional attention to the ways biblical texts are actually heard and lived out in the world around us. The commentary seeks to provide students with diverse materials on the ways in which these texts have been interpreted through the course of history, as well as helping students understand the texts' relevance for today's globalized world. It recognizes the complexities that are involved with being an engaged reader of the Bible, providing a powerful tool for exploring the Bible's multilayered meanings in both their ancient and modern contexts. The commentary seeks to address contemporary issues that are raised by biblical passages. It aspires to be keenly aware of how the contemporary world and its issues and perspectives influence the interpretation of the Bible. Many of the most important insights of contemporary biblical scholarship not only have come from expertise in the world of antiquity but have also been forged in modern struggles for dignity, for equality, for sheer survival, and out of respect for those who have died without seeing justice done. Gaining familiarity with the original contexts in which the biblical writings were produced is essential, but not sufficient, for encouraging competent and discerning interpretation of the Bible's themes today.

Inside the Commentary

Both volumes of *The Fortress Commentary on the Bible* are organized in a similar way. In the beginning of each volume, **Topical Articles** set the stage on which interpretation takes place, naming the issues and concerns that have shaped historical and theological scholarship down to the present. Articles in the *Fortress Commentary on the Old Testament* attend, for example, to the issues that arise when two different religious communities claim the same body of writings as their Scripture, though interpreting those writings quite differently. Articles in the *Fortress Commentary on the New Testament* address the consequences of Christianity's historic claim to appropriate Jewish Scripture and to supplement it with a second collection of writings, the experience of rootlessness and diaspora, and the legacy of apocalypticism. Articles in both volumes reflect on the historical intertwining of Christianity with imperial and colonial power and with indexes of racial and socioeconomic privilege.

Section Introductions in the Old Testament volume provide background to the writings included in the Torah, Historical Writings, Wisdom, Prophetic Writings, and a general introduction to the Apocrypha. The New Testament volume includes articles introducing the Gospels, Acts, the letters associated with Paul, and Hebrews, the General Epistles and Revelation. These articles will address the literary and historical matters, as well as theological themes, that the books in these collections hold in common.

Commentary Entries present accessible and judicious discussion of each biblical book, beginning with an introduction to current thinking regarding the writing's original context and its significance in different reading communities down to the present day. A three-level commentary then follows for each sense division of the book. In some cases, these follow the chapter divisions of a biblical book, but more often, contributors have discerned other outlines, depending on matters of genre, movement, or argument.

The three levels of commentary are the most distinctive organizational feature of these volumes. The first level, "The Text in Its Ancient Context," addresses relevant lexical, exegetical, and literary aspects of the text, along with cultural and archaeological information that may provide additional insight into the historical context. This level of the commentary describes consensus views where these exist in current scholarship and introduces issues of debate clearly and fairly. Our intent here is to convey some sense of the historical and cultural distance between the text's original context and the contemporary reader.

The second level, "The Text in the Interpretive Tradition," discusses themes including Jewish and Christian tradition as well as other religious, literary, and artistic traditions where the biblical texts have attracted interest. This level is shaped by our conviction that we do not apprehend these texts immediately or innocently; rather, even the plain meaning we may regard as self-evident may have been shaped by centuries of appropriation and argument to which we are heirs.

The third level, "The Text in Contemporary Discussion," follows the history of interpretation into the present, drawing brief attention to a range of issues. Our aim here is not to deliver a single answer—"what the text means"—to the contemporary reader, but to highlight unique challenges and interpretive questions. We pay special attention to occasions of dissonance: aspects of the text or of its interpretation that have become questionable, injurious, or even intolerable to some readers today. Our goal is not to provoke a referendum on the value of the text but to stimulate reflection and discussion and, in this way, to empower the reader to reach his or her own judgments about the text.

The approach of this commentary articulates a particular understanding of the work of responsible biblical interpretation. We seek through this commentary to promote intelligent and mature engagement with the Bible, in religious communities and in academic classrooms alike, among pastors, theologians, and ethicists, but also and especially among nonspecialists. Our work together has given us a new appreciation for the vocation of the biblical scholar, as custodians of a treasure of accumulated wisdom from our predecessors; as stewards at a table to which an ever-expanding circle is invited; as neighbors and fellow citizens called to common cause, regardless of our different professions of faith. If the result of our work here is increased curiosity about the Bible, new questions about its import, and new occasions for mutual understanding among its readers, our work will be a success.

Fortress Commentary on the Old Testament

Gale A. Yee
Episcopal Divinity School

Hugh R. Page Jr.
University of Notre Dame

Matthew J. M. Coomber
St. Ambrose University

Fortress Commentary on the New Testament

Margaret Aymer
Interdenominational Theological Center

Cynthia Briggs Kittredge
Seminary of the Southwest

David A. Sánchez
Loyola Marymount University

Reading the Old Testament in Ancient and Contemporary Contexts

Matthew J. M. Coomber

As students file into their desks on the first day of my "Introduction to the Old Testament" course, they are greeted with a PowerPoint slide that simply states, in bold red letters, "Caution: Dangerous Texts Ahead!" The students often respond with the mixture of chuckles and uneasy looks that I intend to provoke. To some extent, the slide is offered tongue in cheek, but not entirely. As with any wry statement, the cautionary slide holds an element of truth. The Old Testament contains powerful teachings and radical ideas that have moved the hearts and minds of both adherents and skeptics for millennia.

While the texts of the Old Testament have had a profound effect on societies and cultures for a long span of time, their texts often take a back seat to the Gospels and the Pauline Letters in popular Christian religion. Even though they constitute well over half of the content of Christian Bibles, very few of my students claim to have read much—if any—of the Old Testament or Apocrypha, despite the fact that I teach at a Roman Catholic university in which the vast majority of the students are Christian. In fact, only a handful of my students claim to have been exposed to the stories of the Old Testament outside of either Sunday school or in episodes of the popular cartoon series *Veggie Tales*. Due to this lack of exposure to the Old Testament, I feel compelled to give them fair warning about what they have gotten themselves into by signing up for what may seem like an innocuous required course. I take it as a professional responsibility to alert them to the fact that a keen examination of the ancient Near Eastern library that sits on their desks has the power to change their lives and forever alter the ways in which they experience the world.

Any collection of books containing calls to wage wars of conquest, to resist the temptation to fight while under threat, thoughts on God's role in governance, and meditations on what it means to live *the good life* has the potential to change lives and even inspire revolutions. To assume that the Bible is harmless is both foolish and irresponsible. After all, the Old Testament's contents have been used by some to support slavery and genocide while inspiring others to engage in such dangerous pursuits as enduring imprisonment, torture, and death in attempts to liberate the oppressed. And just as with using any powerful instrument, be it a car or a surgical blade, reading the Old Testament demands care, responsibility, and substantial consideration from those who put it to use.

Books that promote powerful ideas are complex tools that often belong to the readers as much as—if not more than—their authors. The level of consideration required to read, interpret, and actualize such books is magnified when approaching ancient texts such as those found in the Old Testament. These biblical books bridge multiple theological, cultural, and linguistic worlds, which demand multiple levels of understanding and interpretation. Readers must inhabit three worlds (contexts) when reading any of the books of the Old Testament or Apocrypha, from Genesis to 4 Maccabees: (1) the ancient contexts in which they were written, (2) the modern contexts into which the text is being received, and (3) all of those contexts in between wherein interpreters in each generation have shaped the reading of the texts for their own time and place. *The Fortress Commentary on the Bible: The Old Testament and Apocrypha* approaches these ancient texts with due reverence to this complexity. The purpose of this introduction is to explore a few of the many considerations that are required in reading this ancient Near Eastern scriptural library in its ancient and modern contexts.

A Few Considerations on Receiving Ancient Texts with Modern Minds

The word *context*, whether pertaining to events or a book, looks deceptively singular. A student trying to uncover the context of the US civil rights movement will find many contextual viewing points: those of African Americans who rose up against institutionalized oppression, those of segregationists who tried to maintain the status quo, those within the Johnson administration who worked to find a way forward without losing the Democrats' white voters in the South, and the list goes on.

Challenge of Finding an Ancient or Modern Context

The words *ancient context* and *modern context*, when applied to the Old Testament, also need to be considered in the plural. Considering the ancient context, the books of the Old Testament contain the theologies of diverse communities who lived, wrote, argued, and worked to understand their relationship with the divine under a wide variety of circumstances. An attempt to find a single context for the book of Isaiah, for example, is as complex as finding a single sociohistorical setting of the United States, from the colonial period to the present; it cannot be done. The same is true with the modern context. As these religious texts are received in Chicago or Mumbai, on Wall Street or on skid row, they flow into and take on very different meanings and contexts.

Differing Expectations and Intents of Ancient and Modern Histories

Readers in the age of science have certain expectations when reading a history, and these expectations inform how histories—whether written before or after this age—are received. Modern readers want to know, with scientific precision, when, why, and where events happened. Great value is placed on reconstructions of events that are backed up by reliable sources and with as little interpretive bias as possible. A *good* history of the Battle of the Bulge should include not only dates and locations but also eyewitness accounts of allied forces, Wehrmacht and SS divisions, and civilians. Expectations of accuracy and value in objectivity are a service both to the study of the past and to understanding how these events helped to shape the present. However, when dealing with the Old Testament it is easy to project our appreciation for accuracy and disdain for bias onto the ancient texts, which ultimately is not a fair way to approach these ancient texts.

Long before there was even a concept of "Bible," many of the texts of the Old Testament were passed down through oral tradition, only to be written down and finally canonized centuries later; this is evidenced in the repetitive Torah narratives, such as the creation refrain in Gen. 1:1—2:4a and the lyrical hymn of Deborah in Judges 5. To imagine the original texts as printed, bound, copyrighted, and collected works, as we hold them today, is both inaccurate and misleading. Moreover, assuming the intents and expectations of the oral historian to be akin to those of modern historians is misleading, and focusing on accuracy can limit the scope of a passage's message when the intent of the passage rests in the ideas it promotes. Cultures that employ oral tradition do not make dates, places, or accuracy a priority; rather, they are interested in the telling and retelling of a story to develop an understanding or identity that can answer the questions of the times into which they are received. Take the account of King Solomon's wealth in 2 Chron. 9:22-24, for example.

> King Solomon surpassed all the kings of the earth in wealth and wisdom. All the kings of the earth came to pay homage to Solomon and to listen to the wisdom with which God had endowed him. Each brought his tribute—silver and gold objects, robes, weapons, and spices, horses and mules—in the amount due each year (JPS).

Such an account served a purpose to the ancient author and his audience, but the account was certainly not accurate. Putting aside the issue of transoceanic travel for contemporary rulers in the Americas or the South Pacific, Israel held no such wealth in the tenth century BCE, and such superpowers as Egypt and Assyria would never have been compelled to offer tribute. While questions surrounding the reality of Solomon's wealth are not a center of contentious debate in the public sphere, questions pertaining to the creation of the universe are highly controversial; the front lines of this debate can be seen at the doors of the Creation Museum in Petersburg, Kentucky.

Founded by Ken Ham and Answers in Genesis (AiG), a Christian apologetics organization, the Creation Museum is a prime example of how scientific-age expectations are frequently placed on the ancient texts of the Old Testament. With the motto "Prepare to Believe," the museum promotes Gen. 1:1—2:4a as a scientific explanation for the creation of the cosmos, an event that is said to have occurred around 4,000 BCE, as determined through James Ussher's seventeenth-century-CE biblically based calculations. It is important to consider that the questions the Creation Museum seeks to answer do not likely match the agenda of the authors of Gen. 1:1—2:4a, which is connected to the Babylonian myth the *Enuma Elish* and/or the battle between the Canaanite god Baal and Yam, each of which centers on order's conquest of chaos. It also does not take into consideration that those who canonized the Torah followed this story with another creation story (Gen. 2:4b-25), which is juxtaposed with the first, making it unlikely that the ancient intent was to give a *scientific* account of our origins. Furthermore, the authors of the texts believed that the sky was a firmament that held back a great sky-ocean (Gen. 1:6-8), from which precipitation came when its doors were opened, and that the moon was self-illuminating (Gen. 1:14-18). A key danger in treating Old Testament books with modern historical and scientific expectations is not only receiving inaccurate messages about our past but also failing to realize the intent of the authors and the depth of meaning behind the messages they conveyed.

Projecting Modern Contexts onto the Ancient Past

The oft-repeated notion that only the winners write history is not entirely true, for readers rewrite the histories they receive by projecting their own personal and cultural perspectives onto them. The medievalist Norman Cantor stresses how individuals tend to project their own worldviews and experiences onto the past, thereby reinventing the past in their own image (156–58). Whereas Cantor dealt with issues of secular history, biblical history appears to follow suit, as found in such art pieces as Dutch painter Gerard van Honthorst's piece *King David Playing the Harp*. In the painting van Honthorst depicts the king with European-style attire and instrument. In contextually ambiguous passages, such as the land seizures in Mic. 2:1-4, we find scholars filling in the blanks with characters that make more sense in our time than in the ancient past, such as the mafia (Alfaro, 25). It is difficult for a reader not to project his or her own time and culture onto the text, for that is the reader's primary reference point; to escape doing so is likely not possible. But just as complete objectivity is not attainable, an awareness of its hazards can help readers exercise some degree of control regarding how much they project their present onto the past.

Bringing One's Ideology to the Text

Just as readers bring their notions of history to the Old Testament, so also they bring their ideologies. While attempts to view Old Testament texts through the biblical authors' eyes may be made, one's perceptions can never be entirely freed from one's own experiences, which help shape how a particular idea or story is read. This challenge is a double-edged sword. On one side of the sword, the ideology and experiences of the reader may cloud the text's original meaning and intent, causing unintended—and sometimes intentional—misreadings of a passage. When this occurs, the resulting interpretation often tells us more about the social or ideological location of the reader than the biblical characters who are being interpreted. Albert Schweitzer found that nineteenth-century biographies on the life of the "historical Jesus" turned out to be autobiographies of their authors; romantics uncovered an idealist Jesus, political radicals found a revolutionary, and so on (Schweitzer). On the other side of the sword, one finds an advantage shared by oral tradition. Reading a text through one's own experiences can breathe new life into the text and allow it to speak to current circumstances, as found in postcolonial, feminist, and queer interpretations. Since readers cannot fully remove themselves from their own ideological locations, it is important to acknowledge that a reader's ideas and biases are brought to the text and that much is to be learned by considering various interpretations.

Because ideology plays a role in interpretation, it should be noted that history—and biblical histories, in particular—do not exist in the past, but are very much alive and active in the present. YHWH's granting of land to Abraham's dependents, for example, plays a prominent role in the Israel-Palestine conflict. This is addressed by Keith Whitelam and James Crossley, who find the biblical text shaping modern perceptions of land via cartography. A post-1967 war edition of *The Macmillan Bible Atlas* contains a map of Israel with borders that look remarkably similar to the modern-day border with Gaza—despite great uncertainty surrounding ancient Israel's borders—and that is inscribed with Gen. 13:14-15: "The LORD said to Abram . . . 'Lift up your eyes, and look from the place where you are, northward and southward and eastward and westward; for all the land which you see I will give to you and to your descendants forever'" (RSV; see Whitelam 61–62; Crossley 176). Whether one sees this connection in a positive or negative light, clear political implications of the biblical past can be seen.

Differing Views on the Old Testament's History

Another factor to be considered, which is also highly political, is the lack of consensus pertaining to the historicity of biblical narratives and the state of ancient Israel, ranging from the exodus narrative to the Davidic monarchy. The degree to which these events and histories are *real histories* or *cultural memory* has been the subject of much debate and polemic within the academy. Many scholars agree that the story of the Hebrew exodus out of Egypt is cultural memory, with varying degrees of historical truth, ranging from seeing the Hebrews as an invading force to an indigenous movement within Canaan that rose up against exploitative rulers. But one of the most heated debates in the history of ancient Israel has revolved around the dating of the monarchy and the rise of Judah as a powerful state.

The traditional view, often referred to as the *maximalist* perspective, gives greater credence to the Bible's account of the monarchy's history. Scholars of this persuasion accept, to varying degrees, the Old Testament's stories of the rise of Israel beginning with King Saul and continuing on through the destruction of Israel and Judah. So-called *minimalists* give less credence to biblical accounts, relying more on archaeological and extrabiblical sources to develop their views of the monarchy and the presence of a powerful state, for which they find little evidence. While largely unnoticed outside the academy, the debate has caused great animosity within. Maximalist scholars have been accused of burdening archaeology with the task of upholding the biblical narratives (Davies), while minimalists have been accused of attempting to erase ancient Israel from world history (Halpern).

The purpose of addressing the maximalist/minimalist debate in this introduction is to emphasize that biblical scholarship contains diverse voices and points of view on the Bible's history, which will be seen in the commentaries of this volume. It is good that these different perspectives are aired. When approaching an area of history that is of such great importance to so many, yet with so little definitive information available, it is important to articulate and compare different ideas so as to produce and refine the historical possibilities of the Bible's contexts. In this way we see how differing views of biblical interpretation can work as a dance, where partners can complement each other's work, even if tempers can flare sometimes when partners step on one another's toes.

Reading the Old Testament in Its Ancient Context

It is apparent that contemplating the ancient contexts of the Old Testament requires several areas of consideration. While there is no end to the complexities involved with pursuing a greater understating of the world(s) out of which the books of the Old Testament developed, this section is intended to draw the reader's attention to some of the Old Testament's physical environments, political climates, and theological diversity.

Physical Environments of the Old Testament

The geography and ecology of ancient Palestine can easily be overlooked, but their value for understanding the Old Testament should not be underestimated. While the Old Testament represents diverse social settings that span hundreds of years, all of its authors lived in agrarian societies where land, climate, economics, and religion are inseparable. Due to agrarian societies' dire need to ensure successful and regular harvests—whether for survival or with the additional aspiration of building empire—farming practices become incorporated into religious rituals that end up dictating planting, harvesting, and land management. This strong connection between faith and farming led to rituals that served as an interface between spirituality and socioeconomic activities, effectively erasing the lines between religious and economic practice (Coomber 2013). In the end, the ritualization of agrarian economics helps shape perceptions of the deity or deities to which the rituals are connected: the Feast of Unleavened Bread (Exod. 23:14-17), the barley harvest festival incorporated in the Passover feast (Exodus 12; cf. John 19:29, the wheat-harvest Feast of Weeks, also known as Pentecost (Lev. 23:15-21; cf. Acts 2:1), and the fruit-harvest Feast of Booths (Lev. 23:33-36). Thus geography and ecology affected not only the way ancient Hebrews farmed but also how they came to understand God. Moreover, the geographical regions in which many of them farmed influenced these understandings.

Regions of Ancient Israel

Ancient Israel can be divided into a number of geographical areas, each of which presents its own unique environment. Furthest to the west is the *coastal plain*, which held great economic importance in the way of trade. This is especially visible in the development of manufacturing and shipping cities such as Ekron and Ashkelon. Due to the region's trade potential, it was usually controlled by foreign powers and is not frequently mentioned in the Old Testament (e.g., Judges 16; 2 Kings 16; Jer. 25:20; Amos 1:8; Zeph. 2:4).

The lowland *Shephelah* and the *highlands* are just east of the coastal plain, forming an important region of Israel, which is at the center of most of the Old Testament's stories. This fertile land, composed of low hills and valleys, is good for animal husbandry and the cultivation of grains, cereals, nuts, olives, and grapes. These areas were valuable for both subsistence farming and the production of trade goods, in which surrounding empires could engage. The agrarian potential of this area also made Shephelah and the highlands a target for foreign invasion. This region's political influence was heightened by the cities of Jerusalem, Samaria, and Lachish.

The *Jordan Valley*, east of the highlands, contains the lowest natural surface in the world and is part of a fault that extends into Africa. The valley follows the Jordan River from the city of Dan through the city of Hazor and the Sea of Galilee before flowing into the Dead Sea. Aside from the important role that the Jordan Valley plays in Ezekiel's vision of water flowing out of the temple to bring life to the Dead Sea (Ezekiel 47), the region is rarely mentioned.

To the east of the Jordan Valley is the *Transjordan highlands*, which is often referred to as "beyond the Jordan" (e.g., Josh. 12:1). Extending from the Dead Sea's altitude of 650-feet below sea level to the 9,230-foot peak of Mt. Hermon, this region contains a diverse range of topography and climates that allow for the cultivation of diverse agricultural goods, including grains, fruits, timber, and livestock. The agrarian potential of the area attracted a number of peoples, including the Moabites, the Ammonites, and the Edomites.

Whether valued for their sustaining, trade, or defensive capabilities, the topography of ancient Israel and its surrounding lands influenced its inhabitants' ability or inability to find sustenance and pursue their own interests. When empires such as Assyria and Babylon were on the rise, this region attracted their rulers who sought the earning potential of the land, and these events—or the cultural memories they inspired—influenced the Old Testament authors' stories of defeat and are reflected in their perceptions of God's attitudes toward them.

Climatic Challenges

While the land in and around Israel was some of the most sought after in the ancient Near East, its inhabitants endured serious meteorological challenges. The ancient Israelites lived at the crossroads of subtropical and temperate atmospheric patterns—producing rainy winter seasons and dry summers—and the effects of these patterns shaped the ways in which the Hebrews lived: the resulting erratic precipitation patterns result in a 30 percent chance of insufficient rainfall (Karmon, 27). The unpredictability of each growing season's weather pattern meant that the rainfall of a given season could play out in any number of ways, each demanding specific farming strategies for which farmers had little foresight or room for error. Subsequent failed seasons that diminished surpluses could lead to debt and the selling of family members into slavery or even the extinction of a family line.

Everything in society—from the interests of the poorest farmer to the king—depended on successful harvests and access to their crops, and the strong desire for divine assistance is reflected in Old Testament narratives that emphasize fidelity to YHWH. The seriousness placed on securing favorable rainfall and accessing harvests is clear in warnings against following other deities, such as the weather god Baal (e.g., Judg. 2:11; 2 Kings 3:2; Ps. 106:28; Hosea 9:10), God-given visions that foretell rainfall (Genesis 41), and the granting and withholding of rain as reward or punishment (Deut. 11:11-14; cf. 1 Kings 17–18). Additionally, there are strict rules to protect land access (Leviticus 25) and condemnation against abuses (1 Kings 21; Isa. 5:8-10; Mic. 2:1-4).

The physical environments of the Old Testament authors are an important consideration, because they not only affected the way the authors lived but also helped to shape their views of God and the world around them. From the development of the ancient Hebrews' religious rituals to finding either God's favor or wrath in agrarian events (see Zech. 10:1; 1 Kings 17–18), the topography and climatic environments that affected cultivation played key roles in how the biblical authors perceived and interacted with the divine.

Sociopolitical Contexts of the Old Testament

In addition to the challenges presented by Israel's geographic and climatic setting, its strategic location between the empires of Mesopotamia and northern Africa presented a recurring threat. As these empires invaded the lands of ancient Israel for military and economic reasons, the biblical authors and redactors received and transmitted these events into their religious narratives: foreign invasion was often perceived as divine punishment—with the notable exception of the Persians—and the defeat of foreign forces was perceived as a result of divine favor. Before addressing foreign influences on the Old Testament's ancient contexts, a brief overview of Israel's domestic structures should be considered.

Israel's Domestic Sociopolitical Contexts

While ancient Palestine's Mesopotamian neighbors developed cities and urban economies in the Early Bronze Age (3300–2100 BCE), Palestine largely remained a patchwork of scattered settlements that functioned as a peripheral economy, engaging in trade activity as neighboring empires made it lucrative, and receding into highland agriculture when those powers waned (Coomber 2010, 81–92). Adapting to the demands of waxing and waning empires—rather than taking significant steps toward powerful urban economies of its own—resulted in a marked reliance on subsistence strategies on into the seventh century BCE (Coote and Whitelam).

Biblical accounts of Hebrew societal structures present a patronage system that had its roots in small family units called the *bet av* ("father's house"), which together formed a *mishpahah* ("family" or "clan"), which expanded up to the tribe, or *shevet*. When the monarchy was established, the *malkut* ("kingdom") became the top rung. While the *malkut* and *shevet* held the top two tiers, the phrase "all politics is local" applies to ancient Israel: loyalty structures were strongest at the bottom.

Philip Davies and John Rogerson note that the *bet av*, "father's house," likely had a double meaning (32). While it indicated a family unit that included extended lineage and slaves—excluding daughters who left the family at marriage—it likely also denoted the descendants of a common ancestor, who may not have lived under a single roof (e.g., Gen. 24:38). While the *bet avim* grew through the births of sons and the accumulation of wives and slaves, the danger of collapse due to disease, war, and a lack of birth of sons presented a constant threat. Debt was also a threat to a *bet av*, inspiring legal texts that protected its access to arable land (Leviticus 25; Deut. 25:5). It was the patriarch's responsibility to care for the family's economic well-being, as well as to pass on traditions, the history of the nation, and the laws of God (Deut. 6:7; 11:8-9; 32:46-47). The *bet av* also had power over such judicial matters as those of marriage and slave ownership.

Mishpahah denotes a level of organization based on a recognizable kinship (Numbers 1; 26). It had territorial significance, as seen in tribal border lists of Joshua 13–19, and was responsible for dividing the land. While *mishpahah* is difficult to translate, Norman Gottwald offers the useful definition, "protective association of extended families" (Gottwald 1999, 257). If the immediate or extended families of a citizen who had to sell himself to an alien could not redeem him, the *mishpahah* became the last line of protection from perpetual servitude (Lev. 25:48-49).

Shevet refers to the largest group and unit of territorial organization, which was primarily bound together by residence. Military allegiances appear to have belonged to this level, against both foreign and domestic threats—as seen in the Benjamite battles of Judges 12 and 20–21. Gottwald sees the *shevet* as more of a geographic designation pertaining to clusters of villages and/or clans that gathered for protective purposes rather than as representative bodies within a political system (Gottwald 2001, 35).

The *malkut*, or kingdom, is a source of continued contention in the so-called minimalist/maximalist debate mentioned above. The Old Testament account claims that the kingdom of Israel was founded when Saul became king over the Israelite tribes (1 Samuel 9) and continued through the line of David, after Saul fell out of favor with God. Israel's united monarchy is reported to have spanned 1030 to 930 BCE, when King Rehoboam was rejected by the northern Israelites (1 Kgs. 12:1-20; 2 Chron. 10:1-19), leading to the period of the divided monarchy, with Israel in the north and Judah in the south. These two kingdoms existed side by side until Israel was destroyed by Assyria (734–721 BCE). Judah entered into Assyrian vassalage in the 720s and was destroyed by the Babylonians around 586 BCE. Those who give less credence to the biblical account take note that there is little extrabiblical evidence of a monarchy prior to King Omri, aside from the Tel Dan Stele, which refers to "the House of David," which may refer to a king.

While Israel's domestic organizational landscape played a major role in the development of biblical law and narrative, the biblical authors' interactions with surrounding peoples had profound effects on the stories they told. The main imperial influences, from the premonarchical period to the fall of the Hasmonean Dynasty, were Egypt, Philistine, Assyria, Babylon, Persia, the Greeks, and the Romans.

Israel's Foreign Sociopolitical Contexts

The Egyptian Empire played an important role in the development of the Torah, as seen in the stories of Abram and Sarai (Genesis 12), Joseph (Genesis 37–50), and throughout the entire exodus narrative, interwoven into many areas of the Old Testament. The authors of Exodus used the backdrop of Egypt's powerful *New Kingdom* (1549–1069 BCE) to display their faith in YHWH's power, and other books draw on this narrative as a recurring reminder of the Israelites' debt and obligations toward their god (e.g. Deut. 5:15, 24:17-22, 23:7-8; Ps. 106:21; Ezekiel 20; Amos 2:10; Mic. 6:4), and as a vehicle of praise (Psalms 78; 81; 135; 136). The Jewish holiday of Passover, which is referred to throughout the Old Testament, has its roots in this anti-Egyptian epic. A later and weaker Egypt returns to play a role in the story of Judah's lengthy downfall: King Hezekiah (d. 680s) enters into a failed anti-Assyrian alliance with Egypt (Isaiah 30–31; 36:6-9), and King Zedekiah (d. 580s) enters into a failed anti-Babylonian alliance with Pharaoh Hophra (Ezek. 17:15; Jer. 2:36).

While their point of origins are in dispute (Amos 9:7 puts their origin at Caphtor), the Philistines tried to invade Egypt in 1190 BCE, but were repelled by Ramses III, who settled them in the coastal towns of Gaza, Ashkelon, and Ashdod (Deut. 2:23). From there, they continued their incursions along the coastal plain and perhaps even drove out their Egyptian rulers, under the reign of Ramses IV (d. 1149 BCE). They play a key adversarial role in the book of Judges, as found in the stories of Shamgar (Judg. 3:31) and Samson (Judges 13–16). Their military competencies are reflected in the story of their capture of the ark of the covenant in 1 Sam. 4:1—7:2. Fear of the Philistine threat helped influence the people's decision to choose a king to unite the tribes (1 Sam. 8–9). The biblical authors continued to portray the Philistines as a threat to the Israelites, but Philistine influence in the highlands faded as the power of Assyria grew.

Assyria's fearsome power and influence in the region gave them a villain's role in the Old Testament. The biblical authors perceived Assyria's incursions into Israel and Judah as YHWH's punishment for such transgressions as idolatry and social injustice. While archaeological evidence of Philistine-Israelite interaction is scant, there is plenty of archaeological and extrabiblical evidence of Assyria's impact on Israel and Judah.

From the start of its ninth-century conquests, Assyria was feared for its ruthless force. The psychological impact of Assyria's powerful conscripted forces, iron chariots, siege engines, and public mutilations surface in the writings of the Old Testament authors. The Assyrians enforced submission through power and fear, deporting conquered rulers to prevent uprisings (2 Kings 17:6, 24, 28; 18:11). When uprisings occurred, Assyrian troops were deployed from strategically positioned garrisons to flay, impale, and burn the perpetrators, as portrayed in Assyrian palace-reliefs.

In the late eighth century, both Israel and Judah felt the full weight of Assyria's might. The northern kingdom of Israel was destroyed in 721 BCE after joining an alliance of vassals that stopped paying tribute to Assyria. At the end of the century, King Hezekiah entered Judah into a similar alliance with Egypt (Isaiah 30–31), which resulted in the invasion of his kingdom and the siege of Jerusalem. According to 2 Kgs. 18:13-16, the siege was broken when Hezekiah sent a message of repentance to the Assyrian king, Sennacherib, at Lachish, promising to resume his tribute obligations. Other texts in 2 Kings suggest that Sennacherib abandoned the siege to deal with political unrest at home (19:7, 37) or a plague (19:35-36). Despite his efforts to subvert Sennacherib's dominance of Judah, Hezekiah and his successors continued to rule as vassals.

Under the rule of King Nebuchadnezzar, the Babylonian Empire captured Nineveh in 612, destroyed the Egyptians at the battle of Carchemish in 605, and captured Jerusalem in 597, deporting many inhabitants. After a rebellion by King Zedekiah in 586, the Babylonians destroyed Jerusalem and the temple and deported a significant portion of Judah's population (2 Kings 24; 2 Chronicles 36). The prophets Ezekiel, Jeremiah, and Habakkuk saw Nebuchadnezzar's conquest as YHWH's punishment for the sins of the Judean state (Ezekiel 8–11; Jer. 25:1-14; Hab. 1:6-10). The events of the Babylonian conquest are largely supported by archaeology and extrabiblical literature (Grabbe, 210–13).

Biblical claims of the removal of all Judeans but the poorest "people of the land" (2 Kgs. 24:14-16; 25:12; Jer. 52:16, 28-30) are reflected in the archaeological record, which indicates that inhabited sites decreased by two-thirds, from 116 to 41, and surviving sites shrank from 4.4 to 1.4 hectares, suggesting a population collapse of 85 to 90 percent (Liverani, 195). Such a massive exile plays a formidable role in the Old Testament, as described in the stories of significant characters such as Ezekiel and Daniel. Rage associated with this event is found in Psalm 137, which recounts the horrors of the exile and ends with the chilling words "a blessing on him who seizes your [Babylonian] babies and dashes them against the rocks!" (137:9 JPS). The exiled Hebrews who returned to Palestine after the Persians conquered the Babylonians returned to a destroyed Jerusalem that no longer enjoyed the security of a defensive wall. Some of the returnees helped to reshape Judaism with a flourishing priesthood and the composition of scholarly works and biblical texts. While exile is portrayed in negative terms, many Jews remained in the lands to which they had been deported; this had the effect of spreading Judaism outside the confines of Palestine.

After overthrowing his grandfather King Astyages of the Medes in 553 BCE, Cyrus of Persia (d. 530) rapidly expanded his empire, moving westward into Armenia and Asia Minor and east toward India, and defeated Babylon in 539. But unlike previous conquests, the Old Testament treats Persian dominance as a time of hope. As successor to the Babylonian Empire, King Cyrus instituted a policy of allowing victims of Babylonian exile to return to their homelands, where he sponsored their local religions. To the biblical authors, this policy was met with celebration and as a sign of YHWH's love for his people. The authors of 2 Chron. 36:23 and Ezra 1:2 portray King Cyrus as crediting YHWH with his victories and with the mandate to rebuild the temple in Jerusalem; Ezra 1:7 even portrays the Persian king personally returning the vessels that Nebuchadnezzar had seized from the temple four decades before. While the Bible treats Cyrus's policy of return as inspired by YHWH, Davies and Rogerson note that the practice was neither new nor disinterested, as it served to restore the national culture of a large and culturally varied empire (59). It is important to note the great shift in how the biblical authors treated King Cyrus of Persia, as opposed to the kings of the Assyrians and Babylonians, whom they disdained. In Isaiah 40–50, Cyrus is championed as the great savior of the Judean deportees and of the rebuilding of Jerusalem. In fact, while oracles against foreign nations are a key theme in prophetic oracles, none are directed against Persia. Even when their rulers are compliant with the murder of Jews, they are portrayed as either acting against their own desires or out of ignorance (Daniel 6; Esther).

Like the exile, itself, the return from exile plays an important role in the politics and religion of the Old Testament. Accounts of these events are found in the books of Ezra and Nehemiah. While the Bible presents the return as a blessing from God and a time of joy, it does not seem to have been without its hardships. It can be deduced from Ezra and Nehemiah that resettlement involved various tensions; in Ezra 3:3, those who had remained in Judah during the exile, along with other neighboring peoples, take the Canaanites' role in the book of Joshua: "an evil influence which will, unless strenuously rejected, corrupt the 'people of God'" (Davies and Rogerson, 88). It was during the Persian period that the Jerusalem temple was rebuilt and the priesthood gained power and influence.

The long march of succeeding empires continued with the rise of Alexander the Great, who seized control of the Greek city-states in 336 BCE and conquered the Persian Empire before his death in 323. Unlike previous empires that might make their subjects worship a particular deity or relocate to a different region, the Greek ideal of *Hellenism* posed a particular cultural threat. Hellenism promoted a view in which people were not citizens of a particular region, but of the world, enabling the integration of Greek and regional cultures, thus breaking down barriers that separated local peoples from their foreign rulers. Within a hundred years, Koine Greek had become the lingua franca, and Greek philosophy, educational systems, art and attire, politics, and religion permeated the empire. The consequences of Hellenization had profound linguistic, political, and theological effects on the biblical authors who lived and wrote during this period. Jews who lived outside of Israel became more familiar with the Greek language than Hebrew. By the second century CE, Greek had become so widely spoken among the Jewish community in Alexandria, Egypt, that the Hebrew Bible was translated into Koine Greek, which came to be called the Septuagint.

Greek rule eventually led to the severe oppression of the Jewish people at the hands of the usurper king Antiochus IV (d. 164 BCE), who sought to weed out cultural diversity in the Seleucid Empire. King Antiochus, who called himself *Epiphanes* ("god made manifest"), was known for his erratic character, which manifested itself in his brutal hatred of the Jews. Even his allies referred to him by the nickname *Epimanes*—a play on Epiphanes—meaning "the crazy one." He is known for looting the Jerusalem temple to fund his battles against the Ptolemies and for forbidding the Jewish rite of circumcision and sacred dietary laws.

King Antiochus was also known for instigating treachery among the Jewish leadership, giving Jason—of the pro-Greek Onias family—the high priesthood in return for complying with Antiochus's plans to Hellenize Jerusalem by building a gymnasium and enrolling its people as citizens of Antioch (2 Macc. 4:7). Further strife erupted when Menelaus, another aspirant for the high priesthood, offered Antiochus even greater gifts for the office. The rivalry of Jason and Menelaus led to the sacking of Jerusalem, slaughtering of its citizens, and the looting of its temple (2 Macc. 5:11-23; Josephus 12.5.3 §§246–47). The horrors of life under King Antiochus IV are reflected in the horn that emerges from the fourth beast in the apocalyptic vision of Dan. 7:7-8, and is then slain by the "Ancient One" (7:11).

From stripping the temple to pay for his wars to setting up an altar for Zeus in the temple, King Antiochus IV's brutality against the Jews led to a revolt that started in the Judean village of Modein in 167 BCE and spread rapidly throughout the region—as chronicled in 1 and 2 Maccabees and in Josephus's *Antiquities of the Jews* (c. 100 CE). A guerrilla warfare campaign that was led by Judas Maccabeus eventually liberated and purified the temple—an event celebrated today in the Jewish festival of Hanukkah. The Maccabean revolt drove out the Greeks and expanded the borders to include Galilee. While the revolt was successful in ushering in a period of self-rule, the resulting Hasmonean Dynasty fell prey to the lust for power. As civil conflict broke out between two rival claims to the throne, the Roman general Pompey invaded Judea in 63 BCE, seizing control of the region for his empire. In 40 BCE, the Roman Senate appointed an Edomite convert to Judaism, *Herod the Great*, as king of Judea. Despised by his people, the puppet king had to take Jerusalem by force, from where he ruled harshly.

Each of these empires, vying for control over the Southern Levant, brought with them challenges that helped to shape the Hebrew people by influencing the ways they viewed themselves, their God, and their religious practices.

Religious Contexts of the Old Testament

Despite common perceptions of the Bible as a univocal work, the Old Testament represents diverse theologies of communities that spanned centuries and were influenced by the religious systems of their contemporaries. Babylonian and Canaanite musings over the power of order over chaos, as found in the *Enuma Elish* and Baal narratives, are present in Gen. 1:1—2:4a and referenced in Ps. 74:12-17. The authors of the Bible's Wisdom literature exchanged ideas with their foreign neighbors, as found in parallels between the Babylonian story I Will Praise the Lord of Wisdom and the book of Job, and passages from Proverbs that mirror the words of the Egyptian thinkers Ptah-Hotep and Amen-em-opet (e.g., Prov. 22:4; 22:17—24:22). Understanding the diversity of theological perspectives in the Old Testament can aid both exegesis and hermeneutics by giving the reader greater insight into the biblical authors' ideas of God and uncovering layers of meaning that might otherwise go unnoticed.

Monotheism and Henotheism

It should not be assumed that all Old Testament authors were monotheists: many were *henotheists*. Henotheism promotes a multi-god/dess universe in which the adherent gives allegiance to a supreme primary deity. Elements of this outlook appear to be found in God's decision to create humanity "in our image, after our likeness" (Gen. 1:26 RSV), and in YHWH's anxiety over the man that he created becoming "like one of us" in Gen. 3:22. YHWH also expresses his disgust in that the *sons of God* mated with human women, resulting in the birth of the nephilim (Gen. 6:2-4). In the *Song of Moses*, Moses poses the rhetorical question, "who is like you, O Lord, among the gods?" (Exod. 15:11). The writer of Ps. 95:3 proclaims, "YHWH is a great God, the king of all divine beings," while 97:9 asserts that YHWH is "exalted high above all divine beings." These examples pose a number of questions about the biblical authors' views on the divine. Two that will be briefly addressed here concern the identity of God and the role of the other deities being inferred. The supreme deity of the ancient Hebrews is given several names and titles, representing different personality traits and theological views.

Elohim

The name or title *Elohim*, which is usually translated from the Hebrew into English as "God," makes its first appearance in Genesis 1. The name Elohim is used to identify the Hebrews' supreme deity in several Old Testament texts, including those found in the books of Genesis, Exodus, Psalms, and Job. As in the Bible's priestly creation story (Gen. 1:1—2:4a), Elohim is portrayed as an all-powerful, confident, commanding, and somewhat distant deity, whose supremacy and majesty are emphasized.

YHWH

YHWH is an anthropomorphic god who exhibits tendencies toward both kindness and severity and is self-described as a jealous god who, unlike other ancient Near Eastern gods, demands the exclusive allegiance of his followers. The name YHWH, which is often translated into English as "the LORD"—from the Hebrew *adonay*—makes its first appearance in the second creation story (Gen. 2:4b). The name YHWH carries a sense of mystery. Derived from the Hebrew verb *hawah*, meaning "to be," YHWH is difficult to translate, but means something like "he who is" or "he who causes what is." Some believe that YHWH's origins can be traced to the god YHW, who was worshiped in the northwestern region of the Arabian Peninsula known as Midian: this is where Moses first encounters YHWH (Exodus 3).

YHWH has strong associations with Canaanite culture, which highlights discrepancies between biblical directions for the deity's worship and how the deity was worshiped in popular religion. Whereas the biblical authors convey strict messages that YHWH should be worshiped alone, the remains of Israelite homes reveal that other gods and goddesses, such as Asherah—whom the author(s) of Jeremiah refers to as *the queen of heaven*—were worshiped alongside YHWH (Dever, 176–89). Jeremiah 44 appears to give a glimpse into the popular polytheistic or henotheistic religion of sixth-century-BCE Judah. After YHWH threatens the people for worshiping other gods, the women say that they will not listen but will continue the traditions of their ancestors and give offerings to the queen of heaven, who protected them well (Jer. 44:16-17). Further biblical evidence of Asherah's popularity is found in the biblical authors' continual condemnation of her worship, often symbolized through the presence of pillars and poles, as they worked to direct the people toward monotheism (Deut. 7:5; Judg. 3:7-8; 1 Kgs. 14:15, 23; Jer. 17:17-18).

El

The name or title *El* appears around two hundred times in the Old Testament, with frequent use in the ancestor stories of Genesis and surfacing throughout the Old Testament. Its presence poses some interesting questions.

On one level, El is a common Semitic title for "divine being," and can be read as an appellative for "divinity," often compounded with other words such as *el-shadday* ("God Almighty" [Gen. 17:1; Exod. 6:3; Ezek. 10:5]) and *el-elyon* ("God Most High" [Gen. 14:22; Deut. 32:8-9; Ps. 78:35]). In addition to a title referring to God, El is also the name of the chief god of the Canaanite pantheon. Often portrayed as a bearded king on his throne, and referred to as the "Ancient One," El was worshiped in Canaan and Syria both before and after the emergence of Israel. The frequent use of El for God—and the Canaanite god's prominence in Israel—has led many to conclude that El developed into YHWH. Mark Smith asserts, "The original god of Israel was El. . . . Isra*el* is not a Yahwistic name with the divine element of Yahweh, but an El name" (Smith, 32; emphasis on *el* in "Israel" is mine). A cross-pollination of Canaanite and Hebrew religion is found in the use of Canaanite El imagery to describe the "Ancient One" in Dan. 7:9-10 who sits on a throne with white garments and hair as pure as wool. Furthermore, the description of "one like a human being coming with the clouds of heaven," who "came to the Ancient One and was presented before him" (Dan. 7:13), dovetails with images of the Canaanite god Baal coming before El. Whether or not the authors of Daniel 7 envisioned El, the imprint of Canaanite religion appears to have been stamped on ideas of God and passed down through the generations. While not accepted by biblical authors, popular religion in ancient Israel appears to have had a complex network of deities that fulfilled various roles in daily life. (For a helpful overview on differences between "popular" and "official" religion in ancient Israel, see Stavrakopoulou.)

The idea that El was absorbed into YHWH is also supported by the fact that the chief god of the Canaanite pantheon is never condemned in the Old Testament, but his son Baal, consort Asherah, and other gods face vicious condemnation (Num. 25:2; Deut. 4:3; Judg. 6:30; 1 Kgs. 16:31—18:40). Why would the biblical authors attack lesser Canaanite deities but leave the head god unscathed? One possible answer is that El had become synonymous with YHWH; both share a compassionate disposition toward humanity (Exod. 34:6; Ps. 86:15), use dreams to communicate (Gen. 31:24; 37:5; 1 Kgs. 3:5-15), and have healing powers (cf. *KTU* 1:16.v–vi with Gen. 20:17; Num. 12:13; Ps. 107:20 [Smith, 39]).

The Divine Council

As El served as chief of the Canaanite pantheon, YHWH was head of the *divine council*, whose members were often referred to as "the sons of gods." In Gen. 28:12; 33:1-2; Pss. 29:1 and 89:6-9, we find YHWH at the head of subordinate divine beings who are collectively referred to as the "council of LORD" (Jer. 23:18 and the "congregation of El" (Ps. 82:1). In Psalm 82, God attacks the congregants for their oppressive acts against humanity, for which they are doomed to die like mortals (vv. 5-7). In Job 1:6-7, Job's troubles begin when the divine council convenes with YHWH, and God asks "the satan" where he has been. The satan also appears on the divine council in Zechariah, where YHWH delivers judgment between two members of his entourage. The clearest depiction of the divine council's function is in 1 Kgs. 22:19-22, where YHWH seeks guidance and direction from the council, the members of which confer in open discussion before one spirit approaches YHWH with a proposal. Following a common motif in ancient Mediterranean literature, humans are sometimes transported before God and the divine council, as found in a party feasting with Elohim in Exod. 24:9-11 and Isaiah's commission as prophet in Isaiah 6 (Niditch 2010, 14–17).

Concluding Words on the Complexities of the Ancient Context

Reading the Old Testament in its ancient contexts requires a variety of considerations and an understanding that there are divergent views on these contexts. But this complexity should not discourage readers of the Bible from contemplating the origins of the Old Testament books, because a better understanding of their origins results in a broader understanding of their meanings and potential applications to our modern contexts. The authors of this volume's commentaries have worked to give the reader the best possible overview of the sociohistorical contexts that underlie the books of the Old Testament, opening its texts in new ways so that new meanings can be derived. While this section has highlighted some of the many considerations that need to be addressed when reading the "Very Dangerous Texts Ahead," the variety of contexts out of which the Old

Testament's books emerged is paralleled by the diversity of cultures, faiths, and societies into which they have been received.

Reading the Old Testament in Its Contemporary Contexts

Actively engaging the Old Testament in both its ancient and modern contexts enables readers to discover new levels of meaning that would otherwise go unnoticed. Through acknowledging an Old Testament text's historical setting, exploring how it has been interpreted through the millennia, and noticing the questions and challenges that it raises for our contemporary settings, engaged readers are better able to receive multiple levels of meaning that aid the reader in better understanding the biblical authors' intentions and discerning the passage's potential relevance to conversations that are unfolding today.

The Challenge of Bringing Ancient Context in Line with Modern Contexts

To participate in this process, however, is not a simple task. Beyond working to discern the various levels of meaning within the Old Testament, it is of paramount importance for readers to also acknowledge the preconceptions and biases they bring with them as they work to connect the ancient writings to their own world—an issue that is explored at length below.

As humorously demonstrated in A. J. Jacobs's book *The Year of Living Biblically*, it is important to remember that the texts of the Old Testament were not written for twenty-first-century audiences, but for citizens of the ancient world. As he recounts in his book, Jacobs tried to live as literally as possible according to the laws of the Hebrew Bible for one year. His experiment revealed that to live by the rules of the Hebrew Bible is to live as an outlaw in much of the modern world, whether because the Hebrew Bible calls for the execution of people who wear mixed fibers or because it mandates sacrificing animals in urban centers. This clash of ancient and modern cultures occurred in a very serious way in the tragic murder of Murray Seidman. Mr. Seidman's killer referenced Lev. 20:13 as his motivation for stoning the elderly and mentally disabled man (Masterson).

Conversely, some people, like Charlie Fuqua, assert that engaging with the Old Testament's historical contexts is not required. During the 2012 United States election, Fuqua ran for a seat on the Arkansas state legislature and released a book titled *God's Law: The Only Political Solution*. In his book, Fuqua calls for the creation of legal channels that will facilitate the execution of disobedient children, as commanded in Deut. 21:18-21 (2012, 179). While Fuqua's views represent a fringe group of theomonists that include such Christian reconstructionists as Cornelius Van Til and Rousas John Rushdoony, his example illustrates the importance of contemplating the important differences that exist between the biblical authors' societies and those into which their writings are received today. One must ask questions such as, Did the authors of Deut. 21:18-21 actually seek the execution of disobedient children, or did they pose an extreme example to illustrate a point on child rearing? Another important question to consider is, Did Deut. 21:18-21 originate at a time when resources were so scarce and the production of food so difficult that a child who didn't contribute to—but rather threatened—the common good posed a threat to the community's survival? Growing and cultivating food could certainly be a matter of life and death. Fuqua's failure to engage Deut. 21:18-21, choosing instead to blindly subscribe to the text at face value, is a very serious and dangerous matter, especially considering his aspirations for political office. But while vast differences separate the cultures and societies of the Old Testament authors and the world that we inhabit today, a surprising number of connections do exist.

Whether a Judean farmer or an American physician, we all share such aspects of the universal human experience as love, hate, trust, betrayal, fear, and hope—all of which are reflected both in the Old Testament and in our daily lives. Such themes as women working to find justice in societies that offer little, the quest for love along with its dangers and rewards, and people's struggle to understand their relationships with power, whether personal or political, are all found in the stories of the Old Testament and are still highly relevant to us today.

It should be pointed out, however, that earnestly engaging the Old Testament in its ancient and modern contexts is difficult, even hazardous. Several key considerations that help in an engaged reading of the books of the Old Testament are included here, including issues of biblical ownership, methods of interpretation, and approaches to the reception of its texts.

Whose Bible Is It, Anyway?

While the texts of the Old Testament are commonly used with an air of authority and ownership, their ownership is open to question. So, to whom do they belong? Now that their authors are long dead—and their works have passed through generations and around the world—who is the heir of these works? To which community would they turn and say, "The keys are yours"? One problem with answering this question is that the Old Testament's authors and editors did not represent a unified tradition through which a unified voice could be offered. Furthermore, the faiths and cultures of the twenty-first century CE are so far removed from the ancient authors' that they would most likely be utterly unrecognizable to them. On one level, it is a moot question. Those authors are dead, and they do not get a say regarding who uses their works, or how. Be that as it may, it is an important question to consider, for recognizing that the Old Testament has a number of spiritual heirs with divergent views of the divine underscores the vast interpretive possibilities these texts contain. While many faith traditions draw on the books of the Old Testament, the three largest—in order of appearance—are Judaism, Christianity, and Islam.

The Hebrew Bible (the *Tanakh*) of Judaism is composed of twenty-four books, which are divided into the Torah (Law), the Nebiim (Prophets), and the Ketubim (Writings). The Torah gives accounts of the creation, the establishment of the Hebrew people, and their movement out of captivity in Egypt toward the land that was promised to their ancestors. The public reading of the Torah is a religious ritual that culminates with the annual holiday of *Simchat Torah*, which celebrates its completion. Although the Tanakh forms the whole of Jewish biblical literature, it is supplemented by other interpretive collections.

The Christian *Old Testament*, sometimes referred to as the *First Testament*, sets the books of the Tanakh in a different order and serves as the first section of the *Christian Bible*, as a whole. Canonization of the Old Testament varies among different Christian traditions. Roman Catholicism,

Eastern Orthodoxy, and some Protestant groups include the seven additional books in their canon, as well as additions to the books of Esther and Daniel; these additions are called the *deuterocanon* ("second canon") or *Apocrypha* ("hidden"). Many of the books of the Old Testament are popularly seen as a precursor to the coming of Jesus and his perceived fulfillment of the law.

Islam incorporates many of the figures of the Old Testament into its sacred writings, the Holy Qur'an. Giving particular reverence to the Torah and the Psalms, the Qur'an honors Abraham, Isaac, and Moses as prophetic predecessors to the faith's final and greatest prophet, Muhammad (d. 632 CE).

While each of these traditions draws deep meaning and conviction from the Hebrew Scriptures, they also use them in different ways to reflect their own unique spiritual paths and theologies. The question of which group is the rightful heir of the biblical authors is impossible to answer definitively, since each claims to be in fact the rightful heir. The fact that such a diverse pool of people turns to these texts as sacred Scripture amplifies the many possibilities for Old Testament interpretation.

Evolving Views of the Old Testament and Its Interpretation

Whether or not it is done consciously, all readers of the Old Testament are engaged in some level of interpretation; there are no passive readers of the Bible. When people read the books of the Old Testament, they do so actively, bringing their own presuppositions, experiences, and cultural norms to a text. In essence, readers of the Old Testament bridge the ancient to the modern by way of exegesis and hermeneutics.

Exegesis looks at the texts in their ancient contexts, while hermeneutics works to discern how they relate to a modern reader's situation. Biblical scholars and readers have developed a number of methods for bringing the ancient and the modern together, often with specific objectives and theological motives in mind.

Biblical Literalism

Biblical literalism—which asserts that the Bible is the inerrant word of God, unaltered and untainted by human agency during its transmission from God to humanity—is a prevalent form of interpretation in the United States, practiced commonly within fundamentalist and some evangelical communities. The literal meanings of individual biblical texts were long considered alongside allegorical, moral, and mystical interpretations; it was not until the Reformation's second wave, in the seventeenth century, that literalism became a way to approach the Bible as a whole.

Protestant Christians who broke from the authority of Roman Catholicism found a strong sense of liberation in the idea of gaining access to God's direct word through the Scriptures. If an adherent could access God directly through a Bible, what need did they have for such individual or institutional arbitrators as priests, popes, or the Roman Church? Whereas early Reformers like Martin Luther and John Calvin viewed Scripture as being inspired by God with human involvement in its transmission, some of the second wave of Reformers, such as Amandus Polanus (d. 1610) and Abraham Calov (d. 1686), placed even greater emphasis on the Bible's inerrancy. The movement known as Protestant Scholasticism promoted the idea that any human involvement in the creation of the Bible was strictly mechanical; those who wrote the words were merely tools used by God. This was the first time that the idea of the inerrancy of Scripture as a literal interpretive approach was applied to the Bible—as a whole.

Despite the many developments in biblical interpretation that have occurred between the seventeenth and twenty-first centuries CE, many North American Christians still self-identify as biblical literalists. However, almost nobody practices biblical literalism in the strictest sense, for it would be an almost untenable position. The various contributions by the different religious communities that went into the writing of our biblical texts have resulted in contradicting versions of similar content (cf. Exod. 21:2-8 with Deut. 15:12-13). Given these challenges, how could A. J. Jacobs's experiment in living in strict accord with biblical law have any hope of being tenable, or even legal?

Historical Criticism

The influence of the Enlightenment—with its emphases on reason and searching for facts—gave rise to *the historical-critical movement*, which works to reconstruct the ancient contexts of the Bible. Baruch Spinoza (d. 1677) argued that the same scientific principles that were being applied to other areas of knowledge should be applied to the Bible as well. The results, which are still highly influential on how biblical scholarship is conducted today, have challenged such traditionally held Old Testament notions as the Genesis account(s) of the creation, Moses' composition of the Torah, and the historical validity of the Hebrew exodus out of Egypt, to name a few. Scrutinizing a particular text's origins through asking such questions as, Who wrote the text? For what purpose? and, Under what circumstances? Historical critics work to better understand what lies beneath the text.

Historical criticism's influence on biblical scholarship has shaped the way that many theologians read the Bible by adding to our understanding of the ancient contexts behind biblical texts. *Religionsgeschichte* ("history of religions") is a tool of historical criticism that reads biblical texts in their ancient religious contexts. Another historical-critical tool is *form criticism*, which has gleaned new meaning from such passages as the Song of Deborah (Judges 5) by considering their oral prehistory, reconstructing the *Sitz im Leben* ("original setting"), and analyzing their literary genres.

Social-Scientific Criticism

In the late 1970s—with the publication of Norman Gottwald's *The Tribes of Yahweh*—biblical scholars began to look at the books of the Old Testament through the lens of their sociological settings. Since then, numerous scholars have used societal patterns both to fill in many of the hidden contexts that are simply not addressed in the texts themselves and to better understand the societal motivations behind the Old Testament authors' messages.

One advantage to the social-scientific method of interpretation is its ability to inform hermeneutics (again, the application of biblical texts to modern circumstances). Social-scientific models have proven to be of particular use in shedding light on the contexts and motivations behind biblical texts while opening new ways of understanding how those texts might relate to the modern world (Chaney; Coomber 2011). A tempting misuse of social-scientific models of interpretation, however, is to treat the findings gained through social-scientific models as hard evidence that can stand on its own. Social-scientific models that deal with tribalism, urban development, religious-political interactions, or economic cycles can provide insight into how humans—and their systems—are expected to behave; they do not, however, prove how humans and systems did behave. It is for this reason that social-scientific approaches should be used in tandem with all available data, be it archaeological or literary.

Commenting on the great value of using social-scientific models in the interpretation of biblical texts, Philip Esler writes that their use "fires the social-scientific imagination to ask new questions of data, to which only the data can provide the answers" (Esler, 3). In other words, these models are useful for the interpretation of evidence, not as evidence in and of themselves. Social-scientific criticism has proven especially useful in the development of contextual readings of the Old Testament, which address issues ranging from political interpretations of the Bible to interpretations within such minority groups as LGBT (lesbian, gay, bisexual, and transgender) and disabled communities.

Contextual and Reception Readings and Criticisms

Contextual readings of the Old Testament provide excellent examples of how the ancient stories and ideas of the Old Testament can speak to the modern contexts of diverse communities. These forms of criticism, like social-scientific or literary criticism, often take on an interdisciplinary nature. While a plethora of contextual topics have been covered biblically, those that address issues of empire, gender, and race are briefly covered here.

Empire

Just as issues of empire were integral in the formation of the Old Testament, as addressed in the "Reading the Old Testament in Its Ancient Contexts" section above, Old Testament texts continue to influence the ways people approach issues of empire today. On the one hand, the imagery that celebrates conquest in the invasion of Canaan (Joshua) and the glory of Solomon's kingdom (e.g., 1 Kings 4) could be used to support the building of empire. On the other hand, those who challenge the rise or expansion of empires can draw on anti-imperial readings that condemn the conduct of royals and their exploitation of the citizenry (e.g., Micah 3), and legislation against economic injustice in the Torah, Writings, and Prophets.

Pro-imperial readings of the Old Testament can be seen in the building and expansion of US influence, such as the idea of *Manifest Destiny*, which portrays the Christian European settlement of the United States as God's divine will. Manifest destiny involved a reimagining of the Pilgrims—and later European settlers—as the new Hebrews, pushing aside the Native American peoples—who took on the role of Canaanites—in order to create a new Israel. The Rev. Josiah Strong's publication *Our Country* echoes this sentiment in its assertion that God was charging European Christianity "to dispossess the many weaker races, assimilate others, and mold the remainder" (Strong, 178). Reverberations of the Old Testament–rooted Manifest Destiny still surface in aspects of American exceptionalism, which influences the US political spectrum and can be seen in such approaches to foreign policy as "the Bush Doctrine," which works to spread American-style democracy as a path to lasting peace.

Just as the Old Testament has been used for empire building, it has also been used to challenge empire and its institutions. While the exodus narrative helped to shape the idea of Manifest Destiny, it also became a powerful abolitionist force in attacking the institutions of slavery and segregation. During the abolitionist movement, the powerful imagery of the exodus story gave hope and power to free African Americans and slaves alike. The power of the story was harnessed again in the mid-twentieth century, giving strength to those who struggled for racial equality (Coomber 2012, 123–36). Recent biblical scholarship has also turned to the Old Testament to address various issues of modern-day economic exploitation and neoimperialism (e.g., Gottwald 2011; Boer, ed.; West 2010).

A highly influential outcome of the crossing of Bible and empire has been *postcolonial interpretation*. As European empires spread throughout the world, they brought the Bible and Christianity with them. With the twentieth-century waning of European imperialism, colonized and previously colonized peoples have found their own voices in the Bible, resulting in a variety of new interpretations and new approaches to major Old Testament themes. Postcolonial interpretation has enriched the field from Mercedes García Bachmann's use of Isaiah 58 to address issues of "unwanted fasting" (105–12) to raising questions about whether the Christian canon should be reopened to include the folk stories and traditions of colonized Christian communities that feel unrepresented by the current Bible (Pui Lan).

Gender

Studies in gender have also revealed a wide range of interpretive possibilities and have come to the forefront of biblical scholarship during the past four decades. While often treated as the sex of the body, the word *gender* is a complicated term that addresses a variety of factors of embodiment, including mental and behavioral characteristics. *Masculinity* and *femininity*, for example, take on different attributes and expectations depending on the society or culture in which they exist. While gender is an area of study that is continually developing into various branches, both within and outside of biblical studies, one of its most predominant manifestations in biblical studies is found in *feminist criticism*.

Women have been longtime readers and commentators on biblical texts, even though their work has rarely been given the same consideration as their male counterparts, who have long served as the vanguard of the academy. Hildegard of Bingen (d. 1179) authored a commentary on Genesis 1–2 (Young, 262); R. Roberts (d. 1788) composed numerous sermons on a range of texts for a clergyman acquaintance (Knowles, 418–19); and abolitionist Elizabeth Cady Stanton (d. 1902) helped to publish *The Woman's Bible*. These three women serve as but a few examples of women who have made important contributions to biblical studies, though their work is unknown to many.

Feminist criticism continues to be a very effective mode for recovering women's insights, perspectives, knowledge, and the feminine principle in biblical texts, often rescuing those voices and interpretations from centuries of marginalization by patriarchal and even misogynistic interpretation. Elisabeth Schüssler Fiorenza claims that, unlike many other forms of biblical criticism, feminist biblical studies does not owe its existence to the academy but to social movements for change, and also to a desire for the ongoing pursuit of equal participation and equal rights, which have in practice been restricted to a small group of elite men (Schüssler Fiorenza, 8–9). Schüssler Fiorenza argues that since the Bible has most often been used in these struggles for either "legitimating the status quo of the kyriarchal order of domination *or* for challenging dehumanization, feminist biblical interpretation is best articulated as an integral part of wo/men's struggles for authority and self-determination" (9). Like so many forms of contextual and received readings, feminist criticism can serve as a liberating force by revealing perspectives within the Bible's texts that have otherwise gone unnoticed.

An example of recovering the woman's perspective in the Old Testament is found in feminist commentaries on such texts as Isa. 42:14, in which God says,

> For a long time I have held my peace,
> I have kept still and restrained myself;
> now I will cry out like a woman in labor,
> I will gasp and pant.

Patricia Tull has highlighted the way in which YHWH adopts the power of a woman in labor to emphasize God's own divine power of creation (Tull, 263). Another example of uncovering women's voices to find justice in patriarchal cultures—which work to subvert women's voices and rights—is found in Sharon Pace Jeansonne's treatment of Tamar as a woman who seizes power to find justice in a society that is set up to stop her from doing so (Jeansonne, 98–106).

Feminist criticism—as with most any other form of biblical criticism—is polyvocal, with a broad spectrum of biblical views, including those who have argued that the Bible might be best left alone (Bal, 14). Male scholars have also engaged with feminist-focused readings of Old Testament texts. Daniel Cohen's midrash on Genesis 3, for example, addresses misogynistic interpretations of the Garden of Eden story (Cohen 141–48).

Similar to some of feminist criticism's attempts to reclaim the women's voice in the Bible and address misogynistic interpretation, *queer criticism* works to uncover LGBT perspectives in the Old Testament and messages that are of importance to LGBT communities. Queer interpretation has addressed a number of such topics, including K. Renato Lings's work on homophobic critiques of the destruction of Sodom in Genesis 19—a text often used to condemn homosexuality—in which he argues that attaching homosexuality to the sin of Sodom was a later interpretive development, unrecognized by biblical authors (Lings, 183–207). Others have shed new light on the ways in which biblical texts are interpreted to affect modern-day political decisions, such as the issue of same-sex marriage (see Stahlberg).

Conclusion

To be an engaged reader of the Old Testament involves simultaneously navigating the worlds of the biblical authors and redactors, as well as all those who have interpreted its texts. It is through approaching a biblical text or idea through these multiple angles that the multilayered meanings of the Old Testament books can be unlocked, not only in regard to the authors' intentions, but also in ways that the biblical writers may have never been able to foresee. These multiple intersections with the biblical text help people to have meaningful conversation and debate on topics ranging from climate change, to same-sex marriage, to the international banking crisis, and more. Naturally, being an engaged reader requires considerable effort, but it is through deliberating on biblical texts in all of their complexity that deeper meaning can be found, and more honest—or at least informed—readings of the Bible's contents can be gleaned.

In this volume, the contributors' commentaries provide a tool through which people can develop their engagement with the books of the Old Testament and Apocrypha. Whether approaching this volume as a researcher, educator, member of the clergy, or student, it is the intent of the *Fortress Commentary on the Old Testament* to inform readers about the Old Testament books' historical contexts, interpretive histories, and the modern contexts with which they engage, while also serving as an opening through which the conversation can be expanded.

Works Cited

Alfaro, Juan I. 1989. *Justice and Loyalty: A Commentary on the Book of Micah*. Grand Rapids: Eerdmans.

Bachmann, Mercedes L. García. 2009. "True Fasting and Unwilling Hunger (Isaiah 58)." In *The Bible and the Hermeneutics of Liberation*, edited by A. F. Botta and P. R. Andiñach, 113–31. Atlanta: SBL.

Bal, Mieke. 1989. *Anti-Covenant: Counter-Reading Women's Lives in the Hebrew Bible*. Sheffield: Almond.

Boer, Roland, ed. 2013. *Postcolonialism and the Hebrew Bible: The Next Step*. SemeiaSt 70. Atlanta: SBL.

Cantor, Norman F. 1992. *Inventing the Middle Ages: The Lives, Works, and Ideas of the Great Medievalists of the Twentieth Century*. Cambridge: Lutterworth.

Chaney, Marvin L. 1999. "Whose Sour Grapes? The Addressees of Isaiah 5:1–7 in the Light of Political Economy." In *The Social World of the Hebrew Bible: Twenty-Five Years of the Social Sciences in the Academy*, edited by Ronald A. Simkins and Stephen L. Cook. *Semeia* 87:105–22.

Cohen, Daniel. 2007. "Taste and See: A Midrash on Genesis 3:6 and 3:12." In *Patriarchs, Prophets and Other Villains*, edited by Lisa Isherwood, 141–48. London: Equinox Publishing.

Coomber, Matthew J. M. 2010. *Re-Reading the Prophets through Corporate Globalization: A Cultural-Evolutionary Approach to Understanding Economic Injustice in the Hebrew Bible*. Piscataway, NJ: Gorgias.

———. 2011. "Caught in the Crossfire? Economic Injustice and Prophetic Motivation in Eighth-Century Judah." *BibInt* 19, nos. 4–5:396–432.

———. 2012. "Before Crossing the Jordan: The Telling and Retelling of the Exodus Narrative in African American History." In *Exodus and Deuteronomy: Texts @ Contexts*, edited by Athalya Brenner and Gale A. Yee, 123–36. Minneapolis: Fortress Press.

———. 2013. "Debt as Weapon: Manufacturing Poverty from Judah to Today." *Diaconia: Journal for the Study of Christian Social Practice* 4, no. 2:141–55.

Coote, Robert B., and Keith W. Whitelam. 1987. *The Emergence of Early Israel in Historical Perspective*. Sheffield: Almond.

Crossley, James G. 2008. *Jesus in an Age of Terror: Scholarly Projects for a New American Century*. London: Equinox.

Davies, Philip. 2000. "What Separates a Minimalist from a Maximalist? Not Much." *BAR* 26, no. 2:24–27, 72–73.

Davies, Philip, and John Rogerson. 2005. *The Old Testament World*. 2nd ed. Louisville: Westminster John Knox.

Dever, William G. 2008. *Did God Have a Wife? Archaeology and Folk Religion in Ancient Israel*. Grand Rapids: Eerdmans.

Esler, Philip F. 2005. "Social-Scientific Models in Biblical Interpretation." In *Ancient Israel: The Old Testament in Its Social Context*, edited by Philip Esler, 3–14. London: SCM.

Fuqua, Charles R. 2012. *God's Law: The Only Political Solution*. Salt Lake City: American Book Publishing.

Gottwald, Norman. 1999. *The Tribes of Yahweh: A Sociology of the Religion of Liberated Israel, 1250–1050* BCE. Sheffield: Sheffield Academic Press.

———. 2001. *The Politics of Ancient Israel*. Louisville: Westminster John Knox.

Grabbe, Lester L. 2007. *Ancient Israel: What Do We Know and How Do We Know It?* London: T&T Clark.

Halpern, Baruch. 1995. "Erasing History: The Minimalist Assault on Ancient Israel." *BRev* 11: 26–35, 47.

Jacobs, A. J. 2007. *The Year of Living Biblically: One Man's Humble Quest to Follow the Bible as Literally as Possible*. New York: Simon & Schuster.

Jeansonne, Sharon Pace. 1990. *The Women of Genesis: From Sarah to Potiphar's Wife*. Minneapolis: Fortress Press.

Josephus, Flavius. 1854. *The Works of Flavius Josephus: Comprising the Antiquities of the Jews, a History of the Jewish Wars, and Life of Flavius Josephus, Written by Himself.* Translated by William Whiston. Philadelphia: Jas. B. Smith.

Karmon, Yehuda. 1971. *Israel: A Regional Geography*. London: Wiley-Interscience.

Knapp, A. Bernard. 1988. "Copper Production and Eastern Mediterranean Trade: The Rise of Complex Society in Cyprus." In *State and Society: The Emergence and Development of Social Hierarchy and Political Centralization*, edited by J. Gledhill, B. Bender, and M. T. Larsen, 149–72. London: Unwin Hyman.

Knowles, Michael P. 2012. "Roberts, R. (ca. 1728–88)." In *Handbook of Women Biblical Interpreters*, edited by M. A. Taylor and A. Choi, 418–20. Grand Rapids: Baker Academic.

Kwok Pui-lan. 2003. "Discovering the Bible in the Non-Biblical World." In *Searching the Scriptures: A Feminist Introduction*, edited by Elisabeth Schüssler Fiorenza, 276–88. New York: Crossroad.

Lings, K. Renato. 2007. "Culture Clash in Sodom: Patriarchal Tales of Heroes, Villains, and Manipulation." In *Patriarchs, Prophets and Other Villains*, edited by Lisa Isherwood, 183–207. London: Equinox.

Liverani, Mario. 2007. *Israel's History and the History of Israel*. Translated by Chiara Peri and Philip Davies. London: Equinox.

Masterson, Teresa. 2011. "Man, 70, Stoned to Death for Being Gay." *NBC10 Philadelphia*. Accessed October 14, 2013. http://www.nbcphiladelphia.com/news/local/Man-70-Stoned-to-Death-for-Homosexuality-Police-118243719.html.

Niditch, Susan. 2010. "Experiencing the Divine: Heavenly Visits, Earthly Encounters and the Land of the Dead." In *Religious Diversity in Ancient Israel and Judah*, edited by Francesca Stavrakopoulou and John Barton, 11–22. London: T&T Clark.

Schüssler Fiorenza, Elisabeth. 2013. *Changing Horizons: Explorations in Feminist Interpretation*. Minneapolis: Fortress Press.

Schweitzer, Albert. 1968. *The Quest of the Historical Jesus: A Critical Study of Its Progress from Reimarus to Wrede*. New York: Macmillan.

Smith, Mark S. 2002. *The Early History of God: Yahweh and the Other Deities in Ancient Israel*. Grand Rapids: Eerdmans.

Stahlberg, Lesleigh Cushing. 2008. "Modern Day Moabites: The Bible and the Debate About Same-Sex Marriage." *BibInt* 16:422–75.

Stavrakopoulou, Francesca. 2010. "'Popular' Religion and 'Official' Religion: Practice, Perception, Portrayal." In *Religious Diversity in Ancient Israel and Judah*, edited by Francesca Stavrakopoulou and John Barton, 37–58. New York: T&T Clark.

Strong, Josiah. 1885. *Our Country: Its Possible Future and Its Present Crisis*. New York: The American Home Missionary Society.

Tull, Patricia K. 2012. "Isaiah." In *Women's Bible Commentary: Twentieth-Anniversary Edition*, edited by C. A. Newsom, S. H. Ringe, and J. E. Lapsley, 255–66. Louisville: Westminster John Knox.

West, Gerald. 2010. "The Legacy of Liberation Theologies in South Africa, with an Emphasis on Biblical Hermeneutics." *Studia Historiae Ecclesiasticae* 36, Supplement: 157–83.

Whitelam, Keith W. 2007. "Lines of Power: Mapping Ancient Israel." In *To Break Every Yoke: Essays in Honour of Marvin L. Chaney*, edited by R. B. Coote and N. K. Gottwald, 40–79. Sheffield: Sheffield Phoenix Press.

Young, Abigail. 2012. "Hildegard of Bingen (1098–1179)." In *Handbook of Women Biblical Interpreters*, edited by M. A. Taylor and A. Choi, 259–64. Grand Rapids: Baker Academic.

THE PEOPLE OF GOD AND THE PEOPLES OF THE EARTH

Hugh R. Page Jr.

The Bible Is Just the Beginning

The Bible is preeminently a book about people. That may strike some as a rather odd assertion given the stature enjoyed by the Bible as sacred text containing, in many faith traditions, everything one needs to know about God and salvation. Nonetheless, some of the more important foci of the Old and New Testaments have to do with the saga of the human family and the women and men that are dramatis personae in this unfolding drama. In the twenty-first century CE, our appreciation of how Scripture narrates that story is much more nuanced than it was perhaps a generation or two ago. We are much more aware of the processes by which traditions are shaped and preserved. We have a deeper understanding of the myriad stages through which the inspired words of prophets, poets, and sages proceed before being canonized: as well as of the place the Bible occupies in the global ecology of sacred texts. Moreover, we recognize that many of the world's sacred texts have important things to say about the human condition. Thus perspectives on what it means to be "people of God," women and men in a special relationship with a transcendent being, or members of a large and diverse human family sharing a common terrestrial abode vary widely. Moreover, in today's world, scholarship in fields such as genetics and anthropology is changing the way we think about human origins and notions of personhood.

It is because of new ideas about humanity and its origins that responsible readers of the Bible must, therefore, examine biblical conceptions of personhood, while keeping in mind the ways in which both the human family in general and those individuals called into special relationship with the God of Israel are construed. In so doing, they must also look at how such ideas have shaped, and continue to influence, notions about the world and its inhabitants today; are related to comparable ideas about personhood in other faith traditions; relate to what scientific evidence reveals about the human family; have been complicit in the exploitation of colonized peoples; and stand in relationship to those ideas about the human family articulated in documents such as the United Nations Declaration of Human Rights and the Declaration on the Rights of Indigenous Peoples. Such a task is necessary if we are to enhance the extent to which the Bible can be deployed as a resource in building a more just and equitable global community. Failure to do so may limit the extent to which members of faith communities for which the Bible is authoritative are able to join in meaningful dialogue about the future of our global community and the institutions that support it. It may also inadvertently lend credence to the idea that religious texts and traditions have no place in conversations about those ideals on which a cosmopolitan global community should be based in the future.

The Earth and Its Peoples—A View from the Ethnographic Record

Science has revealed that modern human beings are the result of a remarkable evolutionary process. We share common African ancestry, and our diversity at this point in time bears witness to an array of migratory, climatic, and genetic adaptations that span hundreds of thousands of years. Our cultural landscape is vast and remarkable in its variation. For example, the comprehensive cultural database maintained by Human Relations Area Files at Yale University (see http://www.yale.edu/hraf/collections.htm) contains information on several hundred cultures.

The *Ethnographic Atlas*, a massive project undertaken by George Peter Murdock (1969) and ultimately brought to full fruition in the 1970s, contains information on more than one thousand distinct groups. As an ethnologist, Murdock was particularly interested in both the comparative study of cultures and the identification of behavioral traits that manifest locally, regionally, and internationally (see especially Murdock 1981, 3). His work calls attention to the breadth of lifeways characteristic of peoples around the world. Scholarship continuing in the vein of Murdock's has led to the identification of some 3,500 cultures on which published data are readily available (see, e.g., Price, 10). Such studies have also resulted in the development of templates for comparing social organization, religious beliefs, and other information about the world's disparate peoples (see Ember and Ember; and Murdock et al.). Needless to say, the vision of the human family derived from this research is remarkable. Social scientists see this diverse collage of languages, customs, and religious traditions as the end result of developmental forces that have been operational for *aeons*. It is also for them a mystery to be probed using the critical tools at their disposal. Ethnographic investigations and theory testing have laid bare and will continue to reveal its undiscovered truths. However, humankind has not revealed, and is not likely to yield, the sum total of its secrets to even the most dogged of investigators. Like the stories of primordial reality we encounter in the biblical book of Genesis, such research offers a place from which to begin pondering what it means to be human.

Human life is, of course, dynamic. New social and religious groups are born constantly. The first two decades of the current millennium have even witnessed the dissolution of geopolitical boundaries, the creation of new nation states, and the birth of new religious movements. Thus notions of culture and personhood in our era are anything but static. Our human family continues to grow and with each passing day becomes more diverse and increasingly complex. Research in the social sciences has increased our understanding of how culture and identity evolve. We know more today than ever before about the ways language, physical environment, and other factors contribute to ideas about what it means to be a fully actualized self and to be in relationship with those other selves that are one's family members, friends, and neighbors. It has also shed light on the role that the collection and preservation of religious lore play in this process. Sacred traditions and texts serve as the repositories for stories about how people and the groups in which they are embedded came to be. They also function as points of reference for the nurture of persons and the communities in which they live.

The challenge we face in an era when such traditions are often read narrowly or uncritically—without an eye toward their implicit limitations—is to create charitable and inclusive approaches that allow us to engage and appropriate them. Such strategies necessitate that we become well versed in the ways that stories, both ancient and modern, shape our identities, beliefs, and relationships with one another. Whether one has in mind venerable tales such as the Babylonian *Enuma Elish* and the so-called Priestly account of creation (Gen. 1:1—2:4a), or modern cinematic myths like the *Matrix* or *Prometheus* sagas, narratives of one kind or another provide a context for understanding who we are and how we choose to live. Returning to the Bible itself, it is arguable that one of its central aims is to inform us of what it means to be finite beings that are threads in a sacred cosmic fabric woven, as it were, by a divine and ineffable artisan.

Ancient Near Eastern Lore and Conceptions of Personhood

In the late nineteenth and early twentieth centuries, scholars such as James Frazer and Stith Thompson began looking seriously at cultural practices and folklore from various parts of the world. The results were remarkable, though not without some degree of controversy. Frazer's efforts included his Victorian-era classic *The Golden Bough* (Frazer 1981) and an equally important, if less celebrated, three-volume work titled *Folk-Lore in the Old Testament* (Frazer 1918a; 1918b; 1918c); and Thompson's work on folklore motifs was pioneering insofar as it laid important groundwork for the comparison of tales from around the world. Although questions remain about the aims and theoretical presuppositions of these early works, their efforts, and those of the scholars following in their immediate footsteps, set the stage for much of the social-scientific research we have seen in the twentieth and twenty-first centuries, even in the field of biblical studies.

Among biblical scholars, the pioneers of form criticism and the so-called myth and ritual school found in this body of information—and other information gathered from ancient Near Eastern sources—a treasure trove useful for contextualizing and interpreting key portions of the Old Testament. Among form critics, Hermann Gunkel must be noted. His collection of essays in *What Remains of the Old Testament* and topical studies of literary *Gattungen* ("forms") as such pertain to the Bible in *The Legends of Genesis* and *The Folktale in the Old Testament* repay—even today—careful reading

(1928; 1964; 1987). Among myth and ritual adherents, Sigmund Mowinckel's work deserves pride of place, especially his *Psalmenstudien* (1966). These pioneers' use of ethnological resources in the study of Scripture were paralleled by those of Johannes Pedersen in his two-volume study of ancient Israelite culture (1926–1940) and extended in subsequent generations by Theodor Gaster's efforts to reclaim and expand the work of Frazer (1950; 1959; 1969); Mary Douglas's exploration of the body as social map (1966); Bruce Malina's use of a circum-Mediterranean paradigm to understand the roles of women and men in the Bible (1989); and others whose work has explored the intersections of Jewish, Christian, Mediterranean, and other cultural traditions both ancient and modern.

Several lessons can be gleaned from this body of research. The first is that people are in some ways "hardwired" to create and tell stories. These stories help in making sense of life crises such as birth, maturation, and death. They are also pivotal in defining the self and the social networks into which individual selves are embedded. A second lesson is that one particular genre, creation stories—whether they focus on the birth of deities (theogonies), the universe (cosmogonies), humanity, tribal confederations, monarchies, or all of the aforementioned—have a direct impact on the ways people understand their place in the world. Creation stories define social and ethnic boundaries, reify social and political hierarchies, and ascribe status based on age, gender, and other ontological and ascribed markers. These two factors should inform the ways information about individuals and groups embedded in poetry, rituals, royal inscriptions, and other texts is understood. A few examples from the ancient Near East are particularly illustrative.

The Mesopotamian flood tradition encountered in the Atrahasis myth has, among its more important purposes, articulation of a basic theological anthropology—one that is based on an understanding of the mutable and immutable dimensions of an, at times, capricious cosmos. Human beings are oddly situated in this power-filled and unstable environment. They are remarkable for three reasons. The first is because they are made of the flesh and blood of a divine insurgent and sacrificed because he led a rebellion against the harsh labor imposed on a subset of deities in the pantheon.

> When the gods themselves were men,
> They did the work. They endured the toil.
> The labor was onerous.
> Massive was the effort. The distress was exceedingly great. (Lambert and Millard, 42 [tablet 1.1.1–4], translation my own)

> Let them sacrifice the divine leader.
> Let the gods purify themselves by immersion.
> With his essence—flesh and blood—let Nintu mix the clay,
> So that divinity and humanity may be thoroughly
> Blended in the amalgam.
> For all time let us hear the drumbeat.
> In the flesh of the god let the ghost remain.
> Let her [Nintu] inform him [the slain god] of his token.
> So that there will be no forgetting,
> The spirit will remain. (Lambert and Millard, 58 [tablet 1.4.208–17], translation my own)

The human heartbeat is the "drum" reminding women and men for all time of the immortal lineage that is uniquely their own. The second reason that people are special is due to their being extended kin, as it were, of Atrahasis, the "exceedingly wise one," who managed to survive the great deluge by which all of humanity was destroyed. To them belongs the empowering, yet dangerous, model of this *liminal* ancestor. As William Moran noted more than four decades ago: "The Atrahasis Epic is an assertion of man's importance in the final order of things. It is also a strong criticism of the gods" (Moran, 59).

Humans are also special (see Moran, 60–61) for a third reason: because they are living proof of the imprudence of the gods and goddesses they serve. Created to assume the day-to-day labor deemed too difficult for immortals to bear, the din of their daily existence proved far too disruptive of their divine patrons' and matrons' sleep. Their death was decreed because they were, in a word, "noisy" (Lambert and Millard, 66 [tablet 1.7.354–59]). It is only through the quick-witted intervention of Enki, his personal god, that Atrahasis and his family are able to escape the inundation. Atrahasis is a powerful symbol of what can happen when human perseverance and divine subterfuge are allied.

The Atrahasis myth suggests that people are made of supernatural "stuff" and are heirs to a distinctive lineage. It also emphasizes that in a world filled with danger, the gods who are in control of the fates of women and men do not always have the best interest of the human family in mind. Although all mortals are in a sense beings belonging to and dependent on the gods, the implication of the sobering reality revealed in this myth is that in order to survive, women and men would do well to leverage their inner resources while at the same time relying, should all else fail, on timely divine intervention by those deities with whom they have a special relationship. Such assertions are, of course, in conversation with anthropologies articulated in other lore across a wide spectrum of genres. For example, Gilgamesh—particularly the Old Babylonian version of this Akkadian classic—focuses attention on the unique challenges confronted by one species of individual: monarchs. Of particular interest in this epic are their socialization, capacity to form friendships, quest for lasting renown, and insecurities about death. royal inscriptions, of which exemplars are too numerous to mention, continue in this vein and further define the traits of kings and those subject to their authority. Suzerainty treaties can be said to function in a comparable manner by defining the relationships of sociopolitical aggregates to one another. Sets of laws, like those found in the Code of Hammurabi, reify social status through taxonomies that identify insiders (e.g., king, free men, and those acquitted of offenses) and outsiders (e.g., criminals, widows, and orphans).

Another story, that of the travails of the god Ba'lu from the ancient city of Ugarit, offers a slightly different perspective on human life—this time from West Semitic lore. Unlike the story of Atrahasis, the Ba'lu myth is concerned primarily with how the enigmatic god of the fructifying rains—mainstays of human life—secures his place as head of the pantheon. Although the primary concern of this tale is Ba'lu's contest with rivals for ascendancy to the throne, it lifts the veil concealing the ongoing cosmic struggle between two such forces that inscribe the parameters for human existence: that is, life/fertility, represented by Ba'lu as numen of the storm, and Môtu, the embodiment of death and dissolution. At one point in this saga, he voluntarily submits himself to the authority and power of Môtu. His death, emblematic of nature's cyclic periods of aridity, leads his father 'Ilu, head of the pantheon, and his sister 'Anatu, to bewail its impact on the world. Both give voice to a lament intended, no doubt, to sum up the anguish of all affected by the storm god's departure.

> Ba'lu has died. What is to become of humanity?
> Dagan's child is no more. What will happen to earth's teeming masses? (CAT 1.5.6.23–24; 1.6.1.6–7)

The world and its inhabitants are part of the background landscape against which this divine drama unfolds. Nonetheless, as the narrative progresses, one realizes that each episode has a profound, if at times only partially articulated, impact on the peoples of the earth. Ba'lu returns to life, largely through the intervention of his sister 'Anatu. Eventually, he and Môtu have a fateful encounter that reveals, in no uncertain terms, that they are—and shall remain—in an interminable struggle.

> They fight each other like heroes
> Môtu is strong, as is Ba'lu
> Like raging bulls, they go head to head
> Môtu is strong, as is Ba'lu
> They bite one another like serpents
> Môtu is strong, as is Ba'lu
> Like animals, they beat each other to a pulp
> Môtu falls, Ba'lu collapses. (CAT 1.6.6.16–22)

The two battle to a virtual draw: an indication that the struggle between life and death is ongoing. The hope for "earth's teeming masses" is that the forces of life are able—at the very least—to withstand Death's furious and unrelenting onslaught. To be engaged nobly in the struggle is, therefore, to participate heroically in an age-old struggle that unites every member of the human family as kin. The warp and weft of day-to-day existence finds its ultimate significance in this ongoing cosmic battle. We see a stunning reflex of this mythology in the biblical Song of Songs, where the protagonists are anthropomorphized hypostases of Love (*'ahăbâ*) and Death (*māwet*).

> Seal me to your heart.
> Brand me on your arm.
> Love is equal to Death in its strength.
> Passion rivals Sheol in its ferocity.
> Its flames are a blazing fire.
> It is an eternal inferno. (Song of Songs 8:6, author's own translation)

Additional textual examples from Egypt and Anatolia could be cited, but the above suffice to show how implicit and explicit messaging about people—their nature, connection to one another, and relationship to the divine forces responsible for their creation and support—is conveyed in expressive culture.

The Hebrew Bible, Personhood, and Identity

Biblical references to the earth and its peoples are very much in conversation with these ancient Near Eastern traditions. The opening chapter of the Hebrew Bible contains a remarkable assertion in what scholars have traditionally designated the Priestly account of creation (Gen. 1:1—2:4a): that the world and everything in it is "good." It uses the Hebrew word *ṭôb* to describe its fundamental essence, a word whose semantic range connotes something sweet and pleasurable. Human beings are an important part of the created order. Made on the sixth day, they are distinguished only by gender: male and female. Neither ethnic nor regional markers are noted. All are made according to the divine "form" (*ṣelem*) and "pattern" (*dĕmût*)—that is, God's "image and likeness" according to the NRSV. Theirs are the tasks of reproducing and exercising control of the earth (1:26–28). The word used to describe what will be involved to reach this desired outcome (*kābaš*) connotes a process requiring forceful effort (Oswalt, 430). Also implied here is the idea that this is a laborious enterprise that is both collective and collaborative.

Following this masterful cosmogonic hymn, readers encounter in the remainder of Genesis a "mixed bag" of traditions about the earth's populace representing several sources: fragments of archaic poetry (2:23; 3:14-19; 4:23-24; 49); a descanting creation narrative (2:4b-24); etiological tales (11:1-9); ethnohistorical musings about the origins of particular peoples (4:17-22); an epic about the peregrinations of Israel's ancestors (11:31—36:43); and an extensive novella dealing with a key figure in the national saga: Joseph (37–50). While these materials can be read—as scholarly literature attests—from a variety of perspectives, one thing is very clear: together they tell the story of the God of Israel's relationship with the world and its peoples, some of whom—namely, Abraham, Sarah, and their descendants—are called to take on special responsibilities for the entirety of the human family (12:1-3). In fact, it could be argued that a significant portion of the Genesis tradition (1:1—11:32) has been intended as a creative "riff" on, or response to, Sumero-Akkadian lore (like that found in Atrahasis) about the origins of humanity.

One of the unifying threads holding together the narrative tapestry of Genesis and the remaining books of the Torah/Pentateuch is the story of how the world is affected by the shifting, strained, at times tumultuous, dynamic, and constantly evolving relationships among those who are the offspring of the primordial family. While highlighting theological themes such as *calling* (Exod. 3:1-15); *covenant* (Exod. 6:1-8; 20:1-17); *sin and redemption* (Exod. 32:1-35); *divine immanence and transcendence* (Exod. 25:1—31:18); *holiness* (Lev. 10:3; 20:26); *significant individuals* (Exod. 2:10; 15:20; 2:21; 3:1); *groups* (Exod. 3:8; 6:19); and *events* (Exodus 15; Num. 3:14-16; 9:15-16); these books also articulate a gestalt ("general sketch") for comprehending what it means to be part of a human family. This can entail struggling both to recognize its connectedness and to honor its diversity. It can also involve wrestling with the challenge of managing intergroup crises that influence the welfare of peoples living in proximity; competing for limited resources; and dealing with those changing geopolitical realities that generate population shifts, form new social movements, and give rise to diasporas. It is for this reason that one of the foci of these books, and the sources used therein, is the establishment of social, religious, and other boundaries that determine personhood, group affiliation, and status. For example, the Priestly creation story (Gen. 1—2:4a) can be said to inscribe broad and inclusive parameters for personhood. Since all human beings bear the imprint of the creator's "form" and "pattern," they can be said to belong to a single unified group, for which gender is the only subclassification (1:26-27). The implication of this is that everyone created *by* God belongs *to* God and is therefore part of the "people of God."

Genealogical tables, such as that found in Genesis 10, offer a more nuanced view of group identity based on location, language, and kin group (e.g., 10:5). The story of the Tower of Babel goes a step further in its linkage of linguistic heterogeneity to human hubris and a divine response to quell it (Gen. 11:5-7). Although it can be read simply as an entertaining etiology accounting for the diversity and spread of languages, it does contain a polemical strain resistant to linguistic solidarity, centralized government, and the conscription of resources needed to build monumental structures and to maintain the places—that is, cities—where they are most likely to be found in antiquity. Thus the story seems to be suggesting, on one level, that diversity and difference are preferable to a homogeneity whose consequences, intended or unintended, are to transgress the boundary separating mortals from God.

The block of material inclusive of the ancestral epic and the story of Joseph's rise to Egyptian prominence offers an even more complex picture of the "people of God." On the one hand, the "yes" given by Abram/Abraham to the call of YHWH (Gen. 12:1-3), and the covenant made with him (Gen. 15:18; 17:1-27) by YHWH, serve to distinguish him and his descendants among the "people of God"—that is, as a conduit of blessing to the entirety of the human family (Gen. 12:3). On the other hand, an inversion of status—from "temporary sojourner" to "inheritor" of Canaan (17:6-8)—is also promised, one that sets the stage for what is later described in Joshua and Judges. The story of Joseph's tensions with his brothers, as well as that of the peculiar circumstances leading Jacob and his kin to go to Egypt, set the stage for further musing on several issues. The first is how the kin group through whom all of the "people of God" are to be blessed understands its internal subdivisions (Genesis 49; Deuteronomy 32–33). The second has to do with how the kin group's liberation, covenant at Sinai, sojourn in the wilderness, and occupation of Canaan (Exod. 4:1—20:21; 32:1—35:29; Num. 1:1—36:13; Joshua; and Judges) are construed, particularly in terms of how these sources present Israel's relationship to its neighbors, both as stewards of a unique revelatory experience and part of a larger family of divine offspring. The third concerns the final book of the Pentateuch—Deuteronomy—that serves as the transitional bridge to the Former Prophets. From a literary standpoint, it is a rearticulation and expansion of core precepts first articulated in Exod. 20:1-17. It inscribes very narrow parameters for Israel's self-understanding and relationship to its neighbors. "When you come into the land that the Lord your God is giving you, you must not learn to imitate the abhorrent practices of those nations" (Deut. 18:9).

The book of Deuteronomy has very strict stipulations for the centralization of worship (12:1-28), prophetic practice (18:15-22), the conduct of war (20:1-20), and the care of those without material support (24:14-15, 17-18). All of these grow out of a particular self-understanding, stated most succinctly in what Gerhard von Rad long ago identified as a short creedal statement.

> A wandering Aramean was my ancestor; he went down into Egypt and lived there as an alien, few in number, and there he became a great nation, mighty and populous. When the Egyptians treated us harshly and afflicted us, by imposing hard labor on us, we cried to the LORD, the God of our ancestors; the LORD heard our voice and saw our affliction, our toil, and our oppression. The LORD brought us out of Egypt with a mighty hand and an outstretched arm, with a terrifying display of power, and with signs and wonders; and he brought us into this place and gave us this land, a land flowing with milk and honey. (Deut. 26:5-9)

Israel's identity as an "alien" subject to "hard labor" and "oppression," now liberated by YHWH, is the backdrop against which Deuteronomy's exclusive covenantal obligations are formulated. The jealousy of YHWH (Deut. 4:24) establishes impermeable cultural and ethical borders separating Israel from its neighbors. Deuteronomy and the historical narrative of the occupation of Canaan and the flowering of the monarchy are written in accordance with its principles. This so-called Deuteronomistic History (abbreviated Dtr by some scholars) consists of Joshua, Judges, the books of Samuel, and 1 and 2 Kings. It offers a far more complex, yet ultimately less inclusive, vision of the "people of God."

For example, we encounter the technical designation *ʿam yhwh* ("YHWH's people") in the Pentateuch's oldest strata (e.g., Judg. 5:11, 13—an ancient Hebrew poem; and Num. 11:29; 16:41). Here it refers to either the members of Israel's tribal confederation (Judges) or the Israelite community on the march through the wilderness following its flight from Egypt (Numbers). It is present much more frequently in Dtr, where it denotes those faithful bound by the Deuteronomic covenant (Deut. 27:9—*lĕʿam layhwh*); Israel before the establishment of the monarchy (1 Sam. 2:24); the fallen military contingent that supported Jonathan and Saul (2 Sam. 1:12); and as an *ethnonym* for those under the reign of David (2 Sam. 6:21), Jehu (2 Kgs. 9:6), and Jehoida (2 Kgs. 11:17). We also find the terms *ʿam hāʾĕlōhîm* or *ʿam ʾĕlōhîm* ("people of God") used in reference to the Israelite tribal contingent armed for battle (Judg. 20:2) and to those under David's sovereign rule (2 Sam. 14:13). Beyond these references, we encounter the term "YHWH's people" in 2 Chron. 23:16 (paralleling 2 Kgs. 11:17). Another enigmatic reference—to "the God of Abraham's people"—is found in Ps. 47:9, a poem asserting the universal kingship of *ʾĕlōhîm* ("God").

Although references to "Yahweh's people" and "people of God" do not appear in the Latter Prophets (Isaiah, Jeremiah, Ezekiel, and the Book of the Twelve) or the Writings (outside of the Chronicler), we can certainly detect a keen interest in the world's peoples in many of these books. In some instances, the focus is decidedly polemical. The pointed critique of Israel's neighbors in prophetic oracles is an excellent example (e.g., Isaiah 14–19; Ezekiel 26–30). The bimodal subdivision of humanity in Proverbs (between those who heed Wisdom's voice and others who do not in Proverbs 8–9). A third case in point is the distinction made between "those who lead many to righteousness" in Dan. 12:3) and their opponents. In others, there is an affirmation of the God of Israel's keen interest in building an inclusive eschatological community (e.g., Isa. 66:18-21) and questioning a culture of entitlement and condemnatory rhetoric among Israelite prophets (Jon. 4:9-11). In Jewish apocryphal literature, we also see an interest expressed in the relationship among peoples. In the Greek Addition F to Esther, an editor has called attention to the different "lots" God has assigned to "the people of God" and to "all the nations" (10:10). The author of the Wisdom of Solomon takes a slightly different tack. While adopting a rhetoric that accentuates the difference between the "righteous" and the "ungodly" (Wisdom), it also calls attention to the common ancestry of humanity:

> there is for all one entrance into life, and one way out. (Wis. 18:9)

What we have, therefore, in the Hebrew Bible are multiple visions of what it means to be "people of God" and "peoples of the earth." Some are narrow. Others are selectively inclusive. All must be read with an eye toward genre, the setting in which the text was produced, and the social, political, and religious circumstances it seeks to address.

It goes almost without saying that biblical writers and their initial audiences were concerned with theological issues such as Israel's election and the implications such issues have on the community's holiness and distinctiveness when compared to its neighbors. In light of this special calling, as it were, boundaries—their creation, maintenance, and occasional erasure—take on particular significance. Maintenance is a sign of covenantal fidelity (Deut. 7:1-6) and purity (Lev. 10:1-3). Periodic transgression is, at least in some instances, a necessary survival strategy. Judges is an excellent case in point (see Page). We see evidence in this book of the crossing of bodily, cultural, and other borders as part of what characterizes Israelite life during that bittersweet epoch when "there was no king in Israel" and "people did what was right in their own eyes" (Judg. 21:25). Israel's identity as a people with a unique identity, mission, and teleological objective is, thus, variously articulated in the Hebrew Bible. These overlapping, competing, and complementary ideas of what it means to be a "people of God" among "the earth's peoples" require attentiveness to the religious objectives, political aims, and eschatological foci of the books in which they are found. Therefore, any attempt to fully reconcile all aspects of these disparate conceptions is likely to meet with frustration. Instead, it is perhaps better to recognize that the Hebrew Bible does not speak with a single voice on the issue of what it means to be part of the human family.

Looking beyond the Bible

One could argue that this absence of uniformity in the Hebrew Bible is an invitation not simply to read, but also to query and "talk back to" its books. Among the questions we should ask is what sources—in addition to Scripture—we ought to consult in making sense of who we are, what our relationship should be to one another, and what our place is in the universe. This process is far more involved than turning to Genesis or some other biblical book for a "proof text" (the practice of using a specific text as the final authoritative word on a given issue). Instead, it requires taking into consideration modern geopolitical realities such as globalization and what the pure, applied, and social sciences are telling us about our biological origins, diversity, and connectedness.

It also makes it incumbent on Bible readers to be aware of how documents such as the United Nations Declaration on Human Rights (1948) and the United Nations Declaration on the Rights of Indigenous Peoples (2007) influence how we think about our rights and responsibilities as people of faith and citizens of the world. For example, article 1 of the former states that "all human beings are born free and equal in dignity and rights. They are endowed with reason and conscience and should act towards one another in a spirit of brotherhood" (United Nations General Assembly 2000, 326). An affirmation of this kind shapes the way one thinks about religious texts and traditions that qualify human freedom, equality, dignity, or rights endowed at birth. Furthermore, according to article 18 of the Declaration, "Everyone has the right to freedom of thought, conscience, and religion; this right includes freedom to change his religion or belief, and freedom either alone or in community with others and in public or private, to manifest his religion or belief in teaching, practice, worship, and observance" (United Nations General Assembly 2000, 327). Such texts can't help but influence our reading and deployment of those parts of the Bible that affirm behaviors that affirm or disagree with these statements and the ideals they represent. In the case of those that run counter, a hermeneutic inclusive of exegesis and critical engagement is warranted. Article 7 section 2 of the United Nations Declaration on the Rights of Indigenous Peoples states that "indigenous peoples have the collective right to live in freedom, peace and security as distinct peoples and shall not be subjected to any act of genocide or any other act of violence, including forcibly removing children of the group to another group" (United Nations General Assembly 2007, 5). Moreover, article 8 section 1 affirms that "indigenous peoples and individuals have the right not to be subjected to forced assimilation or destruction of their culture" (United Nations General Assembly 2007, 5). The reading or deployment of biblical passages that appear to celebrate or support behaviors of this kind can be neither ignored nor interpreted in a way that treats lightly the ways they have been used to justify policies that abrogate the rights of indigenous peoples around the world.

Thus, in our current era, perhaps the Bible should be seen less as the single authoritative source from which the final word on what it means to be "people of God" and "people of the earth" is to be found, and more as one of several interlocutors—including lived experience—informing our consideration of what is an unfolding *mystery* about the larger human experience that we are invited to prayerfully ponder.

Works Cited

Douglas, Mary. 1966. *Purity and Danger*. London: ARK.

Eilberg-Schwartz, Howard. 1990. *The Savage in Judaism: Anthropology of Israelite Religion and Ancient Judaism*. Bloomington: Indiana University Press.

Ember, Melvin, and Carol R. Ember, eds. 1999. *Cultures of the World: Selections from the Ten-Volume Encyclopedia of World Cultures*. New York: Macmillan Library Reference USA.

Frazer, James. 1981. *The Golden Bough*. 1890. Reprint, New York: Grammercy.

———. 1918a. *Folk-Lore in the Old Testament*. Vol. 1. London: Macmillan.

———. 1918b. *Folk-Lore in the Old Testament*. Vol. 2. London: Macmillan.

———. 1918c. *Folk-Lore in the Old Testament*. Vol. 3. London: Macmillan.

Gaster, Theodor H. 1950. *Thespis: Ritual, Myth, and Drama in the Ancient Near East*. New York: Harper & Row.

———, ed. 1959. *The New Golden Bough*. New York: Criterion.

———. 1969. *Myth, Legend and Custom in the Old Testament.* New York: Harper & Row.

Gunkel, Hermann. 1928. *What Remains of the Old Testament and Other Essays.* Translated by A. K. Dallas. New York: Macmillan.

———. 1964. *The Legends of Genesis: The Biblical Saga and History.* Translated by W. H. Carruth. Reprint of the introduction to the author's 1901 *Commentary on Genesis.* New York: Schocken.

———. 1987. *The Folktale in the Old Testament.* Translated by M. D. Rutter. Translation of the 1917 ed. Sheffield: Almond.

Lambert, W. G., and A. R. Millard, eds. 1999. *Atra-Hasis: The Babylonian Story of the Flood.* 1969. Reprint, Winona Lake, IN: Eisenbrauns.

Malina, Bruce. 1989. "Dealing with Biblical (Mediterranean) Characters: A Guide for U.S. Consumers." *BTB* 19:127–41.

Moran, William L. 1971. "Atrahasis: The Babylonian Story of the Flood." *Bib* 52:51–61.

Mowinckel, Sigmund. 1966. *Psalmenstudien: 1921–1924.* Amsterdam: Grüner.

Murdock, George Peter. 1969. *Ethnographic Atlas.* 3rd ed. Pittsburgh: University of Pittsburgh Press.

———. 1981. *Atlas of World Cultures.* Pittsburgh: University of Pittsburgh Press.

Murdock, George Peter, C. S. Ford, A. E. Hudson, R. Kennedy, L. W. Simmons, and J. W. M. Whiting. 1987. *Outline of Cultural Materials.* 5th ed. New Haven: Human Relations Area Files.

Oswalt, J. N. 1980. "Kabash." In *Theological Wordbook of the Old Testament*, edited by R. Laird Harris, Gleason L. Archer, and Bruce K. Waltke, 1:430. Chicago: Moody Press.

Page, Hugh R., Jr. 1999. "The Marking of Social, Political, Religious, and Other Boundaries in Biblical Literature—A Case Study Using the Book of Judges." *Research in the Social Scientific Study of Religion* 10:37–55.

Pedersen, Johannes. 1926–1940. *Israel: Its Life and Culture.* 4 vols. London: Oxford University Press.

Price, David H. 2004. *Atlas of World Cultures: A Geographical Guide to Ethnographic Literature.* 1989. Reprint, Caldwell, NJ: Blackburn.

Rad, Gerhard von. 1966. *The Problem of the Hexateuch and Other Essays.* London: SCM.

Thompson, Stith. 2001. *Motif-index of Folk-Literature: A Classification of Narrative Elements in Folk-tales, Ballads, Myths, Fables, Mediaeval Romances, Exempla, Fabliaux, Jest-Books.* Rev. ed. 6 vols. Bloomington: University of Indiana Press.

United Nations General Assembly. 2000. "Universal Declaration of Human Rights (1948)." In *Sourcebook of the World's Religions: An Interfaith Guide to Religion and Spirituality*, edited by J. Beversluis, 325–28. Novato, CA: New World Library.

———. 2007. *United Nations Declaration on the Rights of Indigenous Peoples.* http://www.un.org/esa/socdev/unpfii/documents/DRIPS_en.pdf.

Reading the Christian Old Testament in the Contemporary World

Daniel L. Smith-Christopher

In nineteenth-century Charleston, South Carolina, the Old Testament seemed to assure Episcopal clergyman Frederick Dalcho that slavery was consistent with Christian faith. The same Old Testament, however, particularly Josh. 6:21, just as powerfully inspired fellow Charleston resident and former slave Denmark Vesey to plan a slave revolt. Those involved in the slave revolt felt assured that God would help them "utterly destroy all in the city, both men and women, young and old, with the edge of the sword" (Edgerton 1999, 101–25). In 2010, Steven Hayward, at that time F. K. Weyerhaeuser Fellow at the American Enterprise Institute, published an essay in which he read the story of Joseph in Egypt as a dire warning against government intervention, and suggested that his reading of these texts from Genesis served as a defense of a free-market, private-property economic system. Also in 2010, John Rogerson, professor of Scripture at Sheffield University, began his book on Old Testament theology, written because he, too, believed that the "Old Testament has something to say to today's world(s)," by stating that he wrote as "an Anglican priest . . . a humanist and a socialist" (Rogerson, 11). Dr. James Edwards, of the Center for Immigration Studies, reads some of the Mosaic laws of the Old Testament as defending firm national borders, low tolerance for immigration rights, and concerns for cultural corruption by outsiders (Edwards 2009 n.p., online), while Dr. Lai Ling Elizabeth Ngan of Baylor University, an Asian American scholar, finds that the Old Testament story about God's listening to the prayers of the "foreign woman," namely Hagar, "redefines boundaries that others have inscribed for her"; the story suggests that modern Christians should uphold the dignity of all peoples and resist denigrating people because of physical or racial differences (Ngan 2006, 83).

These are six Christians, all reading their Old Testament in the contemporary world. The fact that not all of these voices are biblical scholars, however, only serves to highlight the fact that reading the Christian Old Testament in the contemporary world is a complex mixture of the scholarly as well as the popular, stereotyped traditional views as well as innovative new insights, and that reading the Old Testament often strikingly divides readers into quite seriously opposing social and political views. Does this mean that reading the Christian Bible (Old or New Testament) in the modern world is a parade example of Cole Porter's 1934 song "Anything Goes"? Is it a matter of some disappointment that we can still agree with Leo Perdue's 1994 observation that "no commanding contemporary theology has yet appeared to form a consensus" (Perdue 1994, 8)?

I would argue that there is no cause for despair. Quite to the contrary! One of the most fascinating aspects of reading the Christian Old Testament in the contemporary world is not simply that there is unprecedented enthusiasm and diversity among scholars and viewpoints in the field but also that *this diversity itself is part of an ongoing debate and discussion.* At the outset, however, we should clarify that we are interested in thinking about serious readings of the Christian Old Testament, and not merely social or political propaganda that lightly seasons its rhetoric with a few Bible verses.

Marketplaces vs. Museums

Biblical scholarship is separated from religious propaganda not only by the fact that biblical scholarship presumes a basic orientation in the relevant historical contexts of the ancient world, familiarity with a diversity of texts both ancient and modern, and the ability to recognize a good argument supported by credible evidence or reasonable suggestions. These are all essential, of course. What really separates biblical scholarship from propaganda is the fact that biblical scholarship in the contemporary world is part of an ongoing discussion—a discussion that knows *and listens* to the challenges of others and seeks to contribute one's own insights *as part of the discussion.* As in all fields of discovery and intellectual endeavor, the success of biblical scholarship is not to be measured by the achievement of some dominant unanimity, but rather is judged by the quality and results of the participation in the scholarly tasks at hand and the *shared perception* that progress is taking place. We are seeing and understanding biblical texts in ever more profound and provocative ways. However, one of the most striking aspects of the rise of simplistic or propagandist use of the Bible is precisely its refusal to engage in dialogue, self-correction, or even acknowledgment of rival views, beyond the occasional ad hominem dismissal of arguments based solely on their association with groups identified by politicized generalizations—for example, "those liberals."

What we are suggesting is that there is an essential *dialogue* in modern, serious reading of the Bible. So, if this essay on reading the Christian Old Testament is not to be a rehearsal of some of the grand theories generally agreed on, now and forever (like a quiet museum tour of accomplishments), it is time for a new guiding image. I am intrigued by suggestions of the Cuban American New Testament scholar Fernando Segovia, who celebrates diversity in dialogue over the Scriptures. Segovia has famously suggested the "marketplace of ideas," rather like Wole Soyinka's discussion of the Silk Road market town Samarkand, as an image of modern sharing and exchanging of multicultural ideas and friendships (see Segovia and Tolbert; Segovia; Soyinka). An introduction to reading the Christian Old Testament in the contemporary world does not need to provide a historical survey of the "great ideas" that led to the present. Good surveys already exist, if European-dominated ideas are one's particular interest (e.g., Ollenburger; Rogerson 1984; Hayes and Prussner). Marketplaces can be elusive, however. They exist within the totality of the lives of people from everywhere, people who set up stalls and shop. Like the night markets of Auckland, New Zealand, or Darwin, Australia, they appear at designated places, at the designated hours, but otherwise there is only quiet. In short, the image of the marketplace suggests that we need a guidebook.

Laura Pulido, Laura Barraclough, and Wendy Cheng have recently published a marvelous, politically informed tour guide titled *A People's Guide to Los Angeles* (2012). The introduction itself is worth the price of admission. In these preliminary observations, the authors reflect on guidebooks and Los Angeles itself.

> *A People's Guide to Los Angeles* is a deliberate political disruption of the way Los Angeles is commonly known and experienced. . . . Guidebooks select sites, put them on a map, and interpret them in terms of their historical and contemporary significance. All such representations are political, because they highlight some perspectives while overlooking others. Struggles over who and what counts as "historic" and worthy of a visit involve decisions about who belongs and who doesn't, who is worth remembering and who can be forgotten, who we have been and who we are becoming.

They continue,

> Mainstream guidebooks typically describe and interpret their sites through the story of one person—almost always a man, and usually the capitalist who invested in a place, or its architect or designer. In doing so, they reinforce an individualized and masculinist way of thinking about history. Meanwhile, the collectives of people who actually created, built, or used the space remain nameless.

It would be difficult to think of a better series of thoughts to begin an essay on reading the Christian Old Testament in the contemporary world, because biblical analysis is rarely, if ever, written without some contemporary concerns in mind. Modern biblical theologies, for example, now usually identify the perspective of the author in the contemporary world (e.g., Brueggemann 1997; Rogerson 2010). Thus I am quite certain that part of the reason I agree with this need for a new image is that I write as a Christian who was born into, and very self-consciously remain informed by, the Quaker tradition. I also learned a great deal of biblical history, language, and theology from my fellow Christian sectarians the Mennonites, and I was first inspired to think seriously about biblical theology in high school by reading Vernard Eller, a theologian from yet another of my sister sectarian movements, the Church of the Brethren (informally known as the Dunkers). This means that I write as a Christian raised on "counterhistories" of the Christian movement—George Fox on Pendle Hill, Margaret Fell at Swarthmore, Conrad Grebel in Zurich, and Alexander Mack in Philadelphia—in addition to the canonical events of Christian history, such as the councils, the division between Rome and the Eastern Orthodox, Calvin, Luther, Wesley, and so on. I am thus well aware that texts, like towns, are susceptible to decisions about which locations are worthy of a visit, and which locations ought to be "memorialized" as deeply important. We could visit the old, established halls memorializing conquest or power—or we can find the marketplaces where we can encounter new ideas, argue with the "stall keepers" (the authors), make offers and listen to the counteroffers. In short, Christian biblical scholarship is tolerant of a variety of particular views of biblical texts, grammar, history, or theological interpretation. It is quite properly intolerant of the refusal to participate in dialogue with others. One of the hallmarks of propagandist abuses of the Bible in the modern world is the virtual absence of dialogue with other serious students of the Bible—a refusal to appear in the marketplace where ideas are examined and challenged.

It might seem that all this "marketplace" talk runs the risk of privileging process rather than results, and thus avoiding the hard work of evaluating whether ideas are good or bad, and then promoting the good. It is a uniquely contemporary heresy, however, to privilege solitary ideas or accomplishments while overlooking the long processes that often lead to any achievements worthy of celebration. Furthermore, to celebrate dialogue in the development of Christian thought about the Bible has sometimes been thought to be a uniquely modern phenomenon. That is already a mistake. What constitutes the "Old Testament," and even whether to have one, have both been matters of serious debate in Christian history.

The Christian Old Testament as a Product of Dialogue

Let us begin with a deceptively simple question: What constitutes the Old Testament? Christians do not even agree on this! Before the early Christian movement that historians now routinely refer to as "orthodox" arose victorious, the determination of what would be the authorized and foundational writings for Christian faith was a lively debate. The so-called *Festal Letter* 39 of Athanasius, which includes the earliest authoritative "list" of a canon of the Christian Bible, is dated to (a surprisingly late) 367 CE. Before then, debates about texts clearly ranged widely, and this does not even address the interesting continued use of noncanonical lore in popular, pre-Reformation medieval theater in the streets and churches of Europe (see Muir).

Furthermore, Athanasius's fourth-century declaration did not really settle the matter. Protestant, Catholic, and Orthodox Christians have each determined to authorize slightly different Old Testaments. Catholics, staying with the collection of Jewish writings that appeared in some of the old Greek translations known as the Septuagint (LXX), have included a series of books in the Old Testament that Protestants do not recognize, which Catholics call "deuterocanonical," and the Orthodox have chosen to include even a few more of these later Jewish (but still pre-Christian) writings. Protestants usually refer to these works as "the Apocrypha." Having said this, however, the difference between Christian canons has fewer implications for biblical scholarship than one might suspect at first. This is primarily because academic biblical studies, including biblical theological work, now tends to overlook specific church doctrines regarding the categories of "canonical," "deuterocanonical," and "noncanonical" writings. In the biblical studies marketplace, no text, artifact, ancient translation, or geographical context is "off limits" to research, comment, and consideration.

Canonical works obviously get the most attention—but it is hardly exclusive—and commentaries and critical analysis of *noncanonical* writing often make significant contributions to the further understanding of the canonical work as well. But we aren't finished with dialogue in relation to the existence of the Old Testament.

In fact, Christianity was marked by diversity in dialogue from the very beginning, as any sober reading of the arguments discussed in the book of Acts clearly reveals. One reason that dialogue is such an important context for thinking about the Old Testament is the fact that *the very existence of a "Christian Old Testament" was not a matter of widespread agreement in the earliest history of Christianity*. The early Christian convert Marcion (c. 85–160) famously proposed that true Christianity ought to discard any connection whatsoever to Judaism and the Jewish tradition; he embraced only a limited number of writings to represent this clean break between Jesus and the Jewish tradition (he proposed only a version of Luke, and ten Pauline epistles). However, the reaction was furious and widespread. W. H. C. Frend argues that Marcion holds the distinction of being "one of the very few opponents of orthodoxy whom Greek and Latin theologians united in damning. For nearly a century after his death . . . he was the arch-heretic" (212). Clearly, not every idea in the marketplace survives. We can stop cynically humming Porter's "Anything Goes" now.

The first Christian centuries, therefore, bequeath a task to all subsequent generations of readers of the "Christian Old Testament," namely, to take these writings into serious consideration when determining the nature of Christian faith. Furthermore, the vast majority of modern Christian communities (Protestant, Catholic, and Orthodox) have agreed with the church fathers and mothers of the first centuries that Christianity does indeed have a "canon," and that the Hebrew writings are part of it. Is this a settled issue, then? Hardly. Before we can speak of ways the Christian Old Testament is being read in the contemporary world, it is important to acknowledge, however briefly, that there are still ways it is *not* being read, and that it is even effectively ignored, in Christian faith and practice. Marcion still haunts us.

Tourism vs. Engagement: Ignoring the Marketplace?

As Aidan Nichols has recently acknowledged for the Catholic Church (2007), and as many others have suggested for other churches (Jenkins 2006, 42–47), a serious tendency remains among many Christian traditions in the modern world to overlook the larger part of their Bible before the Gospel of Matthew begins. Effectively ignoring the witness of the Old Testament for modern Christian faith and practice has sometimes been referred to as "Neo-Marcionism" (Nichols, 81). Even though few modern Christians would explicitly admit to it, the lack of effective education or preaching in Old Testament/Hebrew Bible studies is an alarming prospect for Christian faith and practice. A Christian theology cannot be true to the historic legacy of the faith tradition if it perpetuates such a neo-Marcionite subordination of these texts. This can happen in a number of ways, but it is more typical of popular and/or propagandist readings of the Bible than in biblical scholarship. In fact, some ways of "reading the Christian Old Testament" are simply ways to avoid it!

For example, there is a huge market for "Bible prophecy" books in the United States. One of the most significant criticisms of this popular literature is not only its total neglect of serious biblical scholarship on the prophetic books of the Old Testament but also its exclusive interest in how the books of the Bible may be "decoded" so that they can be understood to refer to contemporary events—as if the eighth-century-BCE book of Amos were actually speaking about twentieth-century Russia, or second-century-BCE portions of the book of Daniel were actually speaking about the twentieth-century ayatollahs of Iran. This "decoding" process usually neglects the historical content of the Old Testament book at hand in favor of what it is "understood" to be saying about modern times. In short, the actual content is merely a code. Its decoded meaning has nothing to do with what is actually written, when it was written, or who may have written it. One effective way of entirely ignoring a biblical book, then, is to completely reconstruct it without regard to its actual content as a historical work. This may not be Marcion's original idea, but he would clearly approve. This radical transformation of the work has little to do with actual study of it, nor is this part of the serious dialogue taking place about how the books of the Old Testament ought to inform contemporary Christian faith and practice.

This case of wildly popular literature on Bible prophecy in the modern world is particularly ironic. While some Christians frequently fault biblical scholars for not accepting the "plain sense" of the biblical text, it is astounding how carefully the various approaches to Bible prophecy omit any engagement with the most straightforward, or "plain," messages of the prophets of ancient Israel, namely, God's concern for the poor and the judgment threatened against the rich and powerful, those who, in the unforgettable images of Amos and Isaiah,

> trample the head of the poor into the dust of the earth,
> and push the afflicted out of the way (Amos 2:7)

or who

> join house to house,
> who add field to field,
> until there is room for no one but you,
> and you are left to live alone
> in the midst of the land! (Isa. 5:8)

No decoding seems necessary here. Radically altering the Old Testament texts beyond any credible historical or theological contexts in the process is clearly to do violence to those texts.

Another even more problematic way to virtually ignore the Old Testament in the Christian tradition is the Christian idea that the Old Testament is "old" and therefore largely replaced by the New Testament. Jesus is thus understood to have so reformed Jewish thought, very much as in Marcion's original proposal, that very little of the Old Testament is left of any real importance for Christian theology (save, perhaps, for the Ten Commandments). The dangers of such a "de-Semiticized" Jesus are legion, beginning with the problem of failing to understand Jesus' own faith tradition. For example, the event universally known as the "cleansing of the temple" is incomprehensible apart from recognizing that Jesus cites two Hebrew prophets in the act (Jer. 7:11 and Isa. 56:7). The reactions to Jesus' famous "reading" in his home synagogue in Luke 4 are equally incomprehensible apart from carefully noting the Old Testament references therein. Such examples can be multiplied throughout the New Testament.

Finally, the Hebrew tradition in both its historic and contemporary expressions is revered by a living people. Contemporary Christian scholarship is increasingly open to dialogue with Jewish biblical scholarship. Even though all Christians share most of the books of the Jewish canon with Judaism, there has been historically a significant difference in Jewish study of the Bible as opposed to Christian study (see summaries in Sommer 2012). One of the important characteristics of modern Christian readings of the Old Testament is that Jewish, Roman Catholic, Orthodox, and Protestant Scripture scholars are all in dialogue and discussion with each other in biblical studies on levels unprecedented before the twentieth century, and these dialogues continue in a variety of academic contexts in the twenty-first century.

Exorcising the ghost of Marcion from contemporary Christian scholarship of the Old Testament properly insists that taking the Old Testament seriously for Christian faith and practice involves a consideration of what Old Testament writings can say to the Christian tradition, not vice versa; Christian tradition should not use the Old Testament to buttress predetermined doctrinal ideas derived from the New Testament. Dictating terms to the Old Testament will never allow it to speak to Christian faith and practice in new and challenging ways. That isn't the way a marketplace works, after all, and trying to fix prices and control commodities only leads to other marketplaces.

The Role of Historical Events in the Old Testament for Christian Faith and Practice

We have already determined that the adjective *Christian* in our title means that we are interested in how the Old Testament speaks to Christian faith and practice, and therefore we are interested in discussing the role of "biblical theology." Here we encounter one of the loudest sectors of our marketplace. There are contemporary scholars (see Barr) who maintain an older tradition that suggests Old Testament scholarship should never be primarily "religious" or "theological," but rather historical, examining texts and other ancient evidence and then handing the results over to the theologians. Thus some scholars believe that biblical theology seeks to identify an exclusively *historical* expression of *past* belief (e.g., What did the ancient Israelites believe?). Indeed, the famous inaugural lecture of Johann Gabler in 1787, considered by some to be the "founding document" of this understanding of biblical theology (Gabler, 497), argued quite forcefully for maintaining a clear separation between biblical theology, defined as an exclusively historical enterprise, on the one hand, and systematic ("dogmatic") theology on the other.

It should be acknowledged that many modern biblical scholars would insist on this same separation between the historical and the theological approaches to Old Testament study and firmly place themselves in the "historical questions only" camp. Some scholars, again citing the late James Barr, have no objection to doing Christian theology based on biblical ideas, but believe that the formulation of these religious ideas ought to be a separate task from the exclusively historical task of Old Testament study. There are others who have doubts about religious belief in general or about the viability or validity of the specific religious traditions that make religious use of these writings. Some biblical scholars self-identify as atheists, for example, and there are even contemporary biblical scholars who openly condemn the very notion of a viable contemporary belief informed by the Bible (e.g., Avalos).

Both versions of the "historical analysis only" argument would maintain that it is not only possible but also necessary for a scholar of biblical texts to refrain from allowing contemporary interests or commitments (religious or otherwise) to "bias" or "interfere" with the task of historical analysis. This proposed form of historical analysis is represented as an activity that seeks to emulate scientific methodology as much as possible. The goal of this approach is thus described as "objective knowledge," or at least a close approximation of objective knowledge, even if these scholars were to acknowledge that certain influences or limitations of a time period certainly apply, such as the state of historical, archaeological, and textual studies at the time. In either case, the result is similar: a form of biblical studies that would be understood entirely as an aspect of historical investigation, no different in kind from determining what Shakespeare or Isaac Newton may have "believed," on religious (or any other) questions. Thus, while some may think or hope that their work could contribute to Christian faith and practice, they would carefully leave that task to others.

Interest-Free Biblical Analysis?

Recent debates, however, forcefully challenge many of the methodological assumptions that a bias-free analysis of historical texts is even a possible, much less laudable, goal. The term *postmodernism* is normally assigned to such challenges. Especially since the work of Thomas Kuhn (who gave us the concept of a "paradigm shift," 1996) and Paul Feyerabend (who calls for an "anarchist theory of knowledge," 2010), even the notion of an "objective" *scientific* analysis (science being the purported, even if largely self-appointed, model of objective analysis for all fields of inquiry) has been largely abandoned as both claim and goal. Motivations or interests do not necessarily poison results, but in the postmodern age, we are always vigilant about their influence, and thus the tendency in postmodernism is to declare such "interests" in the work itself. Does this preclude the possibility of doing biblical theology for modern Christian faith and practice? I contend that the postmodern criticism of a "bias-free" analysis of the Bible not only allows an enterprise of biblical theology but also positively encourages it.

The endless debates about the precise meaning of postmodernism need not distract us from a useful insight associated with this term: *all knowledge is contingent.* What we "know" usually depends on what we seek to know, and thus the questions we think to ask. Furthermore, what we investigate is influenced by own concerns, and we also sort out and determine which of our results are the most important. This is all part of the dialogue of diversity and, in twenty-first-century study of the Christian Old Testament, is now a widely acknowledged working assumption. Few would deny the importance of not only the identification of one's own working interests and assumptions in thinking about how the Christian Old Testament can speak to the modern age but also the retrospective work of placing older Old Testament theological writings in important social and historical contexts in ways that deepen our appreciation of their achievements and limitations (Rogerson 1984).

Is There a "Collapse of History" in Christian Old Testament Study?

There is an interesting debate going on in another sector of the marketplace. In his recent important monographs on the problems of Old Testament biblical theology, Leo Perdue refers to a "collapse of history" in recent biblical studies. One of the ways he formulates this point is to ask: Can these predominantly religious texts really help us reconstruct historical events in ancient Israel? If not, how can it be said that Israel's experience is important for contemporary readers who are seeking to read these texts as a guide to events that inform contemporary faith and practice? Perdue alludes to an important ongoing debate that began in the late twentieth century, a debate about our ability to know much actual history from what is available to us both in the Old Testament texts and in the relevant archaeological work (both ancient texts and artifacts) that supplements the study of biblical texts.

Especially after the publication of Thomas L. Thompson's widely cited monograph *The Historicity of the Patriarchal Narratives* (1974), fiery debates ensued between scholars who were divided (often unfairly) into "camps" called "minimalists" and "maximalists." These terms referred to those who despaired of the ability to be confident about historical events at all (thus "minimalists") and those who thought there was actually a great deal more evidence for biblical history than was often acknowledged (so Dever 2001; 2003). An interesting summary view of some of the historical debates is provided by Grabbe.

However, as some contemporary scholars have pointed out (see Brueggemann), these debates about historical events and biblical narratives mask the importance of answering a previous question, namely, whether *establishing that an event happened—or precisely how it happened—automatically dictates a corresponding religious significance to that event.* Clearly, it does not. Even if I can be convinced, for example, that the measurements of the temple provided in Ezekiel 40–48 are precise, accurate dimensions of the Jerusalem temple during the first millennium BCE, this does not strike me as having monumental importance for Christian faith and practice. It may have quite fascinating historical interest, but *theological* significance? This can also apply to less obscure issues. For example, determining that the texts in the opening chapters of the book of Exodus give us a more or less "historically reliable" report of the actual events of Israelites departing from Egypt does not thereby answer the question: Of what significance is the departure from Egypt *for contemporary Christian faith and practice*? Simply agreeing on the *historical* reliability of a biblical passage leaves considerable ground to cover on questions of *significance*. Simply agreeing on the historical details of the exodus, for example, does not thereby make one a liberation theologian. In fact, precious little of the powerful writings of liberation theology, beginning with the 1968 gathering of bishops in Medellín, Colombia (CELAM), actually debated the historical details of the book of Exodus. It is not that the historical story is insignificant; but rather its historical significance, if any, needs to be *part* of the theological argument, and not the entire task.

What happens when different perspectives can no longer be united on a particular reading of biblical events, especially on the accompanying significance of those events? Dominant and influential Old Testament theologies of the past depended on accepting an assigned weight to particular passages or biblical events that were considered central or guiding concepts, and thus critically important for modern theology. For example, Walter Eichrodt proposed that the idea of God's establishing agreements or "covenants" with God's people represents the central notion of the entire Hebrew Bible (Eichrodt 1961; 1967; the original German volumes were published in 1933 and 1935). Gerhard von Rad's equally influential Old Testament theology (Rad 1962; 1965; German 1957 and 1960) argued for the central importance of certain narratives of faith that Israelites allegedly repeated (he used the term "creeds") as indications of their faith, and thus suggested that Israelites were people who identified with such narratives. There is little doubt that such theological arguments, based on readings of the Old Testament, exerted a powerful influence on Christian theological education throughout the Western world in the twentieth century.

However, what if differing perspectives on the part of modern readers of the Bible—especially influenced by differing life situations (ethnicity, gender, etc.)—suggest to some modern readers that different biblical "events" in the Old Testament (whether unquestionably historical or not) are more important than others? Examples are not difficult to cite. On the one hand, after 1968, Latin American biblical scholars (especially Roman Catholic scholars) determined that the Moses and Exodus stories had a powerful message for them in their modern-day circumstances of economic poverty. On the other hand, Native American (Osage) professor of American studies Robert Allan Warrior famously challenged biblical theologians who celebrated the exodus and the entry to a "promised land" by noting that Native Americans frankly had more in common with the beleaguered Canaanites, reminding us that indigenous peoples continue to have an ambiguous relationship with the legacy of the book of Joshua (see Warrior). Nineteenth-century African American slaves also determined that the Jonah and Daniel stories had powerful messages for them in their circumstances of oppression and suppression (Levine; Cone 1992). Finally, recent suggestions view the conquest of Jerusalem in 587 and the subsequent exile of thousands of Judeans (Albertz; Ahn) as a biblical event with serious theological implications (Brueggemann; Smith-Christopher 2002). Nineteenth-century Maori Christians in New Zealand determined that the prophets were powerful examples of a new form of pantribal leadership that had new potential to unite previously fragmented tribal peoples in opposition to growing European settlement, and some even looked to the Davidic monarchy as a model for a new and culturally unprecedented Maori king, and thus an answer to the power and authority of the British Crown (Elsmore 1985; 1989). Is all this also a "collapse of history"? Or is it really the collapse of *dominant readings* of history in the face of alternative decisions about central ideas, events, and themes?

There is little doubt that some Christian biblical scholars and theologians lament the absence of the dominant Old Testament readings. Such a view arguably represents a kind of wistfulness for the "good old days" when a dominant perspective seemed to influence writing and doing (and teaching!) Old Testament theology in Christian institutions of higher learning. Not only does this "hoped-for dominant" perspective do violence to those who were never part of the "dominant perspective" (because they were either gender or cultural minorities, e.g., women, African American,

Asian American, Latino/Latina, or theological minorities such as Anabaptists, Quakers, or Pentecostals), but it is also arguably built on a largely discredited model of intellectual progress that mimics seventeenth- to twentieth-century Western imperial politics and social values—namely, the (intellectual) goal of domination and the vanquishing of opposition.

Surely an alternative to dominance or conquest is concord, dialogue, and cooperation in common causes. If we are to read the Christian Old Testament, and consider it theologically significant, then that theological significance will have to extend to the entire world. The *emerging* Christian world is now based in the Southern Hemisphere (Jenkins 2002). Reading the Christian Old Testament is thus by necessity a global enterprise. The modern marketplace is diverse indeed, and there are a number of ways to recognize this diversity.

Contemporary Worlds in Dialogue

We have seen that Segovia's "marketplace of ideas" does not so much despair of speaking of the past at all, much less signal a "collapse of history." The issue is not whether history can be written any longer. Rather, the issue is how different histories, and different texts, can be understood to matter in differing contexts. Marketplaces can resist organization. Nevertheless, there are perhaps two general ways of sorting the diversity in view. One way is to focus on the identities of the participants themselves, especially in those cases when they consciously and explicitly draw on these identities in their reading of the Bible. The other is to focus on challenges to the human enterprise in local or global contexts. Many of these challenges will require that we marshal our collective wisdom in order to survive as a species, and there are hardly more urgent reasons for biblical scholars to make their contribution to the ideological, spiritual, and political will of people to act in positive ways.

Text and Experience: The Feminist Pioneering of New Questions

New Testament scholar Elisabeth Schüssler Fiorenza points out that it was early feminist critical studies that largely opened up critical readings of both the New and Old Testaments from a perspective informed by particular "interests" (see Schüssler Fiorenza). One of first of these interests was reviewing the long-presumed subordination of women in the narratives of the Bible. It is interesting to see how this work progressed in a variety of different directions, all inspired by gender-related questions. For some feminist readers of the Bible, restating the often unacknowledged positive and powerful roles of women in the Bible is an important corrective to assumptions about the exclusive biblical focus on men (Gafney; Meyers 1988/2013). Phyllis Trible, on the other hand, pioneered the role of an unvarnished focus on destructive texts featuring violence against women, calling them "texts of terror" and thus highlighting dangerous tendencies within historical biblical cultures themselves (see Trible). Renita Weems, similarly, opened a line of investigation on the prophetic use of violent language associated with feminized subjects and objects that also betrayed violent attitudes (e.g., "Lady Jerusalem," Weems 1995). Kathleen O'Connor, Elizabeth Boase, and Carleen Mandolfo have taken this conversation further, suggesting that there is evidence of an ongoing dialogue with "Lady Jerusalem" that began with the violent imagery noted by

Weems in Hosea and Ezekiel, but then continued to Lamentations and Deutero-Isaiah, suggesting that there is acknowledgment of and even repentance for this violence (see O'Connor; Boase; Mandolfo). There are many other directions that studies can go, many of which explicitly identify as feminist, or gender-interested, analysis (see, e.g., Yee 2003).

The feminist approach, far from being a limiting perspective, has moved methodologically from an interest in one formulation of a "minority" perspective—namely, the role of women—to a comparative interest in how this critical approach relates to other issues of "gendering" and "embodiment" in the Bible (homosexuality, prostitution, especially the vexed question of temple prostitution, foreign wives of mixed marriages, gender in relation to slavery, etc.). This approach can also move beyond questions of gender. These early feminist perspectives quite logically moved toward an interest in those who are considered "marginalized" in Hebrew texts—for example, Edomites, Egyptians, Moabites, those lumped together as "aliens" in the Mosaic laws, foreign workers—for other reasons. Interesting work indeed. But what does it have to do with Christian faith and practice?

While not all feminist analysis of the Bible is done with the hope that it will contribute to a more equitable and egalitarian Christian movement in the contemporary world, a considerable amount is.

Cultural Identities and Social Situations in the Marketplace

Feminism is not the only "contemporary interest" that has driven new questions in Christian biblical analysis. Especially those who hope biblical analysis will affect Christian faith and practice have made significant contributions. Already in narratives of freed slaves in North America, African American readers of the Bible were reflecting on their own insights, especially as a countertheology to the European preachers who constantly preached obedience and subservience (see Raboteau; Hopkins and Cummings). In fact, it is possible to trace a twentieth-century flowering of these early readings, some of which began by reexamining the role of explicitly identified Africans in biblical history (see Felder) in a manner similar to those who reexamined the Old Testament stories explicitly about women. One clear goal was to highlight African presence in the Bible that had been neglected in the face of racial prejudice in the modern world against those of African descent. However, in the wake of important calls for a more assertive black theology in the twentieth century (Cone 1970), this project then expanded in different directions in ways very similar to the expansion of gender-related questions (and often intersecting with gender questions, e.g., in "womanist" analysis; see Weems 1991). In the African American context, the appearance of the groundbreaking work *Stony the Road We Trod* (Felder) was a major contribution to the maturing of contemporary, consciously African American biblical scholarship. Included in this collection were essays that dealt not only with historical-critical analysis of the Bible from an African American perspective, but with the use of the Bible in the history of African American interpretation. Further work on African American history of interpretation (Callahan; Wimbush) continues to make important contributions to unique insights into both the later use of Scripture, but also arguments contributing to historical understanding of the texts themselves. Not only is the role of the Bible in African American history itself the subject of important analysis, but African American biblical analysis is also interested in examining texts that have been used historically to suppress both those of explicitly African descent (for example, to defend slavery) and many non-European peoples. A convergence in methods, and sometimes goals, began to emerge that sought to forge alliances across explicitly named cultural or ethnic categories.

So, even though it has followed a different trajectory than African American scholarship, Latino/Latina literature now also holds an important place in the context of the United States. For example, Justo González, Jean-Paul Ruiz, and Miguel De La Torre (2002; 2007) have published monographs and commentaries on Old Testament themes. Interestingly, however, De La Torre has taken a somewhat pessimistic attitude as to whether cross-cultural analysis of the text will influence the general discipline. De La Torre is clear—Euro-Americans are largely not to be trusted for biblical analysis, because "Euroamerican Christians, either from the fundamentalist right or the far liberal left, probably have more in common with each other and understand each other better than they do Christians on the other side of the racial and ethnic divide" (De La Torre 2007, 125). Nevertheless, serious contributions continue to challenge biblical scholars to take seriously the contributions of those who write Old Testament analysis from an openly acknowledged perspective. Gregory Lee Cuéllar, for example, compares passages of Isaiah to the Mexican and Mexican American folk music style known as the *Corrido*, not only to suggest ways that the biblical texts can be understood in contemporary Mexican American communities, but also to propose potential new readings for the book of Isaiah itself (Cuéllar 2008).

While there have been a number of important works from Asian American biblical scholars in the late twentieth century that consciously draw on Asian themes and identity, a significant milestone was the publication in 2006 of the collected volume *Ways of Being, Ways of Reading*. This volume was comparable in many ways to the impact of the 1991 work *Stony the Road We Trod* in the African American scholarly context. It includes retrospective and survey essays, even very personal reflections on academic work (e.g., Yee 2006), as well as examples of contemporary work of some of the most prominent American scholars using cross-cultural approaches.

Finally, in terms of the American context, it is notable that Randall Bailey, Tat-siong Benny Liew, and Fernando Segovia have initiated a dialogue between Latino/a American, Asian American, and African American scholarship, hoping to find common ground in "minority" analysis of the Bible (Bailey, Liew, and Segovia), suggesting the possibilities of a convergence and maturing of methods of analysis, even as they reject any sort of false consensus on similarity of cultural contexts.

Although it is fair to say that readings explicitly related to specific cultural and ethnic identities and traditions continue in the century, attention has tended to turn toward social, political, and economic locations as another significant source of issues that influence the reading of Scripture. In the last quarter of the twentieth century, a number of Old Testament scholars consciously incorporated sociological and anthropological analysis in their ancient historiography of the Bible (Gottwald; Overholt 1992, 2003), and this dialogue with social sciences certainly continues (Chalcraft). Exegetical issues of the most recent writing in Old Testament studies soon converged on a series of questions closely associated with the influence of Edward Said's classic work *Orientalism*, which further built on the early social theories and the observations of the postcolonial theorists Frantz Fanon and Albert Memmi. Once this dialogue with Said's influence was articulated powerfully in the many works of R. S. Sugirtharajah, the rise of postcolonial approaches to Scripture became a significant movement in the early twenty-first century. Sugirtharajah's now classic compendium *Voices from the Margin* signaled a new energy in "interested perspectives" in the reading of the Bible.

The Rise of Postcolonial Biblical Analysis

We have already noted that Christianity—and its Bible—is seeing profound growth in the Southern Hemisphere in the twenty-first century. Twentieth-century Christians in developing societies, especially India, South America, and Africa, began to assert their own perspectives in the analysis of the Bible. After Said's influential work, they began to identify ways in which previous European scholarship contained certain social and cultural assumptions about Western superiority. They then began readings of the Bible within their past experiences of European colonial presence. In the process of reasserting a cultural and/or national identity, however, they soon realized that a reconstruction of cultural identity in the new world could never go back to a purified "precolonial" state, but must always be in dialogue with the social, political, and philosophical realities of having been deeply affected by Western thought and practice. Although in the context of religion and the Bible, one might better speak of "post-Western-missionaryism," the discussions in biblical studies borrowed a term from social and cultural theory to identify their new reviews of the Bible in their own contexts: *postcolonialism*. Postcolonial biblical exegesis provided special tools for Christians in formerly colonized states (or among indigenous peoples in Western European settled lands, North and South America, Australia, and New Zealand). The questions whether, and to what extent, largely imported biblical scholarship was (and is) tainted by imperial goals of control and economic expansion raised serious concerns about those readings of Scripture that seemed deeply involved in that imperial process (De le Torre 2002). A prime example of attempting to counter Western domination was the Latin American assertion that the exodus is the prime event of the Old Testament—and thus liberation is the prime theological theme. However, it is important to note that these questions were being raised largely by Christian Bible scholars. Not all criticism of colonial and missionary policies rejected Christianity and the Bible as an unwanted imposition (see Roberts); sometimes it rather engaged in the more creative task of rereading the texts.

If "postcolonial" contexts include minorities living in multicultural nations, then Fernando Segovia's "Diasporic" approach to reading Scripture becomes especially suggestive. In the American context, this obviously can include African American, Asian American, and Mexican American readings of particular texts that resonate with themes, motifs, or elements of minority existence such that they lead to expositions of Old Testament texts that are suggestive for all readers of the Bible—and not only to fellow members of particular ethnic or cultural groups.

Ethnic and culturally informed readings challenge the notion that European scholarship has a privileged position in biblical scholarship generally, and in the construction of Christian theologies built from Old Testament texts particularly. What we have learned about diversity in dialogue is that the Christian reading of the Old Testament in the contemporary world will be richer, more learned, and more convincing in both textual and historical analysis only if our marketplace grows in its resemblance to the actual diversity of our worlds. What new insights into particular Old

Testament texts await the future BA, MA, or PhD theses and papers written by young Tibetan, Chinese, Navajo, Roma, or Aboriginal Australian students and scholars? What will they see that the rest of us have too quickly dismissed or completely overlooked? In the twenty-first century, we are likely to benefit from an increase of book titles like that of Senegalese American biblical scholar Aliou Niang: *Faith and Freedom in Galatia and Senegal: The Apostle Paul, Colonies, and Sending Gods*.

Let us reaffirm that diversity ought always to lead to dialogue. Agreements, shared insights, and common convictions that we are all learning from the dialogue ought to deliver even the most cynical from the simplistic hope that we Bible scholars would just please get to "the bottom line." Marketplaces don't have a bottom line! Dialogue and haggling over texts is simply the reality. The invitation, therefore, is to listen and learn. Incidentally, lest Christians think that all this is somehow radically new, those familiar with classic rabbinic dialogue and argumentation over religious texts are aware that dialogue with God and with each other is at the heart of theology.

Issues Driving Contemporary Biblical Analysis

Questions from identities and cultural experiences are not, however, the only major and significant sources of urgency in reading and rereading the Christian Old Testament. A number of contemporary global crises have inspired a renewed examination of the ways in which the Bible can be reread. The modern interest in trauma as the psychosocial reality of a world in crisis has recently gained ground in biblical analysis (see O'Connor; Janzen; Kelle). The millions of humans who flee wars and crises as international refugees have also influenced biblical analysis on ancient exile and deportation (see Ahn). The potential list of pressing issues is depressingly long, of course, but it is possible to examine a few examples to illustrate how this section of the marketplace can be organized. In fact, we can move from an example that is already very old but critically ongoing, war and peace in the Old Testament; to an issue that arguably has its roots in the twentieth century, environmentalism; and finally note the signs of a rising issue so new that it has barely begun to generate serious thought among biblical scholars: evolutionary philosophy, transhumanism, and the nature of the person.

War, Peace, and Violence and the Old Testament

Since the fourth century CE, the Christian church has been faced with direct responsibility for violence. The monarchical descendants of the Roman emperor Constantine made Christianity the official religion of the empire, leading into the Byzantine Empire. Biblical study was now intimately connected to the foreign policy of a powerful military machine, and would continue to have foreign policy implications from that time to the present. The continued relevance of the Bible to issues of war and peace is not difficult to discern in the writings of the Christian warriors and their chaplains on the one hand, and the Christian peacemakers and their communities on the other, throughout Western history especially. A clear majority in this debate has supported more violent interpretations, however regretfully they are sometimes offered.

The Jesus who said, "Love your enemies and pray for those who persecute you" (Matt. 5:44), and the Paul who exhorted, "live peaceably with all" (Rom. 12:18), were effectively trumped in Christian faith and practice very early on by an uncritical admiration for the genocidal Joshua and the conquering David (see Davies). There have been a variety of ways in which Christians have responded to the use of the Old Testament as a moral trump over the pacifist Jesus. Once again, the similarities to the methods of feminist biblical analysis are instructive.

For example, especially since the churches in twentieth-century Europe began to mobilize an opposition to the Cold War threats in their own backyards, innumerable monographs have attempted to reexamine the actual practices of Old Testament violence and warfare, either with explicit admiration (so, famously, Yadin), or appropriate levels of horror (Craigie; Niditch; Collins). In modern Old Testament study, then, one is hopefully exposed to the potential dangers of a casual and unguarded use of biblical texts that are so clearly contrary to contemporary moral judgments and international standards of justice.

Finally, similar to those who sought to lift up exemplary moments previously overlooked, there are those who seek to highlight strongly peaceful passages in the Bible that may even have been in critical dialogue with more violent episodes in the canon and thus reveal an internal dialogue or debate that reveals stronger peace voices among the canonical choir (Enz; Smith-Christopher 2007). This approach articulates how a certain form of Hebrew nonviolence would have been a logical expression of theological tendencies that had their roots in the Servant Songs of Second Isaiah and the universalism of the book of Jonah, where we find openness to the repentance of national enemies like the Assyrians, who are portrayed as repenting ". . . of the violence of their hands." Further developments can affirm the wisdom ethic of peacefulness—an ethic that frequently contrasts self-control over against brute force and earnestly recommends a sober, wise consideration of counsel and diplomacy (Prov. 16:7, 32; 17:27; 24:5-6). In fact, the Wisdom tradition may itself represent precisely a staging place for international discussion, given that wisdom values are as universal in the ancient Near East as any literary themes can be. Ancient Egyptian wisdom, Mesopotamian wisdom, and Greek wisdom all compare quite favorably to ancient Israelite forms.

Texts that reflect an Israelite "exilic" lifestyle, lived in "active nonconformity to the world" (as the famous 1955 Mennonite Church statement puts it), would also build on biblical protests against narrow ethnocentrism (e.g., the book of Ruth, Jacob's apology to Esau, Isaiah 56 and 66, and the striking affirmation in Zechariah 9 of a mixed-race people of God). In fact, there is evidence of a rising protest against violence and narrow self-centeredness (e.g., Ezekiel 40–48) that can be seen to affirm the Deuteronomic critique of the monarchy, and especially the condemnation of the monarchy in the penitential prayers of Ezra 9, Nehemiah 9, and Daniel 9. Thus the fact that there are passages where God is alleged to have called for the massacre of foreign cities does not necessarily cancel out or trump the fact that there are more hopeful passages on this subject as well, texts that openly question whether the stance of the Hebrews toward foreign peoples should be hostile and that envision a different and more peaceful reality (Isaiah 2; 19; Micah 4).

Regrettably, offering a more peaceful reading of the Old Testament will not likely bring about world peace. But if the late Colonel Harry Summers of the Army War College is correct that "it is the passions of the people that are the engines of war" (Summers, 75–76), then perhaps careful biblical analysis will remove at least one major ideological prop and provocation that has certainly been used in the past to excuse quite reprehensible behavior among those who honor the Scriptures (see Trimm).

Environmentalism

Biblical analysis that is driven by ecological concerns can be clearly dated to responses to the famous 1967 article in *Science* by Lynn White, accusing Christianity for providing the "roots" of the ecological crisis in God's injunction to the first couple in Gen. 1:28 to "subdue" and "have dominion" over nature. The late twentieth century then saw an increase of literature that highlighted ways that the Hebrew Bible/Old Testament affirmed a spirituality of care and responsibility for the earth as God's creation. Much of this work owes a great deal to the early writings of Australian biblical scholar Norman Habel (see also Hallman; so now Craven and Kaska; Deane-Drummond). The often-cited "this-worldly" emphasis of much Old Testament ethical discussion, and even the imagery of deep fascination with and appreciation of the created world (Job 38–41; Psalm 147–48), however, continues to inspire further development in pioneering biblical theologies. Genesis portrays God involving Adam in the naming of other creatures (Gen. 2:19) and further records God's intention to "re-create" the world in the Hebrew version of the flood narrative, the basic outlines of which were clearly known to the Jewish people by the time of the Babylonian captivity, and most likely borrowed from Mesopotamian traditions.

A related development is in the direction of animal rights. Concern for animal welfare is not absent from Hebrew law or narrative (Deut. 25:4; Numbers 22). The flood story, of course, involves the considerable responsibility of Noah to preserve animals. The Old Testament strikingly expresses certain visions of peace by referring to changes in the animal kingdom (Isa. 11:6: the wolf living with the lamb) and even hinting that in their first created state, humans were vegetarian (before Gen. 9:4, where eating meat is first explicitly mentioned). Psalm 148 portrays the created animals of the world praising God, and Job famously portrays God's careful attention and knowledge of the details of the animal kingdom (Job 39; on animal rights work, see Linzey 1995; 2009; Miller).

Work in environmentalism more generally, and animal rights specifically, have been parts of a move to appreciate biblical themes that buttress a more responsible care for the earth (Toly and Block). There are, however, some serious economic and even political issues at stake here. On the issue of environmentalism particularly, there has been a serious backlash from those with business interests who see strong environmentalist movements as potential threats to their expansion of industry. Not unexpectedly, then, this reaction has motivated more conservative Christian scholars to reassert a strongly pragmatic and typically short-term ethic of consumption unmitigated by strong concerns for conserving resources in the long term. Christians in this tradition, rarely biblical scholars themselves, are clearly not impressed with nuanced arguments about responsibility for species and their survival. Nor are they likely to be impressed by arguments based largely on Old Testament passages, especially if that concern is perceived as requiring economic sacrifices. An interesting example of this reaction is the work of Steven Hayward, from the conservative think tank the American Enterprise Institute. In a published essay titled "Mere Environmentalism" (the title itself is an homage to evangelical hero C. S. Lewis) and subtitled "A Biblical Perspective on Humans and the Natural World," Hayward suggests that the Genesis narratives promote the hierarchy of creation with humanity at the top. He therefore construes a biblical mandate, not for preservation of the environment, but for a "stewardship" that promotes responsible use of resources and a free-market-driven effort to conquer the "untamed wilderness," and furthermore as free of government intervention as possible. Indeed, Hayward further argues that the story of Joseph in Pharaoh's household is a warning against centralized state control, because Joseph's centralization of resources for the Pharaoh leads directly to the enslavement of the Hebrews. Environmental degradation, therefore, may be a matter calling for repentance, but definitely not for government regulation (33). Finally, Noah offers sacrifice of animals after the flood, Hayward notes, so this story provides no basis for simple preservation, and certainly suggests that animals were to be used for human benefit.

The twenty-first century is likely to see more, rather than less, of this polemical exchange in biblical scholarship. Although more propagandistic approaches have tended to avoid participation in scholarly organizations like the Society of Biblical Literature, we are likely to see more direct engagement over the use, and abuse, of Scripture on various issues of social, and especially economic, importance.

The Nature of the Person: The Rise of Evolutionary Social Science and Philosophy

Finally, it is important in the context of this essay to speculate about issues that may well emerge more fully as the twenty-first century develops. In the wake of Daniel Dennett's polemical 1996 assertion of atheist scientism, titled "Darwin's Dangerous Idea," there is a rise of perspectives represented by the following: "If you believe in a traditional concept of the soul, you should know that there is little doubt that a fuller appreciation of the implications of evolutionary theory . . . is going to destroy that concept"; and, "we must openly acknowledge . . . the collapse of a worldview that has sustained human energies for centuries" (Stanovich, 3). Will biblical studies also be challenged by evolutionary thought? If so, in what way?

In Christian theology and biblical studies, the classic beginning point for discussion of the nature of the human person is the concept of the *imago Dei*, the creation of humanity in the image and likeness of God (Gen. 1:26-27). J. Richard Middleton, for example, seeks to rethink the *imago Dei* debates in a modern context, noting that older Christian theological uses of Genesis 1 were rather strained, and usually presumed that the significance of "the image" and "likeness" of God was precisely human *reason*. Recent discussion has emphasized the royal context of these terms, suggesting that humans are portrayed as royally deputized representations of divine authority and responsibility in the world. Middleton even suggests that the *imago Dei* is, in fact, a politically sophisticated as well as theologically loaded term in Genesis, because here we find the textual staging ground for a narrative culture war against Mesopotamian hegemonic narratives of conquest and subservience. These Mesopotamian narratives were weapons in a philosophical/ideological war that accompanied the invading and conquering armies that conquered both the northern kingdom (722 BCE) and Jerusalem and Judah (597/587).

While it is quite possible to celebrate the theological importance of all humanity from an explicitly evolutionary view of the emergence of *homo sapiens*, it is also clear that some interpretations of human evolution threaten to radically debase and reduce humanity to a mere "sack of genes," with little inherent worth, whose values, art, and faith are mere "spandrels" (that is, accidental and irrelevant by-products) that accompany the real work of genetic reproduction. The value of life is thus no longer inherent in creation, but purely instrumental, as some humans serve as sexual slaves, soldiers, and workers for the shrinking and increasingly ruthless elite. The masses are already once again being pacified by the modern equivalent of bread and circus: ever smaller and more inexpensive sources of digital pornography, graphic violence, and (contra Kant's imperative) the view of fellow humans as means rather than ends.

In this context, religious faith (including, of course, the Bible) is strongly dismissed as "nothing but" the result of evolutionary mechanisms for survival. We perceive deities only because of our ancient and genetically honed "agency detection devices" (instincts that perceive potential threats in the environment). Others suggest that religion was merely a part of a sophisticated social "mate selection" mechanism whereby mates with trustworthy values could be quickly identified. In short, religion is a neural response pattern.

The interesting question is no longer, "Can a biblical scholar believe in evolution and teach Genesis"? Of course they can, and do. What is new is the rising insistence of a form of evolutionary social thought that would dismiss all religious speculation as irrelevant. Such a radically reductionist anthropology seeks to replace the "Eden myth" with an equally implausible and comprehensive "African Savannah myth" that subsumes all humanity into categories of neural survival mechanisms driven by reproductive genes. Does the Old Testament have anything to say in this decidedly modern discussion?

The resources of Wisdom literature and its emphasis on sober assessments of God's moral patterns in the created world provide a foundation beyond Genesis for seeking dialogue with naturalists and biologists. But the issues will continue to press, and will no longer be simply the leisure-time, science-fiction reading of those whose day jobs are in biblical studies. Seeking biblical guidance on the nature of the human person will become increasingly pressing in this century in the light of (1) increased emphasis in the human sciences on "transhumanism," according to which humans can be enhanced by further evolutionary merging with technology; (2) manipulation of genetic information to favor certain human traits (already taking place passively by rejecting human eggs in artificial insemination processes that bear indications of undesired genetic traits); (3) progress in artificial intelligence such that ethical questions are becoming increasingly prominent (when does turning off a machine consist of killing a living being? etc.); (4) further work in cloning; and (5) the location and identification of personhood as directly (and some would say: *only*) a function of neural brain activity, thus raising the possibility of "downloading" human persons into hardware.

Are these exclusively theological issues? Do they have any implications for biblical analysis? Will a biblical analysis arise, for example, driven in part by the prescience of the science fiction writer Philip K. Dick, who anticipated many ethical issues dealing with modern technology? It is possible that biblical scholars will simply suggest that radically new technologies are not the business of textual analysis. However, when those technologies raise serious questions about the nature and value of the human person, it is hard to resist the notion that biblical analysis has something to say to this issue.

Return to the Beginning: Does the Marketplace Matter? Are There Any Real People There?

Finally, we can pick up on a discussion that was left aside at the very beginning of this essay. What about the clashes among various readings of the Old Testament? Is biblical studies hopelessly mired in disagreements such that, in the end, an individual must simply hum along with Porter's "Anything Goes"?

Appearances, especially in the contemporary world, can be deceiving. The reality of extensive and exciting discussion and debate in biblical studies does not mean that the field is wandering aimlessly. Furthermore, the impressive level of publication and discussion does not mean that there is no consensus of methods or results among biblical scholars. Biblical scholars, like professionals in other fields such as medicine, engineering, or astronomy, certainly stay in touch with each other's work, and through international organizations (the largest being the Society of Biblical Literature) continue to pursue common interests, projects, and even enjoy continued debates and disagreements. It is hardly the case, as philosopher Alvin Plantinga somewhat sourly suggests, that biblical scholars can never agree on anything, explaining (for Plantinga, presumably) why Christians usually do not take their work seriously.

Plantinga may be surprised, however. The influence of biblical scholarship on wider Christian practices might be slow in manifesting itself, but it is absolutely clear. Plantinga should be impressed with the articulate, profound, and serious assessment of the importance of biblical analysis in the 1994 document of the Pontifical Biblical Commission titled "The Interpretation of the Bible in the Church." Calling the historical-critical method of biblical analysis "indispensable for the scientific study of the meaning of ancient texts," the document critically assesses, both positively and negatively, many current approaches to biblical analysis common in universities and biblical scholarship, and recommends much of modern biblical scholarship to the Catholic world more widely. Furthermore, the document famously refers to fundamentalist readings of Scripture as "intellectual suicide." Unimpressed with official declarations by hierarchies? One need only examine the textbooks for Catholic *high school* students, including those explicitly recommended by the bishops, to see the profound impact of biblical scholarship on questions of multiple authorship, historicity, the dangers of literalism, and so on.

Only the most conservative Christians today believe that the only way to treasure the significance of the narratives of Genesis is to take them literally, or believe that Moses wrote every word of the Pentateuch. Only the most fundamentalist Christians today would think that the book of Jonah is about surviving in the gullet of a marine animal, or that nearly one-fifth of the entire population of ancient Egypt left with Moses in the thirteenth century BCE. Furthermore, what many Christians in the church pews and Sunday schools *do* know is that a profound Christian faith can be enriched by learning that an unnamed second prophet we call "Second Isaiah" likely reapplied some of the thought of the eighth-century Isaiah of Jerusalem, but also proclaimed radically new thoughts in the late sixth-century BCE when the Persian emperor Cyrus lived. Furthermore, Christians today know much more about the horrific tragedy of the destruction of Jerusalem in 587, and how Lamentations is a powerful poetic response to that tragedy, and how Psalms contains religious poetry from long after the time of David. None of these ideas are shocking to Christians in the churches any more, and none of them are destructive of anything but the most simplistic of readings of the Old Testament.

Finally, what Christians in the churches surely know is that the Bible invites—indeed nearly demands—the careful attention of many different cultures, genders, ages, and contexts who are brought into dialogue as they listen, read, discuss, and debate the meanings and importance of these texts of the Old Testament. There is important historical information we can know, but there is so much more to ask. For those who love only quiet museum tours of "certainties" enclosed in glass cases so that the masses can be enlightened, biblical studies in the contemporary world is not for them. The marketplace is teaming, ebullient, and alive.

Works Cited

Ahn, John. 2010. *Exile as Forced Migrations: A Sociological, Literary, and Theological Approach on the Displacement and Resettlement of the Southern Kingdom of Judah.* Berlin: de Gruyter.

Albertz, Rainer. 2003. *Israel in Exile: The History and Literature of the Sixth Century* B.C.E. Atlanta: Society of Biblical Literature.

Avalos, Hector. 2007. *The End of Biblical Studies.* New York: Prometheus.

Bailey, Randall, Tat-siong Benny Liew, and Fernando F. Segovia, eds. 2009. *They Were All Together in One Place? Toward Minority Biblical Criticism.* Atlanta: Society of Biblical Literature.

Barr, James. 2000. *History and Ideology in the Old Testament: Biblical Studies at the End of a Millennium.* Oxford: Oxford University Press.

Boase, Elizabeth. 2006. *The Fulfillment of Doom? The Dialogic Interaction between the Book of Lamentations and the Pre-Exilic/Early Exilic Prophetic Literature.* London: T&T Clark.

Brueggemann, Walter. 1997. *Theology of the Old Testament: Testimony, Dispute, Advocacy.* Minneapolis: Fortress Press.

Callahan, Allen Dwight. 2006. *The Talking Book: African Americans and the Bible.* New Haven: Yale University Press.

Chalcraft, David. 2006. *Social-Scientific Old Testament Criticism.* London: T&T Clark.

Collins, John J. 2004. *Does the Bible Justify Violence?* Minneapolis: Fortress Press.

Cone, James H. 1970. *A Black Theology of Liberation.* Maryknoll, NY: Orbis.

———. 1992. *The Spirituals and the Blues: An Interpretation.* Maryknoll, NY: Orbis Books.

Craigie, Peter. 1979. *The Problem of War in the Old Testament.* Grand Rapids: Eerdmans.

Craven, Toni, and Mary Jo Kaska. 2011. "The Legacy of Creation in the Hebrew Bible and Apocryphal/Deuterocanonical Books." In *Spirit and Nature: The Study of Christian Spirituality in a Time of Ecological Urgency,* edited by Timothy Hessel-Robinson and Ray Maria McNamara, RSM, 16–48. Eugene, OR: Pickwick.

Cuellar, Gregory L. 2008. *Voices of Marginality: Exile and Return in Second Isaiah 40-55 and the Mexican Immigrant Experience.* New York: Peter Lang.

Davies, Eryl. 2010. *The Immoral Bible: Approaches to Biblical Ethics*. London: T&T Clark.

Deane-Drummond, Celia. 2008. *Eco-Theology*. London: Darton, Longman & Todd.

De La Torre, Miguel. 2002. *Reading the Bible from the Margins*. Maryknoll, NY: Orbis.

———. 2007. *Liberating Jonah: Forming an Ethic of Reconciliation*. Maryknoll, NY: Orbis.

Dennett, Daniel. 1996. *Darwin's Dangerous Idea*. New York: Simon & Schuster.

Dever, William G. 2001. *What Did the Biblical Writers Know and When Did They Know It?* Grand Rapids: Eerdmans.

———. 2003. *Who Were the Early Israelites and Where Did They Come From?* Grand Rapids: Eerdmans.

Edwards, James. 2009. *A Biblical Perspective on Immigration Policy*. Washington, DC: Center for Immigration Studies. http://www.cis.org/ImmigrationBible

Egerton, Douglas R. 1999. *He shall go out free : The lives of Denmark Vesey*. Madison, WI: Madison House, 1999

Eichrodt, Walter. 1961. *Theology of the Old Testament*. Translated by J. A. Baker. Vol. 1. London: SCM.

———. 1967. *Theology of the Old Testament*. Translated by J. A. Baker. Vol. 2. London: SCM.

Elsmore, Bronwyn. 1985. *Like Them That Dream: The Maori and the Old Testament*. Wellington, New Zealand: Tauranga Moana Press.

———. 1989. *Mana from Heaven*. Auckland: Reed.

Enz, Jacob. 2001. *The Christian and Warfare: The Roots of Pacifism in the Old Testament*. Eugene, OR: Wipf & Stock (reprint).

Fanon, Frantz. 1963. *The Wretched of the Earth*. New York: Grove.

Felder, Cain Hope, ed. 1991. *Stony the Road We Trod*. Minneapolis: Fortress Press.

Feyerabend, Paul. 2010. *Against Method*. New York: Verso.

Foskett, Mary F., and Jeffrey Kah-jin Kuan, eds. 2006. *Ways of Being, Ways of Reading: Asian American Biblical Interpretation*. St. Louis: Chalice.

Frend, W. H. C. 1984. *The Rise of Christianity*. Minneapolis: Fortress Press.

Gabler, Johann P. "An Oration on the Proper Distinction between Biblical and Dogmatic Theology and the Specific Objectives of Each." In Ollenburger, *Old Testament Theology*, 497–506.

Gafney, Wilda C. 2008. *Daughters of Miriam: Women Prophets in Ancient Israel*. Minneapolis: Fortress Press.

González, Justo L. 1996. *Santa Biblia: The Bible through Hispanic Eyes*. Nashville: Abingdon.

Gottwald, Norman. 1979. *The Tribes of Yahweh*. Maryknoll, NY: Orbis.

Grabbe, Lester. 2007. *Ancient Israel: What Do We Know and How Do We Know It?* New York: T&T Clark.

Habel, Norman. 1993. *The Land Is Mine: Six Biblical Land Ideologies*. Minneapolis: Fortress Press.

Hallman, David G. 1994. *Ecotheology: Voices from South and North*. Maryknoll, NY: Orbis.

Hayes, John H., and Frederick Prussner. 1984. *Old Testament Theology: Its History and Development*. Atlanta: John Knox.

Hopkins, Dwight N., and George C. L. Cummings, eds. 2003. *Cut Loose Your Stammering Tongue: Black Theology in the Slave Narratives*. Louisville: Westminster John Knox.

Janzen, David. 2012. *The Violent Gift: Trauma's Subversion of the Deuteronomistic History's Narrative*. LHB/OTS 561. London: T&T Clark.

Jenkins, Philip. 2002. *The Next Christendom: The Coming of Global Christianity*. New York: Oxford University Press.

———. 2006. *The New Faces of Christianity: Believing the Bible in the Global South*. New York: Oxford University Press.

Kelle, Brad. 2013. *Ezekiel*. New Beacon Bible Commentary. Kansas City: Beacon Hill.

Kuhn, Thomas. 1996. *The Structure of Scientific Revolutions*. 3rd ed. Chicago: University of Chicago Press.

Levine, Lawrence. 1977. *Black Culture and Black Consciousness.* New York: Oxford University Press.

Linzey, Andrew. 1995. *Animal Theology.* Urbana: University of Illinois Press.

———. 2009. *Creatures of the Same God.* New York: Lantern.

Mandolfo, Carleen. 2007. *Daughter Zion Talks Back to the Prophets.* Atlanta: Society of Biblical Literature.

Meyers, Carol. 1988/2013. *Rediscovering Eve: Ancient Israelite Women in Context.* Oxford: Oxford University Press.

Middleton, J. Richard. 2005. *The Liberating Image: The Imago Dei in Genesis 1.* Grand Rapids: Brazos.

Miller, David. 2011. *Animal Ethics and Theology.* New York: Routledge.

Muir, Lynette R. 1995. *The Biblical Drama of Medieval Europe.* Cambridge: Cambridge University Press.

Niang, Aliou. 2009. *Faith and Freedom in Galatia and Senegal.* Leiden: Brill.

Nichols, Aiden. 2007. *Lovely Like Jerusalem: The Fulfillment of the Old Testament in Christ and the Church.* San Francisco: Ignatius.

Niditch, Susan. 1993. *War and the Hebrew Bible: A Study in the Ethics of Violence.* Oxford: Oxford University Press.

Ngan, Lai Ling Elizabeth. 2006. "Neither Here nor There: Boundary and Identity in the Hagar Story." In Foskett and Kuan, *Ways of Being*, 70–83.

O'Connor, Kathleen. 2002. *Lamentations and the Tears of the World.* Maryknoll, NY: Orbis.

Ollenburger, Ben, ed. 2004. *Old Testament Theology: Flowering and Future, Sources for Biblical and Theological Study.* Winona Lake, IN: Eisenbrauns.

Overholt, Thomas. 1992. *Cultural Anthropology and the Old Testament.* Minneapolis: Fortress Press.

———. 2003. *Channels of Prophecy: The Social Dynamics of Prophetic Activity.* Eugene, OR: Wipf and Stock.

Perdue, Leo. 1994. *The Collapse of History: Reconstructing Old Testament Theology.* Minneapolis: Fortress Press.

Plantinga, Alvin. 2009. "Two (or More) Kings of Scripture Scholarship." In *Oxford Readings in Philosophical Theology*, vol. 2, *Providence, Scripture, and Resurrection*, ed. Michael C. Rea, 266–301. Oxford: Oxford University Press.

Pulido, Laura, Laura Barraclough, and Wendy Cheng, eds. 2012. *A People's Guide to Los Angeles.* Berkeley: University of California Press.

Raboteau, Albert J. 1978. *Slave Religion: The Invisible Institution in the Antebellum South.* New York: Oxford University Press.

Rogerson, John. 1984. *Old Testament Criticism in the Nineteenth Century: England and Germany.* London: SPCK.

———. 2010. *A Theology of the Old Testament.* Minneapolis: Fortress Press.

Roberts, Nathaniel. 2012. "Is Conversion a 'Colonization of Consciousness'?" *Anthropological Theory* 12:271–94.

Ruiz, Jean-Pierre. 2011. *Readings from the Edges: The Bible and People on the Move.* Maryknoll, NY: Orbis.

Said, Edward W. 1979. *Orientalism.* New York: Vintage.

Schüssler Fiorenza, Elisabeth. 2009. *Democratizing Biblical Studies.* Louisville: Westminster John Knox.

Segovia, Fernando F. 2000. *Decolonizing Biblical Studies: A View from the Margins.* Maryknoll, NY: Orbis.

Segovia, Fernando F., and Mary Ann Tolbert, eds. 1985. *Reading from this Place*, vol. 1, *Social Location and Biblical Interpretation in the United States.* Minneapolis: Fortress Press.

Smith-Christopher, Daniel. 2002. *A Biblical Theology of Exile.* Minneapolis: Fortress Press.

———. 2007. *Jonah, Jesus, and Other Good Coyotes: Speaking Peace to Power in the Bible.* Nashville: Abingdon.

Sommer, Benjamin, ed. 2012. *Jewish Concepts of Scripture: A Comparative Introduction.* New York: New York University Press.

Soyinka, Wole. 2003. *Samarkand and Other Markets I Have Known.* New York: Methuen.

Stanovich, Keith. 2004. *The Robot's Rebellion.* Chicago: University of Chicago Press.

Sugirtharajah, R. S., ed. 2006. *Voices from the Margin: Interpreting the Bible in the Third World.* 3rd ed. Maryknoll, NY: Orbis.

Summers, Harry G. 1984. "What Is War?" *Harper's*, May, 75–78.

Toly, Noah J., and Daniel I. Block, eds. 2010. *Keeping God's Earth: The Global Environment in Biblical Perspective.* Downers Grove, IL: IVP Academic.

Thompson, Thomas L. 1974. *The Historicity of the Patriarchal Narratives: The Quest for the Historical Abraham.* Berlin: de Gruyter.

Trible, Phyllis. 1984. *Texts of Terror: Literary-Feminist Readings of Biblical Narratives.* Minneapolis: Fortress Press.

Trimm, Charles. 2012. "Recent Research on Warfare in the Old Testament." *Currents in Biblical Research* 10:171–216.

Rad, Gerhard von. 1962. *Theology of the Old Testament.* Vol. 1. New York: Harper & Row.

———. 1965. *Theology of the Old Testament.* Vol. 2. New York: Harper & Row.

Warrior, Robert Allen. 1996. "Canaanites, Cowboys, and Indians." In *Native and Christian: Indigenous Voices on Religious Identity in the United States and Canada*, edited by James Treat, 93–104. New York: Routledge.

Weems, Renita J. 1991. "Reading Her Way through the Struggle: African American Women and the Bible." In Felder, *Stony the Road We Trod*, 57–77.

———. 1995. *Battered Love: Marriage, Sex, and Violence in the Hebrew Prophets.* Minneapolis: Fortress Press.

White, Lynn, Jr. 1967. "The Historical Roots of Our Ecological Crisis." *Science* 155:1203–7.

Wimbush, Vincent L., ed. 2000. *African Americans and the Bible: Sacred Texts and Social Textures.* New York: Continuum.

Yadin, Yigael. 1963. *The Art of Warfare in Biblical Lands.* London: Weidenfield & Nicolson.

Yee, Gale A. 2003. *Poor Banished Children of Eve: Woman as Evil in the Hebrew Bible.* Minneapolis: Fortress Press.

———. 2006. "Yin/Yang Is Not Me: An Exploration into an Asian-American Biblical Hermeneutics." In Foskett and Kuan, *Ways of Being*, 152–63.

INTRODUCTION TO THE APOCRYPHA

Eileen M. Schuller

Apocrypha is a term applied to various Jewish books of different genres and authors, written in Greek, Hebrew, or Aramaic, from about the third century BCE to the first century CE. These books are not part of the sacred Scriptures of Judaism today; hence they will not be found in a contemporary Jewish Bible (e.g., The Tanakh of the Jewish Publication Society). These books were, however, copied and transmitted by Christian scribes over the centuries. They have been accepted as sacred Scripture by the Roman Catholic and Orthodox churches, and have not been accepted as such by the Protestant churches; hence, they will be found in some contemporary Christian Bibles and not in others. Where they are included, they sometimes appear throughout the Old Testament, with other books of similar genre, and sometimes they are gathered together and placed between the Old and New Testaments (or, less frequently, after the New Testament). Over the centuries, their inclusion or exclusion has often been one of the more visible signs on a popular level of the differences between Catholics and Protestants ("our Bible is bigger/smaller than yours") and reflected at times very sharp polemics over who had the "right" biblical canon (that is, the authoritative list of books accepted as inspired sacred Scripture).

Over the last fifty or sixty years, there has been real shift in how the Apocrypha is approached, both within religious/church contexts and in the scholarly milieu. As the Apocrypha is translated and printed in more editions of the Bible and studied often in a religious studies context in universities, these books are becoming much more widely known. Although faith communities continue to have different views about their authority as Scripture, the value of these books "as significant documents of a most important era in religious history" (quoted in the preface to the Revised Standard Edition, 1957) is increasingly acknowledged, and they have become a significant component in the study of the beginnings of Judaism and Christianity.

We will begin by trying to understand why it is so difficult even to define the term and to draw up an agreed list of texts to be included in this category. Since each book of the Apocrypha is treated individually with its own introduction in the subsequent pages, here we will give only a general overview of the different genres and types of materials that are included in the Apocrypha. We will then conclude with some selective examples of what can be learned from these books and how they have been read and used over the centuries, both theologically and culturally.

Meaning and History of the Term

It is hard to give a short yet comprehensive definition of the term *Apocrypha* since the title has been applied to different collections both in antiquity and in modern times. Indeed, it is only quite recently that "the Apocrypha" has more frequently begun to be used as a singular noun as opposed to Apocrypha with a plural verb, emphasizing the individual books. In 1957, the RSV used the label "the Apocrypha"; the NRSV (1989) uses the designation "the Apocryphal/Deuterocanonical Books."

The word itself is Greek for something that is "hidden away" or "kept secret." Often the connotation is negative: something is kept hidden away because the contents of the books are false or at least not authoritative. (Thus Augustine and Athanasius use the term for books that were never part of the canon and that they considered heretical.) But something can be hidden because it is esoteric, knowledge that is designed only for an elite few. The term is often related to a passage in 2 Esd. 14:45-46 that distinguishes between twenty-four books (the traditional number in the Hebrew canon) that are accessible to everyone, and seventy other books ("Apocrypha") that "were written last" and were kept for the wise, "for in them is the spring of understanding, the fountain of wisdom and the river of knowledge." But there is no evidence that any of the seventy books referred to in 2 Esd. 14:46 overlap with what is presently known as the Apocrypha, and the Apocrypha as now defined is not kept hidden or secret.

The term in the sense that we are using it is very much influenced by the approach of Jerome, a Christian biblical scholar and translator who at the end of the fourth century CE was entrusted by Pope Damasus with preparing a revised Latin version of the Bible (the Vulgate) to replace the existing Latin translations (the so-called Old Latin). Jerome distinguished between the books that were in the Hebrew Bible as known by the Jews of his day and the additional books that were included in the major Greek (Septuagint) Christian Old Testament manuscripts of his day; these latter books he termed Apocrypha. (At times, he did include in this category still other books, such as *Shepherd of Hermas*.) Although Jerome translated the books of the Jewish Bible directly into Latin from their original Hebrew (rather than using the Greek translation), when it came to the Apocrypha, he translated only Tobit and Judith (noting in the prefaces that he had devoted only a single day to Tobit and a single night to Judith). He included the additions to Daniel and Esther but marked in the margins that these were not in the Hebrew Bible. Over time, the Old Latin translations of the rest of the Apocrypha were regularly included in Vulgate Bibles, usually without the notes and prefaces wherein Jerome had made his careful distinctions. With the wide acceptance of the

Vulgate, these books in Latin were read as part of "the Bible" in the Western church, as they were in the Eastern church, where they continued to be copied in Greek manuscripts.

The issue of the Apocrypha came to the fore again in the sixteenth century, when the Protestant Reformers decided to follow the canon of the Hebrew Bible, though for the most part, they did not totally deny a place to those books that were not included. Martin Luther translated these books (with the exception of 1 and 2 Esdras) into German in 1534 and put them in a separate section in his Bible with the heading "Apocrypha," that is, books which are not held as equal to holy Scripture, yet which are useful to read. The 1546 Geneva Bible, with an introduction attributed to John Calvin, made a stronger distinction between "Holy Scripture" and the Apocrypha, considered "profane books," and the latter were sometimes omitted entirely. In the Anglican tradition, these books were kept for "example of life and instruction of manner" but not "to establish any doctrine" (Thirty-Nine Articles); they continued to be heard frequently in church services since they were part of the lectionary of the Book of Common Prayer. After the publication of the King James Version in 1611, the archbishop of Canterbury in 1615 insisted that every Bible that was printed must include these books, though in fact within a few years many editions appeared that did not contain them. Later documents such as the 1647 Westminster Confession adopted a more negative stance: "the books commonly called Apocrypha, not being of divine inspiration, are no part of the canon of the Scripture; and therefore of no authority in the Church of God, nor to be otherwise approved, or made use of, than other human writings."

In this era of controversy over the biblical canon, the Council of Trent in 1546 drew up for the first time a specific and formal list of books that must be included in the Roman Catholic canon and "condemned" anyone "who does not accept these books in their entirety, with all their parts, according to the text usually read in the Catholic church, and as they are in the ancient Vulgate." In terms of their placement, in Catholic Bibles these books were not isolated but integrated, on the basis of genre and historical period; so, for example, Wisdom of Solomon and Ecclesiasticus (Sirach) come with the other Wisdom books after Song of Songs. Books concerned with the exile are grouped together in the following order: Lamentation, Baruch, and the Letter of Jeremiah. Since 1 and 2 Maccabees covered the latest historical period, they are placed at the end of the historical writings. The additions to Esther and Daniel are integrated into these books at relevant places in the narrative, and the additional stories about Daniel (Susanna, and Bel and the Dragon) become the final chapters, 13 and 14, of that book. Three works (Prayer of Manasseh and 1 and 2 Esdras) were not accorded status as canonical books and were put into an appendix after the New Testament in editions of the Vulgate published after the Council of Trent. (Over time, this appendix has disappeared from most Catholic Bibles.) In the terminology introduced by Sextus of Sienna in 1566, a distinction came to be made between "protocanonical" books (books of the Hebrew Bible for which there was no debate about status) and "deuterocanonical" books (those that had been debated).

In the following centuries, the Apocrypha section was often dropped from Protestant Bibles, sometimes for the pragmatic publishing reasons of saving space and cost, at other times in order to distinguish clearly between a Protestant and a Catholic Bible. Indeed, in the nineteenth century, Bible societies in various countries often debated and established formal policies about whether any of their funds could be used for the printing of these books. In 1957, the Apocrypha section of the Revised Standard Version was first published (the New Testament and Old Testament had been available since 1952), containing a rather sparse selection (the books included in the Roman Catholic canon plus 1 and 2 Esdras and the Prayer of Manasseh). The New Revised Standard Version (1989) included many more books in the Apocrypha (see discussion below), and it is in this form that the Apocrypha has become more widely known in both church and academic contexts. Responding to the desire to include these books but recognizing the different authority accorded to them, the "Guidelines for Interconfessional Cooperation in the Bible," published in 1987 by the Secretariat for Promoting Christian Unity (Roman Catholic) and the United Bible Societies (Protestant), agreed that they be published in a separate section.

Content of the Apocrypha

As implied above, there is no set content for "the Apocrypha," and there has been considerable fluidity in the books included in this category, dependent on the time and context. At minimum, the collection includes certain books that are always included in the Roman Catholic, Greek Orthodox, and Slavonic Bibles. These are sometimes counted as seven books plus additions to two books (Daniel and Esther), or as up to twelve books, depending on how the additions are arranged and counted: Tobit, Judith, Wisdom of Solomon, Ecclesiasticus or the Wisdom of Jesus Son of Sirach, Baruch, 1 Maccabees, 2 Maccabees, additions to the book of Esther (107 verses of narrative materials plus the prayers of Mordecai and Esther), additions to the book of Daniel (the Prayer of Azariah and the Song of the Three Young Men (or Three Jews), Susanna, Bel and the Dragon), and Letter of Jeremiah (sometimes included as chapter 6 of Baruch).

A wider version of the Apocrypha includes those books that are regularly part of Greek and Slavonic Bibles, but are not in the Roman Catholic canon (although as we have seen above, some are included in an appendix to the Latin Vulgate). The Orthodox churches have always set discussion about canon less in terms of conciliar decisions and specific lists of books, and more on which books are regularly read and quoted within the community, especially in a liturgical context. Orthodox Bibles, both Greek and Slavonic, include 1 Esdras, Prayer of Manasseh, Psalm 151, and 3 Maccabees; Slavonic Bibles regularly include 2 Esdras. Finally, 4 Maccabees is included because it appears as an appendix in Greek Bibles.

Thus two criteria are crucial for inclusion in the Apocrypha: (1) acceptance by churches (some, not necessarily all) as canonical and (2) inclusion in major fourth- to sixth-century Greek Christian manuscripts (Vaticanus, Sinaiticus, Alexandrinus) or in the Vulgate. Books such as *1 Enoch* and *Jubilees* meet only the first criterion insofar as these two books are accepted as canonical within the Ethiopic church. A work such as the *Psalms of Solomon*, which is included in a sort of appendix to Codex Alexandrinus, meets the second criterion, but this collection of psalms has not been accepted by any church body. The semiexception is 4 Maccabees, which is not canonical for any church but is printed as an appendix in Greek Bibles.

The Apocrypha both overlaps with and should be distinguished from other categories and descriptive titles that are used for related and semioverlapping collections. In the past, sometimes the designation "intertestamental literature" has been applied to books composed between the completion of the last books of Hebrew Bible and earliest of the New Testament books. These books were often grouped together and placed literally between the Old and Testaments, and could be considered to form a "theological bridge between the Testaments" (Harrington, 1). This term, however, is fading from use because of its ambiguity (many of these books may well predate Daniel, and parts of 2 Esdras are later than anything in the New Testament) and because the "inter-" terminology assumes the acceptance of the New Testament as part of the Bible.

From one perspective, the Apocrypha can be considered as part of the larger category of Pseudepigrapha. Many of the books of the Apocrypha are pseudonymous; that is, they are presented as the work of a figure of the past who is clearly not the real author. Thus the book of Baruch, though written probably sometime after 200 BCE, begins, "These are the words of the book that Baruch son of Neriah . . . wrote in Babylon . . . at the time when the Chaldeans took Jerusalem and burned it with fire." The Letter of Jeremiah, a postexilic work in Greek, starts, "A copy of a letter that Jeremiah sent to those who were to be taken to Babylon as exiles." Second Esdras, clearly written after the destruction of Jerusalem in 70 CE, situates itself in the time of the Babylonian conquest, "In the thirtieth year after the destruction of the city, I was in Babylon—I, Salathiel, who am also called Ezra" (2 Esd. 3:1). The royal figure who speaks as "I" in the Wisdom of Solomon continues the tradition already established in the Song of Songs and Proverbs of attributing wisdom works to King Solomon. However, the term *Pseudepigrapha* as introduced by Johann Fabricius in the early eighteenth century is used by many scholars to cover a much wider expanse of any nonbiblical Jewish literature from the Second Temple period, some pseudepigraphic in form (*1*, *2*, and *3 Enoch*, *Testament of Abraham*, *Testament of Moses*, *Syriac Baruch*, *Psalms of Solomon*) and others not (*Jubilees*, *Biblical Antiquities*, *Life of Adam and Eve*). Sometimes, especially in European Catholic scholarship, the term *Apocrypha* is applied to this much larger and more amorphous collection of Jewish works (Charlesworth 1983; Bauckham, Davila, and Panayotov, 2013).

The Dead Sea Scrolls are standardly treated separately since this material was discovered only in 1947–1956 in caves near the northwestern shore of the Dead Sea. This collection of ancient manuscripts includes a number of the Apocrypha: four copies of Tobit in Aramaic and one in Hebrew (4Q196–200), a fragmentary Hebrew copy of Sirach (2Q18; in addition, a copy of Sir. 39:27—43:30 was found at Masada), one copy of the Letter of Jeremiah in Greek in Cave 7, and the Hebrew version of Psalm 151 (in 11QPs[a]). Most of the Dead Sea Scrolls are either copies of the books of the Hebrew Bible (about one-quarter) or previously unknown works (rules, hymns, commentaries), some composed by a distinctive sectarian group (the Essenes or a related group) but others coming from "common Judaism" of the Second Temple period. What canonical status some of these books may have had for the communities that copied them is hard to ascertain; there are more copies of some books like *Enoch* and *Jubilees* than there are of many of the books of the Hebrew Bible, and *Jubilees* is quoted as an authority in a work like the Damascus Document.

The Apocrypha as applied to Jewish literature should be distinguished from the Christian "Apocrypha," that is, a large collection of Christian literature (especially narratives about specific figures such as the *Acts of Paul* and the *Acts of Thecla*) that did not become part of the New Testament canon. Finally, we should note that different traditions give different names to the same work, particularly to the Ezra literature, and this can often generate confusion about precisely what is included (e.g., 1 Esdras = 2 Esdras in Slavonic, 3 Esdras in appendix to Vulgate; 2 Esdras = 3 Esdras in Slavonic, 4 Esdras in Vulgate appendix; includes 5 and 6 Ezra).

Date and Genres of the Apocrypha

In terms of quantity of material, the Apocrypha is a substantial collection. It is about one-fifth of the length of the Old Testament and over two-thirds that of the New Testament (Goodman, 4). Although the books of the Apocrypha are all religious literature from the Jewish community written in the land of Israel and the Diaspora and in the Second Temple period (with the exception of 2 Esdras 1–2, 15–16, which contain somewhat later Christian material), it is often extremely difficult to establish with certainty the exact dates and places or even the original language of composition for individual works.

Some books such as 1 Maccabees, the first part of Baruch (1:1—3:8), and Sirach were certainly written in Hebrew. This is confirmed for Sirach by the fragments in Hebrew that have been found among the Dead Sea Scrolls, and Ben Sira's grandson in his prologue to his Greek translation explicitly reflects on the difficulty of capturing "what was originally expressed in Hebrew." It is likely that Tobit was originally written in Aramaic, but it was translated early on into Hebrew, since there is a Hebrew copy among the Dead Sea Scrolls. The book of Judith may have been written in Hebrew or in Aramaic. Yet all of these books in their totality survived only in Greek translation, and it is the Greek text from the fourth- to sixth-century-CE manuscripts (Vaticanus, Sinaiticus, Alexandrinus) that provides the basis for our modern translations. The exception is 2 Esdras, where translation must be made from the Vulgate. Greek was the original language of many books of the Apocrypha, including the Wisdom of Solomon, 2, 3, and 4 Maccabees, and Prayer of Manasseh. For the books written in Greek, it is often difficult to determine if they were composed in Alexandria or in another major city of the Diaspora. Antioch is often proposed, for instance, as the place of composition for 4 Maccabees, especially since the Maccabean martyrs, whose example is the foundation of the book, were especially venerated there.

For the most part, little can be known of individual authors, only a few of whom are known by name: Jesus son of Eleazar son of Sirach of Jerusalem identifies himself in Sir. 50:27; the name of the author of the unabridged work of five volumes, of which 2 Maccabees is a summary, is given as Jason of Cyrene (2 Macc. 2:19-23). The colophon at the end of the Greek version of Esther mentions "Lysimachus, son of Ptolemy, one of the residents of Jerusalem" (11:1), and it is generally thought that he was the translator of Esther into Greek.

The date of books that treat concrete historical events and persons can be established with some degree of precision or at least within certain boundaries, but for many books only a tentative date or range of dates can be proposed. (Dates of composition will be discussed in more detail in the commentary on individual books.) For example, the historical books 1 and 2 Maccabees were obviously written after the latest events described (134 BCE for 1 Maccabees, 163 BCE for 2 Maccabees). Sirach can be dated most precisely, since the book was translated into Greek by the author's grandson after his arrival in Egypt in 132 BCE (prologue to Sirach, "the thirty-eighth year of the reign of Euergetes"), and so his grandfather must have lived in Jerusalem around 180 BCE. Third Maccabees describes events in Egypt during the reign of King Ptolemy IV Philopator (221–203 BCE), but references to other facets of Egyptian Jewish life (a possible reference in 3 Macc. 2:28 to a poll tax inaugurated in 24 BCE) suggest the book was written considerably later than the events it purports to narrate. Books of prayers and wisdom admonitions are, of course, much more difficult to fit into a specific historical framework. Since Josephus knew and used books such as 1 Esdras, Greek Esther, and 1 Maccabees, this establishes a *terminus ante quem* before the late first century CE. It is generally accepted that 2 Esdras is one of the latest books; chapters 3–14 reflect on the destruction of Jerusalem in 70 CE, and chapters 1–2 and 15–16 are almost certainly additions by Christians authors, perhaps as late as the third century CE.

In terms of genre, historical or quasi-historical works predominate. First Esdras summarizes 2 Chron. 35:1—36:23 and reproduces all of Ezra plus Nehemiah 7:38—8:12. Only 1 Esd. 3:1—5:6 is "new" material, a court tale set in the time of King Xerxes but probably composed sometime later. First Maccabees is a type of theological interpretative history modeled after Deuteronomy–Chronicles. Second Maccabees is much more influenced by the Hellenistic genre of "pathetic history," in which highly charged and emotional language arouses the emotions or "pathos" of the readers. Third Maccabees, also in the Hellenistic style, has nothing to do with the Maccabean crisis of the mid-second century BCE in Judah but rather is a dramatic tale of the suffering and persecution of Jews in Egypt under the Ptolemies in the third century BCE. Fourth Maccabees, although set in the time of the Maccabean martyrs, is a philosophical treatise extolling the supremacy of reason over passion that could have been written in a number of different historical circumstances in the first century CE.

Other books are set in a historical context, but it is generally accepted that they are not intended to report history as such or to be used for recovering historical facts. These moralistic narratives are closer to our modern classification of novels/novellas (Judith, Tobit); some (like the stories in Daniel 1–6, Susanna, Bel and the Dragon) belong to a genre of "tales of the wise man in the court of the foreign ruler."

The wisdom tradition as exemplified in the biblical book of Proverbs is continued in Sirach, both in terms of proverbial sayings and themes (riches and poverty, fear of the Lord, women). However, there are new features, such as longer poetic units that develop a topic rather than individual proverbs, and new themes are introduced (the praise of the ancestors in chapters 44–50, the identification of personified Wisdom with Torah in chapter 24). The Wisdom of Solomon likewise treats standard wisdom themes, but with forms, vocabulary, and philosophical ideas, particularly concerning immortality, that are influenced by Hellenistic genres and philosophical concepts. The wisdom of 2 Esdras is a revealed wisdom, given in a series of seven revelations to Ezra in visions that are interpreted by an angel; this is the only example of a fully developed apocalypse in the Apocrypha.

Thus the books of the Apocrypha, in different ways depending on their genre, open up a window on Second Temple Judaism, both in terms of history and of religious and theological developments. For historical study, they cannot be used in isolation, but when they are combined with the Dead Sea Scrolls, the Pseudepigrapha, and the works of Philo and Josephus, we learn considerable information about this important period of history and religious development, certainly much more information than can be known from the Old and New Testament alone.

Selected Themes in the Apocrypha

On the one hand, it is misleading to treat the Apocrypha as if it were an intentional collection of books, put together because they share common themes or interests or purposes. As we have seen, this is a much more random collection of literature, very diverse in terms of when, where, and by whom individual books were composed. What came to be included in the collection was shaped predominately by issues of canon formation in the Jewish and Christian communities over the centuries. Yet there are certain themes and emphases that do seem to stand out. Other themes, some recurring frequently and some distinctive to particular books, will emerge in the commentaries on individual works.

Given the historical reality of empire and world powers, much of this literature is concerned either explicitly or implicitly with how to "respond to challenges of Hellenism and persevere as a minority culture in a Greek world" (deSilva, 16). An openness to and the adoption of the Greek language, new literary forms, and diverse philosophical ideas (e.g., immortality of the soul) stand along aside the conviction that there are beliefs and values that cannot be abandoned (monotheism, Torah, Sabbath, circumcision, dietary laws; see for instance 1 Macc. 1:54-64 or Tobit's deathbed instruction to his son in 4:5-19).

Beginning with one of the first modern studies of the Apocrypha (Johnson), the frequency and importance of prayer in this literature has often been recognized. The Apocrypha preserves independent prayers (Prayer of Manasseh, Psalm 151), as well as the extended prayers of both penitence and praise that were added to the Hebrew form of Daniel (Prayer of Azariah, Song of the Three Young Men) and Esther (prayers of Esther and Mordecai), the latter of which are particularly to be noted because the Hebrew version of the book has no address to God or even mention of the divine name. Both short prose prayers and longer poetic passages are scattered throughout the narratives of Tobit: the prayers of Tobit (3:1–6), Sarah (3:11–15), Tobias (8:5-7), Raguel (8:15–17); the hymn of Tobit in chapter13; Judith's prayer in chapter 9; the short petitions in 13:4, 7; the victory hymn in 16:1-17; and the penitential prayer of the high priest in 3 Macc. 2:2-20. Even when there is no actual prayer text given, 1 and 2 Maccabees presume that, in time of crisis and battle, the recitation of prayers and hymns are part of the preparation for warfare and the celebration of victory (1 Macc. 4:24, 40; 13:51; 2 Macc. 10:7, 38; 12:37). Although it is sometimes claimed that the introduction of frequent prayers, especially combined with an increased emphasis on angelic intermediaries, indicates that God has become "inaccessible in his holiness" (Kaiser, 3–4), these prayers can be seen rather as expressing a deep conviction of divine involvement that finds expression in a rich and active devotional piety. The prayers within narratives sometimes reflect liturgical practices that were in the process of development, especially in daily set forms of prayer (compare the blessing formularies that became the standardized introduction and conclusion for rabbinic prayers with the blessing formula at the beginning of some of the prayers in Tobit, e.g., "Blessed are you, merciful

God. Blessed is your name forever," 3:11; "Blessed are you, O God of our ancestors, and blessed is your name in all generations forever," 8:5.

Many of the apocryphal books touch on the "mystery of suffering" (Harrington, viii). While a book like Sirach keeps to the traditional view that there is no retribution after death and that sinners are punished in this life (Sir. 40:8-9), other books confront more directly the suffering of the righteous and look for a final vindication, sometimes in the immortality of the soul beyond death (Wisdom of Solomon) or through a direct divine revelation, as in the visions that Ezra sees of the restored Jerusalem or the man from the sea (2 Esdras 10, 13).

It has frequently been noted that women play an important and prominent role in many of these books. Two books, Judith and Susanna, are named after their central female characters, in addition to the book of Esther, where Queen Esther's role is enhanced by the addition of her prayer in the Greek version. Seventeen women are named in these books (Craven, 16), and there are significant women who are not given a name, most notably the mother of the seven martyred sons in 2 Maccabees 7 and 4 Maccabees. The Apocrypha contains some of the most negative material about women (such as Sir. 25:24, the first explicit statement blaming Eve for bringing death into the world). However, the Apocrypha also contains some positive statements about women. These range from the popularistic court tale (1 Esd. 4:13-32) that acknowledges that women are more powerful than the king or wine, indeed that "women rule over you," to the more theological reflections of Sirach 24 and Wisdom of Solomon 7–9, where rich female imagery is used to shape an exalted understanding of Sophia/Wisdom, who tells of her glory in the assembly of the Most High (Sir. 24:2) and who "in every generation . . . passes into holy souls and makes them friends of God and prophets" (Wisd. of Sol. 7:27).

The Use and Influence of the Apocrypha

It is often not clear to what extent individual books of the Apocrypha were known in Judaism after the Second Temple period. We have noted that Josephus used the additions to Esther, 1 Maccabees, and 1 Esdras (rather than the Hebrew Ezra-Nehemiah), but from the second century CE there was a move away from the Septuagint to using translations by Jews such as Aquila and Theodotion that did not include the Apocrypha or the additions to Daniel and Esther. When the rabbis discussed which Hebrew/Aramaic books "rendered the hands unclean" (*m. Yad.* 4:5), the polemic was around books such as Song of Songs and Ecclesiastes rather than books of the Apocrypha. Sirach was the one book quoted and often cited by name by the rabbis, even though it was acknowledged that it was not in the Hebrew Bible. It is often unclear whether the rabbis knew specific books per se or only traditions, such as those about the martyrdom of seven sons. Indeed, the rabbis sometimes focused on traditions not based on apocryphal books. For instance, the Hanukkah story of the oil in the temple that miraculously was sufficient to burn for eight days (*b. Shab.* 21b) is not found in 1 and 2 Maccabees.

During the Renaissance, Jewish interest was sparked in these books, and a translation of most into Hebrew was made in the early sixteenth century. Although historians have always drawn on the data in books such as 1 and 2 Maccabees, in recent centuries most of these books were not widely read by Jews, often being treated with suspicion as Christian literature. The Apocrypha will be part of the forthcoming major three-volume project, *Outside the Bible: Ancient Jewish Writings Related to Scripture*, initiated by the Jewish Publication Society to provide an up-to-date, readily accessible translation of extrabiblical texts for wide circulation in the Jewish and secular communities.

Since the Apocrypha was treated as part of the Old Testament for the most part in the Western and Eastern churches, it is not surprising to find numerous references and allusions in the New Testament and the church fathers. Again, it is often difficult to judge what is a direct quotation from an apocryphal book per se and when Christian authors are simply drawing on a common tradition or general vocabulary—for example, the reference to the martyrs in 2 Maccabees 6–7 and in Heb. 11:35-37, and similar terminology in the Wisdom of Solomon and the letters of Paul and the letter to the Hebrews (e.g., Heb. 1:1-3/Wisd. of Sol. 7.26; 1 Cor. 2:10-16/Jth. 8:14; Rom. 9:3; 10:1/Pr. of Man. 8–9).

The Apocrypha has exerted a significant influence on popular culture, in art, music, and drama, throughout the Middle Ages and into the modern era. The dramatic stories of Judith, Susanna, and the Maccabees have been particularly attractive and have been retold and reenacted in a variety of media: the *Canterbury Tales* (lines 3757–64); lesser-known Scottish ballads; medieval miracle plays; Henry Wadsworth Longfellow's poem on Judas Maccabeus; and Handel's oratorios *Susanna*, *Judas Maccabeus*, and *Alexander Balus*. A recent monograph has explored Judith studies across the disciplines, collecting examples of representations of Judith from the visual arts, music, and drama (see Brine, Ciletti, and Lähnemann). Equally rich studies could be done on the reception and reinterpretation of some of the other books of the Apocrypha.

Bruce Metzger collected some fascinating examples of the often-unrecognized influence of bits and pieces from the Apocrypha in the popular realm. For instance, many people quote the maxim, "Great is truth and strongest of all" (NRSV) or in the King James Version, "Great is Truth, and mighty above all things," without realizing that it comes from 1 Esd. 4:41. Similarly, when singing the Christmas hymn "It Came Upon the Midnight Clear," few people recognize that the identification of the hour of the birth is dependent on a passage in Wisdom of Solomon which declares that "the all-powerful word leaped from heaven" when "night in its swift course was now half gone" (18:14-15). And it was on the basis of 2 Esd. 6:42 and its interpretation of day three of the Genesis creation story that Christopher Columbus set out for India, confident that the seas could not be that vast since the waters were "gathered together in a seventh part of the earth" and six parts were dry land.

The Apocrypha becomes known to many churchgoers through the liturgy. In the Orthodox, Anglican, and Roman Catholic churches, selections from the Apocrypha are regularly read in the prescribed lectionary for Sundays, feasts, and weekdays; however, in the Revised Common Lectionary (an adaptation of the Roman lectionary), which is used in many Protestant churches, whenever a reading from Apocrypha is listed, an alternative from the canonical books is also provided. In lectionaries, the Wisdom of Solomon is the book that is used most frequently (on nine Sundays in the Roman Catholic lectionary). A passage from Wisdom of Solomon, "But the souls of the righteous are in the hand of God" (3:1), is sometimes popular as a funeral reading even in Protestant churches that do not otherwise use the Apocrypha. According to long-standing tradition, on feasts of Mary, the first reading is often a passage about Lady Wisdom from Wisdom of Solomon 7–9 or Sirach 24 or the canticle from Judith 16. In the daily Roman lectionary, substantial portions of Tobit, 1 and 2 Maccabees, and Sirach are read over consecutive days. The liturgical use of the Prayer of Manasseh and the Song of the Three Young Men makes these apocryphal prayers part of contemporary devotional practice.

Works Cited

Bauckham, Richard, James R. Davila, Alexander Panayotov, eds. *Old Testament Pseudepigrapha: More Noncanonical Scriptures*, 2013. Grand Rapids: Eerdmans.

Brine, Kevin R., Elena Ciletti, and Henrike Lähnemann. 2010. *The Sword of Judith: Judith Studies across the Disciplines*. Cambridge: OpenBook.

Charlesworth, James H., 1983. *The Old Testament Pseudepigrapha*. Garden City: Doubleday & Company.

Craven, Toni. 2000. "The Apocrypha/Deuterocanonical Books." In *Women in Scripture*, edited by Carol Meyers, Toni Craven, and Ross S. Kraemer, 12–16. Grand Rapids: Eerdmans.

DeSilva, David A. 2001. *Introducing the Apocrypha: Message, Context, and Significance.* Grand Rapids: Baker Academic.

Feldman, Louis H., James Kugel, and Lawrence H. Schiffman. 2013. *Outside the Bible: Ancient Jewish Writings Related to Scripture.* 3 vols. Philadelphia: Jewish Publication Society; Lincoln: University of Nebraska Press.

Goodman, Martin. 2012. *The Apocrypha*. Oxford Bible Commentary. Oxford: Oxford University Press.

Harrington, Daniel, J. 1999. *Invitation to the Apocrypha.* Grand Rapids: Eerdmans.

Johnson, Norma Burrows. 1948. *Prayer in the Apocrypha and Pseudepigrapha: A Study of the Jewish Concept of God.* Philadelphia: Society of Biblical Literature and Exegesis.

Kaiser, Otto. 2004. *The Old Testament Apocrypha: An Introduction.* Peabody, MA: Hendrickson.

Metzger, Bruce. 1957. *An Introduction to the Apocrypha*. New York: Oxford University Press.

TOBIT

Micah D. Kiel

Introduction

The book of Tobit is a fascinating folktale about a family living in Nineveh during the Assyrian exile. It weaves many different threads, traditions, motifs, and characters into an entertaining tale that also has profound depth.

Historical Context

The book of Tobit makes no overt historical references that allow it to be dated with precision. Based on its original language (Aramaic) and theology (emphasis on unwarranted suffering), a date between 250–175 BCE seems the most likely. The place of its composition is also difficult to discern. Many recent treatments of the book suggest that it may have been composed quite close to, if not within, Jerusalem itself (Fitzmyer; Moore; Kiel).

Canonical and Theological Context

Tobit is a book within the deuterocanonical literature (sometimes also called the Apocrypha). As such, it is deemed canonical by Roman Catholics, but generally not by Protestants. The discovery of the Dead Sea Scrolls (DSS), however, has proved to be a watershed for our understanding of Tobit. Fragments of Tobit have been found among the DSS in both Aramaic and Hebrew, proving that it was written in Aramaic, not Greek. As a result, the philological criterion (that it should not be deemed canonical because it was not written in a semitic language) originally used to justify Tobit's proscription rests on shoddy footing.

Although not canonical for large segments of Christianity, the book of Tobit will prove salutary for anyone interested in studying Scripture. Many Christians, including early pillars of the faith (e.g., Origen, Clement), have read it as "Scripture." Tobit also contributes to an understanding of the biblical world. It is unique as the only text that envisions the Assyrian exile and deportation as its hypothetical historical referent. Tobit provides a more extended picture of quotidian Jewish family life than any other biblical book. Finally, the book of Tobit is a serious piece of narrative theology. Although enshrined in a folktale, it strives to say something profound in conversation with contemporaneous theological formulations. It intentionally engages Deuteronomy, Job, and Sirach as conversation partners. This is a book that had dipped its pen in many inkpots (Nickelsburg 1996, 340) and deserves a place at the table in canon-based theological discussions.

Tobit 1:1—3:17: Tobit and Sarah's Predicaments

The Text in Its Ancient Context

Tobit strives to live a righteous life while in exile, and he succeeds. His paradigmatic righteous activity is burying his kin properly. In Tobit 2, after another burial of one of his people, Tobit must sleep outside, where bird droppings and visits to physicians produce blindness. Tobit suffers: his wife mocks him; his family is suddenly destitute. As a result, he prays for release in 3:1-6. Tobit's prayer asserts his own guilt because of his association with the guilt of his forebears. He can find no way to conceive of his suffering other than that he brought it on himself. The prayer proffers a close connection between act and consequence.

After Tobit's prayer, the narrative flashes to a different city, where a similarly grieving Sarah laments over her demonic affliction (3:11-15). Sarah's prayer, however, brazenly asserts her own innocence in the face of her suffering. The narrative then provides a brief, dramatic glimpse of the heavenly realm. Both of these prayers, we are told, were received before the presence of God, and God sends Raphael to help.

These two prayers contain the two main issues of the book: The first is theodicy, or God's justice in the face of unwarranted suffering. The second is related to the first: a narrative dynamic in which the characters have a limited awareness of their own situations. Although both Tobit and Sarah face severe challenges, the reader knows quite a bit more about God's involvement in alleviating those challenges (in this case, dispatching Raphael to help and heal). This creates dramatic irony and, at the same time, foists on the reader questions about God and human experience: What do we know about God's ways? This is similar to the book of Job, in which the characters in the poetic chapters grope for a reason as to why Job suffers (while the reader knows that God's wager with *ha satan* was behind it the whole time). In Tobit, the characters are similarly in the dark as to the cause of their suffering, but so is the reader. It is not readily apparent why Tobit and Sarah suffer.

The episode in Tob. 3:16-17 bears some similarity to other Jewish literature of the Second Temple period. The prayers of both characters are heard "in the glorious presence of God," which in Greek is the exact description of God's throne in *1 Enoch* 104:1. The episode tells the reader how the story will end—with Tobit's sight restored and Sarah happily married to Tobias. God gives this mission to Raphael, whose name, "God heals," fits his role in the story. Raphael's mission in Tobit is similar to the apocalyptic text *1 Enoch*, in which he is dispatched to bind a demon and bury him in the desert, the same fate that Sarah's menace, Asmodeus, will suffer.

The Text in the Interpretive Tradition

Scenes from Tobit were popular in the history of art, especially in the late-medieval and Renaissance periods. In a time when most artists were restricted to painting only biblical scenes or those that their patrons wanted, available subject matter was quite limited. Tobit provides three specific details rare in biblical narratives: a fish, a named angel, and a dog. Many paintings from the book of Tobit have at least one of these three elements, often all three (e.g., Filippino Lippi's c.-1475 painting *Tobias and the Angel*).

The book also offers drama that many painters attempted to capture. Rembrandt's *Tobit and Anna with the Kid Goat* from 1626, for example, highlights several interpretive issues of the book. In the painting, Tobit, already blind, sanctimoniously folds his hands over his tattered clothing. Anna looms over him, goat tucked under her arm. A dog hides in the shadows. Tobit is annoyed at the goat's bleating, and in Rembrandt's interpretation, Anna is shoving the goat into Tobit's face, as if to make his suffering worse. It represents well the confrontational question Anna asks in the text: "Where are your acts of charity? Where are your righteous deeds? These things are known about you!" (2:14).

The Text in Contemporary Discussion

The opening chapters of Tobit offer an interesting look at gender roles in both ancient and modern contexts. The interaction between Tobit and his wife devolves into a domestic spat. In the ancient context, it is quite possible that the author of Tobit viewed the title character's having to be supported by his wife as an addendum to his suffering (for an example of such thought, see Sir. 25:22).

Modern readers, especially feminist interpreters, read such a scenario differently. Amy-Jill Levine (105–19) has shown the broad disparity in how the two genders are treated in the book. Throughout, the patriarchs are paramount. In their respective prayers that respond to their situations (Tobit's blindness, Sarah's demonic menace), Tobit is the one who embodies the entire story of the nation of Israel, while Sarah does not. The arc of Tobit's story parallels that of the nation as a whole, while the wake of Sarah's affliction is limited only to the disgrace she may bring on her father's reputation (3:15).

Tobit 4:1—7:9: Wisdom Instruction, Disguised Angels, and Mettlesome Fish

The Text in Its Ancient Context

In Tobit 4, Tobit gives his son a series of proverbial wisdom sayings as advice for life. Much of what we find here is sapiential boilerplate—sayings and themes similar to what one would find in Proverbs or Sirach. Two features of this material stand out. The first is its theological underpinnings. All of Tobit's advice is built on the basic assumption that God will reward righteous behavior: "almsgiving delivers from death and keeps you from going into the Darkness" (4:10); "If you serve God you will receive payment" (4:14). The second important feature is that the reader experiences such statements with irony. The one imparting this wisdom, Tobit, is a blinded, impoverished righteous person. Tobit's own words, in light of the events of the narrative as a whole, are shown to be ignorant. The wisdom instruction nevertheless seems to be taken seriously by the author, as it contributes to the complex view of God and retribution that the book embodies (see Macatangay).

In Tobit 5, the angel Raphael appears on the scene, disguised as a human being named Azariah. He agrees to accompany Tobias on his journey to retrieve the money his father had deposited in Rages of Media. Anna is distraught at the prospect of a dangerous journey for her son. Tobit's response, "Do not fear for them . . . for a good angel will accompany him," is another example of the author's penchant for irony.

As the boy and the angel start on their journey, they camp by the River Tigris. A huge fish leaps from the river and attempts to eat Tobias's foot. At Raphael's behest, Tobias grabs hold of the fish, which, as the plot unfolds, becomes a means of sustenance, deliverance, and healing. While birds defecating in Tobit's eyes, fish leaping from rivers, and demons afflicting a woman might all seem like entertaining elements of a well-told folktale, they are also a part of the author's narratological argument about the origin of Tobit's misfortune. We have already observed that Tobit's own explanations might not be sufficient, and telling a story in which the suffering is imposed on the righteous characters by outside forces might hint at a more sectarian origin for the experience of suffering and evil. Birds are seen elsewhere in Jewish literature as related to a demonic menace (*Jub.* 11:10-13; Mark 4:4, 15). The great fish may also be interpreted in a similar way. Many scholars (Nowell; Moore; Kiel) point to how the book of Tobit here evokes Israel's creation mythology in which God destroys a primordial foe as the means of creation (see Ps.74:12-17; Isa. 51:9-11). There are examples of such foes in apocalyptic literature that, like the fish in Tobit, get turned into food (e.g., *1 En.* 60:24; *2 Bar.* 29:4). Tobit, to be sure, is not fully an apocalyptic text, but in its ancient theological context, it seems to be appropriating some of the tenets of that worldview in attempting to address the complicated problem of suffering and evil.

The Text in the Interpretive Tradition

The role of the angel Raphael in the book of Tobit has commonly been read as an anticipation or analogy to the incarnation of Jesus. Bede (d. 735) draws a close parallel between the two: both offered themselves as companions and played a saving role as the embodiment of that companionship (Voicu, 14).

As noted above, that throughout art history the fish and dog in Tobit have been found to be fascinating, so is true of many commentators on Scripture. Ambrose of Milan (d. 397), for instance, says that Raphael intentionally caused the dog to join them (although the text does not say this specifically), which was for protection, and thus those whom Ambrose admonishes should use their voices in defense of Christ (Voicu, 16). Bede reads the story of the fish directly through the lens of a completely developed Christian understanding of the devil. The fish is the devil, and Bede finds in this reading many parallels to the life of Jesus, particularly the passion (Voicu, 17).

The Text in Contemporary Discussion

Two operas have been made of the book of Tobit in the twentieth century. The most recent of them (1999) is by English composer Jonathan Dove with a libretto by David Ian. A small chamber orchestra accompanies the singers. The opera depicts the experience of Tobit's blindness and Sarah's trouble from Asmodeus side by side. Staged music is able to accomplish this in a way that a written narrative cannot, as two characters, disparate in the original source material, can sing in harmony about their respective situations. This becomes a particularly effective interpretation of the story when the two afflicted characters can simultaneously sing of their desire for death. Both Edna (Sarah's mother) and Anna (Tobit's wife) sing together of their concern for their loved ones. Tobit and Sarah themselves slip into a duet that powerfully brings together their respective situations.

Tobit 7:10—10:13: Routing the Demon and Celebrating the Wedding

The Text in Its Ancient Context

Tobit 7–10 narrates the resolution to the main characters' misfortune. Upon arrival in Ecbatana, Raphael and Tobias stay with Raguel. Tobias has heard of Sarah's affliction—some say that it was a demon (7:14)—but Raphael encourages him to pay no heed. Burning the heart and liver of the fish from the river will chase the demon away. This is exactly what happens as the narrative unfolds. Raphael binds the demon hand and foot in Upper Egypt, the wedded couple say a prayer, and they go to sleep.

Raguel, Sarah's father, does not show much hope. He expects to bury another potential son-in-law. He even sends a servant out to dig a hole for the body, another example of humor and irony in the book. This grave also recalls the opening chapters of the book, in which proper burial of the dead instigated the plot in the first place.

These middle chapters of Tobit provide one of the few pieces of literary evidence for ancient Jewish wedding practices, although even here the narrative does not reveal much. Ancient sources suggest an elaborate process to the betrothal period. When examining marriage broadly in the ancient Near East, a contract is often part of the process, and Tob. 7:13 offers the only specific example of such a contract in the entire Old Testament. There is some argument among scholars as to whether such contracts for marriage were used widely within ancient Judaism. In Tobit, the narrative itself condenses the betrothal period because the characters want immediate action—Raguel is keen to hand over his daughter, and Tobias himself refuses to eat or drink anything until the matter is settled (7:11). Thus the needs of the storyteller could explain some of the divergences from what was standard practice in the betrothal and marriage process. The feasting, it seems, was extensive: Raguel forces Tobias to stay for fourteen days of eating and drinking. Tobias, of course, is concerned about his worrying parents.

The Text in the Interpretive Tradition

In his Hymns on Virginity (hymn 22; McVey, 354–60), Ephrem the Syrian (d. 373) interprets the story of Jesus' encounter with the Samaritan woman at the well in John 4 in a way that has been influenced by the story of Sarah from the book of Tobit. As Ephrem recounts the story, the woman at the well is not of questionable sexual repute. Like Sarah, her husbands have been killed before any sexual union, which is what led to a poor reputation: "Blessed are you, woman, because you saw that your husbands were dead, and your reproaches were many. Other men were afraid to take you [in marriage] lest they, like their counterparts, die" (strophe 4). The woman's current husband is only for show, and she lives chastely in that context. Ephrem's "exegesis" here is meant ultimately to avoid any impropriety on the part of Jesus. Jesus could not have approached a sinful woman, and so Ephrem turns her into a paragon of virtue and a victim of unfortunate circumstances, built on the example of Sarah. He says that the woman at the well has been called a harlot, but if she were, her "bad reputation would have wafted to Him" (strophe 5) and the interaction would have been impeded.

The Text in Contemporary Discussion

Given the importance of marriage in the construction of society and the debates regarding its definition, one might be surprised by how few biblical texts discuss marriage in a theological way. At weddings, readings are often taken from Genesis 2 (the two become one flesh) or John 2 (the wedding at Cana). Neither of these texts, however, is primarily about marriage. Tobit 7–8, however, might provide the most robust exposition of a theological understanding of marriage anywhere in the Bible. There are emphases that may not comport well with our modern context, such as the focus on endogamy (marriage of one's own kin) or the dowry. At the same time, the story narrated here is one where the marriage union is a dangerous step. Sarah and Tobias must step out in faith that the demon's curse can be overcome. The prayer on their wedding night is simple yet beautiful. They place their marriage within the long tradition of their ancestors, evoking Adam and Eve as those first to be united. Their prayer is simply to be together, with blessing and old age. While Tobit is not canonical for many Christians, a reading from Tobit 8 might provide a theological interpretation of marriage and give simple expression to hope for the future.

Tobit 11:1—12:22: The Journey Home and Raphael's Revelation

The Text in Its Ancient Context

In Tobit 11, Tobias and Raphael return to worried parents. Anna greets them first, while Tobit stumbles, blind, out the door. Tobias immediately spreads the gall of the fish on Tobit's eyes, his sight returns, and he blesses God and sees his son, the "light of [his] eyes" (11:14). The family then welcomes their new daughter-in-law into their home.

In Tobit 12, Raphael reveals his true identity as one of the seven angels who stands ready before the glory of the Lord (12:15). In this revelation, several of the prominent features of the book of Tobit cohere. At this point, the characters, Tobit in particular, suddenly learn that God's role in their ordeal has been different from that which they had assumed all along. God was working behind the scenes from the outset to alleviate their suffering. This means that with the return of Tobit's sight comes also new theological insight—that both the reasons for his suffering in the first place and what is required for restoration and healing are different than he had been assuming. Based on Tobit's previous statements (e.g., his prayer in Tobit 3), Tobit would have required renewed righteousness for his situation to change. What one finds, instead, is that restoration comes from an incursion by God's agent into human workings.

There are several points of contact here with *1 Enoch* that help further to place Tobit in an ancient theological context. Raphael's role in Tobit is quite similar to the one he plays in *1 Enoch*. In Tob. 3:16-17, Raphael is sent to heal the two characters (Tobit and Sarah), which parallels his being directed to "heal the earth" in *1 En.* 10:7. Also repeated in both Tob. 3:16 and 12:15 is Raphael's self-description as one of the angels who stand "before the glory of God," similar language to that used in *1 En.* 104:1. George Nickelsburg (1988, 67) has noted these similarities and posited similar origins for the traditions that undergird both Tobit and *1 Enoch*. This is just one of the many traditions from ancient Judaism with which the book of Tobit interacts. The author also clearly draws from wisdom traditions similar to Proverbs or Sirach (e.g., Tobit 4 and 14). Ahiqar, a figure known in wisdom circles from other ancient sources, makes two cameos as Tobit's relative. The author assumes that the reader will know the specifics of Ahiqar's tale (Macatangay, 173). The author also interacts with biblical texts, not only those quoted directly (Amos and Nahum), but also more subtly, with texts such as Job or Jonah. While this is a folktale, it is not simple. The breadth of its influences and subtle theological argument belies a depth that needs to be explored.

The Text in the Interpretive Tradition

Although not quoted directly, the angelophany in Tobit 12 provides an important template for certain texts in the New Testament. In particular, the language used to describe Raphael's departure from the earth echoes some of the descriptions of Jesus' ascension in the New Testament. The clearest verbal echo is between Raphael's words in Tob. 12:20, "I am ascending to him who sent me," and those of Jesus in John 16:5, "but now I am going to him who sent me." The active verbs stand out when compared to most ascension scenes, which tend to narrate it with a divine passive construction—for example, "he was lifted up" in Acts 1:9 (Skemp, 54). Vincent Skemp makes a more specific argument that the angelophany in Tobit 12 is a "cultural intertext" for Luke's ascension scene in Luke 24.

The Text in Contemporary Discussion

I once had a student refer to the four-hundred-year gap of God's silence between the Old Testament and the New Testament. Tobit 12 might be a salutary spot to consider, at the very least, as to what can be learned about the intertestamental period as contextual information for those who are interested in the New Testament. Raphael's self-reference as one of the "seven angels who stand ready" is the earliest biblical reference to named angels, predating the references to Michael and Gabriel in the book of Daniel, which dates to the Maccabean period, by at least fifty to one hundred years. Specific interest in heavenly beings—both angels and demons—was increasing in the intertestamental period and on into the first century CE. The book of Tobit, at the very least, fills in some of the background to the development of such thinking and its theological and contextual underpinnings. One of the developments in this period of Judaism is an increasingly heavenly and enthroned God; texts describe God with otherworldly images rather than human metaphors. This makes God less accessible, and angelic intermediaries become necessary to mediate God's presence with the people and to achieve God's ends on the earth. Tobit becomes an important part of our understanding of this context both for early Judaism and nascent Christianity.

Tobit 13:1—14:15: The Future of Jerusalem, Tobit, Tobias, and Their Kin

The Text in Its Ancient Context

The final two chapters of Tobit are written in two different genres. Chapter 13 is a hymn that Tobit sings as a response to his situation. The hymn coordinates the fate of both Tobit and the people of Israel as a whole with God's future restoration of the city of Jerusalem. The first half of Tobit's song of praise finds similarities to kingship psalms and Moses' song in Exod. 15:1-18 (Fitzmyer, 304). The second half becomes more prophetic as it looks forward to a future restoration of Jerusalem, focusing on both the precious stones with which the future city will built (cf. Isa. 54:11-14) and the eschatological gathering of all nations at Jerusalem (cf. Isa. 60:1-4). By culminating Tobit's story with an eschatological hymn, the author argues that this new eschatological perspective is what is required in order to envision both the restoration of Tobit himself and the entire nation. The introspective, intracommunal explanations and hope for the future—marked by a close connection between act and consequence—are no longer apt. Instead, the restoration of Israel will coincide with God's plan for the entire world, all of which will be gathered in praise in Jerusalem. Tobit will be happy if a remnant of his people can survive to see such a thing.

In Tobit 14, the author turns to an entirely different genre of literature, a testament. This literature focuses on a patriarch on his deathbed, imparting wisdom and advice to his children before dying and being given a happy burial. Such a testament is similar to other biblical scenes, such as Jacob's address to his sons in Genesis 48–49. This genre of literature becomes important in some later apocalyptic forms as well, especially the *Testament of the Twelve Patriarchs* (also modeled on Jacob in Genesis 48–49) and the *Testament of Job*. The end of Tobit speaks of the destruction of Nineveh as something to look forward to, but at the time of the author, this is past history. Instead, the author writes in a more apocalyptic way about the future and how things will happen at their "appointed times" (14:4), which shows a deterministic view of time and specific language similar to parts of Daniel.

These final two chapters of the book of Tobit, in their respective genres, frame and interpret the events of Tobit's life. They suggest that, unlike Tobit's insistence early in the book, righteousness cannot guarantee blessing and a peaceful life. The experience of life under foreign rule—or suffering of some sort—has dismantled the underpinnings of such explanations. Instead, the fate of individuals and the nation as a whole are left more radically to God and God's freedom to act on behalf of the remnant of those who endure, faithfully, until the appointed times.

The Text in the Interpretive Tradition

Tobit's description of a future Jerusalem in 13:9-17 in all likelihood influenced the author of Revelation in its own description of the city. The author of Tobit may have been influenced by a text such as Isa. 54:11-12; both of them in turn may have provided language and concepts for the picture of Jerusalem in Rev. 21:9-27. Most modern commentators on Revelation note Tobit as among the intertexts for the author of the Apocalypse.

The Text in Contemporary Discussion

The final two chapters of Tobit portray a change in perspective so drastic that they have long been considered by scholars to be extraneous to the core of the book. The sudden poetic turn to the fate of future Jerusalem and the gathering together of all nations at a rebuilt temple has suggested to some that it was written after the fall of the temple in 70 CE. The discovery of the fragments of Tobit among the Dead Sea Scrolls makes this impossible, as some of the fragments of Tobit 13–14 predate the destruction of the temple. Nevertheless, many scholars still maintain a distinction between the core story (about a family in the Diaspora) and an editorial frame that places that story in the "broader context of the history of Israel" (Collins, 25). A narrative approach to reading the book can find coherence between these sections without positing later redactors as the explanation. By showing a change in Tobit's perspective, the author may be intending to offer a new theological insight—that the explanations Tobit had previously offered are no longer valid. Instead, the author thinks a new eschatological perspective is needed in order for the individual and corporate suffering of the Jewish people to be alleviated. This is the very argument that underlies Raphael's role in the story—that a divine incursion into the human realm is necessary. A revelatory and eschatological perspective is exactly what was missing from Tobit's explanations all along.

What one finds, then, when reading this story, is a complex narrative argument. The author attempts to make a subtle, profound statement about how humans often find themselves stuck between traditional religious formulas and contradictory life experiences. The brilliance of the argument is that the author does not completely shun the traditional explanations, but instead shows how such explanations are of limited explanatory power. God is still free; humans are still dependent on God's willingness to continue to intervene on their behalf. Only by remaining open to what God will do in the future do humans properly understand their past, endure their present, and hope for the future.

Works Cited

Collins, John J. 2005. "The Judaism of the Book of Tobit." In *The Book of Tobit: Text, Tradition, Theology*, edited by Géza Xeravits and József Zsengeller, 23–40. Leiden: Brill.

Fitzmyer, Joseph A. 2003. *Tobit*. Berlin: de Gruyter.

Kiel, Micah D. 2012. *The "Whole Truth": Rethinking Retribution in the Book of Tobit*. London: T&T Clark.

Levine, Amy-Jill. 1992. "Diaspora as Metaphor: Bodies and Boundaries in the Book of Tobit." In *Diaspora Jews and Judaism*, edited by J. Andrew Overmann and Robert S. MacLennan, 105–19. Atlanta: Scholars Press.

Macatangay, Francis M. 2011. *The Wisdom Instruction in the Book of Tobit*. Berlin: de Gruyter.

McVey, Kathleen E. 1989. *Ephrem the Syrian: Hymns*. Mahwah, NJ: Paulist.

Moore, Carey A. 1996. *Tobit: A New Translation with Introduction and Commentary*. AB 40A. New York: Doubleday.

Nickelsburg, George W. E. 1988. "Tobit and Enoch: Distant Cousins with a Recognizable Resemblance." In *SBL 1988 Seminar Papers*, edited by David J. Lull, 54–68. Atlanta: Scholars Press.

———. 1996. "The Search for Tobit's Mixed Ancestry: A Historical and Hermeneutical Odyssey." *RevQ* 8:339–49.

Nowell, Irene. 1983. "The Book of Tobit: Narrative Technique and Theology." PhD diss., Catholic University of America.

Skemp, Vincent. 2005. "Avenues of Intertextuality between Tobit and the New Testament." In *Intertextual Studies in Ben Sira and Tobit*, edited by Jeremy Corley and Vincent T. M. Skemp, 43–70. Washington, DC: Catholic Biblical Association of America.

Voicu, Sever J., ed. 2010. *Apocrypha*. Ancient Christian Commentary on Scripture, Old Testament 15. Downers Grove, IL: InterVarsity Press.

JUDITH

Corrine L. Carvalho

Introduction

The book of Judith tells the fictional story of a Jewish widow who defeats an army through her looks and cunning. While the story has captured the imagination of artists throughout the centuries, it has been largely ignored or viewed as morally problematic by theologians.

Judith was probably written during the Hellenistic period, either under Greek rule or during the Hasmonean period (140–116 BCE; Hopkins). Specific dates have been offered, but none has garnered consensus, in part because the story's message transcends any particular historical setting. The book has been preserved in Greek, but the style of the Greek indicates it is a translation of either a Hebrew or Aramaic original. Judith was not preserved in the Hebrew version of the Tanak, but was included in the Septuagint. Because of this difference, it is considered canonical by Roman Catholic and Orthodox Christians (part of the historical books), but not by Jews or Protestants.

The story is set in a fictional past. The opening verse of the book deliberately confuses historical facts as a cue that the story is fictional. At various times, Christian scholars, perhaps influenced by its placement among the historical books, have searched for the historical veracity of the text, but this approach has now largely been abandoned. Because the historical backdrop of the narrative is deliberately distorted, it is impossible to state the narrative setting of the text. Even the geographical location of the story, a city named Bethulia, is unattested in any other Israelite text.

The book has two halves. Chapters 1–7, which depict an attack on the Israelite city of Bethulia, feature the evil general Holofernes and one of his subordinates, Achior the Ammonite, who warns Holofernes of his hubris. This is answered by chapters 8–16, which narrate the city's deliverance. The turning point is the introduction in 8:1 of Judith, who will venture into the enemy's camp to kill Holofernes. These two halves of the story are brought together at the end: Judith returns to Bethulia and Achior converts, while Holofernes's severed head looks on.

Judith 1:1—4:15: Introducing the Enemy

The Text in Its Ancient Context

The book opens with a seemingly historical notice, but one that clearly sets the book in a fictional past (1:1). It makes the Babylonian Nebuchadnezzar, who destroyed Jerusalem in 586 BCE, the king of the Assyrian city of Nineveh, a city destroyed by the Babylonians in 612 BCE. Both Assyria and Babylon had destroyed parts of Israel, but not at the same time. Historical distortions are a major feature of the book. By recalling Israel's great enemies here, the distortions project Bethulia's enemy onto a cosmic plane. Nebuchadnezzar is cast as an archvillain of a helpless city.

The conflict begins when Judea joins other nations in refusing to support the villain, insulting the honor of this dangerous enemy (1:11). Nebuchadnezzar vows revenge for this insult (1:12), commissioning Holofernes to attack the cities that have insulted him (2:4). Small details in chapters 2 and 3 give snapshots of the terrifying power of Holofernes's army (2:5, 15). They are likened to a swarm of locusts (2:20), who fill fields and ravines with the corpses of those they slaughter (2:8). Like Gog's army in Ezekiel 38, this is an enemy of cosmic proportion.

This cosmic nature is further stressed in 3:8, when Nebuchadnezzar is likened to a god who destroys the sanctuaries of other gods. After this point, Nebuchadnezzar recedes from the action, making him the literary parallel of Yahweh. The action of the rest of the narrative focuses on their envoys: a great general and a small-town widow, both of whom claim that they are serving their god.

Chapter 4 turns its attention to Bethulia, the only rebel land that has refused to capitulate. The city, otherwise unknown, is probably a fictional location. Its name, similar to the Hebrew word for "virgin," recalls a common epithet given to both Zion (Lam. 2:13) and Israel (Jer. 31:4). These first four chapters then use fictional places and mythical time in a story about a fully innocent Judean city attacked by the minions of an evil villain, who claims to be god.

The Text in the Interpretive Tradition

There is not a vibrant history of interpretation of the book of Judith among theologians. In fact, the first full commentary of the book, by Rabanus Maurus, was not written until around 856 CE, although the earliest Christian reference is found in Clement of Rome. Jerome, who viewed Judith as apocryphal, scorned those who wanted to "accept a woman's book" (Brown). Later Christian exegetes, especially in the Middle Ages, read the book as an allegory.

The Text in Contemporary Discussion

The book's creative refashioning of history suggests the story is a kind of mythical realism, where the characters engage the symbolic aspects of Israel's cultural memory. Nebuchadnezzar, not just a foreign king, is the destroyer of Jerusalem. This rhetorical tactic is found in popular culture today. Movies such as *Abraham Lincoln: Vampire Hunter* (2012) or *Cowboys and Aliens* (2011) warp history in order to bring cultural symbols together in creative ways.

The book also plays with the symbolic meaning of space. Biblical scholars have begun to notice how spaces have a symbolic function. In the book of Judith, the city of Bethulia symbolizes the gendered city as vulnerable, innocent, and in need of the male God's protection. The book of Judith plays creatively with Israel's historical spatial symbols in order to exploit its theme of good's triumph over evil.

Judith 5:1—6:21: Achior the Ammonite

The Text in Its Ancient Context

The two characters who understand God's role in this story are Judith and Achior. These characters mirror each other in many ways (Roitman). Both are in dangerous positions while they are in the camp of Holofernes. Their vulnerability is augmented by their marginal social positions (Achior as a foreigner, Judith as a widow). When both of them speak the truth, it puts them at odds with prevailing authorities.

This section features Achior's speech to Holofernes in answer to his query of who would dare oppose him (5:5-21). Achior's answer consists in a thoroughly orthodox retelling of Israel's history. The fact that a foreigner provides the most conventional witness to Israel's past not only foreshadows his eventual conversion to Judaism but also marks him as a righteous foreigner, similar to Ruth the Moabite (Lacocque).

The Assyrians are outraged by both Bethulia's resistance and Achior's speech (5:22—6:4). Holofernes reasserts the divinity of Nebuchadnezzar (6:2). This overreaction to a city that is really no threat to the army shows that the issue is really Bethulia's failure to honor Nebuchadnezzar and accept their subordinate status. This is confirmed in the prayer of the Bethulians, which depicts the Assyrians as arrogant, and their own situation as one of "humiliation" (6:19).

The Text in the Interpretive Tradition

Focus on the character of Achior became lively only in the second half of the twentieth century. Until the 1980s, most biblical scholars had a rather negative view of the narrative quality of the book of Judith. The general consensus was that the book was lopsided, since its main character was not introduced until chapter 8, making chapters 1–7 an overly long introduction to the book. This changed significantly with the work of Toni Craven, who demonstrated that chapters 1–7 were integral to the book's overall structure.

The Text in Contemporary Discussion

This new focus on Achior has led to an appreciation of how the book subverts expected power dynamics. While scholars have always noticed the book's inversion of gender categories, Achior's character demonstrates that the book also plays with other categories of privilege. Both Achior and Judith represent the "other," that is, those communities outside of the privileged circle of elite males within a patriarchal culture. Yet in this book, it is these two others who have the clearest understanding of who God is and, as a result, act with the most courage (Levine).

This text is written in the context of colonization; even if it was penned during the brief period of Israelite independence under the Hasmoneans, the imminent threat of colonization loomed large. The story projects both Achior and Judith as the ideal responses to colonizing threats, one that combines a recognition of the true cosmic power with the courage to stand up to evil.

Judith 7:1—8:36: Attack and Response

The Text in Its Ancient Context

Although Judith's introduction in 8:1 marks a turning point in the book, her reaction to the attack on Bethulia contrasts with the reaction of the rest of the citizens of the city, so the two elements are considered together here. As is true in any communal crisis, the tragedy elicits a variety of responses. The city's dire circumstances are highlighted by the detailed description of the advance of the army (7:1-18), the stopping up of the springs (7:17), and the plight of the whole city captured in the image of listless children and fainting youth (7:22).

The text contains three distinct reactions to the attack: the general population, who want to save lives at all costs (7:23-29), the civic leaders, who choose to wait and see how the situation unfolds (7:30), and Judith, who vehemently opposes both of these options (8:11-27). Although Judith's speech is the longest and most articulate position represented, all three responses invoke the question of sin and blame. The appropriate response depends on whether the attack is a punishment for prior sin to which the people should submit (7:28) or an unwarranted injustice from which God should deliver them (8:18-20). There is no prophetic voice in the text to tell them the correct interpretation, which is why the leaders suggest seeing if God delivers them (confirming their innocence) or allows the disaster to continue (affirming their sinfulness).

Judith's introduction tells the reader that hers is the authoritative voice in this debate. Every element of the text exalts her. She is wise, pious, beautiful, rich, honorable, and esteemed. The lengthy, if chronologically impossible, genealogy exalts her over every other character. She is the most eloquent character in the book, outshining even Holofernes and Achior in her verbal artistry. Her description of the autonomy of God shames her audience in their attempt to manipulate Yahweh. She understands that the fate of Bethulia has national implications, and she engages Israel's traditions in creative ways to depict the disaster as a test. Therefore, when she avers that this particular disaster is a test from God, the reader is ready to acquiesce.

The Text in the Interpretive Tradition

Although the text introduces Judith as a pious widow, the artistic tradition has preferred to depict her after her transformation into a seductress. Medieval interpretations that viewed her as either a type of the Virgin Mary or as an allegory of chastity depend on her description here and at the end of the book.

The Text in Contemporary Discussion

Feminist scholarship on the book has renewed an interest in these opening descriptions of Judith. She has the longest genealogy of any woman in the Bible (Craghan). She seems to own property and conducts her affairs with full autonomy. She is an active character in the book who speaks in public to the city elders. Even before her heroic feat, she is a fascinating counterbalance to the usual way the Bible depicts women.

Judith 9:1—10:10: Judith Going Out

The Text in Its Ancient Context

Before Judith sets out to enact her plan, she prays for success (Eynde). The prayer introduces the theme of sexual violence that will dominate the rest of the book. The author has delayed the identity of Judith's tribe by not listing her tribal ancestor in the genealogy. This identification comes in her invocation of Yahweh as "God of my ancestor Simeon" (9:2). This delayed notice, which highlights the allusion to Simeon, is followed by a description of his revenge for Dinah's rape (Genesis 34). This rape is described not in terms of how Dinah experienced it, who is not even named in the prayer, but how it polluted, disgraced, defiled, and shamed her family. This shift to the communal ramifications justifies Simeon's, and subsequently Judith's revenge.

The sexual theme continues in 10:1-10 with the description of Judith's deliberate transformation of her performance of gender. She changes from a woman who mourns for her husband to that of a seductress. She does so knowing that her beauty gives her power over men.

The Text in the Interpretive Tradition

Throughout the Christian tradition, theologians have tended to view Judith's manipulation of sexual attraction as a bad thing. Both traditional interpreters of the text who would prefer that Judith be a symbol of modesty, as well as some feminists who view her use of sexuality as a reinscription of patriarchal norms, are critical of this element in the text (Efthimiadis-Keith). Craven even suggests that the book does not make it into the Jewish canon because Judith herself "is simply too radical a woman for the tradition to memorialize" (Craven, 117).

The Text in Contemporary Discussion

Behind Judith's prayer is the reality that rape has been used a weapon of war throughout the centuries (Gafney). It is not surprising that this female character, who is about to confront the militarized enemy, should be reminding God to exact vengeance on rapists (Harrington). Rape and other forms of sexual violence are still used as military weapons today. Judith's prayer that God protect women and avenge sexual violence resonates with too many contemporary audiences.

Judith 10:11—12:9: Judith in the Enemy's Camp

The Text in Its Ancient Context

Judith's deliberative plan begins to unfold in this section of the book. Her success requires patience, and the ability to anticipate how the men in the camp will react. The details in the text are exaggerated.

One hundred men take her to Holofernes, whose tent is bejeweled. The general's entrance is grand, while her public acts of subservience are performed perfectly.

Once again, she gives an eloquent speech, but this time it drips with double meanings, ironic references, and cunning deception. Much of what she says seems true. For example, she reaffirms that God can punish Israel's sins through a foreign army (11:10), but she does not say that this particular situation is a test of their faithfulness. She states that she will not run out of food before God has accomplished his purpose (12:4), a purpose that the audience knows is the opposite of what Holofernes expects. She tells outright lies when she claims that the Bethulians are eating food dedicated to God (11:12-15).

Her hidden deception is matched by the ironic truth of the statements that the men in the camp make. For example, at the end of Judith's speech, Holofernes's servants declare, "No other woman . . . speaks so wisely" (11:21), without realizing that her words have just trapped Holofernes through a false sense of security. Perhaps the most ironic statement is found in 11:19, when the soldiers state that women like Judith are worrisome because they have the ability to "beguile the whole world."

Judith's beauty is a major element in this part of the story. The word is repeated seven times here (10:4, 7, 14, 19, 23; and 11:21, 23). While beauty in the Bible often makes a character vulnerable, Judith is able to use her beauty to accomplish her goals (Hopkins). While the threat that her beauty provokes (i.e., rape) has been alluded to in chapter 9, in chapter 10 she can use that beauty without becoming a loose woman (Proverbs 7), a whore (Ezekiel 16 and 23), or a seductive foreigner (Judges 16). To be sure, Judith's power rests in knowing that the Assyrian men would view her as all three of these, but the narrative makes it clear that this is all an act on her part.

The Text in the Interpretive Tradition

One of the biggest problems exegetes have had with the story of Judith is her use of deception. On the one hand, the story depicts her as the paradigm of virtue, through her observation of purity regulations and dietary restrictions, as well as her prayers and fasting. For many Christians, this seems incompatible with a victory wrought by outright lying. This assessment has again contributed to the fact that Judith has not been actively engaged in the theological traditions of Christianity.

The Text in Contemporary Discussion

Advances in the use of sociological analysis have helped clarify how Judith's use of deception was viewed as an exemplary feature of her character (deSilva). Philip Esler in particular has noted that, within the collectivist context of ancient Mediterranean cultures, lying to an outsider, especially one who threatens the security of the insider group, is a sign of group loyalty (2002; 2011). In addition, lying is also an acceptable element of the trickster motif. In a group that does not have enough power to confront an oppressor, subverting their power through trickery can become a valued element of storytelling.

Judith 12:10—13:10: Judith in the Bedroom

The Text in Its Ancient Context

The story reaches its dramatic climax in this section. The motivation for all of Judith's actions thus far is made clear to the audience. She has flattered Holofernes in order to garner his trust. She has gone out to pray regularly to establish an escape route. Even the purpose for her clothing comes into focus; she is literally dressed to kill.

While the whole narrative is rife with allusions to other biblical texts (Lacocque; Henten), this section echoes the story of Jael's execution of Sisera in Judges 4–5 (White). Both victims are generals of an army hostile to Israel. Both assume they are safe when alone with subservient women. Both women gain their trust when the men drink with them. Both men, feeling safe, fall asleep, a sleep that proves fatal. In both stories, there is a sexual undertone. While this is more explicit in Judith, the poetic version of Sisera's death in Judges 5 includes Sisera dying literally between Jael's thighs (5:27), while women talk about the reality of rape in war (Judg. 5:30).

God is offstage in both stories. Some scholars have pursued the fact that God is not a character in Judith (Day), since nowhere does Judith claim that her plan comes from God. Jael is even further removed from God: she is not even an Israelite. In fact, Judges offers no motivation for what she does. Yet the material surrounding both death scenes leads the audience to assume that these are acts of God (Judg. 4:9; Jth. 13:4-5; Eynde).

Perhaps the element that conveys most clearly that God is behind these acts, at least for the ancient audience, is the gender of the executioners. Deborah's oracle that foreshadows Sisera's death centers on the fact that he will die by the hand of a woman. In Judith, the phrase that Holofernes dies "by the hand of a woman" is repeated three times (9:10; 13:15; 16:6), showing that the killer's gender is significant. Since the killing of a warrior by a woman was shameful, the deaths of arrogant Sisera and Holofernes function as a kind of poetic justice.

The Text in the Interpretive Tradition

The most vibrant interpretive history of the book of Judith can be found in the artistic tradition, which has focused on either the actual beheading scene or the two women's return to Bethulia, bagged head in hand (Sölle). Nira Stone traces the Christian development of this type scene in three stages. In medieval art, Judith either represents the church or Mary. During the Renaissance, while she is often cast in nationalistic tones, Gentileschi's artwork in the early seventeenth century poignantly captures the threat of rape that permeates the book. Modern Christian art, Stone's third period, depicts Judith as a feminist heroine.

In medieval Judaism, the book of Judith, which medieval midrash associated with the Maccabean revolt, was used at Hanukkah (Moore). This association of Judith with Hanukkah is found in medieval Jewish art as well (Stone; Tilford). In post-Shoah art, she remains a Jewish heroine who sacrificed herself for her people and a symbol of resistance (Tilford).

The book of Judith has also been the subject of literary and musical retellings (Sölle). From early medieval German poetry to nineteenth-century operas to contemporary films, it is clear that the story of Judith strikes a chord with audiences across the centuries. Audiences can enjoy the suspense and irony of the text when it is freed from its biblical context. Art can play with the elements of the text that strike a universal chord, such as the thrill of the ironic undoing of unbridled claims to power.

The Text in Contemporary Discussion

Psychological analyses of the deaths of Sisera, Shechem (Dinah's rapist), and Holofernes have exploited the sexual overtones of how each man died (Efthimiadis-Keith). Jael pierces Sisera's head with a tent peg, a symbolic reversal of rape. Shechem is slaughtered while recovering from circumcision, a ritual that Amy-Jill Levine likens to a symbolic castration (1992). Judith's decapitation of Holofernes also symbolizes castration (Stocker, p. 117). Through this interpretive lens, the book reflects male anxiety over women's sexual power. This fear is personified on the one hand with Holofernes's servant Bagoas, a eunuch, and, on the other hand with Judith, who is more masculine than all the men in the text.

Judith 13:11—16:25: Judith Triumphant

The Text in Its Ancient Context

The final chapters integrate the themes that permeate the book. This section begins with the visual image of Judith pulling Holofernes's head out of her food bag. The text, however, is less interested in the dripping pate and more focused on Judith's assurance that she "committed no sin" in the commission of this execution (13:16), assuring them that the only body part involved in his seduction was her "face." The author is careful to distance Judith from a reverse rape of the evil general, which ironically reinforces the sexual overtones of the threat of violence found throughout the book.

While the two main heroes of the book represent the other, one of the notable features of these final scenes is the way this other becomes integrated into Bethulian society. Achior the Ammonite converts (14:10), Judith's maid becomes a free woman (16:23), and Judith returns to her life as pious widow (16:21-24). While some scholars seem bothered by the conversion of Achior, because of its prohibition in Deut. 23:3, this element parallels the view of foreigners in other postexilic texts, such as the book of Ruth and Isa. 56:6-8. Similarly, the whole book ends with a summary of Judith's life. This summary reintegrates her into Judean society. Once again, she becomes the honorable widow, living a chaste and pious life, for which she is greatly rewarded.

The ending of the book is satisfying because the fate of each character inverts the honor-shame rhetoric that upheld the colonizing power of the Assyrians. When the Bethulians see the severed head, they praise God, not for killing Holofernes, but for shaming the enemy (13:17). They simultaneously turn and honor Judith as they would a military hero (13:17-20; 15:9-10). It is the male soldier, Achior, who faints at the sight of the head and, when revived, bows down to Judith

(14:6-7). Even Bagoas proclaims that Judith's actions have shamed the supposed god Nebuchadnezzar (14:18).

The last time the audience hears Judith's voice is when she sings the victory song in chapter 16. Modeled after Judges 5, it gives a poetic version of the story of Judith, even referring to her in the third person. That story, however, is framed by her praise of God acting as a divine warrior (16:2), Judith serving as the divine weapon (vv. 5-6), and the battle as a cosmic fight (vv. 14-15). The final verse of the poem (16:17) reveals the purpose for the use of historical figures as symbols of a dehistoricized cosmic fight: the story is a warning to all of Yahweh's enemies of the fate they can expect if they dare attack Judea.

The Text in the Interpretive Tradition

The end of the story is not well represented in visual art. However, Judith's decision to remain celibate reinforces the early church's use of her as a symbol of virginity and chastity. This is seen most clearly in the works of Tertullian, Ambrose, and Jerome (Moore; Tilford).

The Text in Contemporary Discussion

Many contemporary readers of the text resist the praise of Judith. In addition to her use of deceit, the way the text relishes her violence is problematic for some readers. The way the book itself carefully reintegrates Judith back into society shows that her actions were the result of dire circumstances.

It must be remembered, however, that this is a story that reflects the threat of colonization. It reminds readers of privilege that unjust claims to power and the exploitation of others invokes such desires for retaliation. It raises the question of whether armed revolution is always wrong and, even when it is deemed wrong, whether it allows for the fantasies of violent revenge to find expression. The story of Judith is one that can address many different audiences at many different times. Theology's snub of the book is countered by the artistic tradition, where moral taboos have less sway and the power of imaginative engagement with symbols of evil power and the triumph of good resonate for many people.

Works Cited

Brown, William P. 1999. "Judith." In *Dictionary of Biblical Interpretation*, ed. John H. Hayes, 647–50. Nashville: Abingdon.

Craghan, John. 1982. *Esther, Judith, Tobit, Jonah and Ruth*. OTM 16. Wilmington, DE: Michael Glazier.

Craven, Toni. 1983. *Artistry and Faith in the Book of Judith*. SBLDS 70. Chico, CA: Scholars Press.

Day, Linda. 2001. "Faith, Character and Perspective in Judith." *JSOT* 95:71–93.

DeSilva, David A. 2002. *Introducing the Apocrypha: Message, Context, and Significance*. Grand Rapids: Baker Academic.

Efthimiadis-Keith, Helen. 2010. "Judith, Feminist Ethics and Feminist Biblical/Old Testament Interpretation." *JTSA* 138:91–111.

Esler, Philip F. 2002. "Ludic History in the Book of Judith: The Reinvention of Israelite Identity?" *BibInt* 10:107–14.

———. 2011. *Sex, Wives and Warriors: Reading Biblical Narrative with Its Ancient Audience.* Eugene, OR: Cascade.

Eynde, Sabine van den. 2004. "Crying to God: Prayer and Plot in the Book of Judith." *Bib* 85:217–34.

Gafney, Wilda C. 2010. "Judith." In *The People's Companion to the Bible*, edited by Curtiss Paul DeYoung, Wilda C. Gafney, Leticia Guardiola-Sáenz, George E. Tinker, and Frank Yamada, 188–89. Minneapolis: Fortress Press.

Harrington, Daniel J. 2011. "Judith." In *Dictionary of Scripture and Ethics*, edited by Joel B. Green, 433. Grand Rapids: Baker Academic.

Henten, Jan Willem van. 1995. "Judith as Alternative Leader: A Re-Reading of Judith 7–13." In *A Feminist Companion to Esther, Judith and Susanna*, edited by Athalya Brenner, 224–52. London: T&T Clark.

Hopkins, Denise Dombkowski. 2012. "Judith." In *Women's Bible Commentary*, edited by Carol A. Newsom, Sharon H. Ringe, and Jacqueline E. Lapsley, 383–90. 3rd ed. Louisville: Westminster John Knox.

Lacocque, André. 1990. *The Feminine Unconventional: Four Subversive Figures in Israel's Tradition.* OBT. Minneapolis: Fortress Press.

Levine, Amy-Jill. 1992. "Sacrifice and Salvation: Otherness and Domestication in the Book of Judith." In *"No One Spoke Ill of Her": Essays on Judith*, edited by James C. VanderKam, 17–30. SBLEJL 2. Atlanta: Scholars Press.

Moore, Carey A. 1985. *Judith: A New Translation with Introduction and Commentary.* AB 40. Garden City, NY: Doubleday.

Roitman, Adolfo D. 1992. "Achior in the Book of Judith: His Role and Significance." In *"No One Spoke Ill of Her": Essays on Judith*, edited by James C. VanderKam, 31–45. SBLEJL 2. Atlanta: Scholars Press.

Sölle, Dorothee. 1994. *Great Women of the Bible in Art and Literature.* Macon, GA: Mercer University Press.

Stocker, Margarita. *Judith: Sexual Warrior, Women and Power in Western Culture.* New Haven: Yale University Press, 1998.

Stone, Nira. 1992. "Judith and Holofernes: Some Observations on the Development of the Scene in Art." In *"No One Spoke Ill of Her": Essays on Judith*, edited by James C. VanderKam, 73–93. SBLEJL 2. Atlanta: Scholars Press.

Tilford, Nicole. 2012. "Judith and Her Interpreters." In *Women's Bible Commentary*, edited by Carol A. Newsom, Sharon H. Ringe, and Jacqueline E. Lapsley, 391–95. 3rd ed. Louisville: Westminster John Knox.

White, Sidnie Ann. 1992. "In the Steps of Jael and Deborah: Judith as Heroine." In *"No One Spoke Ill of Her": Essays on Judith*, edited by James C. VanderKam, 5–16. SBLEJL 2. Atlanta: Scholars Press.

Esther (the Greek Additions)

Vivian Johnson

Introduction

The book of Greek Esther of the Septuagint innovatively adapts an earlier Hebrew version of the text by adding six additions (additions A–F) and a few marked theological notices (2:20; 4:8; 6:13). In rewriting and updating the story of Esther, the author of Greek Esther gives it an obvious religious tone, having God more directly involved in the action of the story. This feature contrasts sharply with the earlier Masoretic Hebrew text (MT), which does not mention the deity explicitly.

The adaptations Greek Esther makes to the MT speak to the challenges of Jews in coping with multiple and sometimes divergent loyalties in a foreign empire. Greek Esther, MT Esther, and another Greek version of the story, called the Alpha Text (AT) all reveal how Jews attempted "to forge an identity in exile that would allow them both to thrive in their wider societies and to retain their loyalties as Jews" (Koller, 8). Greek Esther seems interested in creating a portrait of Esther that would align with the times of its postexilic audience.

The Text in Its Ancient Context

The marked religious tone occurs at the outset of Greek Esther where, in addition A, God takes center stage as the source of deliverance for the "righteous nation" against whom "every nation" wages war. This cosmic battle occurs in a dream Mordecai has in which God provides him foreknowledge of an impending threat. Mordecai's dream prefaces the content found in the MT, setting the entire story in a grand and universal framework. Indeed, addition B provides details of the Persian king's authorization of a pogrom against Jews, in which he singles out his Jewish inhabitants as contrary to "every nation." The king argues in his edict: "We understand that this people, and it alone, stands constantly in opposition to every nation, perversely following a strange manner of life and laws . . . doing all the harm they can so that our kingdom may not attain stability" (13:5). Thus he unleashes a horrific edict in which he orders the killing of all men, women, and children in a single day (13:6-7). Expanding the content of the royal decree in the MT deepens the need for divine intervention in Greek Esther.

Divine deliverance comes about only after the petitions from Mordecai and Esther for God to avert the annihilation of their people (addition C). Pious protagonists offer a paradigm for people living under hostile authority. Given that the book is named after Esther, her actions in particular come under scrutiny. The book of Greek Esther accentuates her piety, assures her adherence to orthodox Jewish practice, and asserts her sole reliance on the deity for deliverance. These qualities Esther exhibits in this version are noticeably absent in the MT.

Esther's prayer describes dire circumstances in which enemies cause them to undergo "bitter slavery" (14:8). Dissatisfied with the humiliation of their enslavement, Esther laments, they desire also to destroy them completely (14:8-9). Her supplication reinforces the cruelty of the royal decree with its order to destroy all Jews "without pity or restraint" (14:6). These additions evince the fragility of subjected peoples under imperial domination.

After her prayer, Esther exhibits great sangfroid, initially, when she appears before the Persian king in addition D. Her courage lapses at the sight of an angry king who is annoyed by her presence. Esther therefore faints and collapses right before him out of fear. The narrative of Greek Esther at this point reveals the limits of human initiative. Esther cannot achieve a successful outcome all by herself. She needs divine intervention desperately. God comes to her aid by altering "the spirit of the king to gentleness" (15:8). The added details of the MT not only heighten the suspense of the narrative but also underscore the need for divine action in the lives of the people.

Greek Esther affirms that God hears and responds to the needs of the Jewish people. Because God intervenes, the people are saved and addition E notes the reversal of the king's genocidal edict. In this decree, the writer of Greek Esther has the king himself declare God as sovereign, as one who rules over all things (16:17, 21), as one "who always sees everything" (16:4) and directs the kingdom for the Persians "in the most excellent order" (16:15).

Addition F, a colophon, notes the fulfillment of Mordecai's dream and identifies the symbolic elements of his earlier dream. This notice serves to confirm the efficacious nature of the strategy Mordecai and Esther took in their situation.

Although the story takes place in Susa, a city of the Persian Empire, it describes conditions relevant to any imperial context. Esther's deportment then serves as model for subsequent generations to follow as they straddled commitments to their religious heritage with those obligations demanded by the nation imposing its rule on them.

Greek Esther is often dated to the second to first centuries BCE, a precarious time for its Jewish audience. This period saw the heinous xenophobic acts of Antiochus IV (ruled 175–164 BCE), who outlawed Judaism and enforced Hellenism. According to one historian, his measures marked the beginning of Judaism as a persecuted religion (Scheindlin 1998). The story of Greek Esther, then, would resonate well with people experiencing the harshness of foreign domination, especially during this time in Jewish history. Esther describes complete abhorrence to courtly life even though she reigns as queen. She detests all the trappings of royalty and caustically remarks on having to adorn her head with the crown (14:16). Her life, she mourns, has existed without joy since she arrived at the Persian court. The Hebrew version of the story appears to be updated to intensify Esther's condition and uphold her as an exemplar of piety and orthodoxy. She offers a paradigm for how others could manage to live under hostile authority.

The story of Greek Esther befits the genre of literature called novella or short story (Harrington). It has similarities with apocryphal/deuterocanonical books like Tobit and Judith, whose compositions have the didactic purpose of communicating values and ideas that their composers deem important. Tobit, Judith, and Greek Esther all narrate the experience of Jewish characters that must navigate living under foreign rule and peril.

The fervent prayer that Esther offers in the book of Greek Esther encapsulates the pedagogical purpose of the work to show Jews how to live devoutly in unfavorable circumstances. In a few verses, Esther conveys her piety, her loyal observance to Jewish practice, and her complete reliance on the deity to prevent the obliteration of her people. This addition along with all the others that make up Greek Esther enhance its religious character by providing an ideal model for people to emulate as they attempted to maintain their religious convictions in adverse times.

The Text in the Interpretive Tradition

Greek Esther stands in the interpretive tradition of the book of Esther. It appears to be based on the Hebrew version appearing in the Masoretic Text (MT). Noticeably absent in the Hebrew story is the mention of God, and Greek Esther reinterprets the earlier narrative to give it a distinct theological emphasis.

In the Hebrew version of the book of Esther, the deity does not have an overt role in the narrative. Rather, the characters appear to achieve desired ends by their own human agency. Esther appears in this text as a Jewish woman who assimilates fairly well into Persian culture. Although she has strong ties with the Jewish community, especially Mordecai, she works within the system to achieve a favorable outcome for Jews in the Persian Diaspora. When the story of Esther is rewritten in Greek Esther, it resolves troublesome issues that the Hebrew version left open-ended. Did Esther, for example, abide by Jewish dietary restrictions? Did she have marital relations with the Persian king? Did she relish the lavish lifestyle of the Persian court? Esther's prayer addresses each of these concerns. She emphatically proclaims that she has kept *kashrut* and denies having eaten any food or consumed any libation at royal dining events (14:17). Her prayer suggests that she did assume marital sexual obligations with the Persian king, but states categorically that she detested it (14:15). As for her attitude toward living among Persia's most privileged citizens, she decries: "I hate the splendor of the wicked" (14:15).

Greek Esther also clarifies any ambiguity concerning the source of the deliverance. Saving activity lay in the divine realm. God, for example, "changes the spirit of the king to gentleness" (15:8) when Esther approaches the king unbidden to persuade him to revoke the lethal decree. Esther proclaims in her prayer that she has no one to help her but God and that he has been her only source of joy since she was brought to the Persian court (14:14, 18). At the prayer's end, she pleads for God to save her people from the impending threat (14:19).

While the basic story line remains the same, Greek Esther has in fact created a new narrative, where, as one scholar writes, "the scribal manipulation of the base text is so extensive that a recognizably new work is created" (Crawford, 14). Greek Esther takes the detail of the Hebrew story not including any mention of God as its springboard for a strong theological emphasis: Greek Esther mentions the deity more than fifty times. Although the name for the deity, "God" or "Lord," clusters in the additions, Greek Esther also includes the deity several times outside of the additions, integrating them into the main body of the story (2:20; 4:8; 6:1, 13). By rewriting the Hebrew version, Greek Esther does not leave open the possibility that the deliverance of the Jewish population in Persia derived from human ingenuity. Rather, it heightens the role of God and claims unequivocally that their deliverance depends on divine action (e.g., 13:15-17; 14:3, 5-6, 14, 19; 15:8; 6:1).

Greek Esther also reinterprets the story to explain and eradicate any objectionable content of the story. The seemingly unorthodox view of Esther becomes clearly orthodox, and while she may have had intercourse with the Persian king, she hated it. Thereby, her image as an assimilated Jew is recast as a Jewish woman who holds her traditions in the highest regard and observes her customs to the greatest extent possible in a threatening situation.

The Text in Contemporary Discussion

As shown above, Greek Esther and the Hebrew version proffer different views of the story of Esther. Recent discussions on Greek Esther center on the relationship of this narrative to the MT and the AT. One commentator, for example, focuses on all three versions in order to demonstrate their points of similarity and divergence with regard to Esther's character (Day). Another scholar isolates one issue of the narrative, namely, the notice of Esther's keeping her identity secret, to offer a diachronic reading of how each story addresses concerns of the Jewish Diaspora (Halverson-Taylor). Both of these scholars argue that the AT plays a significant part in illuminating Jewish Diaspora issues.

All three versions of the story provide a different understanding of what it takes to have a successful life in an imperial context. While the dating of the AT remains equivocal, it is commonly placed earlier chronologically than the Hebrew. It portrays Esther as a woman whose Jewish descent poses little problem for her Persian neighbors. In the AT edition of Esther, it appears that her ethnicity is recognized throughout the story when the king is surprised that Haman would intend to harm Mordecai, a man from the same ethnic stock as Esther (AT 7:14). This interpretation of the book of Esther could reflect Diaspora communities that sought to meld their Jewish identity with those around them. Following Esther's example of a Jew working within the parameters of Persian policies could result, the AT suggests, in reaching high levels in the foreign government in order to effectuate positive change for Diaspora communities.

The Hebrew shares the cooperative spirit that the AT engenders. However, given that Esther has to keep her Jewish identity secret, it lacks the freedom of religious expression found in the AT

(Halverson-Taylor). A touch of suspense and tension is added with this detail (2:20). Notwithstanding her having to conceal her Jewish heritage, the Hebrew portrays Esther as an assimilated Jew whose winsome qualities facilitate her advance as a high-ranking authority in the Persian government. One critic argues that the Hebrew text of the book Esther, when compared to Greek Esther and the AT, has the widest appeal to audiences of the Jewish Diaspora because of her ability to handle her role as Persian queen and a Jewish leader with skill (Day). She holds these two potentially conflicting roles in delicate balance. By adeptly traversing the arenas of Persians and Jews, she offers another model to Jewish communities to work within the dominant political structure rather than against it.

Greek Esther contrasts sharply with the earlier Alpha and Hebrew texts with its anti-gentile stance. Esther has the strongest connection with the Jewish community in this version. While the Hebrew notes that Esther has to keep her identity a secret, Greek Esther builds on this tension with an apocalyptic preface (addition A), showing the extensive nature of Jewish persecution. The need for her to mask her Jewish roots appears urgent. In an increasingly perilous environment, Greek Esther conveys the import of strict adherence to divine law over that of the imperial overlord. Juxtaposed in the verse speaking of Esther's need to suppress her Jewish identity is the declaration that she maintained her "mode of life" by fearing God and keeping his laws (2:20). Thus, as one critic aptly asserts, the instance of Esther concealing her identity "becomes the occasion to vouch that she maintained the integrity of her identity by keeping the commandments" (Halverson-Taylor, 483).

Greek Esther escalates the sense of danger and could, as mentioned above, point to an audience experiencing persecution or discrimination at the hands of non-Jews. The model Greek Esther provides aligns with both the Hebrew and AT in that a Jew can attain high status in a foreign context and lead a successful existence. It however refocuses the attention to strict Jewish observance and dependence on God, to whom they owe their foremost allegiance.

Greek Esther does not hold canonical status in the Protestant tradition, and it is part of the deuterocanon of Catholic and Orthodox traditions. The attestation of three versions of the story of Esther assists in understanding how it could apply to different contexts of Jews grappling with living in the Diaspora. These stories could also apply to the same context but offer multiple views of how to go about negotiating one's life in an imperial setting. The scholar Linda Day reminds us that when a book became incorporated into a canon, all versions of the book held authority and not just one textual form (Day, 233). She encourages contemporary audiences to broaden "our concept of what can be considered authoritative," as it "opens the possibility for the two Greek versions of the book of Esther, as well as the Masoretic version, to be used by today's faith communities" (Day, 233).

All three versions of the story of Esther deal with how one should one live under imperial rule. In each narration, some acceptance to the imposed government and culture is assumed. The three versions of Esther, however, tackle the degree to which subjects accept the prevailing laws and traditions of the dominant society. Perhaps their ruminations can serve as resources for moderns living in cultures where ethnic traditions come into conflict with those of the dominant culture.

Works Cited

Crawford, Sidnie White. 2008. *Rewriting Scripture in Second Temple Times*. Studies in the Dead Sea Scrolls and Related Literature. Grand Rapids: Eerdmans.

Day, Linda. 1995. *Three Faces of a Queen: Characterization in the Books of Esther*. Sheffield: Sheffield Academic.

Halverson-Taylor, Martien. 2012. "Secrets and Lies: Secrecy Notices (Esther 2:10, 20) and Diasporic Identity in the Book of Esther." *JBL* 131, no. 3:467–85.

Harrington, Daniel. 1999. *Invitation to the Apocrypha*. Grand Rapids: Eerdmans.

Koller, Aaron. 2014. *Esther in Ancient Jewish Thought*. Cambridge: Cambridge University Press.

Scheindlin, Raymond. 1998. *A Short History of the Jewish People*. New York: Oxford University Press.

WISDOM OF SOLOMON

Emerson B. Powery

Introduction

The Wisdom of Solomon was written in Greek and, thereby, was not part of the Hebrew Bible. Its inclusion in the Septuagint and the Vulgate led to its incorporation into the Christian canon. Tracing their canonical traditions back to this earlier period, Roman Catholic and Eastern Orthodox communities still consider Wisdom part of the deuterocanonical collection. Protestants and Jews consider it part of the Apocrypha. Its emphasis on the immortality of the soul had a major influence on Christian theology in the early centuries of the Christian movement.

The Alexandrian author writes as a thoroughly Hellenized Jew who recognizes his immigrant status in a land in which his Egyptian and Greek neighbors mistreat many in the Jewish community (see 19:13-16). He addresses the community and encourages them to live out their faith, even as he employs Greek ideas to modernize Judaism for the new cultural setting. The teacher provides a clear objective in his final words, in a statement addressed to God: "you have not neglected to help [Israel] at all times and in all places" (19:22). As an immigrant in a land he now calls home, he refers to the "holy land" infrequently (see 12:3, 7) and without accompanying language of longing for that land. Rather, he trusts God to assist Israel "in all places." The idea of an Israelite living as an immigrant in foreign territory has many biblical antecedents (see Genesis 37–50; Esther; Daniel 1–6). At various points throughout the treatise, the author assumes the persona of King Solomon—the most internationally remembered figure in Israel's history—in order to detail a message on the origins and actions of wisdom universally available to all (see 7:1-22).

The Alexandrian wisdom teacher addresses three major themes. The first section (1:1—5:23) contrasts the godly with the ungodly, those who fail to follow torah and to do right as the sage teaches (see 1:1, 15; 2:11; 5:6, 18). Apparently, this latter group opposed the sage's challenge to traditional teaching, including his promotion of the concept of the immortal soul. With this idea, the teacher questions established perspectives from the wisdom tradition, including how fertility (see 3:10-19) and longevity of life (see 4:7-12) are distinct signs of God's blessings.

The second section (6:1—10:21) reflects on wisdom's origin, characteristics, and actions. The sage, still assuming the persona of King Solomon, reimagines the specifics of Solomon's prayer for wisdom (8:21—9:18). Unlike the Solomon of old, this Alexandrian teacher connects wisdom to the language of torah in several instances (e.g., 2:11, 12; 6:4, 18; 9:5; 14:16; 16:6; 18:4, 9), even while maintaining wisdom's universal availability (6:9, 12; 7:23).

In the final section of the book, the sage contrasts Egyptians and Israelites through a creative midrash on the ancient exodus tradition (11:1—19:22). His retelling includes specific negative reactions to the issues of idolatry and animal worship (13:1—15:19), both of which stem from the sage's contemporary setting.

The treatise was written in the late first century BCE or in the first half of the first century CE. A few scholars have attempted to situate the book in the specific period of Caligula's reign, circa 38–41 CE (Winston, 23–24; Grabbe, 88). If the latter date is accepted, Philo of Alexandria and Paul of Tarsus are contemporary Jews whose writings provide significant points of comparison. As a book in the wisdom tradition, the Wisdom of Solomon is a late but comparable volume to other wisdom books, including Sirach, a volume translated into Greek in Egypt circa 120 BCE.

The "love of justice" our author advocates (see 1:1) will occasionally cause this interpreter to push back and read *against* the advice of this ancient sage. Justice is contextual, as this ancient literary classic exemplifies, so we must honor our calling for doing what is right in our own context, since those "who do what is right are in God's hands" (3:1 CEB).

Wisdom of Solomon 1:1-15: Seek Wisdom and Justice

The Text in Its Ancient Context

The ancient Jewish author begins abruptly, without any opening formalities. Even the addressees (i.e., "rulers of the earth") are imagined. This sage was too far removed from the seats of power to address them directly. Rather, his audience is fellow Jews in the Alexandrian community, who found themselves increasingly isolated in a land that was becoming more hostile. These "leaders" should seek wisdom (i.e., God) and not put God to the test by committing unjust acts (1:1) or thinking illogically (1:3).

Like other ancient documents in the wisdom tradition, this sage emphasizes the discovery of wisdom as essential for faithful followers (1:4-6; cf. Sir. 1:1-8). The teacher is direct. Wisdom can only be found by those who act justly (1:1, 4) and speak reverently of, and to, God (1:6-11). The outer actions should match a person's inner thoughts. This type of "righteousness" will last forever (1:15). The theme that God's righteous children will live beyond death (1:12-15) is the author's contribution to the wisdom tradition. Many of his contemporaries would question the sage's new theological direction, preferring the older wisdom tradition, "for the fate of humans and the fate of animals is the same" (Eccles. 3:19).

For our author, however, "death" is an unnatural part of life, for which God is not responsible (1:13). This sage reads the Genesis narrative, apparently, as if death were not part of the original design.

The Text in the Interpretive Tradition

Death's origins have attracted much reflection throughout history. Some ancient interpreters thought that righteous souls immediately rise to God while others linger in a nebulous arena separate from the divine (Clarke, 19). Others believed that the unrighteous "disintegrated at death" (Grabbe, 54). Scholars also debate whether the Alexandrian sage refers to a "spiritual" or a "biological death." Either way, the teacher appears not to have connected death and mortality to Adam's sin (see 10:1-2).

The Text in Contemporary Discussion

Whatever specific situation surrounded the ancient teacher, the command to "love justice" (1:1) is universal. The contemporary person of faith should do what is just and right in the world. This is the way of the wise!

To encourage life-giving actions and policies should be standard practice for contemporary wisdom seekers. This coincides with the spirit of the ancient sage's advice that death did not originate with God (see 1:12-14). Rather than seeing death as a necessary *evil*, however, contemporary believers prefer to think (rightly) that death is a natural process of the life God grants.

Wisdom of Solomon 1:16—2:24: The Ungodly Lack Wisdom

The Text in Its Ancient Context

Beginning in 1:16, the sage provides examples of the covenant the "ungodly" made with "death." Despite the label "ungodly," the reference to torah (2:12) indicates that the debate is an intrareligious one. In 2:1-9, the "beliefs" of the "ungodly" appear to draw on the ancient wisdom tradition of Qoheleth, the original Hebrew title for Ecclesiastes. Chapter 2 may be viewed as a brief summary of Ecclesiastes. "Let us enjoy the good things that exist" (2:6) since "our allotted time is the passing of a shadow" (2:5) echoes the ancient wisdom teacher, "There is nothing better for mortals than to eat and drink, and find enjoyment in their toil." (Eccles. 2:24). The Hellenistic Jewish teacher challenges this traditional view of life, death, and the hereafter (as represented in the biblical Wisdom literature itself).

While their confessions are similar to the traditional Israelite faith, their actions belie their intentions: "let our might be our law of right." The sage's opponents desire to attack the *dikaios* (or "the just one," 2:10, 12, 18), and by doing so "test" God (2:17) to see if God will intervene (2:18). To test (or tempt) God shows a lack of wisdom (1:2). They show themselves to be aligned with the "devil's party" by continuing to test and challenge just people (2:24).

The Text in the Interpretive Tradition

Many early Christian interpreters (including Ambrose and Cyril of Alexandria) understood the phrase "God's child" (2:18) to be a reference to the Messiah, that is, Jesus who died at the hands of his Jewish contemporaries because he "opposes our actions" (2:12). But this Christocentric interpretation is not historically instructive for grasping the cultural moment of Judaism in Alexandria. If the "just one" was a reference to a specific person, then our sage probably had a local wise priest in mind who (also) taught the radical teaching of living forever.

The Text in Contemporary Discussion

Competing belief systems are becoming more common in the pluralistic society of the United States. Challenging this competitive framework is one issue for contemporary believers. How do we describe our neighbors? Do we disparage their attempts to wrestle with the divine? Are we like the ancient sage, who refers to his opponents as "ungodly" and disparages their attempts to hold on to older traditions in contemporary settings?

On the other hand, when is it time, as this ancient sage attempts, to challenge the theological (wisdom) tradition of the faith community? Isn't there a message for a time of reassessment of our own theological traditions? Isn't this what liberation theology, in its various guises (e.g., black theology, feminist theology, mujeristic theology, gay/lesbian theology), attempts to do?

Some interpreters suggest that the "righteous one" of 2:12 is representative of many persons who have died untimely deaths fighting for justice: "The pursuit and destruction of the just continues: it is the grist of the mills of history, empire after empire, army after army" (Berrigan, 31).

Wisdom of Solomon 3:1-19: Reward and Punishment after Death

The Text in Its Ancient Context

The sage begins this section (3:1) with a clear statement on the immortality of the godly (cf. 2:23), a fate that the ungodly will not share (3:10-13). The author describes the future state of the godly as one "at peace" (3:3) as they receive "good things" (3:5), and he envisions a meaningful future existence in which the godly will rule over the nations (3:8).

The use of "immortal" language occurs here for the first time in biblical literature. *Athanasia* literally means the opposite of "death" (*thanatos*; see 2:24). For the sage, Wisdom leads her children there (see 8:13, 17), by allowing the wise to do right in the world (see 4:1). More importantly, immortality will mean an ongoing relationship with God (3:9; O'Connor, 172).

Unlike his predecessor in the wisdom tradition (Ben Sira), the author of Wisdom uses the term *psychai* ("soul, life, human being") to refer to a person's earthly "life" (with Sirach) and as a reference for a person's future existence, as a "soul," after death. For Wisdom, a godly person's *psychai* "won't feel the pain of torment" (3:1), will "bear fruit" if barren (3:13), and won't be corrupted (4:11) because "God watches over God's chosen ones" (3:9 CEB).

With his understanding of immortality, the ancient sage calls into question the traditional perspective that God's blessings are visible on earth, including a long life and the presence of children. So the author attacks even the families of the unwise. Their unjust actions must mean that their family is dishonorable (3:10-12). In an honor-shame culture, a community's assessment of a person has a direct impact on that person's family and its communal arrangements (e.g., marriage, bartering). The godliness of "barren" women and "eunuchs"—those without physical descendants—are chief among the sage's examples. It is their godly lives that matter, not their failure to reproduce. It was widely believed that barrenness was due to sin (Winston, 131), but the wisdom tradition had already begun to question this belief (see Sir. 16:3). On the eunuch's spiritual status, the Alexandrian sage chose the prophetic tradition (see Isa. 56:4-5) over the Deuteronomic law (see Deut. 23:1). Reconceptualizing the afterlife allows the sage to challenge the theological idea that "offspring" provided one's future "immortality." In the traditional framework, without children, one's memory died forever.

The Text in the Interpretive Tradition

When the marginalized in a society discover that things on earth are not going according to plan or when they find themselves isolated from the political process, it is not uncommon to imagine a utopian space where they might have some control over their lives. "These promises reverse the reality in which the author's community currently lives" (O'Connor, 173).

The Text in Contemporary Discussion

If God's life and love may be found in acts of justice and *not* in reproductive acts (see 3:13-17), then contemporary followers of wisdom might discover new ways to imagine the political dynamics of same-sex marriage and other gendered relationships in the contemporary church and world. Even those unable to reproduce naturally "will receive a precious gift" for fidelity to God and to others (see 3:14 CEB).

Wisdom of Solomon 4:1-20: Advantages of Godly Living

The Text in Its Ancient Context

This section begins at 3:1, in which the author distinguishes between the "ungodly" (*hoi asebeis* at 3:10) and the "just one" (*ho dikaios* at 3:10), who represents those who do the right thing. The latter believes in life after death, the lens through which this Hellenistic Jewish teacher reinterprets the ancient tradition of wisdom on the blessings of fertility and longevity of life. In this ancient cosmopolitan culture, the author witnesses (and perhaps experiences) the prominence of infertility among local women including, perhaps, family members (4:1-7) and early deaths among honorable people in the community who thus never reach old age (4:1-20).

In chapter 4, the author uses the term "memory" (*mnēmē*) as an inclusio, to set this chapter apart (see 4:1, 19). He recognizes the long-standing role of memory as an ancient way of speaking about "life" beyond one's death (cf. 8:13; Eccles. 2:16; Prov. 1:12 LXX). Yet he moves beyond this idea to include a belief in the (good) soul living after present existence (see 1:15; 2:23). The final section (4:17) stresses God's judgment on the ungodly, including wiping out their "memory" (4:19). Apparently, he has in mind the group who murdered one of the contemporary priests in Alexandria (see 2:17-20).

The Text in the Interpretive Tradition

Although ancient patristic interpretation encouraged the association of the "prolific brood of the ungodly" (4:3 RSV) with the "heretics" of their day, recent scholarship rightfully struggles with this type of reasoning. Older wisdom tradition, in the vein of Job and Ecclesiastes, seems more sophisticated than wisdom's "naive" position that the offspring of the "ungodly" will amount to no good (Grabbe, 49–50). Daniel Berrigan uses even more forceful language: "Is the old canard here resuscitated, the sins of the fathers visited on the progeny? . . . Here, one thinks, wisdom fails the wise" (Berrigan, 62–63).

The Text in Contemporary Discussion

Ancient dualism prevails. Bad things happen to bad people and its reverse, though not exactly in this life according to the Wisdom author!

Is it possible that the Alexandrian sage is *female*? Though this is unlikely, perhaps this male teacher had a barren wife, sister, or close family member. Either way, the sage attempts to lift the theological burden that was placed on infertile females. Infertility is not due to any religious or spiritual wrongdoing on the woman's part. The wise teaching offers a theological challenge to the long-standing religious tradition that childbearing was a sign of divine blessing.

Furthermore, the author questions another *traditional* teaching: longevity of life as a sign of God's blessing. The sage suggests that only the ones who act justly "will be at rest" (4:7); only they will "live a long life in a short span of time" (4:13 CEB).

Just as this Hellenistic teacher read against the grain of his theological heritage, so must later interpreters. The theme of the "useless" children of the ungodly (see 4:3-7) continues the specific issue begun in 3:16-19. Unfortunately, some contemporary Christians still believe that children are punished because of the "iniquity of the fathers" (see Exod. 20:5). This teacher seems not to question this tradition despite his willingness to reassess others. But we must do so in order to avoid the ideological warfare oftentimes imposed on our communities and on our children.

"Do not forget; forgetting is death before death" (Berrigan, 65).

Wisdom of Solomon 5:1-23: Reflections on the Final Judgment

The Text in Its Ancient Context

The first section (5:2-14) describes the (re)action of the ungodly, more so than the godly (5:1), as the Alexandrian sage imagines a final judgment scene. Beginning in 4:19, the sage describes the loss of any memory of the ungodly: "it passes like the remembrance of a guest who stays but a day" (5:14). In traditional wisdom teaching, ancestors are expected to live on in their children's memory (see Prov. 20:7).

First, the sage imagines the thoughts of the ungodly at the final judgment when they will meet again the "just one" (*dikaios*, see 5:1) whom they murdered (cf. 2:12-20). The intent is to recall the figure in chapter 2, so the plurals in the NRSV—all the way through the passage—are misleading.

Second, the sage questions the value of "wealth" (5:8, *ploutos*), even though traditional wisdom thinking promotes wealth as a by-product of wisdom (see 7:11, 13; 8:18). It is still less valuable than wisdom itself (see 7:8; 8:5).

The second half of this chapter covers the rewards for the godly (5:15-16; cf. 3:5), before the teacher shifts into an unexpected discussion about apocalyptic warfare (5:17-20) and the role of the cosmos in the battle (5:20b-23). The arrival of God as a military warrior may have been borrowed from the earlier prophetic tradition (see Isa. 59:15-17; see below).

The Text in the Interpretive Tradition

The Alexandrian sage's depiction of God's preparation for battle in a cosmic apocalyptic war has a history in the earlier biblical tradition and is picked up (from Wisdom?) in later Christian circles, as encouragement for believers as well.

Isaiah	Wisdom of Solomon	Ephesians
(see Isa. 59:15-17)	(see 5:17-20)	(see 6:13-17)
"God"	"the Lord"	believers
——	——	Belt of truth
Breastplate of righteousness	Breastplate of righteousness	Breastplate of righteousness
Helmet of salvation	Helmet of impartial justice	Shoes to spread peace
Garments of vengeance	Shield of holiness	Shield of faith
Mantle of fury	Sword of anger	Helmet of salvation
	Sword of God's word	

The Text in Contemporary Discussion

"The arc of the universe is long, but it bends toward justice." The words of Martin Luther King Jr. seem to echo this ancient wisdom book. Many attempting to do what is right in the world have considered God/the cosmos/justice/wisdom on the side of their work. As the sage will state later, "the universe itself comes to the defense of those who do what is right" (16:17 CEB; cf. 16:15-19; 19:13-17). And we hope they are right!

Wisdom of Solomon 6:1-21: Rulers Should Seek Wisdom

The Text in Its Ancient Context

Addressing "kings" (6:1) recalls the opening address in 1:1 and continues the critique of "rulers" that began at 5:23. Though the sage imagines an audience of rulers, he has the people of his community in mind, especially those who oppose his views about "right" living and future rewards (see chapters 2–4). The fruits of following wisdom include living and ruling forever (6:18, 21).

While imagining kings, the sage offers the common theological perspective that all sovereignty originates with God (cf. Sir. 10:4-5; Rom. 13:1-7). Rulers must follow God's law, or else God will turn against them (6:4-5). Of course, no Egyptian ruler would feel obligated to follow Jewish law. But the sage's Jewish community would (Collins, 192). Furthermore, the teacher follows biblical tradition closely in advocating for God's judgment on those rulers who judge unjustly (cf. Job 12:17-20; 34:24-30; Ezek. 21:25-27). God has higher expectations for "rulers" than for the "lowly"

(6:6-8), a comparison that Sirach also makes (Sir. 10:14-16). The poor receive God's great mercy (Berrigan, 82).

In 6:12-21, the sage introduces the origins of wisdom, a discussion that will take up several chapters (see Wis. 6–9). The sage builds on the language of Proverbs 8 to explore the characteristics of Wisdom. Wisdom seeks those who seek her (cf. Prov. 8:17; Wis. 6:12-15). Moving beyond the tradition of Proverbs, however, those who desire her—in our sage's view—should follow torah (6:18). This chapter provides the clearest connection between torah and Wisdom in the book (6:4; 9:5; 14:16; 16:6; 18:4, 9).

The Text in the Interpretive Tradition

The apostle Paul and the Alexandrian sage may be drawing on a common Jewish tradition on the relationship between God and civil authorities. Both agree that human sovereignty derives authority from God (cf. Wis. 6:3-8 with Rom. 13:1-8). But their similarities end there. For the Alexandrian sage, earthly rulers should follow God's law or else they lose divine covering. That is, God will act against them (6:4-5). On the other hand, Paul is less concerned with the way rulers govern than with those who fall under their civil authority (Rom. 13:1, 5).

The Text in Contemporary Discussion

What advice can the colonized give to the colonizer? "Your power stems from our God!" is one example. The colonized can presume that earthly authority is no true authority at all. They can hope for right treatment and justice in the land, demanding that God's law be followed.

On the other hand, is there only "wisdom" in the religious tradition (e.g., torah)? In our modern, secular state, those political leaders who frequently tend to govern from a religious (think "Christian") perspective tend to be more warlike and economically myopic, representing corporate interests rather than the wider democratic citizenry.

Wisdom of Solomon 6:22—8:1: A Treatise on Wisdom

The Text in Its Ancient Context

In chapters 6–9, attention shifts to Wisdom (cf. 6–9), which occurs twenty-five times (of its thirty uses) in chapters 6–10. At 6:22, the sage addresses the "origins" of wisdom, although the theme of immortality remains (see 6:18-19; 8:17).

Here in 7:5-6, the author again assumes the personification of "King Solomon" and discusses how he gained wisdom. This is a retelling of 1 Kgs. 3:5-15, in which King Solomon receives wisdom from God (7:7). The Solomon of old asked for a discerning mind to govern (see 1 Kgs. 3:9), a theme the sage examines more carefully in the following section (Wis. 8:9-15). Because of his original request, Solomon was also granted other gifts of wealth and fame (1 Kgs. 3:13; Wis. 7:11-12).

According to the sage, securing wisdom by prayer (7:7) differs from Solomon's dream in 1 Kgs. 3:5, in which he hears from YHWH. Perhaps the sage shared Ben Sira's general cultural condemnation of dreams, unless verifiably originating with God (see Sir. 34:1-8). The sage also moves beyond the biblical tradition in claiming Solomon's "friendship" with God (7:14, 27), a label that places Solomon on par with Abraham (see 2 Chron. 20:7) and Moses (see Exod. 33:11 LXX; Winston, 188). And Solomon's love for wisdom (7:10; cf. 6:17-18) may be an interpretive extension of Solomon's love for YHWH in the earlier account (cf. 1 Kgs. 3:3).

With wisdom comes *vast* knowledge (7:17-20): cosmology, astronomy, biology, botany, and more. Wisdom's "mobility" emphasizes that, as a spirit (see 1:6), it resides anywhere that is "pure" (7:23-24; Collins, 198). Wisdom and God are closely aligned, but they are not the same. For the sage, God guides wisdom (7:15).

If the sage has only the "traditional" prophets in mind (7:27), as those in whom wisdom resides, then he is similar to Sirach (see Sir. 1:1, 9; 46:13, 15; 48:1, 8, 22; 49:7, 10). If not, then the Alexandrian sage may be encouraging a continuing prophetic tradition through wisdom's presence.

The Text in the Interpretive Tradition

In later Christian circles (e.g., Dionysius of Alexandria, Ambrose, Augustine) beginning with Hebrews, Christians will transfer the language about wisdom to the Christ figure (Voicu, 99–100). As wisdom is the "breath of the power of God," a "pure emanation," and a "reflection of eternal light" (7:25-26), so is Christ the "reflection of God's glory and the exact imprint of God's very being" (Heb. 1:3). The transfer of wisdom's characteristics to Christ will improve the popularity of the Wisdom of Solomon in early Christian circles.

The Text in Contemporary Discussion

Contemporary seekers of wisdom should appreciate the fictional Solomon's desire for wisdom above all else. To possess wisdom—or, rather, to be possessed by Wisdom—will enhance one's human journey beyond all other values (see 7:11).

Wisdom of Solomon 8:2—9:18: Solomon's Desire and Prayer for Wisdom

The Text in Its Ancient Context

The sage's character, "Solomon," personifies "Wisdom." He sought her as a "bride" (8:2), pursuing her since his youth. All true Wisdom seekers do this (cf. Sir. 51:13-22). Solomon brought her "to live with me" (8:9), so that they might share their lives together (8:16). Most significantly, Wisdom provided "good counsel" and assisted Solomon in governance (8:9-15). Solomon stresses this further when he describes the specifics of his prayer for Wisdom (9:5-8, 12). Wisdom is the only one who understands how God works in the world (9:9), and without her Solomon knew he would fail (9:13-18). So, Solomon loved Wisdom (cf. 7:10).

And, God "loves" Wisdom too (8:3), even as God loves those who seek Wisdom (7:28). Wisdom has an intimacy with God and thereby "knows God's secret ways" (8:4 CEB), working intimately with God in the affairs of the world. Initiation language (*mystis*) is used to describe Wisdom as an "initiate" in the knowledge of God. This same term (*mystis*) is used for the cultic initiate into the mystery religions (cf. 12:5). Those who seek wisdom and love it will find it (see 6:12), even as Solomon did (7:10). Other "rulers"—and all people—should also love right actions (1:1) and those who do work alongside Wisdom (8:7) to accomplish their goals. Since God loves Wisdom, God also loves those who do right (4:10).

Before describing his prayer, Solomon describes his preparation, since Wisdom only enters "holy beings" (7:27; 10:16). His own "good soul" entered a pure body (8:20; 9:15), which prepared the way for the reception of Wisdom. Inappropriate bodies may "weigh down" good souls (9:15). In the sage's Hellenistic theology, only the soul will resurrect (see 3:1; also, Collins, 186).

The Text in the Interpretive Tradition

Biblical scholars have rightly recognized the female imagery of Wisdom that would not have been lost on the sage's readers. This is "Woman Wisdom," whose desire for relationship fits neatly into a Hellenistic setting in which Isis, the Egyptian goddess, is prominent (Tanzer, 293; Collins, 203–4; O'Connor, 175). With the sage's theological perspective, Jews need no longer look outside of Judaism for this type of intimate relationship. Wisdom (*sophia*) is so closely associated with God as God's "breath," "mirror," and "image" (see 7:25-26) that it is easy to claim that she and God are one: "To see her, therefore, is to see God. To relate to her is to relate to God. She is God, not a new god or a second god, but God poetically imaged as woman" (O'Connor, 178).

The Text in Contemporary Discussion

Contemporary discussions about God's *male*ness—with constant inconsiderate and unquestioned use of male pronouns—must deal with this ancient sage's attempts to imagine God's *female*ness. According to Wisdom of Solomon, God does nothing in the world except through *Sophia*.

Wisdom of Solomon 10:1-21: Wisdom Guides the Heroes of Israel

The Text in Its Ancient Context

Wisdom/Sophia language continues in chapter 10 (four times). The sage connects Sophia's actions to Israel's history and tells how Sophia guided (seven) heroes to do what was right. Wisdom not only led prominent heroes but also guided the people of Israel (10:15–11:14; cf. 18:20) from their bondage in Egypt. She may have "entered" Moses' soul (10:16; cf. 7:27), but the sage concentrates on her activity among all people (10:15-21). The sage uses the adjective *dikaion* ("just, right, fair") to define Wisdom's servants (10:4, 5, 6, 10, 13, 20), a term associated with the earlier theme of those who do what is right (see 3:1; 4:7; 5:1, 15).

There are a few surprises in this list. For example, apparently only Adam committed the "transgression" in the garden; there is no mention of Eve (see 10:1), although Sophia is present. The sage blames the flood on Cain's murder of Abel (10:2-4), although he knows the fuller Genesis tradition (see 14:6). Among the heroes, Jacob receives the most attention. Jacob's lesson about "holy things," though unclear, distinguishes his character's description (10:10). Wisdom teaches the knowledge of "hidden" things (see 7:21-22), since only she understands "heavenly things" (cf. 9:16-17). Perhaps this is a vague reference to Jacob's struggle with God in the "contest" of verse 12 (see Gen. 32:22-31), as the Revised Standard Version may capture ("knowledge of angels"). Here Wisdom represents God in that ancient struggle.

Compared to other lists of Jewish heroes (e.g., Sirach 44–50; 1 Macc. 2:49-64), this Alexandrian teacher highlights Wisdom's involvement and care in the lives of Israel's leaders. The heroes remain unnamed, since the sage's objective is to emphasize Sophia's role in their protection and salvation (Collins, 215).

The Text in the Interpretive Tradition

The author of Hebrews provides his own hero list, which shares parallels with Wisdom 10 (e.g., Noah, Abraham, Jacob, Moses). In Hebrews, names are specified, however, and the author emphasizes activities lived out by faith. Our Alexandrian sage focuses instead on the significant role Wisdom played in each of the unnamed representatives of Israel. In later Christian reflections on Wisdom 10 (e.g., Augustine), Christ will replace Wisdom's role as the one who, for example, "released" Adam from his "crime" (Voicu, 123).

The Text in Contemporary Discussion

Jacob's struggle with Sophia in order to secure wisdom may model contemporary struggles to secure knowledge and wisdom in the modern world. It is an arduous task and not easily accomplished, but earned through diligent perseverance. At the end of the day, it may not simply be "godliness" alone, however, that allows one to succeed as the ancient sage believes (see 10:12). To be clear, those who do what is right are on Wisdom's path.

Wisdom of Solomon 11:1—12:2: The Role of Wisdom in Israel's Exodus from Egypt

The Text in Its Ancient Context

Focusing less on Israel's individual heroes (chapter 10), the sage concentrates on Wisdom's contributions to Israel's history in the specific event of the exodus. The history of Israel's escape from Egyptian bondage would have had an immediate appeal for his Alexandrian audience, some of whom sensed hostility from their Egyptian neighbors (cf. 19:13-15). There is significantly less wisdom language in this final section (after 10:21, *Sophia* does not appear until 14:2, 5), though she is the implied subject at 11:1 (as the NRSV suggests). Referring to Moses as a "holy prophet" recalls the role of Wisdom as well (cf. 7:27). Despite some scholarly claims, the absence of "God" language in chapter 11 actually begins to shift the focus from Wisdom to God—as the primary acting agent (O'Connor, 183; cf. Clarke, 73; Collins, 180; Berrigan, 119; Tanzer, 294).

The sage views the worship of animals, which his contemporary neighbors practice, as a part of God's punishment for the Egyptians (11:15; cf. Rom. 1:23). God did not simply allow it; God initiated this misguided religious practice (11:15-17). The Creator of the world would have no difficulty forming the necessary creatures for this experiment, since God formed the original creations "out of formless matter" (11:17). The idea of preexistent matter was shared widely by other Jewish and Greek thinkers (e.g., Philo and Plato; see Grabbe, 65). This is *not* creation *ex nihilo*, which had only been expressed a few generations earlier (cf. 2 Macc. 7:28: "God made these things from nothing"; CEB). The sage supports the more widely held process of creation elsewhere as well (see 1:14; 2:23; 10:1; 11:17; 13:3).

In this passage, punishment is not the final word (11:20b—12:2). Rather, God's mercy is driven by God's love for all creation (11:24).

The Text in the Interpretive Tradition

Citing 11:17, Augustine claims—in his unfinished commentary on Genesis—that the "formless matter" was *also* created by God (Voicu, 131). This allowed later Christian thinkers to maintain the logic of a creation *ex nihilo* (cf. 2 Macc 7:28; Heb. 11:3).

The Text in Contemporary Discussion

It is worth exploring the relationship between memory and religious discourse in light of its occurrence in this treatise (see 11:12). For example, the sage provides a biased retelling (i.e., a way to remember) of Israel's "goodness" and Egypt's "evil" as indicative of wisdom's presence with one group and not the other. Other uses of memory correlate. The memory of virtue will live on (4:1), while the memory of the ungodly will disappear (4:19); and "Solomon's" memory was preserved because of wisdom (8:13). What do we remember about our past, our histories, and the other? And what part of that memory are we willing to pass along to shape present relationships and communities?

Wisdom of Solomon 12:3-27: God's Treatment of the Gentiles

The Text in Its Ancient Context

The sage continues his defense of God's mercy and fairness with God's treatment of the nations (12:8-18; cf. 11:23-26). Similar to Philo and Josephus, he justifies Israel's conquest of Canaan (Winston, 238). Canaanites had polluted the land. Yet God did not massacre them swiftly, allowing them an "opportunity to repent" (12:10; cf. 12:20).

The teacher concludes that the ancient practice of human sacrifice was the cause for God's anger (12:3-7). Only here, in Wisdom, does the author consider a special relationship between God and the "holy land" (12:3, 7), an expression rare in biblical literature (cf. 2 Macc. 1:7). On the other hand, this Alexandrian Jew does not express any desire himself to return to Judea. Unlike Ben Sira, the sage offers no preferential treatment to Jerusalem (19:22; cf. Sir. 24:8-12; Fuller, 34–35). The ambivalence of this immigrant is apropos.

His defense of God's mercy still allows room for proper judgment for the sage's Egyptian community. The sage begins here (12:23-27) an argument that will continue through chapter 15: God allowed the Egyptians to follow their own paths, which ended up in the ungodly worship of all sorts of creatures and animals.

The Text in the Interpretive Tradition

Has God been fair with the gentiles? According to the sage, God is sovereign yet fair and patient with wrongdoers. Divine patience is indicative of God's inevitable mercy, which Israel should also expect (12:19-22). Yet the sage's God is on Israel's side and not on the side of the majority population. This is the voice of the immigrant who has entered into another land; the sage echoes the voice of those who feel abused in foreign territory (cf. 19:13-15).

The Text in Contemporary Discussion

The questions of theodicy, alluded to in 12:12, are age-old questions. In the sage's wisdom tradition, no one should question God. In the contemporary world, however, theodicy questions loom large. The sage provides one theological perspective: "You always do what's right" (12:15 CEB). Unfortunately, this kind of thinking may lead to the idea that whatever we see in the world is due to God's actions and is thereby "righteous." Many fundamentalists think this way. Others rightly question this approach, wondering whether "God" could be responsible for all of the destruction and chaos in the contemporary world, or, more likely, whether it was due to human machinations.

Wisdom of Solomon 13:1-19: Gentiles and Idolatry

The Text in Its Ancient Context

In chapters 13–15, a lengthy digression, the sage attacks gentile religious practices. He wrestles with whether gentiles are guilty for their failure to acknowledge God and, therefore, should receive God's full judgment (12:27; 13:6-9). The sage claims (similar to Paul the apostle) that gentiles appreciated creation but failed to recognize its Creator (13:1; cf. Rom. 1:19-21). The outcome was the worship of created things, failing to recognize "a corresponding perception of their Creator" (Wis. 13:5).

This Jewish teacher stands in a long line of traditional opponents to idolatry (13:10-19; cf. Isa. 44:9-20; Jer. 10:1-16). In order to attack meaningless prayers to idols (Wis. 13:17-19), the sage explains the overtly human process of idol-making (13:11-16). Attacks on idolatry increased in the Hellenistic period (cf. 1 Corinthians 8; see Collins, 209). During his attack, the sage provides a window into why ancient people prayed: possessions, marriages, children, health, and safe travel (13:17-18). The sage does not condemn *why* gentiles pray, only *to what* they pray.

The Text in the Interpretive Tradition

The similarity between Wisdom 13 and Romans 1 has been widely discussed in scholarly literature. Whether Paul is dependent on the Alexandrian sage could only be determined if scholars were more certain about the historical circumstances surrounding Wisdom. The present consensus is that both authors share a common tradition and condemnation of gentile idolatry. Douglas Campbell has recently challenged this consensus, arguing that the words of Romans 1:18-32 are not Paul's position but his representation of an opponent's teaching in the Roman community who is closely aligned with the thinking of the Wisdom of Solomon.

The Text in Contemporary Discussion

Why people pray today parallels the ancients of Alexandria. Possessions, marriage, children, health, and safety still resonate for many people. But where are the prayers on behalf of the other, those least like us? Where are the prayers for those who struggle for citizenship (i.e., immigrants), for those whose sexual identities cause political and theological debate (i.e., LGBT persons), and for those who seek religious solace through alternative means (i.e., Muslims)? Where are those prayers in the ancient world? And where are those prayers today?

Wisdom of Solomon 14:1-31: The Origin of Idols

The Text in Its Ancient Context

The sage continues his attack on idolatry with a specific example: travel at sea. In the ancient world, sea travel was notoriously precarious (14:2-7), so prayers were plentiful (13:18). This wisdom teacher argues that God is the real protector of any voyage (14:3-4). The final references to "wisdom" in the book occur here (cf. 14:2, 5). The author links the "giants" to the flood (14:6), providing a closer reading of the Genesis narrative (see Gen. 6:1-4) than the earlier suggestion that Cain's actions led to the flood (see 10:3). The sage stands in a long line of biblical authors who view idolatry as the greatest offense to God (cf. Isa. 44:9-20; Jer. 10:1-16). According to Wisdom, God "hates" the idols and their designers (14:9).

The sage, then, offers two examples on the origins of idols: (1) a grieving father creates an image to remember a lost child (14:15-16); (2) an image is produced to remember the emperor (14:17-20). High infant mortality was commonplace in the first century, so many religious acts memorialized the tragic loss of the young (Winston, 274). Child veneration, however, was not common. In the second scenario, the emperor cult is initiated from the earlier practice (14:16-17), a practice perhaps common in the sage's experience. With "secret rites and initiations" surrounding the idol (14:15, 23), the sage seems to refer to the "mystery cults" of Egypt, perhaps those associated with the Isis cult.

Finally, there are other ramifications from these idolatrous practices (14:22-31), including the sage's charge that these religious rituals include murdering children (14:23; cf. 12:5), a common rhetorical attack in antiquity used against other religious groups. The "sacrifice" of a child may be more symbolic than real. Compare Paul's language of "death" for the practice of baptism (see Rom. 6:4-5). In the sage's mind, idolatry is the cause of all evil (14:27), a theme commonly shared by Jews.

The Text in the Interpretive Tradition

The language of 14:7—"blessed is the wood by which righteousness comes"—would have attracted Christian readers for other intentions than the sage's. Some scholars suggest that the verse is a later

Christian interpolation (Collins, 210n70). Others disagree (Winston, 267), preferring to locate the sage's use of wood as a reference to Noah's ark in the immediate context.

Early Christian theologians—for example, Epiphanius of Salamis and Augustine—will blame demons for the origins of idolatry. Epiphanius wrote that idols "are the products of wicked demons and of the human mind full of impulses to pleasure, since each of us is led to make his own passion an object of veneration" (*Ancoratus* 102.5–7; Voicu, 153). This moves beyond Wisdom, but may reflect Pauline thinking (see 1 Cor. 10:20).

The Text in Contemporary Discussion

In the ancient world, the sage follows a long tradition of recognizing idolatry as the one thing the God of love "hates" (see 14:9, 27). For many, idolatry is the cause of all that is evil in the world (see 14:27). What contemporary "idols," created by human hands, distort the image of God among us?

Wisdom of Solomon 15:1—16:1: God's Mercy toward Israel

The Text in Its Ancient Context

In chapter 15, the sage returns to the earlier theme of God's mercy toward Israel (cf. 11:20-26). The teacher links this mercy (at 15:3) to the theme of immortality (*athanasias*) that was prominent earlier in the book (cf. 3:4; 4:1; 8:13, 17). Knowing God (15:3) or wisdom (8:13, 17) will lead to immortality. The opposite of immortality is not sin for the Alexandrian sage. "Sin" has a more specific meaning in Wisdom. It refers to idolatry (see 11:16; 14:13) or the creation of idols that lead to the religious practice (15:13). So the sage's claim that "we will not sin" (15:2) is a statement of the unattractiveness of idol worship for the Alexandrian Jewish community (15:4-6; cf. 14:17-20). In the sage's theology, idolatry is the "origin of all evil" (14:27).

He reiterates how foolish it is to create idols themselves (15:7-13). Performing this egregious sin (15:13), that is, creating idols, for profit is no excuse (15:12). Even more foolish are those who worship these human-made creatures (15:14-16:1). The sage joins the common chorus of monotheists that idols have no life in themselves (15:17; cf. Ps. 115:4-8; 1 Cor. 8:7). The sage distinguishes between the lifeless idols and the humans who created them, whose own souls are loaned to them for the short period of their human existence (15:8, 11, 16), a popular idea in the Greco-Roman world (Winston, 286–87). His focused attack on idolatry does not ignore his particular critique of Egyptian animal worship (15:18—16:1; 11:15-20).

The Text in the Interpretive Tradition

In early Christianity, a significant debate ensued as to whether souls preexist the created body in which they reside (so Origen) or are created at the same moment (so Tertullian, Jerome) when it enters the body. The language of "borrowed" souls (in 15:8, 16) seems to support Origen's position, which was later condemned. The latter position seems to be supported by 15:11, although early Christians disagreed whether the soul derived from one's parents (i.e., traducianism) or from God at the moment of one's birth (i.e., creationism, with respect to the soul).

The Text in Contemporary Discussion

The label "sin" has specific cultural contexts. For this Jewish teacher, there is no greater sin than idolatry (14:27). Just as ancient Jewish and Christian believers find idolatry to be opposed to the divine will, contemporary followers of God view racism as opposed to God's purposes. Racism is a theological problem, since people who think of other people as inferior make a direct statement about the Creator of all. So sin is not just theological but also cultural.

Wisdom of Solomon 16:2-29: God Protects Israel

The Text in Its Ancient Context

The author assures his listeners—using the classic story of the exodus—that God cares for Israel in their present surroundings in Egypt. Sometimes God's "wrath" (against Israel) appeared (6:5, 11), but it was only for brief moments of discipline. In light of the sage's attack on idolatry, the irony (and indirectness) of 16:5-8 should not be missed (Grabbe, 66). Under God's command, Moses created a bronze serpent (Num. 21:8-9) to symbolize God's salvation. The sage recognizes the potential conflict; people were "saved, not by the thing that was beheld, / but by you, the Savior of all" (16:7; cf. 16:12). Unlike Sirach (see Sir. 38:6-15), the sage emphasizes God alone as the agent of healing, not any mediating object (Wis. 16:12, 26).

The sage takes other liberties with the earlier biblical story in his retelling: the destructive role of fire (16:16-19, 22-23), the heavenly bread suiting each person's taste (16:21). The major point of this retelling is how nature took sides, operating in Israel's favor: "the universe defends the righteous" (16:17). This is a common theme throughout the book (see 5:17, 20; 16:24; 19:6). Finally, the sage stipulates the practice of praying twice daily, before sunrise and again at sunset (16:28). Ben Sira shares the example of early morning prayers (Sir. 39:5); the author of Daniel advocates praying thrice daily (Dan. 6:10).

The Text in the Interpretive Tradition

A late contemporary of the sage, the author of the Gospel of John will also find a religious analogy in Moses' bronze serpent: "And just as Moses lifted up the serpent in the wilderness, so must the Son of Man be lifted up, that whoever believes in him may have eternal life" (John 3:14-15). For the Alexandrian sage, God's "word" is the salvific force (16:6, 26). For John, it is the "Son of Man" who is defined as the "word" (*logos*) who was "in the beginning with God" (John 1:2), in language reminiscent of the sage's conception of Wisdom: "All things came into being through him, and without him not one thing came into being" (John 1:3; cf. Wis. 7:22).

The Text in Contemporary Discussion

The sage expounds no greater wisdom than at 16:17: "for the universe defends the righteous." In another place and time, Rev. Martin Luther King Jr. put it this way: "the moral arc of the universe bends towards justice." Both sages make a theological assumption that the cosmos leans toward those who do what is right. King did not share with the ancient sage the view that right actions always come from "our" side, those who may be situated like us religiously, politically, or geographically. Unfortunately, the sage could not see through his own wisdom. For King, those who act *justly* can come from any walk of life and should be included in the beloved community.

Wisdom of Solomon 17:1-21: The Ignorance of the Ungodly

The Text in Its Ancient Context

The sage continues to address God (17:1), as if in a prayer (cf. 16:28). But here he concentrates his efforts on the ignorance of the ungodly (17:1-21), oblivious to their wrongdoing that gives them a false sense of hope (17:13). The author imagines psychological torment and emotional warfare on the enemies of Israel, and he offers a midrash on the fatal night of Israel's escape from bondage (17:5). His creative literary expression about this occasion is unmatched in biblical literature.

The darkness that overwhelmed them (17:2, 10, 14, 18, 21), despite the light that allowed others in the whole world to do its business (17:20), was based on the three-day darkness that covered Egypt (see Exod. 10:21-23). Darkness of this kind comes on those who presumably are not taught torah (17:1), who depend on magic (17:7; 18:13), and who let fear drive their ignorance (17:13, 15, 19).

The language of "holy nation" (17:2) is not common in Wisdom. Here "nation" (*ethnos*) refers to the *people* and not the *land* and is the only use of *ethnos* for Israel in the book (cf. 3:8; 6:2; 8:14; 10:5, 15; 12:12; 14:11; 15:15). The author prefers *laon hosion* ("holy people") throughout his account (see "holy ones," 4:15; 10:17; 18:1, 5, 9; and "your people," 9:7; 12:19; 16:2, 20; 18:7; 19:5, 22).

The Text in the Interpretive Tradition

Samuel Cheon has argued that the Alexandrian teacher—whom he calls Pseudo-Solomon—was not interested in a careful explanation of the exodus account (Cheon, 109). Chapter 17 is an excellent case in point. Darkness was present in the biblical account (Exod. 10:21-23), but Pseudo-Solomon has interests beyond the text (e.g., ghosts, 17:3-4). As Cheon suggests, this sage was much more invested in applying the ancient story to his contemporary setting than explaining obscure elements of the biblical account.

The Text in Contemporary Discussion

The chapter reads like an ancient description of what we may classify today as clinical depression, a mood disorder in which feelings of sadness, loss, or anger inhibit common, everyday practices. The challenges of living peacefully in today's society can sometimes be hindered by fear, as the ancient sage writes: "For fear is nothing but a giving up of the helps that come from reason" (17:12). This kind of fear drives ignorance (17:13, 15, 19). As Ernest Clarke observes, "It is this psychological analysis of fear (17:11-13) which the writer developed in his exegesis of Exod. 10:23-4" (Clarke, 113):

Wisdom of Solomon 18:1-25: God's Deliverance from Egypt

The Text in Its Ancient Context

The sage returns to God's protection of Israel (see Wisdom of Solomon 16). Just as darkness surrounded the enemy (18:4; cf. 17:2, 10, 14, 18, 21), so an incredible light brightened up Israel's path (18:1). The physical light of Exodus (Exod. 10:23) in the sage's retelling also becomes a metaphor for torah (18:4; cf. 5:6-7). In this way, the author introduces the law into the story (18:4), just as he included torah as the "symbol of deliverance" earlier (see 16:6). For the sage, the law was granted *before* Israel's departure from Egypt (18:9) and provided crucial guidance during Israel's journey in the wilderness. Later rabbis will promulgate the idea of a preexistent torah (before creation). Here, the sage alludes to torah's universal design through Israel (18:4).

The specific deliverance of Exodus is repeated here (18:5-9; cf. 16:2-29). Despite their enemies' request for forgiveness (18:2)—a scene absent from the original account (see Exod. 10:17)—God's annihilation of Egyptian children was inevitable (18:10-13). Egyptian magic hindered them from belief (18:13; 17:7), and their nightmares were fulfilled (18:14-19; 17:14-15).

Israel does not fully escape punishment and death either (18:20), as the sage focuses on a later period in Israel's wilderness journey (Num. 16:46-48). A priest was needed to fight the plague. Its punishment did not last long since their high priest—unnamed here as the heroes of chapter 10 were—intervened. The sage emphasizes the significant role of this ancient hero, Aaron (18:20-25). The high priest utilized prayer, along with incense, to intervene (18:21; Num. 16:48). He reminded God—who is implied as the "destroyer" here—of the divine promises and "covenants" (18:22), symbols the "destroyer" feared (18:24-25). Unlike Numbers, the sage is reluctant to name God directly throughout this section.

The Text in the Interpretive Tradition

Some scholars consider 18:4 as evidence of a missionary impulse in ancient Judaism (see Collins, 154). Martin Goodman has convincingly argued against any such inclination in Jewish Hellenistic literature. The Alexandrian sage probably did not view his teaching in this way—as encouragement to the Greeks and Egyptians to participate in Judaism—even if he understood torah and wisdom as having universal implications (see 6:24; 9:3). His teaching was directed at other Jews.

The Text in Contemporary Discussion

God's destruction of the "enemy" is a theological problem in contemporary circles (Berrigan, 190), especially when innocent children are involved (18:5, 10, 12). The sage has his own theological dilemma, in that he reluctantly depicts God as striking Israel, as the indirect language of 18:20-24 suggests (cf. Num. 16:46-48). Some scholars highlight the absence of Lady Wisdom in this final segment, and the return of the God of violence (Tanzer, 294; Berrigan, 191).

Wisdom of Solomon 19:1-22: God Defeats Israel's Enemies

The Text in Its Ancient Context

After a long reflection on Israel's exodus from Egypt (starting in 11:1), the sage finally turns to the final destruction of the Egyptians, their drowning in the sea (19:1-5). The teacher highlights God's foreknowledge as an attempt to relieve God of any wrongdoing: "for God knew in advance even their future actions" (19:1; cf. 12:10-11). After all, it was nature again that protected God's people (19:6-12), a theme emphasized earlier (16:17, 24-25). Furthermore, these "sinners . . . justly suffered" (19:13) because of their mistreatment of the immigrants living among them (19:13-15).

The author's discussion of the immigrant is relevant to his own contemporary society. Some citizens treated strangers oddly from the very beginning (19:14)—an apparent allusion to the Sodomites of Genesis 19—while other citizens mistreated them after the immigrants had received the rights of citizenship (19:16). This latter group refers to the Egyptians and their oppression of their Jewish neighbors in Alexandria (Winston, 329). By implication, Egyptian mistreatment would again lead to their punishment.

The Alexandrian sage closes the treatise almost as abruptly as he began (19:18-22). First, as a teacher in the wisdom tradition, he reminds his audience of the importance of observation (19:18). What he observes is how nature defends those who do right, a theme discussed throughout the book (16:17, 24-25). More importantly, behind nature stands the Creator, whom the sage addresses in his closing words. The sage affirms God's faithfulness toward Israel (19:22; Sir. 51:3) in a closing doxology (Grabbe, 17).

The Text in the Interpretive Tradition

The author writes as an immigrant who hopes to encourage the immigrant community in which he resides. There is also ambivalence in his perspective. On the one hand, he labels the mistreatment he experiences in the foreign land (19:14). On the other hand, he does not encourage the community to return home. In fact, he refers infrequently to Judea and does not express any longing to return there (12:3, 7). In the final verse of the book, he confesses trust in God to protect and guide Israel "in all places" (19:22).

The Text in Contemporary Discussion

Treatment of the stranger or immigrant is a common motif in biblical literature. This sage provides something profound—perhaps even unique—in biblical literature. Nature itself—as God's representative in the world scene—operates on behalf of the immigrant. Of course, in this instance, the author speaks as the immigrant and not as the host.

Works Cited

Berrigan, Daniel. 2001. *Wisdom: The Feminine Face of God.* Lanham, MD: Sheed & Ward.

Campbell, Douglas. 2009. *The Deliverance of God: An Apocalyptic Rereading of Justification in Paul.* Grand Rapids: Eerdmans.

Cheon, Samuel. 1997. *The Exodus Story in the Wisdom of Solomon: A Study in Biblical Interpretation.* Sheffield: Sheffield Academic.

Clarke, Ernest G. 1973. *The Wisdom of Solomon.* CBC. Cambridge: Cambridge University Press.

Collins, John J. 1997. *Jewish Wisdom in the Hellenistic Age.* OTL. London: T&T Clark.

Fuller, Michael E. 2006. *The Restoration of Israel.* Berlin: de Gruyter.

Goodman, Martin. 1994. *Mission and Conversion: Proselytizing in the Religious History of the Roman Empire.* Oxford: Clarendon.

Grabbe, Lester L. 1997. *Wisdom of Solomon.* Sheffield: Sheffield Academic.

O'Connor, Kathleen M. 1988. *The Wisdom Literature.* Message of Biblical Spirituality. Collegeville, MN: Michael Glazier.

Origen. *On First Principles.*

Tanzer, Sarah J. 2012. "Wisdom of Solomon." In *Women's Bible Commentary*, edited by Carol A. Newsom, Sharon H. Ringe, and Jacqueline E. Lapsley, , 404–9. 3rd ed. Louisville: Westminster John Knox.

Voicu, Sever, ed. 2010. "Commentary on Wisdom of Solomon." In *Apocrypha*, 34–175. Ancient Christian Commentary on Scripture, Old Testament 15. Downers Grove, IL: InterVarsity Press.

Winston, David. 1979: *The Wisdom of Solomon.* AB 43. New York: Doubleday.

SIRACH

Stacy Davis

Introduction

Sirach's author identifies himself in 50:27.

> Instruction in understanding and knowledge
>   I have written in this book,
> Jesus son of Eleazar son of Sirach of Jerusalem.

Most likely a teacher (Sir. 39:32-34), Ben Sira, as he is commonly called, left in written form the results of decades of oral instruction. Unlike most biblical books, Sirach's date can be determined from intertextual evidence. The praise of the high priest Simon (219–196 BCE) in Sirach 50 and the silence regarding the Maccabean revolt (175–164 BCE) suggest that Ben Sira completed his work in the 180s. His grandson translated the book from Hebrew to Greek after 132 BCE, "the thirty-eighth year of the reign of Euergetes" (prologue).

Catholic and Orthodox traditions recognize and include Sirach as part of their Hebrew Scriptures; Sirach appears between the Wisdom of Solomon and Isaiah in Catholic Bibles and between Wisdom and Hosea in Orthodox ones. Protestants do not consider Sirach canonical, although the book sometimes is printed in study Bibles, including the NRSV. Sirach was not included in the Jewish Tanak, but remained a part of Jewish tradition, cited in the Talmud and by Nachmanides (Koperski, 262).

Historical/Cultural Context

By the time Ben Sira was writing, in the first quarter of the second century BCE, the Greeks had controlled Palestine for 150 years; first by the Ptolemies and then the Seleucids. The Ptolemies had followed the Persian approach to governance—rule benevolently in exchange for timely tax revenue. Jewish communities paid their taxes and therefore lived peacefully. Peace notwithstanding, Jews supported the Seleucid rise to power under Antiochus III (223–187 BCE). He rewarded them with a three-year tax release. Temple workers specifically received some permanent tax relief. Religious freedom for Jews remained intact from Ptolemaic rule, although it disappeared shortly after Ben Sira completed his work (Di Lella 1992, 933; Perdue, 245). Culturally, Hellenization, or the adoption of Greek ideas and customs, was the word of the day. The extent of Ben Sira's acceptance and incorporation of Hellenization remains debatable, as the following section will indicate.

What was Ben Sira's view of Hellenization? Scholarly answers to the question vary and depend on an understanding of Sirach's purpose. Alexander A. Di Lella argues that Ben Sira's "purpose was not to condemn Hellenism as such, but rather to demonstrate to Jews and even gentiles of good will that true wisdom is to be found primarily in Jerusalem and not in Athens" (1992, 933). Leo G. Perdue suggests that Ben Sira "[attempts] . . . the forging of a somewhat uneasy synthesis between older Israelite and Jewish wisdom and Hellenistic *paideia*" (Perdue, 246). Sirach's breadth of topics lends itself to both arguments. While Ben Sira certainly reinforces belief in Israel's God and Jewish traditions, he also uncritically shows Hellenistic cultural influences, as his views about friendship and gender will indicate. As a whole, the book defends the writer's self-identification as a man "whose mind poured forth wisdom" (Sir. 50:27). Readers of Ben Sira's work "might make even greater progress in living according to the law" (prologue).

Literary Forms

Sirach contains several specific literary forms, including proverbs ("Birds roost with their own kind, / so honesty comes home to those who practice it" ([Sir. 27:9]), hymns, prayers, and what may be called teaching narratives, or stories designed to inform the reader how (and how not) to behave (see the discussion on table etiquette in Sir. 31:12-24). The proverbs and stories are scattered throughout Sirach, giving the author's point of view about themes such as wisdom, divine retribution, virtues, vices, and gender relations. While Sirach begins with a hymn, other hymns and prayers appear throughout the book.

Although the book uses clear literary forms, dividing the book into units is difficult at best. The number of large sections ranges from three to eight (nine including the conclusion following the hymn to the ancestors), and no consensus exists regarding the number of subsections, particularly in Sirach 1–38 (Di Lella 1992, 936–37; Perdue, 247; Clifford, 118–20). Additionally, Sirach has no linear thematic structure. The *Anchor Bible Dictionary* entry "Wisdom of Ben-Sira" (Di Lella 1992) sequentially divides the book's fifty-one chapters but then discusses the work thematically, with sections on the book's style, sources, and major theological themes. Richard Clifford follows the same approach. Burton Mack and Benjamin G. Wright III perhaps say it best: "The nature of the material in this large collection of wisdom proverbs and poetry prohibits neat organization and frustrates prolonged linear reading" (Mack and Wright, 1380). Yet the book's final form remains linear in some sense. The difficulty may be a consequence of Sirach's overall purpose. Alexander A. Di Lella notes that the book "is a kind of handbook of moral behavior for the early second-century BC Jew" (1992, 936). To that end, its purpose is similar to the easier-to-divide but still anthology-like Proverbs (Perdue, 77; Clifford, 43). With that in mind, this essay will approach Sirach thematically, form-critically, and linearly. The texts will be discussed in chapter-and-verse order, beginning with Sir. 1:1 and ending with 51:30. The following divisions, therefore, are neither definitive nor arbitrary; their purpose is to enable the reader to follow the linear pattern in which Sirach attained its final form, while noticing important and repeated ideas and themes in the book as a whole.

Sirach 1:1—10:31 Prologue and the Beginning of Wisdom

The Text in Its Ancient Context

Ben Sira's grandson writes a brief prologue that explains both the purpose of his grandfather's work and offers an apology for any translation problems. Sirach as a whole is designed to help those who want to follow the torah and live well. The grandson, living in Egypt, worked tirelessly to translate the work from Hebrew into Greek.

The book itself then begins with a hymn. Ben Sira's hymns exemplify intertextuality, with allusions to Job, Genesis, and Proverbs (Perdue, 249, 259; Clifford, 122–23). The sage's opening hymn (Sir. 1:1-10) glorifies God as the Creator and therefore the source of wisdom (cf. Job 28). He concludes that "those who love [God]" will receive wisdom (Sir. 1:10). The hymns reinforce older traditions about God's majesty and the wonders of the created world. Yet they are also distinctive products of Hellenistic Judaism. Praising the God of Israel as the genuine and authoritative source of wisdom may be a response to *1 Enoch*'s apocalyptic claim that Enoch himself knows the universe's mysteries as well as a reaction to the Greek argument that such mysteries can be solved through scientific inquiry (Corley 2003, 269–85).

For Ben Sira, almost all proper behavior comes directly from fear of the Lord. A poem on the topic immediately follows the opening hymn to wisdom in Sirach 1, with the fear of the Lord being "the beginning . . . [the] fullness . . . the crown . . . [and] the root of wisdom" (1:14, 16, 18, 20). The ones who fear God enjoy length of days, riches, and good health (Sir. 1:12-13, 17-18).

Ben Sira then connects fear of the Lord to patience and steadfastness, both with God and with people. Followers of God must expect difficult times and not allow those times to weaken their resolve (Sir. 2:1-18). Additionally, they must honor their parents both as minor children and as adults, caring for elderly parents with love and patience (Sir. 3:1-16). Ben Sira argues that those who fear the Lord will be humble and obedient. The humble stick to their own tasks and concerns and do not exceed their own limits or capabilities by moving beyond the torah into mysticism or apocalypticism, the things that are "too difficult," "hidden," and "beyond you" (Sir. 3:21-23; Prockter, 245–52; Wright, 126). As a result, they are also wise (Sir. 3:17-29). The wise and humble not only care for family members but also for the poor and needy, blessing them with alms and offering justice when it is within their power to do so (Sir. 3:30—4:10).

As a wisdom text, Sirach's fifty-one chapters are full of the subject. But in some specific passages, Ben Sira offers praise of wisdom's advantages to those who seek it. The texts all take a gendered, heterosexual perspective regarding the acquisition and benefits of wisdom, which is feminine both in Hebrew (*ḥokmâ*) and Greek (*sophia*). According to Sir. 4:14-15, "Those who serve her [wisdom] minister to the Holy One; the Lord loves those who love her. Those who obey her will judge the nations, and all who listen to her will live secure." Both of these occupations, priest and judge, belonged to men in second-century Palestine. Wisdom is also the mother who teaches her sons how to prosper (Clifford, 126). Chapter 5 acts as a type of transition, in which Ben Sira offers a variety of pieces of wise advice. One must remain humble even if wealthy, repent speedily in order to avoid divine retribution, and be slow to speak and therefore avoid shame.

Ben Sira warns his readers that calmness of mind is the key to being a good friend and that not everyone who looks and acts like a friend deserves the title; some behave like friends when it is advantageous for them, but later reveal themselves as enemies (Sir. 6:7-13). Righteous, loyal friends are priceless (Sir. 6:14-15), and "those who fear the Lord will find them" (Sir. 6:16). Jeremy Corley argues that Ben Sira may have been familiar with ancient Greek and Egyptian ideas about friendship, especially from the Greek poet Theognis and traditions found in the Egyptian Papyrus Insinger. Corley concludes that "either he [Ben Sira] knows such works (directly or indirectly), or else he is familiar with at least their thought world" (2002, 213).

The lessons that Wisdom wants to teach her sons and the rewards she wants to bestow in Sirach 4 cannot be learned without patience (Sir. 6:19-22), perseverance (Sir. 6:24-31), and wise counsel (Sir. 6:34-36). As a transition to a lengthy list of dos and don'ts (mostly don'ts) in Sir. 7:1-9:9, Ben Sira reminds the reader to

> Reflect on the statutes of the Lord,
> and meditate at all times on his commandments.
> It is he who will give insight to your mind,
> and your desire for wisdom will be granted. (Sir. 6:37)

This insight should include the following important reminders: do not perform bad acts (Sir. 7:1-3); do not seek power (Sir. 7:4-7); do not break the commandments or neglect religious duties (Sir. 7:8-14); do not be lazy or arrogant (Sir. 7:15-17); do not mistreat a good friend, a good wife, a good slave, or a good farm animal (Sir. 7:18-23, 26); do not "show yourself too indulgent with [daughters]," but look out for their virginity and marry them off (Sir. 7:23-25); and do not neglect your parents, the priests, the poor, mourners, or the sick (Sir. 7:27-36). Additionally, one should avoid arguments with the rich and powerful as well as the sinful and foolish, respect the old and wise, stay away from lending, and keep one's thoughts to oneself (Sir. 8:1-19). The last rule applies to a man's relationships with women as well; the wise man will not allow a woman, whether a virgin, a prostitute, or another man's wife, to tempt him and therefore take away his strength (Sir. 9:1-7). The mention of different themes and ideas one right after another is similar to the structure of Proverbs 1–9, in which talk of wisdom is interspersed with practical advice about how to live well.

In spite of Ben Sira's warnings about the dangers of interpersonal relationships, friends do matter. To avoid false friends, the sage encourages his reader to

> Let your conversation be with intelligent people,
> and let all your discussion be about the law of the Most High.
> Let the righteous be your dinner companions,
> and let your glory be in the fear of the Lord. (Sir. 9:15-16)

Having this fear could make someone a competent leader one day, if it is God's will (Sir. 9:17—10:5).

For Ben Sira, vices include pride and anger, which can be avoided through remembrance of one's mortality. God dislikes and punishes pride (Sir. 10:7, 13-17), because

> the beginning of human pride is to forsake the Lord;
> the heart has withdrawn from its Maker. (Sir. 10:12)

Additionally, Ben Sira suggests that pride makes little sense.

> How can dust and ashes be proud?
> Even in life the human body decays.
> A long illness baffles the physician;
> the king of today will die tomorrow. (Sir. 10:9-10)

Those who are born to die should not exalt themselves, and they should also restrain their anger. Only those who fear God deserve praise, regardless of their social status (Sir. 10:19-25).

Ben Sira returns to the theme of humility in this unit's final section. To be humble is to be honorable; Sir. 10:28 states that you should "honor yourself with humility, / and give yourself the esteem you deserve." This suggests that humility should not be confused with humiliation.

The Text in the Interpretive Tradition

The Jewish canon excludes Sirach, but the praise of God for creation and the importance of wisdom remain fundamental parts of Jewish liturgy and tradition. Psalm 29, which is sung in some Conservative synagogues during the procession of the Torah, echoes Sirach's praise of God through a description of nature. Comparisons can also be made between Sirach and Christian tradition. The argument that wisdom is God's gift (Sir. 1:10) sounds like Paul's insistence on grace as God's gift in the book of Romans. Centuries later, the Catholic "Dogmatic Constitution on Divine Revelation," *Dei Verbum*, calls creation one source for such revelation (§3).

Sirach's admonition against repetitive prayers in 7:14 ("Do not repeat yourself when you pray") reappears in Matt. 6:7—"When you are praying, do not heap up empty phrases as the Gentiles do; for they think that they will be heard because of their many words." The author's response to such ineffective prayers is to give what Christians now know as the Lord's Prayer. Matthew's critique of lengthy prayers does not appear in Luke's citation of the prayer, and Luke condenses the prayer into two verses as opposed to Matthew's five. Both in Ben Sira's day and in the time of the first followers of Jesus, there appeared to be distaste for long-winded petitions, and Matthew's author specifically links such prayers to gentiles in a way Ben Sira does not.

The virtues Ben Sira describes appear as fundamentals in other religious traditions. Just as Sirach links right living to the fear of the Lord, the Qur'an connects proper behavior to obedience to Allah. In the instructions for the hajj, believers also should sacrifice properly designated animals (22:25-34, 36-37) and speak to the "humble whose hearts fill with awe whenever God is mentioned, who endure whatever happens to them with patience, who keep up the prayer, who give to others out of Our provision to them" (22:34-35). Allah's humble servants respond to others with compassion, pray regularly, use money moderately, and only worship God (25:63-68). The Qur'an also links friendship to the final judgment, and those who chose evil companions will regret their poor decision (25:27-29). By extension, unrighteous friends are not true friends at all, as Sirach 9 suggests. In Hindu tradition, deities and saints, represented by statues or photos, may receive food and incense offerings as signs of respect (Knott, 58, 60). Moderation pervades Buddhist teaching. Buddhists call the Noble Eightfold Path the Middle Path because of its insistence on moderation or finding happiness neither "through sensual pleasures" nor "through self-mortification" (Adiele, 162). Such moderate living includes no alcohol consumption, to give one example (Adiele, 163). While each religion applies the virtues in specific ways, Sirach's general ideas of humility, sacrifice, and moderation remain important spiritual practices and disciplines.

The Text in Contemporary Discussion

Michael Eric Dyson, a Baptist minister, uses religion and cultural criticism to define proper and improper pride in his volume for the New York Public Library and Oxford University Press series on the seven deadly sins. Using Aristotle and his own Christian tradition, Dyson argues that proper pride enables a person to appreciate fully their gifts and talents without vanity or apology. He concludes, "If thinking too highly of oneself is a sin, then the Aristotelian vice of thinking too lowly of oneself qualifies as well. At a minimum, it signifies a rejection of God's creation, even if the creature is the source of doubt about her worth. Thus, to take pride in one's person, one's achievements, one's moral worth . . . is to affirm and embrace the character of God reflected in one's own soul" (Dyson, 24). Improper pride manifests itself in racism and nationalism, both of which glorify accidental attributes at the expense of others who do not possess a particular skin color or passport stamp (Dyson, 43–57, 85–118). Dyson offers a view of pride that is less limiting that Ben Sira's insistence that pride "was not created for human beings" (Sir. 10:18).

Sirach's discussion of children's responsibilities toward their parents, however, resonates with religious and cultural ideas both in the West and the East. In a discussion of the Fourth Commandment ("Honor your father and your mother"), the *Catechism of the Catholic Church* states that "as much as they can, they [children] must give them [parents] material and moral support in old age and in times of illness, loneliness, or distress" (2218). The proof for such responsibility is Sir. 3:2-6, 12-13, and 16, which the catechism quotes directly. Whether Catholic or not, elder care remains a source of anxiety for adult children and a hugely profitable business in the United States. Businesses such as A Place for Mom offer assisted-living and nursing-home referrals, and children have an array of additional options for parental care, including in-home nursing care and attempting to do the work themselves. Yet such care comes at a great cost, not only in terms of money (often thousands of dollars a month) but also in terms of social stigma, particularly for those children who live with aging and infirm parents. Men who live with their mothers, for example, are not considered honorable. In contemporary musical group TLC's words, they are "scrubs," and even a woman who follows the catechism religiously stated to this author that such a man would never find a spouse. In Asian cultures, where for centuries it was assumed that parents would be supported by their children, the system is breaking down with devastating consequences.

The rate of elderly suicide in South Korea is "nearly four times the rich-country average" ("Poor Spirits"), particularly among the rural elderly, whose children have moved away and have not taken their parents with them. In India, where sons are expected to care for their mothers, the tension between mothers-in-law and daughters-in-law can be unbearable, with the mothers trying to rule the household and, more recently, the daughters fighting back. This pushback has resulted in the creation of charities to help elderly widows whose families have abandoned them. After centuries of daughter-in-law mistreatment, the mothers-in-law are now the mistreated ("Curse of the Mummyji"). While Sirach mentions the duties of children, adult children today are less willing to accept the parent-child hierarchy that the biblical text describes.

Sirach 11:1—16:23: A Balanced Life

The Text in Its Ancient Context

Ben Sira warns that appearances deceive; therefore, the wise person will listen and think before making a judgment. Once a decision is made, however, the person should honor their obligations and work hard (Sir. 11:1-26). The reason is as follows:

> For it is easy for the Lord on the day of death
> to reward individuals according to their conduct. (Sir. 11:26)

The importance of proper decision making is connected to friendship. Finding true friends proves difficult (Sir. 11:29—12:18). Ben Sira notes that

> A friend is not known in prosperity,
> nor is an enemy hidden in adversity.
> One's enemies are friendly when one prospers,
> but in adversity even one's friend disappears. (Sir. 12:8-9)

Such friends should be chosen from one's own social station, lest a rich or powerful friend impoverish and humiliate the less wealthy and cultured acquaintance. Additionally, sinners and the righteous should not socially interact; just like the rich and the poor, they have nothing in common (Sir. 13:1-24).

And yet, anyone who holds their tongue and remains optimistic, rich or poor, can be counted as happy (Sir. 13:25—14:2). One way to be happy is to treat oneself and others well. To do otherwise is foolish, since all will die one day and cannot take their goods with them. Ben Sira argues,

> My child, treat yourself well, according to your means,
> and present worthy offerings to the Lord. . . .
> Do good to friends before you die,
> and reach out and give to them as much as you can.
> Do not deprive yourself of a day's enjoyment;
> do not let your share of desired good pass by you. (Sir. 14:11, 13-14)

Such words remind the reader that the wise life need not be the ascetic life and sounds similar to Qoheleth's arguments a few centuries earlier and the Epicureans about a century before (Furley, 261, 263).

Ben Sira returns to the image of Woman Wisdom in chapters 14 and 15. The man "who camps near her house / and fastens his tent peg to her walls / [and] who pitches his tent near her" (Sir. 14:24-25) will find wisdom—"she will come to meet him like a mother, / and like a young bride she will welcome him" (Sir. 15:2). His rewards will include good reputation and joy (Sir. 15:5-6). But just like a bride, wisdom must be chosen. If people choose to disobey the commandments, they have only themselves to blame (Sir. 15:11-20). This belief in human choice appears famously in Deut. 30:15-20 and Josh. 24:14-15.

Like Proverbs, Sirach argues for the principle of divine retribution: God rewards the righteous and punishes the wicked. Because God sees all people, God will punish wrongdoers, whether few or many, and will bless the righteous; additionally, the ungodly may not live for long (Sir. 16:1-23). The lengthy discussion of retribution in chapter 16 reappears in shorter passages throughout the book.

The Text in the Interpretive Tradition

Wisdom's personification as female not only fits the gendered nouns of biblical language but also serves as a means of placing the biblical faiths within their historical context. Jews and Christians were surrounded by cultures that had goddesses as well as gods. To insist on the supremacy and exclusivity of one male deity was culturally odd. Making wisdom a feminine being in service of the divine, while not creating a consort for God, did at least offer some alternative to the constant glorification of God as "he." Judith Hadley notes that the worship of the Queen of Heaven condemned in Jeremiah 7 and 44 also may have been a response to male religious dominance (Hadley, 30–51). Today, Jews and Christians include female images in their liturgy and worship. Jewish congregations still sing the hymn *Lekha Dodi* to bring in the Sabbath, praised as the "bride, O Queen Sabbath" (*Lekha Dodi*). The hymn dates from the mid-sixteenth century. A synagogue in South Bend, Indiana, has bimah (altar) decorations that quote Prov. 3:18: "She [Wisdom] is a tree of life to those who lay hold of her." Catholic and Orthodox traditions venerate Mary as the Queen of Heaven and the Mother of God in mysteries of the rosary and on feast days. Medieval artwork of Mary's assumption into heaven and her coronation show the glorification of a woman in a male-centered heaven and earth.

The Text in Contemporary Discussion

Claudia V. Camp notes the connections between friendship and economics in Sirach. Those who make friends with the poor will benefit when their friends' fortunes change (Camp 1991, 16). Such seemingly practical advice echoes the ancient idea of friendship as patronage, or a relationship between unequal parties (Malina, 100–102). What appears to be missing, however, is the concept of friendship as mutuality, when two people with common interests, ideas, or social standing develop and maintain a relationship. While Ben Sira hints at the joy of good friends, the hint almost disappears under the warnings about all the ways friendship can go off the rails. Recent scientific studies of female animals suggest that "affiliative, longlasting, and mutually beneficial relationships between females turn out to be the basic unit of social life" (Angier, 1–2). Faith Adiele says that she needs "reliable friends with whom I feel comfortable" (Adiele, 134), and she also may be saying something universal about "baboons, humans and other group-minded kinds" (Angier, 2). As an ancient man, Ben Sira could not have envisioned the ways in which friendship would evolve among women, and men, too—as the popularity of the word *bromance* to describe close male friendship indicates.

Sirach 16:24—19:30: The Two Ways

The Text in Its Ancient Context

Sirach 16–18 praises God's creation of the earth, with emphasis on humankind in general and Israel in particular. All of God's works are orderly and good, similar to the assessment of creation in Genesis 1. Distinctively, the hymn also supports the belief in divine retribution and encourages repentance. Leo Perdue notes that "Ben Sira is the first sage to bring sapiential teaching about creation into the normative traditions of Israelite faith that focused on salvation history" (Perdue, 262, see also 284).

Creation, however, will not be enjoyed by the immoderate. Ben Sira urges people to use care in financial decisions (almsgiving, saving resources, feasting) and personal interactions (sexual conduct, alcohol use; Sir. 18:15—19:3). Sirach's numerous passages about the tongue have a similar message: use sparingly. As the sage says,

> Never repeat a conversation,
> and you will lose nothing at all. (Sir. 19:7)

People should avoid gossip or telling what they have heard, especially if the tale refers to someone close to them, lest they be guilty of spreading lies (Sir. 19:4-17).

Ben Sira's few comparisons of wisdom and folly both reinforce and disregard common Wisdom literature motifs. Sirach 19 insists that "the whole of wisdom is fear of the Lord" (19:20; cf. 21:11), a virtue that will be discussed later in this essay. Additionally, the wise will keep the commandments. Wisdom, however, cannot automatically function as a synonym for knowledge and intelligence, because both can be used for negative purposes. Fools know evil and/or behave unjustly (Sir. 19:24-28). And while Ben Sira personifies Wisdom as female, he does not do so with folly.

The Text in the Interpretive Tradition

Themes from Sirach's warnings about wisdom and folly appear in the New Testament and rabbinic literature. Ben Sira's warning that "there is a cleverness that is detestable . . . exact but unjust" (Sir. 19:23, 25) finds a parallel in Paul's claim that "God's foolishness is wiser than human wisdom" (1 Cor. 1:25). Earthly wisdom may not be the same thing as righteousness, a much more important characteristic (Sir. 19:24; 1 Cor. 1:22, 26-27).

The Text in Contemporary Discussion

Because Sirach does not personify folly, scholarship about Wisdom and Folly often focuses exclusively on Proverbs 1–9 (Estes, 151–69) or solely on Ben Sira's characterization of Woman Wisdom (Angel, 152–58). But other scholars have noted that Ben Sira's exclusion of Woman Folly is not unique; Qumran literature does not include her either, and Woman Wisdom appears infrequently (Goff, 20–38). In an intertextual comparison of Qoheleth, Ben Sira, and the opening chapters of Exodus, J. E. Owens argues that "Pharaoh is folly!" because he does not listen to counsel or act prudently (Owens, 235). Pharaoh's behavior in Exodus 5–10 contrasts with the wise man of Sirach 21 and 37. Whether personified or not, wisdom and foolishness are identifiable traits whose effects can be seen in ancient texts and contemporary life. Calling someone a fool today often conjures up the same images that Ben Sira describes—someone lacking knowledge and behaving badly. While Sirach limits its definition of the wise and foolish to men, today women too can receive either title, depending on the assessment of their actions. Wisdom and folly no longer reside solely in a man's world, as the musician Pink's 2006 song "Stupid Girls" humorously and profanely observes.

Sirach 20:1—22:26: The Importance of Proper Behavior

The Text in Its Ancient Context

The wise know when to be silent, because poorly timed comments or outright lies produce nothing but trouble (Sir. 20:1-8, 20-26). A list of what the NRSV calls paradoxes (Sir. 20:9-19) interrupts the two-part discussion of speech and how to use words wisely. Most of these paradoxes are financial.

> There is the gift that profits you nothing,
> and the gift to be paid back double. . . .
> Some buy much for little,
> but pay for it seven times over. (Sir. 20:10, 12)

The ideal wise man, however, can avoid these paradoxes through proper living. This man speaks at the right time and avoids sinful acts and people (Sir. 20:27—21:7, 9-10). Returning to the importance of proper financial planning, Ben Sira warns that

> whoever builds his house with other people's money
> is like one who gathers stones for his burial mound. (Sir. 21:8)

Fools, unfortunately, cannot be educated or taught restraint; their mouths move constantly and say nothing useful, and they find themselves in the wrong place at the wrong time (Sir. 21:14-28). Fools include lazy people, who are compared to unclean stones and animal waste (Sir. 22:1-2). Before returning to his recurring theme of friendship, Ben Sira warns about badly behaved children, particularly daughters. Their birth is already "a loss" (Sir. 22:3) that can only be mitigated if they marry. In contrast,

> An impudent daughter disgraces father and husband,
> and is despised by both. (Sir. 22:5)

To avoid such disgrace, corporal punishment is in order (Sir. 22:6). Regarding equal social relations, in order to keep one's friends, one must be wise; such wisdom includes keeping their secrets and helping them during difficult times (Sir. 22:19-26).

The Text in the Interpretive Tradition

While the New Testament rarely personifies wisdom (Matt. 11:19 is one brief exception), Jesus' first followers valued the virtue. Parables condemn fools who do not prepare their souls for the final judgment and praise the wise who do (Matt. 25:1-12; Luke 12:13-21). The author of the book of James states, "If any of you is lacking in wisdom, ask God, who gives to all generously and ungrudgingly, and it will be given you" (1:5). Again, Ben Sira does not personify folly as female, but Revelation contains a good woman/bad woman binary. The "woman clothed with the sun" (Rev. 12:1) who gives birth to the Messiah contrasts with "the great whore who is seated on many waters" and is "clothed in purple and scarlet" (Rev. 17:1, 4).

The Text in Contemporary Discussion

In a culture now saturated with speech, written and verbal, Ben Sira's warnings about communication can easily go unheard. With Facebook, Twitter, talk radio, politically slanted news programming, and a proliferation of talk shows, thoughtless speech and constant chatter seem to be the new normal. But modern sages do exist. A college professor runs properfacebooketiquette.com, advising readers that knowing what to say and when enables them "to be . . . more comfortable, pleasant and happy [people]." Numerous sites are devoted to Twitter etiquette, and dummies.com warns that you should not "share information that you might regret making public." And the same noisy culture also offers examples of the benefits of silence, from the ashram visitors in *Eat Pray Love*, to the French Carthusian monks who hardly talk in the documentary *Into Great Silence*, to those who use quiet to protest hateful speech against LGBT students during the annual National Day of Silence. Ben Sira's observation that "honor and dishonor come from speaking" (Sir. 5:13) remains true today, and people still may choose whether to use their communication abilities for good or ill (Sir. 15:15-17).

Sirach 22:27—24:34: God Is Watching

The Text in Its Ancient Context

Sirach contains two petitions and a prayer of thanksgiving. Each of the book's three prayers has some connection either to a theme within Sirach particularly or the Hebrew Bible generally. Ben Sira's first prayer asks the following questions:

> Who will set a guard over my mouth,
> and an effective seal upon my lips,

so that I may not fall because of them,
 and my tongue may not destroy me? (Sir. 22:27)

Who will set whips over my thoughts,
 and the discipline of wisdom over my mind,
so as not to spare me in my errors,
 and not overlook my sins? (Sir. 23:2)

Assuming that his prayer is answered, God will save him from foolish words and unclean thoughts. The importance of controlling the tongue and limiting bad behavior reappears throughout the book.

Ben Sira then warns against all manner of oaths,

for as a servant who is constantly under scrutiny
 will not lack bruises,
so also the person who always swears and utters the Name
 will never be cleansed from sin.
The one who swears many oaths is full of iniquity,
 and the scourge will not leave his house. (Sir. 23:10-11)

Additionally, sinful, undisciplined fools may be identified through their bad language (Sir. 23:12-15).

Other sinners think God is blind and forgetful and foolishly engage in fornication and adultery, but those men will be caught and punished (Sir. 23:16-21). So will a woman who produces children through adultery, "[disobeying] the law of the Most High" (Sir. 23:23). She and her children will be punished, and

Those who survive her will recognize
 that nothing is better than the fear of the Lord,
and nothing sweeter than to heed the commandments of the Lord. (Sir. 23:27)

After describing foolish behavior, Ben Sira allows Wisdom to speak for herself in chapter 24. Scholars have noted the parallels between this chapter and Proverbs 8 (Skehan, 365–79; Perdue, 264; Rogers 1996, 148, 150–51; Clifford, 123; Hayward, 33–34). Yet Ben Sira offers innovation as well. Not only is Wisdom God's creation (Sir. 24:3), but she also rules the earth and its inhabitants (Sir. 24:6; Perdue, 268; Rogers 1996, 148–53). She resides, however, in the Jerusalem temple, smells like the fragrances used there, and joins herself to the Mosaic torah (Sir. 24:8-12, 15, 23). Ben Sira's poem emphasizes Second Temple Judaism's focus on Scripture as sacred and the importance of ritual practice (Perdue, 250, 271). The poem may also function as a defense of the temple against Jewish opponents like the Samaritans and the Essenes, and Hellenistic claims about Greece as the home of wisdom and philosophy (Hayward, 38–46). The most-sought-after woman on earth obeyed God's order and chose Israel as her man.

The Text in the Interpretive Tradition

Sirach 22:27—23:1 asks God for deliverance from an out-of-control mouth. The author of James, while not praying for help, agrees in 3:1-12 with Ben Sira's assessment of the tongue as a tool of destruction, or "a restless evil, full of deadly poison" (James 3:9). Sophie Laws and Walter T. Wilson note that "the concern for such sins [of speech] is also prominent in wisdom literature" (Laws and Wilson, 2055). A number of Christian traditions include praying the Psalter as a spiritual practice, perhaps as a way to control one's speech. Previously limited often to clergy or those in religious orders, the Divine Office or the Liturgy of the Hours has become more common among Catholic and Protestant laity. Phyllis Tickle's *The Divine Hours* series is one example of the daily practice of utilizing the Psalms for their original purpose as prayers.

And in the Qur'an, just as in the Tanak and the Bible, adultery counts as a sin (17:32). Because God sees everything, women and men should "lower their eyes and guard their private parts" (24:30-31; cf. Sir. 23:18-20). Anthropologist Clifford Geertz argues that only through studying humans in particular can anything be said about humanity in general (Geertz, 52). The repetition of the same vices and their categorization as such across time and tradition suggests that certain states of being may be universal and perhaps even innate.

The Text in Contemporary Discussion

Most scholarly discourse about Sirach and Wisdom emphasizes the poem in chapter 24. Wisdom, the world traveler, makes her home in Jerusalem, a place greater than Greece; and she is described as superior to Isis, the premier Egyptian goddess (Hayward, 31–46; Rogers 1996, 141–56). Torah and Wisdom are connected, but Wisdom cannot be contained fully by anything, including torah (Rogers 2004, 114–21). Ben Sira may even give Wisdom masculine traits outside of chapter 24 (Camp 2005, 378, 386). Yet Ben Sira, while usually describing Wisdom as a woman, limits her benefits to men. Because of the parallels with Proverbs, another wisdom text written to instruct men, the limitation makes sense. But it need not be the last word. The Hebrew Bible contains examples of wise women, from Deborah the prophetess and judge to the prophetess Huldah and the wise women of Tekoa (2 Sam. 14:1-20) and Abel (2 Sam. 20:16-22). Their stories indicate that even within a patriarchal society, women too could be examples of the blessings of wisdom and help themselves and the men around them. If wisdom is a woman, then she has female and male devotees.

Sirach 25:1—29:28: Managing Social Relationships

The Text in Its Ancient Context

Harmonious domestic relations are praiseworthy (Sir. 25:1-11), but they can be difficult across gender lines. For the sage, women embody the worst type of evil and anger, and that warning begins his discussion of marriage and fatherhood, which fits perfectly in his patriarchal cultural context. He distinguishes first between good and bad wives. Good wives are quiet, organized, and chaste. If they happen to be physically attractive, then that is even better (Sir. 26:13-18). As with all good gifts, "the man who fears the Lord" receives her (Sir. 26:3); also, "a wife's charm delights her husband" (Sir. 26:13). But the husband with a bad wife will suffer. Such unattractive, loud, disobedient, and overbearing women torment their husbands, who should choose divorce if their wives refuse to behave (Sir. 25:16-26). And wives who support their husbands financially, drink excessively, or commit adultery are bad too (Sir. 26:7-9). While Sir. 26:10 mentions a "headstrong daughter," the text most likely refers to adulterous wives (Mack and Wright, 1413; Greenfield, 171).

Just as proper behavior comes from fear of the Lord, improper behavior comes from a lack of that fear. While Ben Sira hates to see strong men suffer from poverty (Sir. 26:28), he also claims that business and commercial transactions often lead to sin, because of the desire to acquire more (Sir. 26:29—27:1). He states,

> As a stake is driven firmly into a fissure between stones,
> so sin is wedged in between selling and buying. (Sir. 27:2)

The passage could have ended there, but it does not; Ben Sira adds one more verse for the reader's information.

> If a person is not steadfast in the fear of the Lord,
> his house will be quickly overthrown. (Sir. 27:3)

And being overthrown remains a possibility in life; such challenges show a person's worth, particularly when they speak (Sir. 27:4-7).

Ben Sira continues to remind the reader of the inevitability of divine retribution. According to him,

> If you pursue justice, you will attain it
> and wear it like a glorious robe.
> Birds roost with their own kind,
> so honesty comes home to those who practice it.
> A lion lies in wait for prey;
> so does sin for evildoers. (Sir. 27:8-10)

Scholars have noted Sirach's repeated imperatives regarding the tongue, including an additional warning against swearing and combative language in Sir. 27:11-15. Alexander A. Di Lella notes that "the book contains more material on the use and abuse of the tongue/lips/mouth/palate (all organs of speech) than any other book of the Old Testament" (1996, 32). Linking speech to the ancient ideals of honor and shame, Ben Sira borrows ideas not only from other Hebrew wisdom texts but also Egyptian literature (Di Lella 1996, 37, 41).

And once again, poor control of the tongue will cost a person their friends. Failure to remain loyal, particularly through a public, verbal betrayal of a friend's confidence, guarantees the friendship's demise (Sir. 27:16-21). And for men at this time, reputation meant everything; its loss, particularly by a friend's deeds, would be unforgivable (Malina, 50–55).

The angry increase their sins (and the likelihood of negative divine retribution) and cannot expect God's forgiveness, since they refuse to forgive others (Sir. 27:30—28:11). Ben Sira asks,

> If a mere mortal harbors wrath,
> who will make an atoning sacrifice for his sins? (Sir. 28:5)

The implied answer is no one, and the sage then reminds the reader of two eternal truths, death and the law.

> Remember the end of your life, and set enmity aside;
> remember corruption and death, and be true to the commandments.
> Remember the commandments, and do not be angry with your neighbor;
> remember the covenant of the Most High, and overlook faults. (Sir. 28:6-7)

This recollection leads a person away from anger and toward virtue.

Just like anger, negative speech regularly destroys individuals and communities (Sir. 28:13-18). In contrast, the righteous will be spared the destruction caused by the tongue (Sir. 28:19-23). Ben Sira advises the reader to take seriously the power of their lips.

> As you fence in your property with thorns,
> so make a door and a bolt for your mouth.
> As you lock up your silver and gold,
> so make balances and scales for your words.
> Take care not to err with your tongue,
> and fall victim to one lying in wait. (Sir. 28:24-26)

In other words, watch your mouth.

And finally, watch your wallet (Sir. 29:1-28). While one should make loans, Ben Sira warns that some loans simply will not be repaid. The poor, relatives, and friends should be helped "for the commandment's sake" (Sir. 29:9), but guaranteeing another's debts is risky. The sage warns,

> Assist your neighbor to the best of your ability,
> but be careful not to fall yourself. (Sir. 29:20)

It is better to be poor and have your own home than to rely on the hospitality of others, which could happen if one is too kind and therefore loose with one's finances.

The Text in the Interpretive Tradition

Before modern feminist and nationalist movements, patriarchal views about wives and daughters dominated religious and social ideology and practice. In Hindu myth and Scripture, women's religious and domestic duties are synonymous; they care for their parents when single and their husbands when married (Knott, 44, 81–82). Although Buddhist texts such as *Anguttara Nikaya* 4.55 (see Bhikkhu 1997a) praise mutuality and harmony in marriage, other texts such as *Digha Nikaya* 31 assume that a woman belongs in the home (see Kelly, Sawyer, and Yareham). The Qur'an gives women the option of divorce if their marriages fail (4:128), but husbands can settle arguments by giving their wives the silent treatment or one slap (4:34). Times, however, have changed traditions. Hindu nationalist movements led women out of the home and into political life, later leading to increased activism on behalf of women's economic and domestic equality (Knott, 82–87). US converts to Buddhism resist and reject the traditions of segregated meditation centers and the androcentric practices and leadership assumed in Buddhist texts (see Gross). Muslim women also are experiencing similar transitions, placing ancient texts and traditions in conversation with modern realities (see Huq). Across geographical and religious space, women now speak for themselves, as opposed to men solely defining their roles and responsibilities.

Divine retribution remained a part of biblically based religions and non-Western traditions long after Ben Sira. The contemporary cliché that you reap what you sow comes from Paul in Gal. 6:7-8, although Stephen Travis describes the passage as an example of people receiving the results of their choices and not "retributive judgment" (Travis, 81). In the eighth-century Asauchiyama myth from Japan, a spirit kills a group of women who break a taboo and allow men to see them weave at night on a body loom (Palmer, 223–32). At the end of the medieval era, Rabbi Joseph Albo argued that divine retribution, especially in the next life, makes up an indispensable part of divine law (Ehrlich, 277, 282–83, 288). And after decades of apocalyptic preaching and natural disasters being interpreted as God's punishment for sin, the Christian Venetians decided to repent. As proof, in 1516 they created a ghetto for the Jews (Crouzet-Pavan, 163–79). In this case, a belief in divine retribution led to a specific social action with long-term ramifications.

Ben Sira's analysis of sins repeats itself in the other major world religions. Sirach 28:2 is in the Lord's Prayer (Matt. 6:12; Luke 11:4). Buddhist teaching warns that the angry may live a short life and "be reborn in a body which is ugly" ("Culakammavibhanga Sutta" 3.204). Lord Krishna states in the *Bhagavad Gita* that "there are three gates leading to this hell [separation from the divine and miserable human existence]—lust, anger, and greed (16.21; see Prabhupada). Thousands of years later, a young London blogger Farhanah Diman quoted the verse as an opening to a cautionary secular tale about perfectionism (Diman). The seriousness of particular bad acts remains a part of religion in general, regardless of the particular faith tradition.

Buddhists, Hindus, and Muslims place the same high value on silence and careful speech as Ben Sira. The Noble Eightfold Path asks Buddhists to engage in right speech, meaning no "lies, slander, verbal abuse, gossip" (Adiele, 162). According to Iti 1.25, "the person who lies, who transgress in this one thing, transcending concern for the world beyond: there's no evil he might not do" (Bhikkhu 2001). The author of a blog for Buddhist laypeople cites the passage in order to encourage truth-telling, stating that "one result of my own efforts to speak truthfully is that I speak less often than I used to" ("The Truth Will Set Us Free"). Like Buddhism, Hinduism also includes a vow of silence, *mauna*, which some observe through limiting speech at certain days and times. The benefits include getting rest and avoiding the consequences of negative and thoughtless words ("Silence Is Golden"). The Qur'an also encourages proper speech: "Believers, do not be like those who insulted Moses—God cleared him of their allegations and he was highly honoured in God's eyes. Believers, be mindful of God, speak in a direct fashion and to good purpose, and he will put your deeds right for you and forgive you your sins" (33:69-71). The faithful also should practice silence, because "God does not like bad words to be made public unless someone has been wronged: He is all hearing and all knowing" (4:148). Ben Sira's insistence on careful speech is an interreligious and cross-cultural commonplace.

The Text in Contemporary Discussion

Buddhist Robert A. F. Thurman, in his volume on anger for the Seven Deadly Sins series mentioned above, uses the Buddhist wisdom teacher Shantideva's writings to describe anger and how to free oneself from it in an increasingly angry and hostile world. Because anger in Buddhist tradition is an addiction, rehabilitation is necessary to transform anger through mindfully practicing patience. One recognizes that irritating things will happen and that being angry about them will not make the irritations go away. One then learns to make peace with any human sources of those irritations. In a world where anger management classes can be part of a court-ordered punishment, usually because the defendant has committed a crime out of anger, Thurman's work is timely.

Sirach 30:1—42:14: Honor and Shame

The Text in Its Ancient Context

Only when discussing food, wine, and party etiquette does Ben Sira's advice sound more secular than religious. Food should be enjoyed (Sir. 30:18-25), but one should not eat everything in sight at a dinner party (Sir. 31:12-18). Wine too is a blessing, as long as the drinker does not overindulge (Sir. 31:25-31). Ben Sira claims that moderation leads to good health.

> In everything you do be moderate,
>   and no sickness will overtake you. (Sir. 31:22b)

The same rule applies at a party. Hosts should be attentive, but guests should limit their speech and their visit in order to have the best possible time (Sir. 32:1-13). Ben Sira's lengthy discussion of etiquette is interrupted by a warning against loving money (Sir. 31:1-11), which may be loosely connected to the money that one will spend on food and wine.

Similar to Sirach 7–8, Sir. 32:14—34:13 is a list of various wisdom ideals that are not necessarily connected to each other. The wise will trust in God's providence (Sir. 32:14—33:6). They will also know that God has made some days and people more important and special than others (Sir. 33:7-14). They will remain financially independent throughout their lives, treating all of their slaves well but not giving them too much time off (Sir. 33:20-33). And they will place their trust in God and not in their dreams (Sir. 34:1-8). In this discourse, Ben Sira offers himself as a model for others, having learned from older teachers (Sir. 33:16-17).

> Consider that I have not labored for myself alone,
>   but for all who seek instruction.
> Hear me, you who are great among the people,
>   and you leaders of the congregation, pay heed! (Sir. 33:18-19)

He also concludes that as a world traveler, he knows a great deal and is qualified to teach others (Sir. 34:9-13).

These qualifications, however, are nothing without fear of the Lord. Those who fear God will receive God's strength and protection (Sir. 34:14-20). Fearing God means doing what ought to be done, such as offering regular and generous sacrifices with joy (Sir. 35:1-13). Ben Sira insists,

> Do not appear before the Lord empty-handed,
> for all that you offer is in fulfillment of the commandment. (Sir. 35:6-7)

Imperfect animals or animals poached from the poor, however, will not be acknowledged (Sir. 34:21-27). Sirach's emphasis on the fear of the Lord appears not only in other Hebrew Bible texts but also generally in the ancient Near East (Perdue, 252; Clifford, 127). Ben Sira describes the fear of the Lord in terms of divine retribution from Deuteronomy; those who honor God will be blessed (Di Lella 1997, 188–204). Therefore, fear of God "is the fundamental attitude one needs to live wisely and thus enjoy all the good things of life" (Clifford, 121). Similar to *Jubilees*, Sirach links fear of the Lord to an occupation, specifically his own work as a scribe (Wright, 128–29).

Fear of the Lord is closely linked to divine retribution. God will respond to the mistreated and/or vulnerable by punishing their oppressors (Sir. 35:14-26). Ben Sira then prays that God will do just that. In the prayer, theology and historical context come to the forefront. Ben Sira asks God to show divine power by protecting Israel against non-Israelites, rewarding faithful Jews and punishing their enemies. Such calls for divine retribution appear in all three divisions of the Hebrew Bible, including Deut. 28:1-14; Zephaniah 2–3; and Psalm 137. Not only will God's actions prove that God is the only deity (Sir. 36:5, 22), but they will also inspire the faithful Israelites.

> As you have used us to show your holiness to them,
> so use them to show your glory to us. (Sir. 36:4)

Additionally, the prayer "against foreign nations" (Sir. 36:3) may be a response to the second-century-BCE stress between Judaism and Hellenism that eventually led to the Maccabean revolt (Perdue, 245).

After his prayer, Ben Sira returns to practical advice. A man should use wisdom in picking the right wife, and the bachelor life is not to be trusted (Sir. 36:23-31). Using proper judgment and picking friends also go hand in hand. Sirach 37 warns that

> Every friend says, "I too am a friend";
> but some friends are friends only in name. (Sir. 37:1)

Such friends will not remain loyal during difficult times (Sir. 37:4). If one has a friend who remains constant even in difficulty, then one ought to show the same faithfulness in kind (Sir. 37:5-6). Regarding the warning in Sirach 37 that not all friends are true friends, Jeremy Corley notes, "This observation is a commonplace of ancient Greek writing" (2002, 72). Ben Sira's insistence that a friendship cannot survive public betrayal places the sage firmly "within a social system based on honor and shame" (Corley 2002, 202). Continuing with the theme of choice, one should not take advice from just anyone, but only from a follower of the torah, oneself, and God (Sir. 37:7-15).

Unlike the foolish, the wise think and speak carefully, bringing honor and blessing on themselves (Sir. 37:16-26). The connection of wisdom to moderate behavior and obedience to God appears in Prov. 1:7; 10:8, Eccles. 5:1-7; and Job 28:28, to name only a few examples. Unlike Proverbs, however, Sirach's Woman Wisdom has no corresponding Woman Folly as a rival. Instead, a fool is simply a man (Sir. 19:26-28; 21:19-20), and his opposite also is a man (Sir. 37:22-26).

Before offering another hymn, Ben Sira gives the reader additional practical advice. People should eat moderately; in case that advice is not followed, however, going to a doctor, who is a blessing from God, is a wise course of action (Sir. 37:27—38:15). Mourning, too, should be done in moderation, lest the mourner put themselves in an early grave (Sir. 38:16-23). Regarding occupations, those who work with their hands keep a community thriving, but they are not wise men. That honor belongs to scribes such as Ben Sira (Sir. 38:24—39:11).

Retribution and praise of the orderliness of creation reappear in Sir. 39:12-35. Not only are "all the works of the Lord . . . very good," but even troubles like famine are God's tools for punishing the wicked (Sir. 39:16, 28-31). The world is good and orderly, but it is also difficult, full of hard labor; such labor, however, will be even harder for sinners (Sir. 40:1-11). While the ungodly will neither live long nor enjoy financial blessings, the righteous will exist for all time because of their good deeds and reputation (Sir. 40:12-17; 41:5-14). Their lives, if blessed, will include a good wife, good friends, and food; they will neither beg nor shrink from their inevitable death (Sir. 40:18—41:4). Ben Sira's ideas about retribution resonate with other examples of Wisdom literature and non-Israelite historiography. The first lengthy passage in Proverbs warns that those who plot crimes

> lie in wait—to kill themselves!
>   and set an ambush—for their own lives!
> Such is the end of all who are greedy for gain;
>   it takes away the life of its possessors. (Prov. 1:18-19)

Proverbs concludes with the honors that competent wives and mothers receive as rewards for their work (Prov. 31:28-31). Job and his friends debate the legitimacy and effectiveness of divine retribution for twenty-eight chapters. Ecclesiastes insists on the absurdities and mysteries of life, but mentions divine retribution as well: "For to the one who pleases him God gives wisdom and knowledge and joy; but to the sinner he gives the work of gathering and heaping, only to give to one who pleases God. This also is vanity and a chasing after wind" (Eccles. 2:26). And belief in divine retribution was not limited to the Jews. Herodotus's *Histories*, written centuries before Sirach, argues in favor of the concept. While sometimes delayed or carried out by mortals, the gods' vengeance on the wicked is just and inevitable (Harrison, 101–22).

Ben Sira also warns that certain actions create shame—bad sexual behavior, lying, committing a crime, breaking a promise, bad manners, and gossiping (Sir. 41:15—42:1). In contrast, one should not be ashamed of the torah, proper judgment, sharing one's resources, earning a living, and keeping the household inferiors (women, children, and slaves) under control (Sir. 42:1-8).

And Sir. 42:9-14 distinctly describes daughters as a great source of potential shame. When unmarried, they may get pregnant or become old maids; when married, they may be sexually unfaithful and/or be infertile. The anxious father must "see that there is no lattice in her room, / no spot that overlooks the approaches to the house" as one way to protect his honor (Sir. 42:11).

Sirach's association of females with male dishonor appears both before and after the sage's time. Classical Athenian women must be domesticated through marriage, kept in the house as much as possible, and be sexually faithful at all times (Davis, 13, 36, 44). Written in the same century as Sirach, 2 Macc. 3:19, describing a state of emergency in which people gather outside to pray, notes that "some of the young women who were kept indoors ran together to the gates, and some to the walls, while others peered out of the windows." Ben Sira's warnings about controlling daughters reappear in *b. Sanh.* 100b, centuries later (Greenfield, 167–73). In opposition to the common identification of Eve with the woman in Sir. 25:24, Teresa Ann Ellis uses textual analysis to argue that the woman is Hesiod's Pandora (Ellis, 723–42), responsible for all the evil in the world (Davis, 25). And all women, in Ben Sira's worldview, have the potential to turn bad. Claudia V. Camp concludes, "It is as if, in Ben Sira's drive to master life amid anxiety and arbitrary reversals of fortune, women—especially as sexual beings—epitomize all that is potentially out of control" (1991, 36).

The Text in the Interpretive Tradition

Sirach 36:1-22, titled "A Prayer for God's People" in the NRSV, contains elements that appear in Jewish liturgy and tradition. While the texts that describe the Maccabean revolt are not part of the Jewish canon, the annual festival of Hanukkah commemorates the Jewish people's successful defense of their traditions and defeat of their Greek enemies. Ben Sira's prayer was answered. Purim, described in the book of Esther, is another yearly celebration of Jewish triumph over genocidal enemies.

Ben Sira's arguments about true versus false friends appear in Hindu, Buddhist, and Islamic traditions. The *Mahabharata* states that "a friend capable of listening to beneficial counsels, and also of doing good, is exceedingly rare"; one should therefore pick friends of good character, those "who continue unchanged (in their attachment) like a red blanket made of wool (which does not easily change its colour)" (Ganguli). Although the Third Noble Truth can be interpreted as a call to "detachment, [to] not needing people" (Adiele, 134), the Buddha insists in *Samyutta Nikaya* 45.2 that "admirable friendship, admirable companionship, admirable camaraderie is actually the whole of the holy life" (Bhikkhu 1997b). In another teaching, *Digha Nikaya* 31.15 and 21, the Buddha warns against "four enemies disguised as friends: the taker, the talker, the flatterer, and the reckless companion"; true friends, however, come in four types—"the helper, the friend who endures in good times and bad, the mentor, and the compassionate friend" (Kelly, Sawyer, and Yareham).

The Talmud, like Sirach, links wisdom to righteousness and restraint. One passage states: "A favourite saying of Raba was: The goal of wisdom is repentance and good deeds, so that a man should not study Torah and Mishnah and then despise his father and mother and teacher and his superior in wisdom and rank, as it says, The fear of the Lord is the beginning of wisdom, a good understanding have all that they do thereafter" (*b. Ber.* 17a; see Simon). Another saying reads: "Hence the Sages said: Silence is better for the wise, and how much more so for fools, as it is said, Even a fool, when he holds his peace, is counted wise" (*b. Pesah.* 99a; see *English Babylonian Talmud*). The previous passages, in abbreviated form, frequently pop in a Google search of "Talmud and wisdom," because of their ubiquity on Jewish websites and blogs. But Christians too have appropriated wisdom for various purposes. Elizabeth A. Johnson's classic *She Who Is: The Mystery of*

God in Feminist Theological Discourse links wisdom, or Sophia, to the Holy Spirit. And the revised Saint Mary's College (Notre Dame, IN) general education curriculum is called the Sophia Program because of the word's meaning and significance in a Catholic, all-women's college context.

The Text in Contemporary Discussion

Scholars have recently noted Ben Sira's advice about party behavior. Sirach 32:10 reveals "the two-sided sense of shame. Controlled speech yields proper shame in the sense of modesty" (Camp 1991, 19). Moderate behavior brings praise—and perhaps future party invitations. Using Sirach to interpret Last Supper narratives, J. Bohnen concludes that in John, Jesus identifies Judas as the traitor through proper host etiquette; in Matthew, however, Judas identifies himself through poor guest etiquette (Bohnen, 259–83). Neither Camp nor Bohnen, however, mentions Sir. 31:21.

> If you are overstuffed with food,
> get up to vomit, and you will have relief.

While Ben Sira writes before the development of *vomitoriums* in the Roman Empire (Prose, 25), the idea of bulimic behavior as a response to gluttony already had traction. This ancient practice is not modern bulimia nervosa (see "Bulimia Nervosa Fact Sheet"). But in a culture simultaneously obsessed with eating well and being thin (Miles, 99; Prose, 77–79), Ben Sira's advice raises a red flag. When "over half the females between the ages of eighteen and twenty-five would prefer to be run over by a truck than be fat" (Martin, 1), simply enjoying a meal, even a large one, without guilt or nausea may be the most moderate advice of all (Martin, 281–82, 285).

In a 2011 article, Bradley Gregory argues persuasively for the connection between Ben Sira's description of retribution in chapter 35 and the prayer for Israel in chapter 36. Since justice for the poor and oppressed Jews has been inexplicably delayed, Ben Sira prays that it will now come. Textually, Gregory's thesis holds. But in the modern era, historical events have challenged the theological implications of divine retribution, and no event more than the Holocaust. Job's question—why do the innocent suffer?—has been asked by survivors and all trying to understand what Jews call the horror. For Elie Wiesel, no satisfactory answer exists; as he writes in his classic text *Night*, his experiences in the camps destroy his faith in God. For those who choose to remain theists, divine retribution may seem far too simplistic. The idea that God will punish the guilty may sound like wish fulfillment. In the midst of suffering, God will make things right and orderly, even as the world appears to be out of sorts. And the Bible is full of this idea. Process theology, however, argues that while God is everywhere, human behavior, good and bad, creates consequences for other beings (see processandfaith.org). Human free will led to the abolitionist movement as well as the Holocaust. Choice also undergirds Deuteronomy's description of retribution (Deut. 30:15-20), so whether God can, does, will, or should override human agency remains unclear, both in the Bible and in contemporary theology.

Perhaps the most provocative prayer for modern readers in the book of Sirach is chapter 36. Theological us-versus-them language, common in the Hebrew Bible, deuterocanonical literature, and the New Testament, bore bitter historical fruit. Christian anti-Judaism and forced conversion of American indigenous peoples are two pieces of that fruit. Because the Psalms often lack religiously or culturally inclusive language, contemporary people of faith may have to write their own psalms. The Conservative Jewish "A Prayer for Our Country" (the United States) is one example, and it concludes with what can be described as a prayer from the prophet Micah.

> nation shall not lift up sword against nation,
> neither shall they learn war any more. (Mic. 4:3)

The Bible can be a resource for modern prayer; as with all resources, selectivity may be necessary.

Ben Sira's discussion of daughters assumes the hegemony of marriage and male control of women's sexuality. But in the United States, single women have come into their own as an identity category, not just as daughters waiting to become wives. In the 2012 election, 68 percent of single women voted for President Obama, becoming the group equivalent of a swing state (see Scott). HBO has jumpstarted popular discourse in the last fifteen years. *Sex and the City* portrays four unapologetically sexual, thirtysomething women. No anxious guardian fathers appear; instead, the women seek protection via each other. *Girls* portrays four sexually active, twentysomething women with physically and/or emotionally absent fathers. But single women's empowerment is about more than sex. Because more women earn college degrees and therefore higher-paying jobs, marriage as an economic necessity is less of a cultural reality. And that leaves women free to develop relationships on their own terms, in "a place where single women can live and thrive as themselves" (Bolick). In Ben Sira's time, men should "marry down" (Camp 1991, 29). So, who did wealthy women marry? Today, the answer can be no one, and that answer marks an incredible and ongoing shift in gender relations.

Sirach 42:15—50:29: Songs of Praise

The Text in Its Ancient Context

Sirach's fourth hymn expands the praise of creation, including the sun, moon, stars, and the rainbow. Thunderstorms and wintry weather also receive praise, because they are instruments of the all-knowing God. As a transition to his final hymn, Ben Sira writes,

> We could say more but could never say enough;
> let the final word be: "He is the all." (Sir. 43:27)

The hymn in honor of our ancestors (Sirach 44–50) uses traditions and texts from the Torah and the Prophets. The sage honors great men in Israelite history, including patriarchs, priests, kings, prophets, and leaders, with the priests Aaron and Simon son of Onias receiving the lengthiest sections. The hymn concludes with a prayer for blessings on Israel and a reminder that "if they put them [Ben Sira's teachings] into practice, they will be equal to anything" (Sir. 50:29). Even as Ben Sira resists Hellenistic claims about the source of wisdom in other texts, he uses Hellenistic literary forms (the encomium in Sirach 44–50) to do so (Perdue, 245, 276; Clifford, 125).

The Text in the Interpretive Tradition

Just as Ben Sira honors the ancestors, there are prayers of blessing for the patriarchs and matriarchs during Shabbat services. Sirach 42–43 concludes that to see creation is to see God's glory. No direct textual references to Sirach appear in Paul or *Dei Verbum*, but the focus on creation and praise is a fundamental part of Christian hymnody, from Saint Francis's *Canticle of the Creatures* to Pierpoint's "For the Beauty of the Earth."

The Text in Contemporary Discussion

The most recent scholarship focuses on the final hymn in Sirach 44–50. The hymn's composition displays a numerical order designed to show God's orderliness (Corley 2007), and the ancestors receive praise for their piety and not merely their celebrity (Redmond). Feminist analysis, however, notes the gender(ed) trouble the hymn presents. Wisdom literature personifies Wisdom as feminine, reinforcing a heteronormative ideal to male students and readers—in other words, a male God gives a woman to obedient male followers. Ben Sira's description of wisdom will be no exception (Clifford, 126), but the connection he makes between wisdom and the priestly cult is even more male-centered. No woman appears in his final hymn. Claudia V. Camp argues that the hymn creates a "monument to the male textual body" (2002, 79) through its discussion of male ancestors and the male-dominated temple site. Ideally, Ben Sira desires an all-male space, but "Lady" Wisdom makes that impossible (Camp 2002). Camp warns that "this book [Sirach] is one of the most ideologically oppressive pieces of literature imaginable" (2002, 69). Precisely because Ben Sira is a man of his time, not all of his words, even the praise of God and men, fit comfortably in today's time.

Sirach 51:1-30: The Sage's Last Words

The Text in Its Ancient Context

Ben Sira concludes his work with a prayer and a poem. In the prayer, he thanks God for deliverance from enemies and "many troubles" (Sir. 51:3). Alexander A. Di Lella notes that the prayer, "a classical Hebrew poem" (1986, 407), borrows heavily from the Psalter and can easily be described as a psalm of thanksgiving (1986, 395–407). In the poem, Ben Sira claims that he has sought wisdom his entire life and therefore is capable of teaching those who need her. His students, if they apply themselves, will gain financial and spiritual rewards.

The Text in the Interpretive Tradition

While Sir. 51:1-12 is not in the Psalms, both Jews and Christians regularly echo the text's praise of God for salvation from human enemies and troubles; such praises are part of synagogue liturgies and the Divine Office. The Qur'an makes a similar point; the believer should pray when in danger and "when you are safe again, remember God, for He has taught you what you did not know" (2:239).

The Text in Contemporary Discussion

Bing searches are not definitive, but they indicate that wisdom images are much less gendered than Sirach's. Wisdom does not appear as a woman whom one should desire; instead, it is a pithy one- or two-line statement on a poster. And desire has disappeared—wisdom does not seem to be sought for its own sake. Ben Sira would be disappointed.

Works Cited

Adiele, Faith. 2004. *Meeting Faith: The Forest Journals of a Black Buddhist Nun*. New York: W. W. Norton.

Angel, Andrew. 2007. "From Wild Men to Wise and Wicked Women: An Investigation into Male Heterosexuality in Second Temple Interpretations of the Ladies Wisdom and Folly." In *A Question of Sex? Gender Difference in the Hebrew Bible and Beyond*, edited by Deborah W. Rooke, 145–61. Sheffield: Sheffield Phoenix.

Angier, Natalie. 2012. "The Spirit of Sisterhood Is in the Air and on Air." *New York Times*. April 24, D1–D2.

Bhikkhu, Thanissaro, trans. 1997a. *Anguttara Nikaya: Samajivina Sutta: Living in Tune*. *Access to Insight*. www.accesstoinsight.org/tipitaka/an/an04/an04.055.than.html.

———. 1997b. *Samyutta Nikaya: Upaddha Sutta: Half (of the Holy Life)*. *Access to Insight*. http://www.accesstoinsight.org/tipitaka/sn/sn45/sn45.002.than.html.

———, trans. 2001. *Itivuttaka: The Group of Ones (Iti 1-27)*. *Access to Insight*. http://www.accesstoinsight.org/tipitaka/kn/iti/iti.1.001-027.than.html.

Bohnen, J. 2000. "'Watch How You're Eating': Judas and Jesus and Table Manners: An Intertextual Reading of John 13:26, Matthew 26:23 and Sirach 31:12—32:13." *Scriptura* 74:259–83.

Bolick, Kate. 2011. "All the Single Ladies." November. *The Atlantic*. http://www.theatlantic.com/magazine/archive/2011/11/all-the-single-ladies/308654/.

"Bulimia Nervosa Fact Sheet." 2012. *Office on Women's Health, U.S. Department of Health and Human Services*. www.womenshealth.gov/publications/our-publications/fact-sheet/bulimia-nervosa.html.

Camp, Claudia V. 1991. "Understanding a Patriarchy: Women in Second Century Jerusalem through the Eyes of Ben Sira." In *"Women Like This": New Perspectives on Jewish Women in the Greco Roman World*, edited by Amy-Jill Levine, 1–39. Atlanta: Scholars Press.

———. 2002. "Storied Space, or, Ben Sira 'Tells' a Temple." In *"Imagining" Biblical Worlds: Studies in Spatial, Social and Historical Constructs in Honor of James W. Flanagan*, edited by David M. Gunn and Paula M. McNutt, 64–80. Sheffield: Sheffield Academic.

———. 2005. "Becoming Canon: Women, Texts, and Scribes in Proverbs and Sirach." In *Seeking Out the Wisdom of the Ancients: Essays Offered to Honor Michael V. Fox on the Occasion of His Sixty-Fifth Birthday*, edited by Ronald L. Troxel, Kelvin G. Friebel, and Dennis R. Magary, 371–87. Winona Lake, IN: Eisenbrauns.

Catechism of the Catholic Church. 1995. New York: Doubleday.

Clifford, Richard J. 1998. *The Wisdom Literature*. Nashville: Abingdon.

Corley, Jeremy. 2002. *Ben Sira's Teaching on Friendship*. Providence: Brown University Press.

———. 2003. "Wisdom versus Apocalyptic and Science in Sirach 1, 1-10." In *Wisdom and Apocalypticism in the Dead Sea Scrolls and in the Biblical Tradition*, edited by F. García Martínez, 269–85. Leuven: Leuven University Press.

———. 2007. "A Numerical Structure in Sirach 44:1—50:24." *CBQ* 69, no. 1:43–63.

Crouzet-Pavan, Elisabeth. 1992. "Venice between Jerusalem, Byzantium, and Divine Retribution: The Origins of the Ghetto." Translated by Sharon Neeman. In *Jews, Christians, and Muslims in the Mediterranean World after 1492*, edited by Alisa Meyuhas Ginio, 163–79. London: Cass.

"Culakammavibhanga Sutta." 2000. In *366 Readings from Buddhism*, edited by Robert Van de Weyer, reading 3/19. Cleveland: Pilgrim.

"Curse of the Mummyji." 2013–2014. *The Economist*. December 21–January 3, 59–62.

Davis, Stacy. 1996. "Sex and Violence, Savagery and Madness: Women in Athens and Euripides' *Bacchae*." Senior Honors Project, the University of Tulsa.

Kelly, John, Sue Sawyer, and Victoria Yareham, trans. 2005. *Digha Nikaya: Sigalovada Sutta: The Buddha's Advice to Sigalaka. Access to Insight*. http://www.accesstoinsight.org/tipitaka/dn/dn.31.0.ksw0.html.

Di Lella, Alexander A. 1986. "Sirach 51:1-12: Poetic Structure and Analysis of Ben Sira's Psalm." *CBQ* 48:395–407.

———. 1992. "Wisdom of Ben-Sira." In *ABD* 6:931–45.

———. 1996. "Use and Abuse of the Tongue: Ben Sira 5,9–6,1." In *"Jedes Ding hat seine Zeit" Studien zur israelitischen und altorientalischen Weisheit Diethelm Michel zum 65. Geburtstag*, edited by Anja A. Diesel, Reinhard G. Lehmann, Eckart Otto, and Andreas Wagner, 33–47. Berlin: de Gruyter.

———. 1997. "Fear of the Lord and Belief and Hope in the Lord amid Trials: Sirach 2:1-18." In *Wisdom, You Are My Sister: Studies in Honor of Ronald E. Murphy, O.Carm., on the Occasion of His Eightieth Birthday*, edited by Michael L. Barré, SS, 188–204. Washington, DC: Catholic Biblical Association of America.

Diman, Farhanah. 2011. "'Hell has 3 gates—Lust, Anger, and Greed'—Bhagavad Gita." Blog post, March 22.

"Dogmatic Constitution on Divine Revelation: *Dei Verbum*." 1965. The Vatican. www.vatican.va/archive/hist_councils/ii_vatican_council/documents/vat- ii_const_19651118_dei-verbum_en.html.

Dyson, Michael Eric. 2006. *Pride*. The Seven Deadly Sins. New York: New York Public Library/Oxford University Press.

Ehrlich, Dror. 2011. "Does R. Joseph Albo Succeed in Proving the Dogmatic Necessity of Divine Retribution?" *JSQ* 18:277–89.

Ellis, Teresa Ann. 2011. "Is Eve the 'Woman' in Sirach 25:24?" *CBQ* 73:723–42.

English Babylonian Talmud. n.d. Tractate Pesachim. www.halakhah.com/pdf/moed/Pesachim.pdf.

Estes, Daniel J. 2010. "What Makes the Strange Woman of Proverbs 1–9 Strange?" In *Ethical and Unethical in the Old Testament: God and Humans in Dialogue*, edited by Katharine J. Dell, 151–69. New York: T&T Clark.

Furley, David John. 1998. "Epicurus." In *The Oxford Companion to Classical Civilization*, edited by Simon Hornblower and Antony Spawforth, 261–63. Oxford: Oxford University Press.

Ganguli, Sri Kisari Mohan, trans. n.d. "Santi Parva." In *The Mahabharata*. www.hinduism.co.za/friendsh.htm.

Geertz, Clifford. 1973. *The Interpretation of Cultures*. New York: Basic.

Goff, Matthew. 2010. "Looking for Sapiential Dualism at Qumran." In *Dualism in Qumran*, edited by Géza G. Xeravits, 20–38. New York: T&T Clark.

Greenfield, Jonas C. 1990. "Ben Sira 42.9-10 and Its Talmudic Paraphrase." In *A Tribute to Geza Vermes: Essays on Jewish and Christian Literature and History*, edited by Philip R. Davies and Richard T. White, 167–73. Sheffield: JSOT Press.

Gregory, Bradley C. 2011. "The Relationship between the Poor in Judea and Israel under Foreign Rule: Sirach 35:14-26 among Second Temple Prayers and Hymns." *Journal for the Study of Judaism* 42:311–27.

Gross, Rita M. July 2005. "How American Women Are Changing Buddhism." *Shambhala Sun*. www.shambhalasun.com/index.php?option=com_content&task=view&id=1319.

Hadley, Judith M. 2001. "The Queen of Heaven—Who Is She?" In *A Feminist Companion to Prophets and Daniel*, edited by Athalya Brenner, 30–53. 2nd series. London: Sheffield.

Harrison, Thomas. 1997. "Herodotus and the Certainty of Divine Retribution." In *What Is a God? Studies in the Nature of Greek Divinity*, edited by Alan B. Lloyd, 101–22. London: Duckworth.

Hayward, C. T. R. 1999. "Sirach and Wisdom's Dwelling Place." In *Where Shall Wisdom Be Found? Wisdom in the Bible, the Church and the Contemporary World*, edited by Stephen C. Barton, 31–46. London: T&T Clark.

Huq, Corine. 2012. *Rights and Wrongs: The Story of Women in Islam*. Women Make Movies. DVD.

Koperski, Veronica. 2003. "Sirach and Wisdom: A Plea for Canonicity." In *The Biblical Canons*, edited by J.-M. Auwers and H. J. De Jonge, 255–64. Leuven: Leuven University Press.

Knott, Kim. 2000. *Hinduism: A Very Short Introduction*. Oxford: Oxford University Press.

Laws, Sophie, and Walter T. Wilson. 2006. "James." In *The HarperCollins Study Bible*, edited by Harold W. Attridge, 2052–58. New York: HarperCollins.

Mack, Burton, and Benjamin G. Wright III. 2006. "Sirach." In *The HarperCollins Study Bible*, edited by Harold W. Attridge, 1378–451. New York: HarperCollins.

Malina, Bruce J. 1993. *The New Testament World: Insights from Cultural Anthropology*. Rev. ed. Louisville: Westminster John Knox.

Martin, Courtney E. 2007. *Perfect Girls, Starving Daughters: The Frightening New Normalcy of Hating Your Body*. New York: Free Press.

Miles, Sara. 2007. *Take This Bread: A Radical Conversion*. New York: Ballantine.

Owens, J. Edward. 2005. "'Come, Let Us Be Wise': Qoheleth and Ben Sira on True Wisdom, with an Ear to Pharaoh's Folly." In *Intertextual Studies in Ben Sira and Tobit: Essays in Honor of Alexander A. Di Lella, O.F.M.*, edited by Jeremy Corley and Vincent Skemp, 227–40. Washington, DC: Catholic Biblical Association of America.

Palmer, Edwina. 2007. "A Striking Tale of Weaving Taboos and Divine Retribution: A Reinterpretation of the Asauchiyama Myth in *Harima Fudoki*." *Asian Folklore Studies* 66:223–32.

Perdue, Leo G. 1994. *Wisdom and Creation: The Theology of Wisdom Literature*. Nashville: Abingdon.

"Poor Spirits." 2013. *The Economist*. December 7. http://www.economist.com/news/asia/21591211-loneliness-and-poverty-are-killers-poor-spirits.

Prabhupada, A. C. Bhaktivedanta Swami. 1972. *Bhagavad Gita*. www.asitis.com/16/.

Prockter, Lewis J. 1990. "Torah as a Fence against Apocalyptic Speculation: Ben Sira 3:17-24." In *Proceedings of the Tenth World Congress of Jewish Studies, Jerusalem, August 16–24, 1989: Division A: The Bible and Its World*, 245–52. Jerusalem: World Union of Jewish Studies.

Prose, Francine. 2003. *Gluttony*. The Seven Deadly Sins. New York: New York Public Library/Oxford University Press.

Qur'an, The. 2010. Trans. M. A. S. Abdel Haleem. Oxford: Oxford University Press.

Redmond, Eric D. 2001. "Prelude to the Praise of the Ancestors, Sirach 44:1-15. *HUCA* 72:1–14.

Rogers, Jessie F. 1996. "Wisdom and Creation in Sirach 24." *JNSL* 22, no. 2:141–56.

———. 2004. "'It Overflows Like the Euphrates with Understanding': Another Look at the Relationship between Law and Wisdom in Sirach." In *Of Scribes and Sages: Early Jewish Interpretation and Transmission of Scripture* Vol. 1, *Ancient Versions and Traditions*, edited by Craig A. Evans, 114–21. London: T&T Clark.

Scott, Beth. 2012. "Women and the 2012 Election." AAUW website. www.aauw.org/2012/11/7/women-and-the-2012-election/.

"Silence Is Golden." 1997. *Hinduism Today*. June. www.hinduismtoday.com/modules/smartsection/item.php?itemid=4881.

Simon, Maurice, trans. n.d. *Babylonian Talmud, Tractate Berakoth*. Edited by Isidore Epstein. *Come and Hear*. www.comeandhear.com/berakoth/berakoth_17.html.

Skehan, Patrick W. 1979. "Structures in Poems on Wisdom: Proverbs 8 and Sirach 24." *CBQ* 41:365–79.

Thurman, Robert A. F. 2005. *Anger*. The Seven Deadly Sins. New York: New York Public Library/Oxford University Press.

Travis, Stephen H. 2008. *Christ and the Judgement of God: The Limits of Divine Retribution in New Testament Thought*. Peabody, MA: Hendrickson.

"The Truth Will Set Us Free." 2013. *The Buddha's Advice to Laypeople* weblog entry. http://buddhasadvice.wordpress.com/2013/01/18/the-truth-will-set-us-free/.

Twitter for Dummies cheat sheet. www.dummies.com/how-to/content/twitter-for-dummies-cheat-sheet.html.

Wiesel, Elie. 1988. *The Night Trilogy: Night, Dawn, The Accident*. New York: Hill and Wang.

Wright, Benjamin G. 2009. "Jubilees, Sirach, and Sapiential Tradition." In *Enoch and the Mosaic Torah: The Evidence of Jubilees*, edited by Gabriele Boccaccini and Giovanni Ibba, 116–30. Grand Rapids: Eerdmans.

BARUCH

Karina Martin Hogan

Introduction

The book of Baruch is falsely attributed to Jeremiah's scribe and companion, Baruch son of Neriah. For most of its history, it was believed to be by Baruch, so it followed the book of Jeremiah in most manuscripts of the Septuagint and followed Lamentations (believed to be by Jeremiah) in the Vulgate. In reality, it was compiled centuries after the lifetimes of the historical Jeremiah and Baruch, probably in the mid-second century BCE. It has been called "a mosaic of older biblical passages" (Moore, 259), but it combines biblical traditions in innovative ways. Baruch is recognized as canonical by the Roman Catholic and Orthodox churches; it is classified as among the Apocrypha by Protestants.

The book consists of three originally separate compositions, with an introduction probably added by the compiler. The first half of the book consists of the prose introduction (1:1-14) and a lengthy prose prayer (1:15—3:8) that begins with a confession of sins and ends with a petition for deliverance, parallel to the prayer in Daniel 9. The second half of the book is made up of two poems, probably by different authors. The first (3:9—4:4), which imitates the language of Deuteronomy, Proverbs, and Job, is about the elusiveness of wisdom and ends by identifying wisdom with the Torah of Moses. The final part of the book (4:5—5:9) is a poem that alludes extensively to Isaiah 40–66 and part of it parallels *Ps. Sol.* 11, a noncanonical psalm. The various parts of the book are unified by the theme and setting of the Babylonian exile.

The prose portions of the book were almost certainly composed in Hebrew and were probably translated into Greek by the same person who revised the Septuagint translation of Jeremiah (Tov, 111–33). It is somewhat less certain, but still likely, that the two poems were written in Hebrew; if so, they were probably translated into Greek by a more fluent translator (Burke, 23–26). The other extant ancient versions (Latin, Syriac, Coptic, Ethiopic, Arabic, and Armenian) are derived from the Septuagint (Greek) version. The most likely historical setting for the composition of Baruch, despite its fictive setting in the Babylonian exile, is in the land of Israel, shortly after the Maccabean revolt (167–160 BCE), although scholarly opinions on the date of composition range from c. 300 BCE to after 70 CE (Steck, 285–303).

Baruch 1:1-14: Narrative Introduction

The Text in Its Ancient Context

The text confers authority on its putative author, Baruch, by giving him a lengthy genealogy (1:1; cf. Jer. 32:12). The book is presented both as a speech to the exiles in Babylon, including the exiled king Jeconiah (Jehoiachin), and as a letter to the people left behind in Jerusalem. In the book of Jeremiah, conversely, Baruch and Jeremiah are among those left behind in Jerusalem (though they were later taken to Egypt, according to Jer. 43:1-7), and Jeremiah writes a letter to the exiles in Babylon (Jer. 29:1-23). Baruch's location in Babylon "by the river Sud" (1:4; otherwise unknown) and "in the fifth year" (1:2) recalls the opening of the book of Ezekiel (Ezek. 1:1-2). The fifth year of the exile was 593 BCE, whereas Jerusalem was not actually destroyed until 586. Other anachronisms include the return of the temple vessels to Jerusalem by Baruch, along with a donation from the exiles (1:8-10); according to Ezra 1, this took place at the end of the exile (in 538). Further, Belshazzar is incorrectly identified as the son of Nebuchadnezzar (1:11), probably based on Daniel 5.

The Text in the Interpretive Tradition

Baruch is the protagonist of two later Jewish apocalypses, *2 Baruch* and *3 Baruch,* and of a collection of legends about him and Jeremiah called *4 Baruch* or *Paraleipomena Jeremiou.* In none of these Pseudepigrapha, all preserved by Christians, does Baruch go to Babylon. *Second Baruch* ends with a letter (*2 Bar.* 78–87) that Baruch sent to the exiles in both Babylon and Assyria (the "nine and a half tribes" exiled from the northern kingdom). The tradition that Baruch went to Babylon himself is known from several rabbinic sources, though it is unlikely that they are directly dependent on the book of Baruch. In the Babylonian Talmud, Baruch is considered both a prophet and a priest (*b. Meg.* 14b) and the teacher of Ezra in Babylon (*b. Meg.* 16b). His presence in the exile is also attested in *y. Sanh.* 1:2, *Song Rab.* 5:5, and *S. 'Olam Rab.* 26.

The Text in Contemporary Discussion

The placement of Baruch in the Babylonian exile is significant because the exile of the Jewish people due to their sins is the theme that unifies the diverse parts of the book of Baruch. In contemporary theological discourse, exile can function as a symbol for alienation from the dominant culture. The message of the book is about maintaining Jewish identity and resisting assimilation, which has contemporary resonance. On the other hand, in 1:11, the exiles ask the people in Jerusalem to pray for King Nebuchadnezzar and his son, which suggests adaptation to a life under foreign domination (see also Ezra 6:10; Jer. 29:7). There is a tension throughout the book, as in contemporary Jewish experience, between exile as an existential necessity and a yearning for both literal and metaphorical return to the land of Israel.

Baruch 1:15—3:8: Penitential Prayer

The Text in Its Ancient Context

This long prose prayer combines a communal confession of sins (1:15—2:10), in which God is referred to in the third person, with a petition for mercy and deliverance (2:11—3:8) addressed directly to God. This combination of confession and petition is typical of prayers contained in texts of Second Temple Judaism (Werline), but the closest parallel is the prayer in Daniel 9, which many scholars think is an older prayer incorporated by the author of Daniel 7–12. The confession of sins consists mainly of verbatim parallels with Daniel 9:7-14, but the mention of cannibalism of children in 2:3 is not found in Daniel's prayer. It is threatened in the Torah (2:2; cf. Lev. 26:29; Deut. 28:53) and alluded to elsewhere (2 Kgs. 6:28-29; Jer. 19:9; Lam. 2:20; 4:10; Ezek. 5:10) as the ultimate expression of social disintegration in times of war.

The prayer of petition parallels Dan. 9:15-19, but with many more expansions than are present in the confession of sins. Most of these expansions contain language drawn from Jeremiah; for example, the command to serve the king of Babylon and its accompanying threats (2:21-25) is a pastiche of phrases that are often repeated in Jeremiah. Even the long quotation attributed to Moses (2:29-35) consists mainly of phrases from Jeremiah. The idea that the dead cannot praise God (2:17)—as an argument for saving those who are near death (2:18)—is found in the Psalms (6:5; 30:9; 88:10-12; 115:17) and in Isa. 38:18. The concluding paragraph (3:1-8) summarizes the message of the whole prayer: Israel is in exile because of their sins and those of their ancestors, but they have repented and are imploring God's mercy, aware that their punishment is deserved.

The Text in the Interpretive Tradition

Although this prayer is part of an instructional letter from Baruch to the people living in the ruins of Jerusalem, Baruch also prays on behalf of the people in exile. Baruch does not play the part of intercessor for his people in Jeremiah, but he takes on that prophetic role here, and even more explicitly in the later books attributed to Baruch. In *2 Baruch*, Baruch prays for mercy on his people (48:1-24) and also advises his people, both in Jerusalem and in exile, to repent and pray for mercy (77:2-10; 84:10-11). In *4 Baruch*, both Baruch and Jeremiah are such powerful intercessors that God has to ask them to leave Jerusalem so that he can deliver it to the Chaldeans: their prayers are "like a firm pillar in the middle of it, and like an unbreachable wall encircling it" (1:2). Thus the penitential prayer in Baruch established his reputation as an intercessor and an advocate of repentance.

The Text in Contemporary Discussion

The structure of the penitential prayer in Baruch can be found in penitential prayers in both Judaism and Christianity to this day: a communal acknowledgment of sins is followed by a recollection of God's forgiveness of his people's sins in the past and a petition for God's mercy in the present.

Such prayers can be useful reminders of the social dimension of sin: morality is not purely a matter between an individual and God, but involves taking responsibility for creating a more just society. The prayer in Baruch serves as a warning against self-righteousness and complacency, since Israel's history of continual disobedience (1:19) can be read as paradigmatic of human history. Human societies rarely live up to their ideals, and penitential prayer can be a vehicle for acknowledging collective failures and renewing a commitment to social justice.

Baruch 3:9—4:4: Wisdom Poem

The Text in Its Ancient Context

For this poem in praise of wisdom, the poet draws on several models in biblical Wisdom literature, but especially Job 28, a poem about the elusiveness of wisdom. The poem is connected to the previous prose portions of Baruch in that it addresses Israel in exile (3:10-11), in Deuteronomic language (3:9), explaining their predicament as the result of having "forsaken the fountain of wisdom" (3:12). The bulk of the poem (3:15-28) is devoted to the thesis that no one from other nations, no matter how rich or powerful, has been able to acquire wisdom. In 3:29-30, the poet alludes to Deut. 30:12-13 in order to introduce the association between wisdom and the divine gift of the Torah to Israel. Unlike Job 28, which declares the inaccessibility of wisdom to everyone but God, the wisdom poem of Baruch emphasizes the election of Israel, to whom alone God gave "the whole way of knowledge" (3:36; cf. 3:27). The next verse, "Afterward she appeared on earth and lived with humankind" (3:37), has been viewed by some scholars as a Christian interpolation, but it is consistent with the actions of personified Wisdom in Prov. 8:1-4, 31; Sir. 24:10-12; and Wis. 9:10-11.

The identification of wisdom with "the book of the commandments of God, the law that endures forever" (4:1), recalls Sir. 24:23, but whereas the Wisdom of Ben Sira maintains a more universal understanding of Torah-wisdom (Sir. 24:25-34), Baruch celebrates Israel's exclusive claim to the Torah as its advantage over other nations (Bar. 4:3-4). This difference in outlook may be attributed to the persecution of the Judeans under Antiochus IV Epiphanes, which happened just after Ben Sira wrote his book and probably shortly before the composition of Baruch (see introduction). Since that persecution aimed "to compel the Jews to forsake the laws of their ancestors," according to 2 Macc. 6:1, the Baruch poet may be appealing to ethnic pride in order to motivate his people to return to Torah observance.

The Text in the Interpretive Tradition

This section of Baruch was very important in early Christianity for establishing a relationship between Wisdom and Christ. Baruch's reinterpretation (in 3:29-30) of the famous verses of Deuteronomy about the Torah being "very near to you" (Deut. 30:12-14) as applying to Wisdom made it possible for Paul (in Rom. 10:6-8) to read those same verses as referring to Christ. Therefore, a number of church fathers (including Irenaeus, Clement, Origen, Tertullian, Ambrose, and Hilary) understood 3:37 (3:38 in the Greek), about Wisdom appearing on earth, by analogy with John 1:14, to refer to the incarnation of the preexistent Christ (Tull, 420). While the subject of Bar. 3:38 in the

Greek is apparently Wisdom (feminine), in the Vulgate the subject has become masculine, apparently referring to Christ (or God).

The Text in Contemporary Discussion

It is refreshing from a feminist perspective that this passage presents Wisdom as feminine but not eroticized (in contrast to Proverbs 1–9 and Sirach 51, for example), and that a feminine divine hypostasis could be identified with Christ in early Christianity. Nevertheless, the main message of the poem, that only Israel out of all the nations possesses wisdom, sounds disturbingly ethnocentric to contemporary ears. Clearly, it is possible to identify the Torah as the main source of Israel's wisdom (as Deut. 4:6-8 does) without claiming that Israel has exclusive access to wisdom, since Ben Sira manages to depict the Torah as a source of wisdom for the whole world (24:23-34). The contrast between Ben Sira and Baruch on this point (see "The Text in Its Ancient Context" above) is instructive, because it shows that extreme positions sometimes reflect the need to maintain group identity in the face of persecution or pressure to assimilate.

Baruch 4:5—5:9: Consolation Poem

The Text in Its Ancient Context

The final section of Baruch is a poem of consolation and encouragement, which falls into three parts: An introductory address to Israel (4:5-9a), a discourse spoken by personified Zion (4:9b-29), and a prophetic speech addressed to Jerusalem, again personified (4:30–5:9). The introductory verses serve a similar function to the introductory verses of the wisdom poem (3:9-13): they explain why Israel is in exile, using language drawn from Deuteronomy (in this case, Deuteronomy 32, the Song of Moses). Whereas Deut. 32:16-18, which Bar. 4:7-8 is based on, applies maternal imagery to God, here the maternal role is assigned primarily to Jerusalem/Zion and God is presented as an involved (4:8) but angry father (4:6, 9).

The character of Zion that emerges in her speech (4:9b-29) is complex, combining features of the debased daughter Zion of Lamentations with the comforted and comforting mother Zion of Isaiah 49–55. At first, she addresses the "neighbors of Zion," asking them to "remember the capture of [her] sons and daughters, which the Everlasting brought upon them" (4:10, 14). The speaker's tone is a bit reproachful toward God, like that of Zion in Lamentations 2, but at the same time she acknowledges that it is actually her children (i.e., the inhabitants of Jerusalem) who are to blame for her bereavement (4:12-13). In the second half of her speech (4:17-29), she exhorts her children to "take courage" and "cry to God" (4:21) for deliverance from their enemies. The "neighbors of Zion" are invoked again, this time as proleptic witnesses to the salvation of God's people (4:24). Zion concludes by urging her children to "return with tenfold zeal to seek him" (4:28). Although the language of the poem evokes the Babylonian exile, the message makes sense in the aftermath of the persecution of the inhabitants of Jerusalem by Antiochus IV Epiphanes. In particular, the concern with the perception of Israel by her "neighbors" reflects the perspective of the Jews as a subject people dispersed throughout the Hellenistic empire.

The book of Baruch closes with a prophetic speech of consolation to Jerusalem/Zion (4:30—5:9). Answering Zion's lament about the ruthlessness of her enemies (4:15-16), the prophet (speaking for God) announces the downfall of her unnamed oppressors (5:31-35). This vengeful form of consolation is familiar from the prophets of the Babylonian exile and postexilic periods (e.g., Isaiah 47, Obadiah), but it was equally acceptable in the Maccabean period (e.g., Jth. 16:1-12, 17). The image of Jerusalem seeing her "children . . . gathered from east and west" (4:37; 5:5) is also drawn from exilic prophecy (see Isa. 43:5-6; 60:4), but it is the first of several verbal parallels with *Ps. Sol.* 11 (here, 11:2). The motifs in Bar. 5:1-4 of Jerusalem putting on God's glory as a garment and being given a new name have a parallel in *Ps. Sol.* 11:7-8 (cf. Isa. 52:1-2; 62:2, 12), and the sequence of images in Bar. 5:7-9 resembles *Ps. Sol.* 11:4-6. Scholars disagree about the direction of influence, but there is clearly some relationship between the two poems. At the same time, most of the imagery in both poems is found in Isaiah 40–66.

The Text in the Interpretive Tradition

Although it is not clear that it was directly influenced by Baruch, the apocalypse *2 Baruch*, written in response to the destruction of Jerusalem by the Romans in 70 CE, makes use of the personification of Zion as a mother (3:1-3; 10:16) and includes many of the same motifs as this poem. For example, *2 Bar.* 67–68 contrasts the present boasting of "Babylon" (= Rome) over Zion's defeat with the future glorification of Zion and downfall of their enemies (see *2 Bar.* 82). There is a brief mention of the ingathering of the exiles (78:7). Nevertheless, there is a new emphasis in *2 Baruch* on Zion as an eternal, heavenly city (4:1; 32:4; cf. Gal. 4:26; Heb. 11:16), a belief also found in two other apocalypses written around the same time, *4 Ezra* and Revelation. Those apocalypses are also in continuity with the consolation poem in Baruch in that they personify Jerusalem (as a mother in *4 Ezra* 10:7; as a bride in Rev. 21:2, 9), and they offer consolation for the destruction of the earthly Jerusalem by promising that the heavenly Zion will be revealed on earth in the end times (*4 Ezra* 7:26; 10:54; Rev. 21:3, 10).

The Text in Contemporary Discussion

Like the wisdom poem, the consolation poem has appealing features for feminist readers: the feminine personification of Zion is not sexually degraded or abused, in contrast to some prophetic instances of it (e.g., Ezekiel 16, 23). She takes on some of God's parental role (4:8) and addresses her daughters as well as sons (4:10, 14, 16), frequently using the gender-neutral term for children, *tekna* (Tull, 421). Zion is a strong female figure, combining pathos with exhortation, who commands God's attention on behalf of her "children." God's response acknowledges that she embodies the collective moral agency of her people, when he urges her to "put on the robe of the righteousness that comes from God" (5:2). On the other hand, the consolation poem shares some of the wisdom poem's triumphalism, seeming to relish the suffering of Israel's enemies (4:25, 31-35). At least it allows a middle ground for the "neighbors of Zion," who serve as witnesses to Israel's suffering and redemption (4:14, 24). The poem's underlying Deuteronomic assumption (which it shares with the rest of the book of Baruch) that Israel is to blame for its historical suffering must be rejected in a post-Holocaust world.

Works Cited

Burke, David G. 1982. *The Poetry of Baruch: A Reconstruction and Analysis of the Original Hebrew Text of Baruch 3:9—5:9.* SBLSCS 10. Chico, CA: Scholars Press.

Moore, Carey A. 1977. *Daniel, Esther and Jeremiah: The Additions, A New Translation with Introduction and Commentary.* AB 44. Garden City, NY: Doubleday.

Saldarini, Anthony J. 2001."The Book of Baruch: Introduction, Commentary and Reflections." In *The New Interpreter's Bible.* Vol. 6, *Introduction to Prophetic Literature, Isaiah, Jeremiah, Baruch, Letter of Jeremiah, Lamentations, Ezekiel,* edited by Leander Keck, 929–82. Nashville: Abingdon.

Steck, Odil Hannes. 1993. *Das apocryphe Baruchbuch: Studien zu Rezeption und Konzentration "kanonischer" Überlieferung.* Göttingen: Vandenhoeck & Ruprecht.

Tov, Emmanuel. 1976. *The Septuagint Translation of Jeremiah and Baruch: A Discussion of an Early Revision of the LXX of Jeremiah 29–52 and Bar 1:1—3:8.* HSM 8. Missoula, MT: Scholars Press.

Tull, Patricia K. 2012. "Baruch." In *Women's Bible Commentary, Third Edition,* edited by Carol A. Newsom, Sharon H. Ringe, and Jacqueline E. Lapsley, 418–22. Louisville: Westminster John Knox.

Werline, Rodney A. 1998. *Penitential Prayer in Second Temple Judaism: The Development of a Religious Institution.* SBLEJL 13. Atlanta: Scholars Press.

THE LETTER OF JEREMIAH

Patricia K. Tull

Introduction

The Letter (or Epistle) of Jeremiah (Ep. Jer.) is only extant today in Greek and its dependent translations, but several verbal confusions can best be explained as misreadings of an original Hebrew manuscript (Moore, 323). In the earliest Greek Bibles, it is found as an independent work following the book of Lamentations, but in the Vulgate and subsequent English translations, it was appended as the sixth chapter of Baruch, which, like Lamentations, was secondarily associated with Jeremiah. In the NRSV, where it appears immediately following Baruch and is numbered as chapter 6, it is nevertheless presented as a separate book.

The Letter of Jeremiah repeatedly asserts the absurdity of idol worship. Parodies of idols and idol worship are also found in the deuterocanonical Bel and the Dragon (Daniel 14), Wisd. of Sol. 13:10-19; 15:7-13, and the pseudepigraphic book of *Jubilees* (e.g., 12:2-5; 20:8-9). The parody in the Letter of Jeremiah is clearly influenced by the polemics against idolatry in Jer. 10:1-16 and elsewhere (see Deut. 4:27-28; Pss. 115:3-8; 135:15-18; Isa. 40:18-20; 41:7; 44:9-20; 46:1-7; Hab. 2:18-19). In fact, as will be seen below, it echoes many of their arguments. Its form as a letter written by Jeremiah to Judeans being taken captive to Babylon follows the tradition of Jeremiah 29, in which the prophet writes to those in exile. It is one of several Diaspora writings associated with Jeremiah and Baruch, epistolary writings intended to strengthen Jewish identity and unity (Doering, 44). These include Baruch and several other noncanonical writings now classified as Pseudepigrapha, Targum, and Qumran texts.

The letter consists of an introduction and ten further sections deriding the worth of Babylonian gods, which the writer equates with the human-made idols that represent them. Each of these arguments concludes with a variation on the exhortation in verse 16, "From this it is evident that they are not gods; so do not fear them" (see also vv. 23, 29, 65, and 69) or the rhetorical question in verse

40, "Why then must anyone think that they are gods, or call them gods?" (see also vv. 44, 52, 56, 64). The arguments do not build toward a case. Rather, topics are strung together in a manner described as "catchword and catchthought associations" (Roth, 20). For instance, discussion of priests' dishonest behavior in verse 28 precedes discussion of the ungenerous behavior of their wives (v. 28), which leads to description of their pollution by contact with women during unclean periods (v. 29), which leads to the objection against women serving in the temple at all (v. 30), which leads to the listing of behaviors of the male priests to which the writer objects (vv. 31-33) (Dancy, 199).

The Text in Its Ancient Context

6:1-7: Introductory Words

The Vulgate and NJB number differently from the NRSV. In the Vulgate and NJB, the first verse of the Letter of Jeremiah is Bar. 5:9b, and the letter proper begins on verse 1. Internally, there are other variations in the numbering. This commentary follows the NRSV verses. Unlike the letter Jeremiah sent to captives in Jeremiah 29 instructing them to settle peaceably in Babylon, this one is delivered before the exiles leave Jerusalem, warning them of challenges they will meet in their new land. Whereas Jer. 29:10 warned of an exile of seventy years, Ep. Jer. 6:3 warns of an exile of up to seven generations. Commentators disagree over whether this is meant to reach to the writer's own timeframe, like the "seventy weeks" of years in Dan 9:2, or whether it simply indicates a very long time.

Throughout the book, beginning in verses 4 and 5, the word *theoi* ("gods") is used forty times to describe the figures of "silver and gold and wood." This usage, rather than the more common "idols," emphasizes the writer's equation of the Babylonian gods with the human-made objects representing them. Only in the final verse (see discussion below) does the word *eidola* ("idols") appear at all ("idols" in vv. 44 and 63 of the NRSV is a gloss for "them" or "these things").

6:8-73: Ten Arguments against Idolatry

Idols are helpless to act for themselves (6:8-16). The first of ten sections arguing the uselessness of Babylonian gods emphasizes their incapacity. Active verbs are all associated with craftspeople who produce them and worshipers who clothe and ornament them. Actions associated with the gods are negative: they cannot speak or defend themselves against rust, corrosion, violence, or theft. Even the weapons held by gods heighten their ineffectuality, since they are helpless to use these symbols of power. In verses 10-11, their attendants are accused of stealing from them.

The reductionistic argument being leveled against these gods—that they possess no reality beyond their manufactured representations—first appears here. It is the same argument that was made in Isaiah 40–46: the irrationality of worshiping objects that were made by humans (Isa. 40:19-20; 41:7; 44:11-17; cf. Jer. 10:9), objects that cannot move or act (Isa. 40:20; 44:18).

This section concludes, as subsequent ones will, with a refrain that repeats the point that what Babylonians are worshiping are not gods. Therefore, as the first and last several refrains exhort, they are not to be feared (see Jer. 10:5).

They suffer indignities without defending themselves (6:17-23). This second group of verses intensifies the argument. The gods are not even sound vessels, but are as useless as broken dishes (cf. Jer. 22:28; Hosea 8:8), their eyes filled with dust stirred up by their worshipers. They are locked up like criminals for their own protection. No matter how many lamps are lit for them, they cannot see (cf. Deut. 4:27-28; Pss. 115:3-8; 135:15-18), nor notice the soot blackening their faces. They are subject to destruction by insects and desecration by bats, cats, and birds. A refrain much like that in verse 16 concludes this section.

They are helpless when carried about (6:24-29). The arguments repeat themselves in variation here. Once again, the need to be cleaned is mentioned. They have no sensibilities—this time, no feeling. Though expensive, they cannot even breathe (cf. Ps. 135:17; Jer. 10:14; 51:17; Hab. 2:19). The need to carry them about is repeated (see v. 4 and Isa. 46:2; Jer. 10:5). Like the Philistine god Dagon in 1 Sam. 5:3-4, they fall to the ground and must wait for humans to right them. As in verse 18, where they were compared to prisoners, here also the writer's associations are damning: gifts brought to them resemble those given to the dead. Once again, the corruption of priests—and now their wives as well—is showcased, and the gods are even desecrated by unclean women.

They are unable to help humans in need (6:30-40a). What the gods cannot do dominates this section. All activity is attributed to women who feed them and priests who howl and shout at them. The gods cannot make or depose a king, bestow wealth or punish neglect, rescue from death or even from foes, or do anything a just God would do, such as to heal the disabled or help the helpless.

Prostitutes serve them (6:40b-44). Ironically, these gods, though mute themselves, are invoked to awaken tongues, which of course they cannot do. A ritual practice of cult prostitution inimical to Israelite practice and very similar to one related by Herodotus (*History* 1.199) is described.

They are made and managed by humans (6:45-52). Once again the gods' human-made construction and need for human protection are described.

They cannot help humans (6:53-56). An array of actions Scripture attributes to Israel's God are denied the Babylonian gods: They cannot appoint kings, bring rain, judge, or deliver—in fact, in case of fire, they cannot even save themselves.

Other human-made and natural objects are more valuable (6:57-65). In what may be the letter's most original statement, the claim is made not only that it is better to be a human king, but also that it is better to be a useful household utensil, a protective door, or a wooden pillar: even though standing still, they actually serve some purpose. Furthermore, elements of the heavens—sun, moon, stars, lightning, wind, clouds, and fire—likewise serve useful purposes, but these gods lack power to do anything of use.

They cannot do anything that others can (6:66-69).

It is better not to have idols (6:70-73). "Scarecrow in a cucumber field" here echoes Jer. 10:5. Commentators note significant distinctions in the final verse, the only verse to actually mention *eidola*, "idols," and the only verse to suggest that readers themselves might possess them.

The Text in the Interpretive Tradition

Most of what is known of later interpretation of this letter is the near silence with which it seems to have been received. Second Maccabees 2:2, written close to the end of the second century BCE, may allude to it: "The prophet [Jeremiah], after giving them the law, instructed those who were being deported not to forget the commandments of the Lord, or to be led astray in their thoughts on seeing the gold and silver statues and their adornment." A Greek fragment of verses 43-44 was found in Qumran cave 7. But the letter was neither included in the Jewish Bible nor widely discussed among early Christian writers. It may have influenced the second-century-CE *Apologia* of Aristides of Athens, which defends Christianity to Hadrian. Though brief passages were quoted by Tertullian and Cyprian, only the fourth-century Sicilian rhetorician Firmicus Maternus quoted it extensively (Moore, 324).

The Text in Contemporary Discussion

The Letter of Jeremiah raises the question, important in many religions, of the distinction between an idol and an icon. Iconic worship in the ancient world, both within and around Judea, was more subtle than this description of fetishism suggests. Babylonian inscriptions concerning the rites of idol initiation show goldsmith and carpenter ritually denying having made the statue, and the deity being invited to descend from heaven to indwell it (Jacobsen, 15–32). Such rituals indicate clearly the worshipers' awareness of the distinction between gold and god. To their worshipers, idols were understood to be wood and stone, and yet more as well. Parallels to the Jewish Torah scroll as more than mere parchment and ink, or the Christian Eucharist as more than mere bread and wine, might well be drawn. Every faith is vulnerable to ridicule, since its rituals reflect belief in unseen truths underlying perceived realities. The contemporary challenge in a multifaith world is to employ empathetic curiosity to seek to understand, rather than to denigrate, the faith of others. The depiction of another's belief as a straw figure, easily ridiculed and thus rendered nonthreatening, has in recent history gone hand in hand with arrogant theology, colonial domination, and interreligious violence.

Yet Ancient Judea did not stand in the same relationship to Babylon and subsequent foreign rulers in which contemporary Westerners stand to interfaith neighbors. Their overwhelming religious challenge was not so much getting along in a multicultural world as community survival in a world of other possibilities, possibilities made all the more attractive because of the participation of the powerful. Vivian L. Johnson has sympathetically described arguments similar to those in the Letter of Jeremiah that were made by leaders of her own Pentecostal faith, arguments used, as these were, to "thwart the attraction of other religions by presenting them as idolatrous" (Johnson, 311)—and, by extension, to counter the threat of assimilation to American popular culture by naming as idolatry secular attractions such as clothing, music, dancing, and consumerism.

Though we cannot, it would be instructive to know more about the debate through which the Letter of Jeremiah was excluded from Jewish Scripture, and the precise causes of its lack of attention among earliest Christians living in a Greco-Roman environment in which cultic figures remained important. Access to such a debate might more subtly have nuanced later similar views, such as those of the Reformers against Catholicism and those of Western missionaries encountering indigenous religions.

Works Cited

Dancy, John Christopher. 1972. *The Shorter Books of the Apocrypha: Tobit, Judith, Rest of Esther, Baruch, Letter of Jeremiah, Additions to Daniel and Prayer of Manasseh.* Cambridge: Cambridge University Press.

Doering, Lutz. 2005. "Jeremiah and the 'Diaspora Letters' in Ancient Judaism: Epistolary Communication with the Golah as Medium for Dealing with the Present." In *Reading the Present in the Qumran Library*, edited by Kristin de Troyer and Armin Lange, 43–72. Atlanta: Society of Biblical Literature.

Jacobsen, Thorkild. 1987. "The Graven Image." In *Ancient Israelite Religion: Essays in Honor of Frank Moore Cross*, edited by Patrick D. Miller, Paul D. Hanson, and S. Dean McBride, 15–32. Philadelphia: Fortress Press.

Johnson, Vivian L. 2010. "Letter of Jeremiah." In *The Africana Bible: Reading Israel's Scriptures from Africa and the African Diaspora*, edited by Hugh R. Page Jr., 310–11 Minneapolis: Fortress Press.

Moore, Carey A. 1977. *Daniel, Esther and Jeremiah: The Additions*. AB 44. Garden City, NY: Doubleday.

Roth, Wolfgang. 1975. "'For Life, He Appeals to Death' (Wis 13:18): A Study of Old Testament Idol Parodies." *CBQ* 37:21–47.

Tull, Patricia K. 2012. "The Letter of Jeremiah." In *The Women's Bible Commentary*, edited by Carol A. Newsom, Sharon H. Ringe, and Jacqueline Lapsley, 423–25. 3rd ed. Louisville: Westminster John Knox.

Introduction to All Additions to Daniel

Lawrence M. Wills

The Greek and Latin versions of Daniel (and many versions dependent on them) contained three additions that were not included in the Jewish and Protestant canons of the Bible: the Prayer of Azariah and the Song of the Three Young Men (or Three Jews), Susanna, and Bel and the Dragon. The origins of these writings may be as old as the earliest parts of the Daniel tradition, composed anytime after the sixth century BCE. They may, like the other chapters of Daniel, have been composed in Hebrew or Aramaic, although no such ancient versions have been found. The latest they could have been written is the period of the incorporation of these chapters into the version of the book of Daniel in the Greek Bible, about the first century BCE. The additions were evidently written independently of each other, and some of them may not have originally been associated with the Daniel tradition (the names of Daniel and the three friends having been inserted at key points).

PRAYER OF AZARIAH AND THE SONG OF THE THREE YOUNG MEN

Lawrence M. Wills

Introduction

In Daniel 3, Daniel's three companions are thrown into the fiery furnace and emerge unharmed. The Prayer of Azariah and the Song of the Three Young Men (or Three Jews), inserted between Dan. 3:23 and 3:24, are the prayers uttered by these three. Similar prayers can be found in narrative works of the Bible (1 Samuel 2; 2 Samuel 22; Jonah 2; Judith 16; Additions to Esther 14:11-19). The theme of the Prayer of Azariah and the Song of the Three Young Men is communal confession, in a pattern of threat/prayer/redemption/praise of God, a well-established pattern in Israel from the exodus paradigm to the Deuteronomistic theology of the Historical Books. Yet it is important to take note of the differing themes of these texts before they were brought together (Nickelsburg, 26–27); the Prayer of Azariah and the Song of the Three Young Men differ in tone from each other, and in some ways from the tone of Daniel 1–6 as well.

The situation of Daniel and his friends is often likened to martyrdom, but what we find here is actually a subtly different paradigm. The young men do not die, although they are willing to testify bravely to their loyalty to God. This is rather a wisdom paradigm: the wise and righteous Jew who remains steadfastly loyal to God will be protected and saved; indeed, will somehow escape death (Wisdom of Solomon 2–5). It is important that originally Daniel was not a prophet but a wise courtier, and an intensification of the ideal sage found in the book of Proverbs.

The Text in Its Ancient Context

The form of the Prayer of Azariah (vv. 3-22) owes much to the psalms of national lament (e.g., Psalms 44, 74, 79, 80). In contrast to these, however, Azariah also *blesses* God for *punishing* Israel for its sins (vv. 3–5), reflecting the penitential theology found also in Daniel 9, Ezra 9, Nehemiah 9, and Baruch 1–3. This confession-of-sin motif, though plausible for the postexilic setting of the narrative, is different from the tone of the stories in Daniel 1–6; the latter depict "blameless" protagonists who have no apparent reason to confess their sins.

The contrite hearts of the three Jews will be accepted as a substitute for sacrifice (Horst and Newman, 190). The idea that sacrifices, though important, are yet not as important as devotion to God's moral and legal demands has a strong background among the prophets (Jer. 7:22-23; Hosea 6:6; Mic. 6:8), but here there is a new focus on the "contrite heart and humble spirit." This substitute sacrifice could be understood as the giving of the lives of the three men themselves, a sacrificial gift that they are prepared to offer. This would then link this scene with the martyrdom theme in Daniel 7–12 (Collins, 203). Alternatively, the sacrifice could also be the prayer itself (Horst and Newman, 186). At Qumran, some texts seem to emphasize the function of prayers and songs as a direct worship of God and a local substitute for temple liturgy.

The tone of the Song of the Three Young Men (vv. 28-68) is so different from the Prayer of Azariah that it is often suggested that they circulated separately before being inserted into Daniel 3. While Azariah is a penitential lament, the Song is a two-part communal confession of praise. In addition, in early Christian usage, the two parts of the Song were often divided between verses 34 and 35. The first part of the Song (vv. 29-34) is a royal enthronement hymn: God rules the heavens as a king would rule on earth (cf. Psalms 96–97). This part of the Song addresses God directly, but the second part (vv. 35–68) exhorts all creation to bless God (cf. Psalm 148). There is a downward progression from the highest cosmological powers and angels (vv. 36-41), elements of the atmosphere (vv. 42-51), to the earth and its creatures (vv. 52-59), and those who worship God (vv. 60–68). The second line of each verse was likely an antiphonal communal response (cf. Psalm 136). This section of the Song perhaps betrays an origin somewhat different from the wisdom and visions of the Daniel tradition; the command for the priests to bless God (v. 62) may suggest a temple setting for the song's composition. The servants (v. 63) are not likely prophets, as is sometimes the case, but priests or other orders of temple functionaries.

The Text in the Interpretive Tradition

The quality of the poetry here was once disparaged. In a classic reference work, C. W. Bennett (630) characterizes Azariah and the Three Jews as "mostly secondary and imitative," but this anthological aspect actually renders these texts *more* a model for the common person, more a *liturgical* experience. In the words of more-recent scholars, "The words that echo the Torah should arise spontaneously on the lips of the faithful . . . ; the prayers of the young men should be emulated by those in similar danger. . . . Such long, scripturalised prayers were depicted as performative exemplars" (Horst and Newman, 180).

These texts were reflected in the Jewish texts of 1 Macc. 2:59-60 and 3 Macc. 6:6-7, and in the Christian text of Justin Martyr's *Apology* 1.46. Verses 16-17, which relate the burning of the three as a substitute for sacrifice—their anticipated martyrdom—are perhaps the most important verses theologically. They simultaneously reflect new thinking on the significance of sacrifice apart from the temple, serving later as a metaphor for asceticism as sacrifice, and establishing a paradigm for martyrdom.

Among Christians, Azariah and the Song of the Three Young Men were separated and included as numbers 7 and 8 of the fifteen odes appended to the book of Psalms in some early Christian versions of the Bible. Both parts are sung in the Matins service in the Eastern Orthodox Church. The feast day of the three was the same as Daniel's, December 17, and they are commemorated on the two Sundays before the Nativity of Christ and on Holy Saturday. Like many texts of the Apocrypha, they also remained in use in the Lutheran Church; there the three, with Daniel, are commemorated as prophets on December 17. The fiery furnace is also featured in the Orthodox liturgy on Holy Saturday. Although Azariah and his companions are technically not martyrs because they do not die, and they anticipate that God will deliver them, the scene of the three Jews in the fiery furnace was also taken up in Christian art. Along with Jonah and the whale, it symbolized martyrdom and the hope of salvation. (See esp. the Catacomb of Priscilla in Rome, third–fourth centuries CE.)

The Text in Contemporary Discussion

In contemporary ascetical theology, ancient prayers such as this are often adopted as a way of connecting to a deep tradition of prayer that transcends time and modernity. The fact that the three Jews appear in Christian theology as a type of martyrdom and resurrection only adds to the power of this book for a traditional reading in spirituality and ascetical theology. In addition, in response to present-day discussions of ethnic, racial, and sexual identity, many scholars now note the way some ancient texts shaped ancient Jewish notions of identity, especially prayers, hymns, and narratives such as those found in the Daniel tradition. These texts often respond to ethnic conflict and competition, and reveal a strong sense of how Jews are to understand their values and their place among other peoples.

Works Cited

Bennett, C. W. 1913. "Prayer of Azariah and Song of the Three Children." In *Apocrypha and Pseudepigrapha of the Old Testament in English*, edited by R. H. Charles, 1:625–37. Oxford: Clarendon.

Collins, John J. 1993. *Daniel*. Hermeneia. Minneapolis: Fortress Press.

Horst, Pieter van der, and Judith H. Newman. 2008. *Early Jewish Prayers in Greek*. Berlin and New York: de Gruyter.

Nickelsburg, George W. E. 2005. *Jewish Literature between the Bible and the Mishnah*. 2nd ed. Minneapolis: Fortress Press.

Wills, Lawrence M. 2006. "Ascetic Theology Before Asceticism? Jewish Narratives and the Decentering of the Self." *JAAR* 74, no. 4:902–25.

SUSANNA

Nyasha Junior

Introduction

The book of Susanna involves a married Jewish woman whom two elders attempt to coerce into a sexual encounter. When she refuses, they accuse her of adultery. Due to Daniel's intervention at Susanna's trial, she is acquitted, and the elders are punished. The book of Susanna is included in the Protestant Apocrypha and is considered to be deuterocanonical (literally "second canon") in the Roman Catholic and Orthodox canons. It is one of the three additions to the Greek book of Daniel, including the Prayer of Azariah and the Song of the Three Young Men (or Three Jews), and Bel and the Dragon. The book of Susanna is not found in the Jewish Tanakh. The text of Susanna was probably written during the late Persian or Hellenistic periods. Two ancient Greek texts, the Old Greek and Theodotion, provide the earliest texts of Susanna. For reasons now lost to us, the early Christian church chose to use Theodotion's version of Daniel (with additions) instead of the Old Greek version.

Verses 1-27: Susanna and the Two Elders

The Text in Its Ancient Context

The book of Susanna is set in Babylon and appears to take place during the time of the Babylonian exile (c. sixth century BCE). The key character, Susanna, is a beautiful, God-fearing woman who is married to a wealthy Jewish man named Joakim. The primary conflict in the story takes place when two elders attempt to coerce Susanna into a sexual encounter with them. On a hot day, Susanna goes to bathe in her garden. She instructs her two maids to bring her toiletries, and while they are gone, two elders who serve as judges proposition her. Unless she has sex with them, they will claim that a young man was with her. She cries out with a loud voice and refuses, a significant detail in light of Deut. 22:24, which requires the death penalty for both the man and the woman if an engaged woman who is assaulted does not cry out when assault takes place in the city. The presupposition is that if an assault takes place in the city, someone will hear the woman's cries and come to her aid. A woman who does not cry out during an attack in the city is presumed guilty. When the people in Susanna's house hear the noise and come into the garden, instead of responding by assisting Susanna, they listen to the story offered by the elders (vv. 24-27). Susanna's cry is the last time she speaks in the text. She does not speak in her defense here or during the trial.

The Text in the Interpretive Tradition

The story of Susanna, especially the bath scene, has a rich history in Christian visual interpretation. Representations of the Susanna story appear in catacombs and sarcophagi in early Christian art (Smith). Also, Susanna was a popular figure for painters and sculptors, especially during the Renaissance era (Clanton). The text does not specify that Susanna was in the bath or undressed when the elders confront her, but many artists depict Susanna as nude or in various states of undress, including sixteenth-century Italian painter Tintoretto, seventeenth-century Dutch painter Rembrandt van Rijn, and seventeenth-century Italian painter Artemisia Gentileschi. Yet, unlike the nudes of other artists who tend to eroticize the interaction of Susanna and the elders, Gentileschi's *Susanna and the Elders* (1610) depicts a fearful Susanna in a defensive posture with the two menacing elders leaning over the wall. Mary Garrard argues that this unusual portrayal of Susanna may be related to Gentileschi's personal experience of sexual trauma by her painting teacher Agostino Tassi. Gentileschi's sympathetic treatment need not be self-referential, but it is a distinctive artistic choice in contrast to the work of her contemporaries.

The Text in Contemporary Discussion

Given the attempted sexual encounter in Susanna, scholars often link the book of Susanna with other so-called seduction scenes such as the story of Joseph and Potiphar's wife in which Joseph refuses the demands of Potiphar's wife (Genesis 39) and the David and Bathsheba encounter (2 Samuel 11). Since the elders' proposition involves coercion, Jennifer Glancy questions the linking of Susanna with seduction texts and examines reasons why many interpreters do not regard the incident between Susanna and the elders as an attempted rape.

The book of Susanna does not label the interaction between Susanna and the elders. Nor does the story fit neatly within our contemporary legal definitions or social frameworks. Nevertheless, it illustrates how those in power attempt to take advantage of their position and authority, and such abuses of power remain problematic in our contemporary period. For example, in 1991, at the confirmation hearings for then Supreme Court nominee Clarence Thomas, Thomas's former employee Anita Hill testified at the hearings and alleged that Thomas had engaged in repeated, unwanted sexual advances toward her. Although Thomas denied Hill's claims, the televised hearings focused attention on the issue of sexual harassment in the United States. More recently, numerous abuse-of-power allegations have been made against various high-profile organizations such as the Boy Scouts of America, Pennsylvania State University, and the Roman Catholic Church.

Verses 28-64: Susanna's Trial

The Text in Its Ancient Context

The day after the incident with the elders, Susanna is accused of adultery, tried, and condemned to death (see Lev. 20:10; Deut. 22:22). After being moved by the holy spirit of God, a young man, Daniel, comes forward to demand an examination of the charges against Susanna. According to Deuteronomy, at least two witnesses are necessary to convict someone of a crime (Deut. 19:15-16). Thus the charges against Susanna are allowed to stand because of the testimony of the two elders. Yet Daniel's skilled interrogation of the two men results in Susanna's acquittal. He notes that the Israelites have condemned Susanna without proper investigation (v. 48), which is required according to Mosaic law (Deut. 19:18). By separating the elders and questioning them individually, Daniel proves that the elders have lied and falsely accused Susanna. Since someone found to be a false witness will be punished in the same way as the person who was initially charged (Deut. 19:16-19), the elders are put to death "in accordance with the law of Moses" (v. 62).

The Text in the Interpretive Tradition

In his commentary on Daniel, Hippolytus of Rome, a third-century-CE Christian theologian and martyr, offers an allegorical reading of Susanna. He interprets Susanna as the church and her husband Joakim as Christ. The two elders are identified as two groups that oppose the church, those "of the circumcision" and the gentiles. Hippolytus contrasts Jezebel's adornment with makeup (2 Kgs. 9:30) with Susanna's adornment with faith, chastity, and sanctity. He admonishes believers to imitate Susanna.

The Text in Contemporary Discussion

Susanna is typically regarded as a positive female character by many ancient and contemporary interpreters. Susanna is active and is named and speaks on her own behalf in courageously refusing the two elders. Yet, while Susanna's family praises her (in Theodotion's account), she is not present at the end of the story. She does not save herself. Instead, in the dramatic trial scene and interrogation, Daniel plays the role of hero (Glancy). Recent scholarship has noted important and overlooked issues of gender and ethnicity in interpreting Susanna. For example, Amy-Jill Levine notes the importance of women's bodies in biblical texts and explains how Susanna serves as a metaphor for the Diasporic community. Susanna is vulnerable and shamed but remains faithful. Similarly, the Diasporic community has experienced shame and faces threats to its continued existence.

The book of Susanna illustrates how those in positions of authority can take advantage of the vulnerable. Furthermore, it points out the ways in which even those with privilege can be vulnerable.

Although Susanna is married and enjoys status and wealth, the accusation of two men of advanced age and status places her at risk of being put to death without due process. Unlike Ruth, she is not a poor widow without the protection of the paterfamilias. Yet her husband and family do not speak on her behalf. Her community does not demand that the authorities properly examine the situation or ascertain the facts. The elders, who have taken advantage of other women (v. 57), serve in positions of power.

Among nonprofessional readers, Susanna is probably not as well known as other female biblical characters such as Miriam, Deborah, or Mary since Susanna is one of apocryphal/deuterocanonical books. Although this text is not well known, it offers relevant and poignant questions regarding the complexities of power and privilege.

Works Cited

Clanton, Dan W., Jr. 2006. *The Good, The Bold, and The Beautiful: The Story of Susanna and Its Renaissance Interpretations*. New York: T&T Clark.

Garrard, Mary. 1989. "Susanna." In *Artemisia Gentileschi: The Image of the Female Hero in Italian Baroque Art*, 183–209. Princeton: Princeton University Press.

Glancy, Jennifer A. 1993. "The Accused: Susanna and Her Readers." *JSOT* 58:103–16.

Hippolytus. 1994. "On Daniel." In *ANF* 5:177–94.

Levine, Amy-Jill. 1995. "'Hemmed In on Every Side': Jews and Women in the Book of Susanna." In *Reading from This Place*. Vol. 1, *Social Location and Biblical Interpretation in the United States*, edited by Fernando E. Segovia and Mary Ann Tolbert, 175–90. Minneapolis: Fortress Press.

Smith, Kathryn A. 1993. "Inventing Marital Chastity: The Iconography of Susanna and the Elders in Early Christian Art." *Oxford Art Journal* 16:3–24.

BEL AND THE DRAGON

Lawrence M. Wills

Introduction

Bel and the Dragon appears as chapter 14 of the book of Daniel in the Greek versions of the Bible (and those dependent on them). From the period of the exile on, Jews came to live in foreign lands ruled by powerful kings. Administration was carried out in the king's courts, where wise and well-trained scribes could rise to become powerful courtiers. The new genre of "court legend" appeared, which in narrative form treated the trials and triumphs of wise figures who counseled the king. These texts were exciting and highly entertaining, but they also encapsulated the affirmations of identity of the people who told them. Non-Jewish examples can be found in Herodotus and later Persian literature, and Daniel 1–6 is also composed of court legends, as are Esther and, at a local court level, Susanna. (The story of Joseph in Genesis 37–50 appears to be a forerunner.) Like Daniel 1–6, Bel and the Dragon begins in the reign of a famous monarch, but although Dan. 5:31 and 6:28 introduce a historically inaccurate king, "Darius the Mede," Bel gets the personages right: Astyages was the last king of the Medes, and Cyrus the Persian defeated him in 550 BCE.

The Text in Its Ancient Context

The theme of this particular court legend is the parody of idols, which after the exile became a literary commonplace in a number of different genres in the Hebrew Bible (Pss. 115:4-8; 135:15-18; Isa. 40:18-20; 44:9-20; 46:6-7; Jer. 10:3-9; Hab. 2:18-19; Wisd. of Sol. 13:1—15:17; Epistle of Jeremiah; Nickelsburg, 24–27, 210–11). The message of the idol parodies is that the representations of the foreign gods are simply wood and stone, or in the case of the so-called dragon, a very mortal beast; the foreign peoples are foolish to revere them. The God of Israel, the truly "living God," rules history and is to be contrasted both with the "idols made with hands" and with the large snake. The "pitch, fat, and hair," for instance, that Daniel feeds the snake are not magical or miraculous but are everyday substances that evidently swell up in the serpent's stomach. The Jewish idol-parody narratives, both inside and outside the Bible, present a naturalistic exposé of the folly of idolatry. It was the nature of such polemic to affirm Jewish identity by exaggerating the distinction between the beliefs and practices of Jews and others, although the beliefs and practices were actually much more similar than these satires would indicate. After all, Jews provided food sacrifices for their God as well, and the other peoples held a much more sophisticated view of the representation of the gods than these texts suggest.

There are three parts to this story: the exposure of the priests of Bel (vv. 1-22), the destruction of the dragon (vv. 23-27), and the punishment and vindication of Daniel (vv. 28-42). The first two parts are "trickster tales," in which the brash courtier Daniel demonstrates the inferiority of idol worship. They are told humorously and ironically, even whimsically (Wills 1990, 129–38; Wills 1995, 40–67). In verse 18, for example, the king exclaims about Bel, "In you there is no deceit!" even though we have just learned that the priests of Bel and their families deceive everyone (except Daniel), and in the process eat all of the food laid out for the god. Some of the irony probes deeper theological issues as well. In verse 6, Cyrus applies the lofty theological idea of a "living God" to a god whose impressive deed is to gorge on vast quantities of food; lofty theological ideas are misunderstood on a mundane level (see v. 24). This sort of irony—lofty theological ideas misunderstood on a mundane level—is also explored in the Gospel of John (3:3-4; 4:10-15). The foreign kings are also often humorously depicted as being slow-witted. This conveys the message that the great empires were able to function solely through the efforts of the wise courtiers. Still, it is important to note that Cyrus the Persian, a positive king in Israelite history (Isa. 41:2-3; 45:1), is here sympathetic to Daniel's position; it is the Babylonian courtiers, a competing ethnic group, who persecute Daniel and unrealistically force the king's hand (cf. Dan. 3:8-12; 6:6-9).

The religious and political symbols in this story are crucial to its meaning. Bel is the East Semitic form of the Northwest Semitic Baal, meaning "lord," found also in the Hebrew Bible. In Babylonian mythology, Bel, "lord," almost always refers to Marduk, and is satirized, for instance, in Isa. 46:1. Bel and the Dragon is thus a narrative satire of Bel. Herodotus (*History* 1.183) includes information about a statue of Bel in Babylon eighteen feet tall made of gold, to which Nebuchadnezzar offered provisions of food and drink. Babylonians also believed that Bel/Marduk destroyed a mythological serpent or chaos monster (see Job 7:12; Ps. 74:13-14; Isa. 27:1), and serpents are a recurring motif in ancient Near Eastern mythology. Cyrus of Persia claimed to have been chosen by Bel, the Babylonian god, to liberate the Babylonians from their king (see Isa. 45:1-8).

By the end, Daniel's brashness has landed him in trouble, and the third part shows an adaptation of the trickster motif to the "higher wisdom" of the Daniel tradition: God will protect the wise and righteous worshiper. In legends and folktales, there is also often a "fitting end": the villain is executed by the very means he or she had originally devised for the protagonist (cf. Dan. 3:22, Esth. 7:8-10). It is not plausible that in the polytheistic empires a major deity like Bel would have been treated contemptuously in this way, but one may assume here a degree of poetic license that the audience also recognized. The structure of this court legend—the wise courtier suffers a fall from a position of honor, is persecuted by the non-Jewish courtiers, but is vindicated and reinstated—is similar to the plot structure of Daniel 3 and 6. The den of lions appears as well in both Bel and in Daniel 6, but neither exhibits a clear dependence on the other. Bel and the Dragon was thus probably not written for inclusion in the book of Daniel, but circulated independently, as an alternative telling of the "Daniel in the lions' den" motif.

The Text in the Interpretive Tradition

There are no references to the additions to Daniel among the texts from Qumran or in the first-century Jewish authors Josephus or Philo, and as they were not canonical in the Jewish Scriptures, they are not commented on in rabbinic tradition. Although Bel and the Dragon is similar to Daniel 6—in both, Daniel is thrown into a lions' den—in Bel there is also a temporary intervention of the prophet Habakkuk (vv. 33-39); here the Daniel and Habakkuk traditions come together. As a result, in Christian art, there is a tradition of Habakkuk and Daniel together in the lions' den. Especially famous are a wooden panel in the door of the Basilica of Santa Sabina in Rome (c. 430 CE) and a sculpture by Gian Lorenzo Bernini (1655). While modern viewers of this art may assume that Habakkuk's image comes from the book by that name, it actually derives from Bel and the Dragon.

The Text in Contemporary Discussion

The story of Bel and the Dragon, like the court legends in Daniel 1–6 and Esther, emphasizes the challenge of remaining faithful to God and God's law in a broader world ruled by foreign kings. These ancient stories have postcolonial interest in that they depict a Jewish minority in a world controlled by great empires. In the modern world, where the rulers may be Jewish, Christian, Muslim, of some other faith, or of no faith at all, the image of one who will witness to his or her faith—or even to "freedom" or some other ideal—to the point of death is very strong. But in addition, such stories as this should be recognized for the way they construct and affirm the identity of the audience. The faith to be confessed is laid out, especially in the prayers and hymns, at the same time that the threats of the other peoples are depicted in sharp contrast. All of the narratives of the Daniel tradition, which were likely created separately, speak to the maintenance of identity in a threatening colonial world, and as global issues become more central in theological discourse, the postcolonial reading of Bel and the Dragon and the rest of the Daniel tradition will likely find an increased role as well.

Works Cited

Nickelsburg, George W. E. 2005. *Jewish Literature between the Bible and the Mishnah.* 2nd ed. Minneapolis: Fortress Press.

Wills, Lawrence M. 1990. *The Jew in the Court of the Foreign King: Ancient Jewish Court Legends.* Minneapolis: Fortress Press.

———. 1995. *The Jewish Novel in the Ancient World.* Ithaca, NY: Cornell University Press.

1 MACCABEES

Michael S. Moore

The first book of Maccabees depicts the aftermath of Alexander's fourth-century-BCE advance into Syria-Palestine. The story is told from an ideological perspective dominated by the pragmatic mindset of enfranchised Judean landowners resolutely opposed to the Hellenistic culture of acquisition that is invasively challenging their way of life (Schwartz 1993; Moore 2011, 168–201). Differing from other Jewish groups, these landowners view the world through stained-glass windows colored by outrage and disgust over anything "foreign," "oppressive," or "Greek."

1 Maccabees 1:1-64: Alexander's Aftermath

The Text in Its Ancient Context

The opening paragraph breaks down into two sections, one focused on *external* conflicts (vv. 1-9 and 16-64), the other on *internal* conflicts affecting the Jews trying to eke out a living in Yehud, a satrapy tucked away in the northwestern corner of the Persian Empire (vv. 10-15). Here the Macedonian conqueror Alexander appears not as "the Great," but as a rapacious colonialist hailing from the "land of the Kittim" (Hebrew code word for "northern foreigners"), a "foolish and childish" adolescent (Philo, *Cher.* 63) determined to "strike down" (Gk. *patassō*; see 1 Macc. 1:1) the Persian emperor Darius III and take over his kingdom. Where the Greek version of Daniel uses this verb to depict this West-versus-East conflict as a he-goat forcefully "striking" a helpless ram (*patassō*; see Dan. 8:7), 1 Maccabees uses it to create a grammatical construction designed to express emphasis, albeit translating it here into "clumsy, semitizing Greek" (Schwartz 1989, 380).

After the death of Alexander, his surviving lieutenants go to war with each other like wild dogs fighting over a fresh carcass, violently carving up his empire into several more-governable chunks (*CHJ* 2:45-52), forever revolutionizing Middle Eastern life through a development the writer of

1 Maccabees condescendingly describes as "the multiplication of evils" (1 Macc. 1:9). Other Jews, however, are not nearly so defensive about the Greeks or Greek culture. Capitulating to peer pressure from patrons and colleagues, the Jewish historian Josephus even goes so far as to describe Alexander's invasion as "the leading of God's will" (*Ant.* 2.348), while many of his countrymen fall all over themselves trying to enter with them into all sorts of "covenants" (Gk. *diathēkē*; 1 Macc. 1:11; Moore 2004). The author of 1 Maccabees summarily refers to such covenanters as "sons of lawlessness" (1 Macc. 1:11, another telltale Semitism, like "sons of disobedience" in Eph. 2:2), while others decide to leave Jerusalem and "wait things out" in xenophobic cocoons affixed to the northwestern bank of the Dead Sea (Moore 2011, 189–201). Against this pluralistic backdrop, the Jews in 1 Maccabees pick up weapons and fight, taking on the Greeks and their mercenaries while displaying in the process a form of patriotic nationalism quite unlike anything else within Second Temple Judaism.

The Text in the Interpretive Tradition

Many contemporary critics see in 1 Maccabees a reliable witness to the impact of Alexandrian colonialism (Grabbe 2008b, 5–7), not only in its attention to sociohistorical detail, but also in its focus on the consequences of colonialism generally (Victor, 77–108). One of the more obvious of these consequences has to do with the ways and means by which various Jews imagine the function and purpose of circumcision, a complicated custom within the Middle East generally, but certainly within Judaism specifically (see Livesey). For example, where 1 Maccabees depicts this rite as a mark of allegiance to Hasmonean rule (1:15; a position echoed by Josephus, *Ant.* 12.265), the book of *Jubilees* interprets it as a mark of adherence to the Lord's "eternal ordinance" (*Jub.* 15:25-34). Where 2 Maccabees identifies it as a sign of pious sacrifice (6:10-17), 4 Maccabees champions it as a symbol of pious rationalism's supremacy over irrational emotivism (4:25). Where Josephus identifies circumcision as the most obvious symbol of monotheistic Judaism (*Ant.* 20.38–48), Philo more broadly classifies it as a symbol of divine-human fellowship (*QG* 3.46–52; *Migr.* 86–105). Given the breadth of this diversity, Paul's refusal to ascribe salvific power to the rite of circumcision inevitably challenges the beliefs of his rabbinic colleagues, thereby forcing him (1) to take a stand against what he perceives to be a stubbornly misguided religion driven by forces all-too-content to prioritize the trivial (the *flesh*) over the essential (the *spirit*; Gal. 3:3; Murphy-O'Connor); and (2) to refocus attention on that part of the human anatomy most in need of radical surgery (Rom. 2:29; citing Deut. 10:16).

The Text in Contemporary Discussion

As contemporary critics are making clear, the dynamic governing the process of group identity formation accelerates considerably whenever and wherever colonialism raises its ugly head (Tafjel). Prejudice and persecution continue to affect the lives of many today, particularly those who are perceived, for whatever reason, to be ethnically, linguistically, and/or religiously "odd" (Merskin, 3–105). Persecuted communities thus continue to gravitate, like the Maccabeans of old, to recognizable identity markers able to produce refuge and safety from the dangers of cultural assimilation and religious defilement. For example, as circumcision operated as a primary identity marker among colonialized Jews in the Second Temple period, contemporary Muslims gravitate to mosques requiring women to wear the hijab (headscarf), or to mosques championing the implementation of sharia law over against their more assimilated neighbors who permit the Jeffersonian separation of mosque and state (Jasser, 282). Again, certain sects of modern Judaism distinguish themselves from gentiles (and each other) by whether or not the men trim their sideburns "properly" (Becher, 286). Similarly, Christians gravitate to "contemporary" versus "traditional" worship, or to "welcoming-and-affirming" versus "welcoming-but-not-affirming" churches (Grenz). Each of these cases helps illustrate the kinds of decisions Second Temple Jews had to face with regard to circumcision, Sabbath observance, and other, less conspicuous forms of identity-marking. Regardless of religious *content*, each case illustrates the same anthropological *process* (Roy, 23–148).

1 Maccabees 2:1—9:22: The Maccabean Revolt

The Text in Its Ancient Context

The classic East-versus-West conflict portrayed in 1 Maccabees comes to a violent head when a country priest from the village of Modein (approximately twenty-one kilometers northwest of Jerusalem) finds his anger stretched to the breaking point and publicly assassinates a Greek tax official alongside an unnamed Judean villager who, in clear violation of the Mosaic code, caves in to the "pressure" of worshiping "other gods" (Gk. *katanagkazō*; 1 Macc. 2:15; see Exod. 20:1-6). This assassination sparks a grassroots revolt that the writer of 1 Maccabees associates with the spirit of Phineas, another priest driven by righteous indignation to "protect the law" via public assassination (Num. 25:6-13). The writer, in other words, is saying to his readers, "What Mattathias does is nothing new. He simply follows Phineas's example." The leaders of this grassroots revolt include the priest Mattathias and three of his sons—Judah, Jonathan, and Simon.

Whatever his intentions, however, Mattathias soon capitulates to a leadership model that is just as pagan, violent, and repressive as that practiced by his enemies. This is not the only instance of religious violence associated with Mattathias's name. For example, in lieu of offering Jewish children the *opportunity* of participating in the rite of circumcision, the text clearly states that Mattathias and his disciples zealously *force* it on many of them, going so far as to "strike down" anyone they consider unfit for duty (Gk. *patassō*; 1 Macc. 2:44; this is the same verb used to describe Alexander's "striking" of Darius in 1 Macc. 1:1). After Mattathias's death, then, it comes as no surprise that the son on whom he lays his mantle—Judah—quickly distances himself from such extremism, focusing instead on more immediate pragmatic concerns like military defense strategy (Klawans, 155) and international diplomacy (Mandell). To protect the homeland from further attack, Mattathias even organizes a militia and trains it to fight against the battle-hardened mercenaries perennially hired to keep the Jews "in line" (Bar-Kochva 1989). Lacing his training lectures with biblical stories of past victories, Mattathias makes sure to expose his students to those sections of the Bible he deems most able to inspire them sufficiently to fight for hearth and home (Berthelot). Succinctly put, the narrator of 1 Maccabees portrays Judah ben Mattathias as a "second David," and the account of his days as a guerrilla leader as an updated version of David's days as an "outlaw on the run" (Himmelfarb, 80).

The Text in the Interpretive Tradition

Where 1 Maccabees focuses on Mattathias's decision to "strike down" (again, Gk. *patassō*; see 1 Macc. 1:1; 2:44) the "lawless," tear down their altars, and circumcise their children "by force" (Gk. *en ischui*; 1 Macc. 2:46), Josephus highlights these same three projects (*Ant.* 12.278). Other than Josephus, though, few other texts have much to say about Judah or his activities (with the obvious exception of 2 Maccabees; see below). Preoccupied with other concerns, the Pharisaic rabbis remain conspicuously silent in the documents for which they are most obviously responsible (Targum, Mishnah, Talmud, Tosefta, Midrash), while the Nazarene library preserved in the Greek New Testament refrains from mentioning him at all. Should the Zealots be the most likely successors of the Maccabees (Farmer, 182–83, contra Josephus, *J.W.* 2.117–18), then the silence of this group seems somewhat less surprising. Why? Because zealot fringe groups have a long history of camouflaging their literary footprints (Sivan and Friedman).

The Text in Contemporary Discussion

With a few exceptions, this silence remains in place until the twentieth century—the most violent century in human history. Apart from a few artistic compositions (e.g., Handel's 1746 oratorio *Judas Maccabaeus*), interest in Judah Maccabaeus used to be limited to the annual holiday seder around the candles of Hanukkah. Early in the twentieth century, however, some Jews (later called "Zionists") began to take an interest in Judah's life in their literary attempts to throw off the shackles of Teutonic oppression. In their zeal, they often blur the boundaries separating contemporary discourse from ancient narrative as they enlist others to follow their "impossible dream," the creation of a democratic Jewish state to shelter the survivors of the Holocaust. Lamenting the "contemptible role" Jews are forced to play in the 1930s, one writer expresses his astonishment that the world would allow something as barbaric as a "concentration camp" to imprison and destroy "a people which once had its Maccabees" (Pinsker, 87). Another dares to imagine, in this dark and lonely time, that a "wondrous generation of Jews" will someday "spring into existence," and that good people everywhere will someday support the creation of a new nation where "the Maccabeans will rise again" (Herzl, 102). Looking for ways to substantiate this hope, one enthusiastic student goes to the Psalter, where he imagines that the "sons of Adam" to whom the Lord gives "the earth" (Ps. 115:16) actually refers to "Maccabean warriors" destined to "acquire earthly life for themselves and their nation" (Klausner, 3:29).

Building on these sentiments, several Zionists began pushing hard for the next logical step: the development of a "Maccabean philosophy of military nationalism" into a workable model for transforming Arab Palestine into a functioning Jewish state (Jabotinsky). As is widely known, debate over the efficacy and propriety of such a philosophy continues to polarize the politics of the Middle East, repeatedly igniting what seems to most Westerners to be endless arguments both pro (Kahane) and con (Sprinzak). Perhaps no response is so poignantly eloquent, however, as that voiced by Holocaust survivor and Pulitzer Prize–winning novelist Elie Wiesel, who in his 1960 novel *Dawn* narrates the story of a troubled Holocaust survivor who, after surviving the horrors of the camps, soon finds himself forced to assume the role of a guerrilla fighter, thereby ironically prolonging his exposure to suffering and destruction and death. One of Wiesel's biographers tellingly describes this protagonist as "a twentieth century Maccabee struggling for the liberation of the . . . Jewish spirit" (Downing, 141).

1 Maccabees 9:23—12:53: Marginalizing Hebrew Religion

The Text in Its Ancient Context

When Judah dies, his brother Jonathan inherits a tenuous situation in which a bureaucrat named Bacchides, the handpicked emissary of King Demetrius I (d. 150 BCE), stands on Judea's throat. In spite of this uncomfortable beginning, Jonathan soon turns the tables on Bacchides and the rest of his neighbors. In fact, this strategy becomes so successful, one might well compare his leadership style with that exercised by his ancestor Jacob—another wheeler-dealer able to summon up the savoir faire necessary to outfox his opponents (Genesis 27–35). Where Judah Maccabaeus has to bear the brunt of facing a united enemy, however, Jonathan's success hangs on how well he can manipulate his enemies into turning against one another. Where Judah helps Judea weather wave after wave of foreign attack, Jonathan negotiates with his hostile neighbors in ways designed to humiliate and embarrass them.

Marginalized and diminished by this politicking, the office of high priest loses considerable religious traction (VanderKam, 251–71). Compared to previous high priests, like the "tyrannical" Menelaus (2 Macc. 4:25) and the "ungodly" Alcimus (1 Macc. 7:9), Jonathan's decision to procure the office for himself looks relatively innocuous at first glance. He's worse than some, yet better than others. Yet whatever the social, economic, and political factors responsible for his decisions, the high priesthood significantly loses its "religious mediator" and "spiritual advisor" components, replacing them with those more aligned with the roles of "bureaucratic administrator" and "cultic figurehead" (Rooke, 266–302).

The Text in the Interpretive Tradition

Apart from Josephus's narrative of these events (*Ant.* 13.1–194), few writers have much to say about Jonathan or his contribution to the establishment of what soon becomes, under the leadership of his brother Simon, a full-fledged Hasmonean "state" (Goodblatt, 1–27). Even less can be said about the impact of the high priesthood on Judean religious life. Since Jonathan does not descend from the line of Aaron (Moore 1996), some hypothetically associate his name with the figure of the "wicked priest," the cryptic figure in the Dead Sea Scrolls who is so adamantly condemned by the puritan community of the Essenes (1QpHab 8:8). Whatever the validity of this association (Woude), the fact remains that the integrity of the office of the high priest takes a beating in this time period, a fact underlined by the lopsidedly negative depiction of it generated by the Nazarenes (Metzner).

On trial for his life, for example, Paul laments, "Brothers, up to this day I have lived my life with a clear conscience before God," after which Ananias the high priest orders those standing next to him to punch him in the face. At this Paul angrily responds, "May God strike *you*, you whitewashed wall! How dare you sit there, judging me according to the law, when contrary to the law you order me to be struck?" (Acts 23:1-5).

The Text in Contemporary Discussion

Similar tensions continue to afflict the lives and families of modern religious leaders. Where Jonathan the high priest has to deal with the fallout generated by Hebraic-versus-Hellenistic religious models, postmodern believers have to deal with ministry models in which such specific intangibles that are unique to ministry as building a sense of community, growing within an ecclesiastical communion, and the inclusion of spirituality are covertly ignored, if not overtly ridiculed. As the present text shows, the relationship between religion and popular culture can be paradoxically complex. Religion can have a powerful impact on popular culture, but popular culture can exercise just as much influence on religious leaders and their priorities (Kyle). Whatever the direction of influence, it is becoming increasingly difficult to find "successful" pastors who are appreciated more for their commitment to a "suffering servant" ministry model than to a "televangelist" ministry model (Schultze). The media culture is just too strong for many religious leaders to resist, especially if they want to keep their jobs and support their families (Postman).

Globally, these tensions may be either directly or indirectly responsible for various kinds of puritan extremism (Juergensmeyer). Such analysis may be too simplistic (Berlinerblau), but no one can deny that just as Essenes rise up against Sadducees, so also do Taliban rise up against corrupt Sunni Muslims, Hasidim against Reform Jews, and US Anglicanism against Episcopalians.

1 Maccabees 13:1—16:24: Reestablishing a Nation

The Text in Its Ancient Context

Like the Saul–David–Solomon sequence in Samuel–Kings and the warlord–monarchy–colony sequence within Hebrew history generally, the Judah–Jonathan–Simon sequence follows a recognizable pattern, one sociologists call "routinization" (Weber). Like his brothers, Simon registers a number of military, diplomatic, and cultural successes. But unlike his brothers, he receives for his efforts the largesse of a grateful people who reward him with honors and awards not unlike those conferred on other civic benefactors in the Hellenistic world. Conspicuously posted on bronze tablets, one of these awards proclaims Simon's civic achievements as well as several of his official titles, all bestowed on him by the "great assembly of the priests and the people and the rulers of the nation and the elders of the country" (1 Macc. 14:28). These include the titles of "governor" (*hēgoumenos*; Lucian, *Alex.* 44), "commander" (*stratēgos*, Aristotle, *Ath. Pol.* 4.2), "ethnarch" (*ethnarchos*; Origen, *De princ.* 4.1.3), "high priest" (*archiereus*, Herodotus, *Hist.* 2.37), and "friend of the king" (*philos basileōs*; see Richardson, 208).

The Text in the Interpretive Tradition

To this list of titles, Josephus adds one more, "benefactor" (*euergetēs*, *Ant.* 13.214), one of the most important functionaries in every Greek *polis* (Gardner). Taken together, these titles identify Simon as a force to be reckoned with in the eastern Levant, a reality confirmed by the fact that the next generation of Hasmonean leaders comes through *his* seed, not that of his brothers. Public international recognition of Simon thus signifies a major development in Hasmonean history.

The Text in Contemporary Discussion

Sociologically, religious groups tend to develop according to the following sequence: sects develop into communities, which in turn develop into denominations (Troeltsch, 331–43). Exceptions occur, of course, but generally speaking, the "routinization" pattern holds just as true for Muslim (Brumberg, 98–151) and Jewish communities (Cohen, 6–7, 44–45) as it does for Christian communities (Goldstein). Never does it proceed *in reverso* because the "routinization of charisma" is a one-way street. What this means, practically speaking, is that all religious groups can benefit from understanding where they fit within this "routinization" sequence. Just as Judah is not the right candidate for the position given to his brother Simon, so not every congregation needs a high-powered entrepreneurial pastor to serve the Lord faithfully and effectively (Davis). And just as Jonathan is not the appropriate candidate for the position given to Simon, so not every congregation needs a postmodern radical thinker to fulfill the gospel mandate (Galli). Pastoral search committees, to cite only one group of contemporary constituents, need to understand how "routinization" works if they expect to find the right "fit" for the congregations in which they serve.

Works Cited

Bar-Kochva, Bezalel. 1989. *Judas Maccabaeus: The Jewish Struggle Against the Seleucids.* Cambridge: Cambridge University Press.

Becher, Mordechai. 2005. *Gateway to Judaism: The What, How, and Why of Jewish Life.* Brooklyn, NY: Shaar Press.

Berlinerblau, Jacques. 2012. *How to Be Secular: A Call to Arms for Religious Freedom.* Boston: Houghton Mifflin Harcourt.

Berthelot, Katell. 2005. "The Biblical Conquest of the Promised Land and the Hasmonean Wars According to 1 and 2 Maccabees." In *The Books of the Maccabees: History, Theology, Ideology*, edited by Géza Xeravits and József Zsengellér, 45–60. Leiden: Brill.

Brumberg, Daniel. 2001. *Reinventing Khomeini: The Struggle for Reform in Iran.* Chicago: University of Chicago Press.

Cohen, Michael. 2012. *The Birth of Conservative Judaism: Solomon Schechter's Disciples and the Creation of an American Religious Movement.* New York: Columbia University Press.

Davis, Marshall. 2006. *More Than a Purpose: An Evangelical Response to Rick Warren and the Megachurch Movement.* Enumclaw, WA: WinePress.

Downing, Frederick L. 2008. *Elie Wiesel: A Religious Biography.* Macon, GA: Mercer University Press.

Farmer, William R. 1956. *Maccabees, Zealots, and Josephus.* New York: Columbia University Press.

Galli, Mark. 2011. "What's Up with Hell?" *Christianity Today* 55:63–65.

Gardner, Gregg. 2007. "Jewish Leadership and Hellenistic Civic Benefaction in the Second Century BCE." *JBL* 126:327–43.

Goldstein, Warren S. 2011. "The Dialectics of Religious Conflict: Church–Sect, Denomination and the Culture Wars." *Culture and Religion: An Interdisciplinary Journal* 12:77–99.

Goodblatt, David. 2006. *Elements of Ancient Jewish Nationalism*. Cambridge: Cambridge University Press.

Grabbe, Lester L. 2008a. "The High Priest." In *A History of Judaism and the Jews in the Second Temple Period*. Vol. 2, *The Coming of the Greeks*, 225–29. London: T&T Clark.

———. 2008b. "The Relevance of Post-Colonial Theory." In *A History of Judaism and the Jews in the Second Temple Period*. Vol. 2, *The Coming of the Greeks*, 5–7. London: T&T Clark.

Grenz, Stanley. 1998. *Welcoming but Not Affirming*. Louisville: Westminster John Knox.

Herzl, Theodor. 1904. *A Jewish State*. New York: Maccabaean.

Himmelfarb, Martha. 2008. "'He Was Renowned to the Ends of the Earth' (1 Macc. 3:9): Judaism and Hellenism in 1 Maccabees." In *Jewish Literatures and Cultures*, edited by Anita Norich and Yaron Eliav, 77–98. Providence: Brown Judaic Studies.

Jabotinsky, Vladimir. 1923. "The Iron Wall." In *Israel and the Middle East: Documents and Readings on Society, Politics, and Foreign Relations, pre-1948 to the Present*, edited by Itamar Rabinovich and Jehuda Reinharz, 41–43. Waltham, MA: Brandeis University Press, 2007.

Jasser, M. Zuhdi. 2012. *A Battle for the Soul of Islam: An American Muslim Patriot's Fight to Save His Faith*. New York: Simon & Schuster.

Juergensmeyer, Mark. 2008. *Global Rebellion: Religious Challenges to the Secular State, from Christian Militias to al Qaeda*. Berkeley: University of California Press.

Kahane, Meir. 1972. *Never Again!* New York: Pyramid Books.

Klausner, Joseph. 1952. *Historya shel ha-bayit ha-sheni*. 5 vols. Jerusalem: Achiasaf.

Klawans, Jonathan. 2012. *Josephus and the Theologies of Ancient Judaism*. New York: Oxford University Press.

Kyle, Richard. 2006. *Evangelicalism: An Americanized Christianity*. New Brunswick, NJ: Transaction.

Livesey, Nina E. 2010. *Circumcision as a Malleable Symbol*. Tübingen: Mohr Siebeck.

Mandell, Sara. 1991. "Did the Maccabees Believe That They Had a Valid Treaty with Rome?" *CBQ* 53:202–20.

Merskin, Debra L. 2010: *Media, Minorities, and Meaning: A Critical Introduction*. New York: Peter Lang.

Metzner, Rainer. 2010. *Kaiphas. Der Hohepriester jenes Jahres: Geschichte und Deutung*. Leiden: Brill.

Moore, Michael S. 1996. "Role Preemption in the Israelite Priesthood." *VT* 46:316–29.

———. 2004. "Big Dreams and Broken Promises: Solomon's Treaty with Hiram in Its International Context." *BBR* 14:205–21.

———. 2011. *WealthWatch: A Study of Socioeconomic Conflict in the Bible*. Eugene, OR: Pickwick.

Murphy-O'Connor, Jerome. 1998. *Paul: A Critical Life*. Oxford: Oxford University Press.

Pinsker, Lev S. 1944. *Road to Freedom*. New York: Scopus.

Postman, Neil. 1985: *Amusing Ourselves to Death: Public Discourse in the Age of Show Business*. New York: Viking.

Richardson, Peter. 1996. *Herod: King of the Jews and Friend of the Romans*. Columbia: University of South Carolina Press.

Rooke, Deborah. 2000. *Zadok's Heirs: The Role and Development of the High Priesthood in Ancient Israel*. New York: Oxford University Press.

Roy, Olivier. 2010. *Holy Ignorance: When Religion and Culture Part Ways*. New York: Columbia University Press.

Schultze, Quentin J. 2003. *Televangelism and American Culture: The Business of Popular Religion*. Eugene, OR: Wipf & Stock.

Schwartz, Seth. 1989. "The 'Judaism' of Samaria and Galilee in Josephus's Version of the Letter of Demetrius I to Jonathan (*Antiquities* 13.48-57)." *HTR* 82:377–91.

———. 1993. "A Note on the Social Type and Political Ideology of the Hasmonean Family." *JBL* 112:305–9.

Sivan, Emmanuel, and Menachem Friedman, eds. 1990. *Religious Radicalism and Politics in the Middle East*. Albany: State University of New York Press.

Sprinzak, Ehud. 1999. *Brother against Brother: Violence and Extremism in Israeli Politics*. New York: Free Press.

Tafjel, Henri, ed. 2010. *Social Identity and Intergroup Relations*. Cambridge: Cambridge University Press.

Troeltsch, Ernst. 1992 (1912). *The Social Teaching of the Christian Churches*. Louisville: Westminster John Knox.

VanderKam, James C. 2004. *From Joshua to Caiaphas: High Priests after the Exile*. Minneapolis: Fortress Press.

Victor, Royce M. 2010. "Hellenism and Material Culture in Israel." In *Colonial Education and Class Formation in Early Judaism: A Postcolonial Reading*, 77–108. London: T&T Clark.

Weber, Max. 2009 (1922). *The Theory of Social and Economic Organization*. Edited and translated by Talcott Parsons. New York: Free Press.

Woude, A. S. van der. 1982. "Wicked Priest or Wicked Priests? Reflections on the Identification of the Wicked Priest in the Habakkuk Commentary." *JJS* 33:349–59.

2 MACCABEES

Michael S. Moore

Introduction

The second book of Maccabees covers much the same historical ground as the first, only from a perspective much more intentionally Hellenistic, focused on the life of the guerrilla warrior Judah Maccabaeus and his efforts to save Judea from the colonialist oppressions of Judah's Greek ruler, King Antiochus IV Epiphanes (d. 164 BCE).

2 Maccabees 1:1—2.32: An Invitation to Diaspora Jews

The Text in Its Ancient Context

Two prefatory letters introduce this document, one addressed to Alexandrian Jews from their cousins in Jerusalem, the other to a Jewish scholar named Aristobulus—a tutor of Egyptian king Ptolemy VII—from Judah Maccabaeus and the Jerusalem Council. The purpose of these letters is to invite Egyptian readers up to Jerusalem to celebrate the Festivals of Tabernacles and Hanukkah. Underneath the pleasantries, however, the primary goal of these letters is to encourage Egyptian Jews to come over and participate in a purification ceremony designed to cleanse the Jerusalem temple from years of gentile defilement (1 Macc. 4:41-51), thereby providing for these émigrés the opportunity to either affirm or reaffirm their loyalty to *this* shrine over all others (Frey).

Fleshing out the rationale for these invitations, the author, who describes himself as the "epitomizer" of a much larger five-volume history (Gk. *epitomein*; 2 Macc. 2:23), relates two legends to "prove" to his Diaspora cousins that the sacred fire to be used in this purification ritual is not a "strange fire"; that is, it will not have the same deleterious effect on them as does the "strange fire" in Lev. 10:1 on Aaron's sons Nadab and Abihu. The first legend claims that this fire comes directly from Solomon's temple, having been propitiously saved from extinction by their priestly ancestors before the Babylonian invasion and destruction (2 Kgs. 24:1-17). The second legend then claims that Nehemiah rediscovers this sacred fire in a hidden cistern after it has transformed into a thick, oily liquid (2 Macc. 1:20-21; Lange).

The Text in the Interpretive Tradition

Two socioreligious concerns drive these invitations, each grounded in the ideological world of priestly torah reflection (Knohl, 8–40). First, the Palestinian Jews responsible for issuing the invitations believe that full protection from cultic defilement can only occur at one divinely designated place (Deut. 12:5; Philo, *Spec. Laws* 1.66–70). Second, they believe the Jerusalem temple to be that place. This view is challenged in one of the Dead Sea Scrolls (the *Halakic Letter*, 4Q394–99) and the Greek New Testament (Matt. 12:6; Luke 21:5-6), but reaffirmed and promoted in one of the longest of the Dead Sea scrolls, the *Temple Scroll* (11Q19 45:10). The focus of this ideology tends to blur, however, as Jerusalem's festival celebrations transform the city into an international circus attended by Diaspora Jews eager to replace the rituals of torah with the indigenous ritual traditions of their adopted countries (see John 2:13-21; Acts 2:5-11).

The Text in Contemporary Discussion

Similar concerns influence contemporary religious behavior. First, whether or not postmodern Westerners will admit it, "defilement" continues to be a very real problem, whether for believers or nonbelievers, monotheists or polytheists, religionists or secularists, Christians or Jews (Kristeva, 56–89). Anthropologists have long known that unimpeded defilement tends to breed cultures of despair (Douglas) that are myopically focused on death and denial instead of life and renewal (Mjaaland), even when "suffering and evil, on the one hand, and the indelible memory of hope on the other" combine to expose, however faintly, the possibility of an antidote (Moltmann, 141). Engaging the problem of defilement seriously—that is, through healthy ritual (Ramshaw) instead of rhetorical hypocrisy (Molnar), escapist demagoguery (Aslan), or worse, perverse ideology (Heschel)—can be difficult for many Westerners to imagine, much less recognize or embrace. Even when the spiritual survival of a generation is at stake (Solzhenitsyn), Westerners can delude themselves into thinking that purification from defilement is solely a private, individual affair. From a biblical perspective, however, true purification cannot be imagined apart from active participation in the "fellowship of the Spirit" (2 Cor. 3:17-18; Phil. 2:1-6).

A second concern is that in spite of all their good intentions, the Protestant Reformers are largely responsible for fostering a religious legacy more attuned to the polyphonic melodies of sociopolitical pluralism than the concordial harmonies of sacral unity (Littell, 102–28), thereby invalidating for many the possibility "of a religiously pluralistic, yet Christian, confessional political order" (Kozinski, 113–14). Today most "Protestants" (a quaint holdover term) devote little attention to questions of religious unity (Putnam and Campbell, 1–36) or spiritual development (Foster) because many are far more preoccupied with questions of particularized romance and consumptive politics. Paul's query to the Corinthians has therefore lost none of its sting: "Do you not know that you [plural] are God's temple and that God's Spirit resides (author trans.) in you [plural]?" (1 Cor. 3:16).

2 Maccabees 3:1—7:42: Martyrs and Martyrdom

The Text in Its Ancient Context

According to the summary prayer in 2 Macc. 8:2-4, colonialist oppression affects Judean life in three areas: the *temple*, the *city*, and the *people*. Since ancient temples served both economic and religious functions, it's not surprising to find at the beginning of 2 Maccabees a nasty narrative focused on a vicious socioeconomic conflict dividing temple employees. One of the temple captains—a Benjamite named Simon—openly challenges the methods by which his boss, the high priest Onias III, manages "the administration of the city market" (2 Macc. 3:4), basically accusing him of so much corruption. Delighted to learn of this conflict, some Greek bureaucrats quickly manipulate it to their advantage in pursuit of their primary goal: the confiscation of temple funds (Moore 2011, 173–77).

Greek geographer Pausanias (d. 180 CE) observes that every Hellenistic "city" (*polis*) must have a "municipal office," a "marketplace," a "public fountain," a "theater," and a "school" (*gymnasion*; *Descr.* 10.4.1; see Moore 2013). Thus Jason's attempt to build a *gymnasion* in Jerusalem may represent nothing more than a good-faith attempt to integrate Jewish life into Hellenistic culture (Dequeker). Regardless of his motives, however, the author of 2 Maccabees will have none of it, condemning this development in no uncertain terms, labeling it a primary example of foreign "corruption" (2 Macc. 4:7).

Where the Aramaic book of Daniel condemns Babylonian oppressors for their persecution of innocent Hebrews, 2 Maccabees dramatically focuses attention on one particularly violent Greek oppressor, Antiochus IV Epiphanes, and his penchant for torturing Jewish civilians by the most hideous means imaginable (Shepkaru). The epitomizer gives three examples. In the first example, Antiochus's henchmen parade two Jewish mothers through the streets of Jerusalem before throwing them to their deaths, along with their nursing infants, from the top of the city wall. Their crime? Circumcising their children in accordance with the Mosaic law (Gen. 17:12-14). The second example addresses an occurrence in which Antiochus's men try to force an elderly gentleman named Eleazar to violate torah by eating pork (Lev. 11:7-8), only to hear him refuse via a most eloquent testimonial to the many spiritual advantages of submitting to a "noble death" (2 Macc. 6:24-28). In the third example, seven brothers and their mother perish in one of the most drawn-out, grisly scenes in all the Bible, a depiction as horrifying and revolting as the rape-murder-dissection scene that concludes the book of Judges (Judg. 19:1-30).

The Text in the Interpretive Tradition

Martyr stories like these eventually coalesce into a literary trajectory on which sit the philosophical speeches of 4 Maccabees (deSilva), the Talmud's account of Rabbi Akiba's execution (Boustan, 58–61), the Greek account of Polycarp's execution (McCready), the Latin account of Perpetua's passion (Heffernan), the Arabic account of the earliest Muslim martyrs (Afsaruddin), and the Gospel accounts of the passion (Boff). Whether the Nazarenes "prolong and supersede" an indigenously Jewish martyr tradition (Frend, 31) or draw from a broader Greco-Roman martyr tradition in their understanding of the passion is difficult to determine, but it is less difficult to see how intentionally all these stories focus on a common desire to bear "witness" (Gk. *martyria*) to the power of God in the midst of injustice, even when such witness leads to torture and death (Rouwhorst).

The Text in Contemporary Discussion

For obvious reasons, martyrdom is never something widely embraced by the majority, whether that majority be Jewish (Sprinzak), Christian (Hefley and Hefley), Muslim (Kurzman), or agnostic (Mitchell). Most difficult today is the problem of definition. What, exactly, *is* "martyrdom"? How much truth *actually* adheres to the oft-cited proverb, "One man's terrorist is another man's martyr"? Is martyrdom always "religious" in nature? Does it always possess the element of transcendence, or does each act of "martyrdom" depend on the life circumstances of this or that particular "martyr"? If "a poet immortalizes himself through his poetic art, and a moral teacher through his wise sayings," do martyrs achieve fame by transfusing "invaluable fresh blood" into the groups with which they are most obviously identified (Atkins, 550)? Does martyrdom consist only of self-infliction, or can it also include elements of "collateral damage"? To be specific, does Jesus of Nazareth's voluntary decision to suffer and die on a Roman cross truly compare to Mohamed Atta's voluntary decision to pilot American Airlines flight number 11 into the north tower of the World Trade Center on September 11, 2011? If so, how does one explain why Jesus goes so far out of his way to protect everyone around him from bodily harm, both enemies as well as friends?

2 Maccabees 8:1—15:39: Faith under Pressure

The Text in Its Ancient Context

Responding to the systematic injustices perpetrated by Antiochus and his court, 2 Maccabees claims that God will miraculously intervene to save his people whenever and wherever God sees fit. Three angels miraculously shield the Jerusalem temple from foreign attack (2 Macc. 3:25-28), five angels miraculously protect Judah Maccabaeus from foreign attack (2 Macc. 10:29-31), and an angelic horseman successfully rides with Judah into battle against foreign mercenaries (2 Macc. 11:8). Overt theological commentary sometimes perforates these texts to explain these divine interventions, using statements like "the wrath of the Lord turned to mercy" (2 Macc. 8:5) or "the Lord no longer showed mercy to him" (2 Macc. 9:13). Though never simply relying on the "miracle option," Judah Maccabaeus often asks the deity for help (2 Macc. 8:16-21; 10:25-27; 12:5, 15, 28, 36; 13:10-12; 15:8-11), especially after "seeing" the prophet Jeremiah giving him a "holy sword" (*hagian rhomphaian*; 2 Macc. 15:16) in a "waking vision" (*hypar*; 2 Macc. 15:11; n.b. the same word association in Homer, *Od.* 19.547).

The epitomizer of 2 Maccabees also wants his readers to know that Judah's opponents, like foreigners throughout Hebrew history (Moore 1998), can confess the supremacy of Israel's God and be blessed, especially after being humbled by the terrifying experience of divine intervention. Struck down by such an experience, the taxman Heliodorus immediately vows eternal loyalty to Israel's deity, addressing him as "Lord" and "Savior" while the Jewish high priest benevolently administers his "atonement" (Gk. *hilasmos*; 2 Macc. 3:33; see 1 John 2:2). So available is this blessing, even Antiochus IV Epiphanes experiences attitudinal transformation when the Lord "strikes" him (Gk. *pattassō*; 2 Macc. 9:5) with an "incurable and invisible plague" (cf. the use of *pattassō* in 1 Macc. 1:1; 2:44). Not only does the king's "conversion" make it possible for him to realize and experience the torture he previously inflicts on others, but it also destroys his plan to turn Jerusalem into a "cemetery of Jews" (2 Macc. 9:4), replacing it instead with a positive communiqué declaring the city's inhabitants "equal to the citizens of Athens" (2 Macc. 9:14-15).

The Text in the Interpretive Tradition

Where 2 Maccabees emphasizes the phenomenon of miraculous intervention, 3 and 4 Maccabees stretch this emphasis to the point of preferential reliance (Eve, 244). The Talmud also weighs in with "miracle stories" of its own. For example, when a pious man considers repairing a breach in his fence but refrains from taking action because the job might carry over to the Sabbath, a "miracle occurs" (Heb *nēs na'ăśeh*, lit. "is made") when a caper bush sprouts into existence ex nihilo at the spot of the breach, thereby providing him with enough income to replace that which might otherwise have been lost (*b. Shab.* 150b). Again, when a widower with an infant child suddenly develops the biological capability to nurse it, one rabbi labels this a "miracle" (Heb *nēs*), attributing it to the man's "superiority" (*gĕdōl*). Another rabbi, however, disagrees, attributing it rather to his "inferiority" (*gĕrō'â*). Weighing both opinions, still another rabbi states what eventually becomes the rabbinic *via media*: Miracles can and do "happen" (*mitḥārîš*), but only rarely do they "produce" (*'ăbārû*, lit. "thicken into") any real benefit to their recipients (*b. Shab.* 53b). Discussions like these illustrate how many pre-Enlightenment Jews try to explain their understanding of the natural-versus-supernatural polarity, championing neither while denying neither (Chajes).

Miracle stories in the Greek New Testament operate more from a desire to affirm God's interventional power—as in 2 Maccabees—than to explain the natural-supernatural polarity, as in Talmud (Kahl). Where the Fourth Gospel describes Christ's miracles via the Greek word *sēmeia* ("signs"; John 2:11; 4:54; 20:30), the Synoptic Gospels avoid this term, preferring instead the Greek word *dynameis*, or "deeds of power" (Matt. 11:20-23; Mark 6:2; Luke 10:13). Why? Because the Nazarenes believe that Jesus of Nazareth—not this or that angelic figure—is the final, primary conduit of divine power on earth (Schenck).

The Text in Contemporary Discussion

Western children of the European Enlightenment tend to bristle at this kind of discussion because many of us suffer deep resistance to the possibility that anything (or Anyone) can be perceived by something other than the five senses (Craig), much less consider the possibility that a supernatural, personal, and loving God can and will visit his creation to protect, rescue, and/or salvage his loved ones from the scourge of defilement. Yet if the force responsible for what physicists call "the big bang" is, in fact, a divine Creator, does it make any sense to imagine this person "running up and down the corridors of the hotel he created like a bewildered bellhop trying to find the right key" (Rogers, 16)? The contents of 2 Macc. 8:1—15:39 give food for thought that might be able to address such skepticism.

Works Cited

Afsaruddin, Asma. 2006. "Competing Perspectives on *Jihad* and 'Martyrdom' in Early Islamic Sources." In *Witnesses to Faith? Martyrdom in Christianity and Islam*, edited by Brian Wicker, 15–32. Burlington, VT: Ashgate.

Aslan, Reza. 2010. *Beyond Fundamentalism: Confronting Religious Extremism in the Age of Globalization*. New York: Random House.

Atkins, Stephen E., ed. 2011. *The 9/11 Encyclopedia*. New York: ABC-Clio.

Boff, Leonardo. 2011. *Passion of Christ, Passion of the World*. Maryknoll, NY: Orbis.

Boustan, Ra'anan S. 2005. *From Martyr to Mystic: Rabbinic Martyrology and the Making of Merkavah Mysticism*. Tübingen: Mohr Siebeck.

Chajes, Jeffrey H. 2007. "*Entzauberung* and Jewish Modernity: On 'Magic,' Enlightenment, and Faith." In *Early Modern Culture and Haskalah: Reconsidering the Borderlines of Modern Jewish History*, edited by David B. Ruderman and Shmuel Feiner, 191–200. Göttingen: Vandenhoeck & Ruprecht.

Craig, William Lane. 2000. "Naturalism and Cosmology." In *Naturalism: A Critical Analysis*, edited by William Lane Craig and J. P. Moreland, 215–52. London: Routledge.

Dequeker, L. 1993. "Jason's Gymnasium in Jerusalem (2 Macc 4:7–17): The Failure of a Cultural Experiment." *Bijdragen* 54:371–92.

DeSilva, David. 1998. *4 Maccabees*. Sheffield: Sheffield Academic Press.

Douglas, Mary. 1966. *Purity and Danger: An Analysis of Concepts of Pollution and Taboo*. London: Routledge.

Eve, Eric. 2002. *The Jewish Context of Jesus' Miracles*. Sheffield: Sheffield Academic Press.

Foster, Richard. 1998. *Celebration of Discipline*. San Francisco: HarperSanFrancisco.

Frend, W. H. C. 1965. *Martyrdom and Persecution in the Early Church*. London: Blackwell.

Frey, Jorg. 1999. "Temple and Rival Temple: The Cases of Elephantine, Mt. Gerizim, and Leontopolis." In *Gemeinde ohne Tempel*, edited by Beate Ego et al., 171–204. Tübingen: Mohr Siebeck.

Heffernan, Thomas J. 2012. *The Passion of Perpetua and Felicity*. New York: Oxford University Press.

Hefley, James C., and Marti Hefley. 2004. *By Their Blood: Christian Martyrs from the Twentieth Century and Beyond*. Grand Rapids: Baker Books.

Heschel, Susannah. 2008. *The Aryan Jesus: Christian Theologians and the Bible in Nazi Germany*. Princeton: Princeton University Press.

Kahl, Werner. 1994. *New Testament Miracle-Stories in Their Religious-Historical Setting*. Göttingen: Vandenhoeck & Ruprecht.

Knohl, Israel. 2007. *The Sanctuary of Silence: The Priestly Torah and the Holiness School*. Winona Lake, IN: Eisenbrauns.

Kozinski, Thaddeus J. 2012. *The Political Problem of Religious Pluralism, and Why Philosophers Can't Solve It*. Lanham, MD: Lexington.

Kristeva, Julia. 1982. *Powers of Horror: An Essay on Abjection*. New York: Columbia University Press.

Kurzman, Charles. 2011. *The Missing Martyrs: Why There Are So Few Muslim Terrorists*. New York: Oxford University Press.

Lange, Armin. 2007. "2 Maccabees 2:13-15: Library or Canon." In *The Books of the Maccabees: History, Theology, Ideology*, edited by Géza Xeravits and József Zsengellér, 155–67. Leiden: Brill.

Littell, Franklin H. 2007. *From State Church to Pluralism: A Protestant Interpretation of Religion in America*. New Brunswick, NJ: Aldine Transaction.

McCready, Wayne O. 2005. "Martyrdom: In Accordance with the Gospel." In *Religious Rivalries and the Struggle for Success in Sardis and Smyrna*, ed. Richard S. Ascough, 141–55. Waterloo, ON: Wilfrid Laurier University Press.

Mitchell, Jolyon P. 2012. *Martyrdom: A Very Short Introduction*. New York: Oxford University Press.

Mjaaland, Marius Timmann. 2011. "Suicide and Despair." In *Kierkegaard and Death*, edited by Patrick Stokes and Adam Buben, 81–100. Bloomington: Indiana University Press.

Molnar, Thomas Steven. 1987. *The Pagan Temptation*. Grand Rapids: Eerdmans.

Moltmann, Jürgen. 1968. "Resurrection as Hope." *HTR* 61:129–47.

Moore, Michael S. 1998. "Ruth the Moabite and the Blessing of Foreigners." *CBQ* 60:203-17.

———. 2011. *WealthWatch: A Study of Socioeconomic Conflict in the Bible*. Eugene, OR: Pickwick.

———. 2013. "Civic and Voluntary Associations in the Greco-Roman World." In *The World of the New Testament: Cultural, Social, and Historical Contexts*, edited by Joel B. Green and Lee Martin McDonald, 149–55. Grand Rapids: Baker Academic.

Putnam, Robert, and David Campbell, 2010. *American Grace: How Religion Divides and Unites Us*. New York: Simon & Schuster.

Ramshaw, Elaine. 1987. *Ritual and Pastoral Care*. Philadelphia: Fortress Press.

Rogers, Adrian. 1997. *Believe in Miracles, But Trust in Jesus*. Wheaton, IL: Crossway.

Rouwhorst, Gerard. 2005. "The Emergence of the Cult of the Maccabean Martyrs in Late Antique Christianity." In *More Than a Memory: The Discourse of Martyrdom and the Construction of Christian Identity in the History of Christianity*, edited by Johan Leemans, 81–96. Leuven: Peeters.

Schenck, Kenneth L. 2009. "The Worship of Jesus among Early Christians: The Evidence of Hebrews." In *Jesus and Paul: Global Perspectives in Honor of James D. G. Dunn for His 70th Birthday*, edited by B. J. Oropeza, C. K. Robertson, and Douglas C. Mohrmann, 114–26. London: T&T Clark.

Shepkaru, Shmuel. 2006. *Jewish Martyrs in the Pagan and Christian Worlds*. Cambridge: Cambridge University Press.

Solzhenitsyn, Alexander. 1976. *Warning to the West*. New York: Farrar, Straus & Giroux.

Sprinzak, Ehud. 2000. "Israel's Radical Right and the Countdown to the Rabin Assassination." In *The Assassination of Yitzhak Rabin*, edited by Yoram Peri, 96–128. Palo Alto: Stanford University Press.

1 ESDRAS

Daniel L. Smith-Christopher

Introduction

As with many characters of the Hebrew Bible (e.g., Jeremiah, Baruch, Esther, Daniel), Ezra has been the subject of continued interest in late Jewish works, only some of which (e.g., 1 Esdras) appear in editions of the Septuagint (Bird, 34). Sara Japhet points out that Josephus makes use of 1 Esdras in combination with Ezra-Nehemiah in his biblical "summaries," despite the work being absent from significant discussion in Jewish sources. First Esdras was used more widely in early Christian traditions, but as Michael Bird, Japhet, and Jacob Myers all note, not without significant criticism.

The most important initial observation about 1 Esdras is the relation of the work to 2 Chronicles, Ezra, and Nehemiah. Thus, any commentary, however brief, must begin with some form of the following chart:

1 Esd. 1:1-22	2 Chron. 35:1-19
1 Esd. 1:23-24	*unique* to 1 Esdras (summary of Josiah's reign)
1 Esd. 1:25-33	2 Chron. 35:20-27
1 Esd. 1:34-58	2 Chron. 36:1-21
1 Esd. 2:1-15	Ezra 1:1-11
1 Esd. 2:16-30	Ezra 4:6-24 (out of the sequence in MT Ezra)
1 Esd. 3:1—5:6	*unique* to 1 Esdras (the three youths/guards)
1 Esd. 5:7-46	Ezra 2:1-70
1 Esd. 5:47-66	Ezra 3:1-13
1 Esd. 5:67-73	Ezra 4:1-5
1 Esd. 6:1-22	Ezra 5:1-17
1 Esd. 6:23-34	Ezra 6:1-12

1 Esd. 7:1-15	Ezra 6:13-22
1 Esd. 8:1-27	Ezra 7:1-28
1 Esd. 8:28-67	Ezra 8:1-36
1 Esd. 8:68-90	Ezra 9:1-15
1 Esd. 8:91-96	Ezra 10:1-5
1 Esd. 9:1-36	Ezra 10: 6-44
1 Esd. 9:37-55	Neh. 7:73—8:12

While Bird (3–16, 22–26) has recently reviewed text-critical issues, it is generally agreed that the three most significant literary issues raised by 1 Esdras (Japhet, 752) are as follows:

1. The story of the three guards (3:1—5:6). Zipora Talshir (1999, 6) is surely correct to suggest that this long story must be central to 1 Esdras as a unique work, as it represents the single most important difference with the canonical versions.

2. The editorial comment in 1:23-24 with regard to the reign of Josiah leads to the question: Is Ezra to be compared with Josiah—thus explaining why we begin with Josiah and end with Ezra as an inclusio (Bird, 18)?

3. The rearrangement of the material that appears in the MT at Ezra 4:6-24 so that it comes immediately following the material found in the MT at Ezra 1 apparently magnifies the problems facing the returning community, and shifts the list of returnees under Jeshua and Zerubbabel to later in the book of 1 Esdras.

1 Esdras 1:1-58: Passover and Temple Restoration

The Text in Its Ancient Context

The opening narrative of the book, paralleled in 2 Chron. 35:1-19, focuses on the Passover celebration under Josiah. The emphasis is on large-scale preparations, the meticulous care given to the ritually appropriate steps, and the beneficence of the Persian king in providing meat to the people from royal herds (2,600 sheep, 300 calves, etc.). Central to the opening lines, however, is the restoration of the ark in the temple. The Passover, in other words, is the occasion for the renewal of the temple itself and its role among the people. Josiah is explicitly compared to David and Solomon, but Josiah's celebration exceeded all the kings of Israel (1:20-21). Nevertheless, the theme from Jeremiah that the exile was God's response to royal and priestly corruption is strongly maintained. Blame is shared among "leaders and priests" (1:49).

The Text in the Interpretive Tradition

Talshir (1999) concludes that the work does indeed begin with this note of praise for Josiah (against those who propose a "lost" beginning). Myers (28–29) suggests that the emphasis on Josiah's righteousness draws a stronger contrast with the sins of the people faced by Ezra at a later age. Bird, however, suggests that beginning with Josiah magnifies Ezra's accomplishments at the end—what Josiah could not fully accomplish, Ezra does (Bird, 18)! It is interesting that 1:50 features a reference to a single "messenger." Was this understood to be a particular reference to Jeremiah, and thus a verification of Jeremiah's promise of seventy years (Jeremiah 29)?

The Text in Contemporary Discussion

Like many discussions of the monarchy, the sheer power and wealth of the central administration ought not be overlooked. The benevolence of Josiah raises ambiguous issues with regard to the privileges of the central power. On the one hand, the text attempts to praise generosity; on the other hand, it highlights the rather shocking excess of the king's holdings. The wealthy always attempt to divert attention from their greed by emphasizing their generosity and philanthropy. The praise of the generosity of the wealthy is the public face of bitter oppression and misappropriation of resources. A healthy skepticism is in order when reading any monarchy, especially in ancient Israelite experience. While Bird suggests that there is a "distinct absence of Judean militancy" in the attitude toward foreign rule in 1 Esdras (Bird, 19), it is also true that verses 34-58 contain no recognition of the *validity* of foreign strength or sovereignty (cf. John 19:11).

1 Esdras 2:1-30: Cyrus and the Restoration

The Text in Its Ancient Context

First Esdras, like Ezra, summarizes the story of Cyrus's giving the Israelites permission to rebuild their temple. In the text, Cyrus himself piously says he has been instructed by the God of the Israelites to do so. The captured temple vessels are returned, money is raised, and a delegation is headed by a certain "Sheshbazzar." However, opposition back in the land is strong. Jerusalem is called a "rebellious city," and the local Persian officials seem to express concern that the city itself is being revived, and not merely the temple.

The Text in the Interpretive Tradition

Talshir (2001, 105) notes that the entire Persian period is summarized quickly, emphasizing the direct fulfillment of Jeremiah's prophecy. Furthermore, 1 Esdras presents a linear view of history rather than the somewhat jumbled perspectives of Ezra 1–4. It is widely noted (e.g., Myers, 37) that the biblical image of Cyrus, emphasizing his piety and kindness toward the Judeans, is consistently maintained in the Bible, and is especially contrasted with more negative treatment by later Persian rulers. The discussion about the later ruler Artaxerxes, therefore, is reminiscent of a pharaoh "who did not know Joseph" (Exod. 1:8). Consistent with this, 1 Esdras uses the work stoppage to create a dramatic pause in the narrative to introduce the tale of Zerubbabel.

The Text in Contemporary Discussion

While it is often suggested that the reports of Cyrus are intended to show God's concern and care, a perspective informed by the experience of colonized and/or minority peoples may suggest the reality of constant Imperial red tape, the need to appeal to authorities for everything, and the threats of constant harassment. Here, as in the Daniel stories, opposition to the Hebrew community then creates occasions for a test of Judean character and faith.

1 Esdras 3:1—4:63: Speaking Truth

The Text in Its Ancient Context

The contest among members of Darius's court, found only in this text, is "the literary summit of the document" (Bird, 142). Darius is introduced as the most powerful man on the earth, with an emphasis on all the people under his rule. Whatever else the story is intended to communicate, it cannot be understood apart from this carefully constructed description of the worldly power of the emperor! The youths write their answer to the question: What is strongest? The answers of the three are (1) wine, (2) the king, and (3) women, but ultimately truth! The three youths appear to seek rewards; they wish to share in the power of Darius and the opulence of his rule and wealth. This is an important element for later in the story. Zerubbabel does not accept the offer of power or wealth, but instead asks for the restoration of Jerusalem and the freedom of the people from harassment and interference of local officials. The story contrasts the God of truth and wisdom to the power of the Persian officials. Cleverness, faithfulness, and wisdom (e.g., truth) prevail over brute strength (see Prov. 11:14; 24:6).

The Text in the Interpretive Tradition

The story clearly intends to magnify the role of Zerubbabel, who secures more from Darius than either Ezra or Nehemiah in the MT (Talshir 1999, 47). There is no doubt who is responsible for Darius's change of heart; it is the blessed brilliance of Zerubbabel in facing down, Daniel-like, the challenge of a ruler. Indeed, Talshir proposes, finally, that Zerubbabel's persona is constructed from "pieces" of the Nehemiah tradition and is clearly intended to replace him in the story of the Persian-period restoration (1999, 56–57). It seems hardly a coincidence that the same ruler who favored Daniel (Daniel 6) is here shown as favoring Zerubbabel. However, was this story written for its present position in the book of 1 Esdras? It has a clear beginning and ending, and no connections with the material surrounding it, and is an entirely different kind of literature from the rest of 1 Esdras (Talshir 1999, 58–59). Bird emphasizes "Hellenistic characteristics" (143–44), and suggests that the final element, "Truth," was added to "religionize a philosophical discussion" (145). Finally, Stacy Davis strongly challenges the values of the story as once again seeing women as "powerful only insofar as they can manipulate men" (201) and furthermore notes feminist critique of this story beginning already with Mary Wollstonecraft in 1792 (Davis, 201; cf. Schuller, 236).

The Text in Contemporary Discussion

"Strength" is understood as closely related to the emperor's power of privilege. The argument for wine centers on how wine makes one forget their lowly state and ignore their proper place! A person might "forget kings and satraps," and "talk in talents" (comparing money to words). The second argues for the importance of the king himself, but the argument is entirely centered on the violent power of the ruler to make war. Zerubbabel's answer is the height of irony. Because men do all manner of things to please women, they are considered even more powerful than the king himself. But then, out of the blue, Zerubbabel shocks the reader with a direct reference to the sexual enslavement of the emperor to his concubine—who is even named! Zerubbabel's courageous challenge to the king is reminiscent of Nathan's challenge to David, and even more, to Daniel's laughter—whose name means *laughter*—at Nebuchadnezzar for believing that an idol consumed food (the story of Bel). In short, Zerubbabel is mocking the ruler of the world. Zerubbabel then rounds on the king with a fourth power—the God of Truth! That God and truth are seen together is clear from the close association between the creator and truth in verses 33-41. Bird certainly understates when he wonders if this tale reflects "Deuteronomistic misgivings about Kings" (162).

1 Esdras 5:1-46: The List of Returnees

The Text in Its Ancient Context

This is another copy of the famous "Golah List" ("List of Exiles") that also appears in both Ezra 2 and Nehemiah 7. Leaders are named first, followed by very large "families" named for either an ancestor or a village/town name. This is followed by priests, Levites, and temple servants, and then an interesting series of references to certain groups that could not establish their lineage, suggesting that there was some controversy surrounding who is legitimately to be included in this roll.

The Text in the Interpretive Tradition

There has been considerable controversy about what this list actually intends to portray—a census of the "true Israel" living in Judah at a particular time? A utopian list of the number of people who returned with Zerubbabel in a kind of "exodus" entourage heading back to the land? The large numbers in the first section (families and villagers) furthermore raise questions about what is actually being enumerated here since the numbers seem too large for simple "families." Klein (1643) suggests that the list may have been intended to show that the community is composed almost entirely of returnees, which he notes does "not conform to historical fact."

The Text in Contemporary Discussion

Official lists of population always serve an authoritarian goal (cf. 2 Samuel 24) because lists are intended to exclude as much as include—as the controversies around some of the members clearly state. Census information is power, and control. Often the powerful want lists to control financial assistance provided by the state (e.g., carefully excluding people from tribal/indigenous membership [even "authenticity"] in countries that conquered an indigenous people for their land, sorting "legal" from "illegal," and thus "legitimate," etc.). If the people can be enticed into fighting among themselves, all the better for the powerful. In short, we seriously mistake the significance of this list if we do not read it in the context of the interference and harassment by the Persian administration.

1 Esdras 5:47-73: Temple Building

The Text in Its Ancient Context

The text returns to the narrative provided in Ezra about the beginnings of the building of the temple. Notable in this discussion is the local opposition. Although it is implied that some of the "people of the land" joined in, the force of the text seems to be aimed at excluding those whose offer to help was considered interference. In response, then, the local officials write their protests to the emperor, which temporarily halts the work. Having introduced the story of the three youths, the reason for another work stoppage seems awkward here, but it is forced on the editor by the materials borrowed from Ezra-Nehemiah.

The Text in the Interpretive Tradition

As Talshir notes (2001, 320–21), 1 Esdras expands on the opposition activities that led to a halt of the building project—referring to "cutting off supplies," "hindering the building," "plots and demagoguery and uprisings"—and implies that this opposition activity prevented progress throughout the reign of Cyrus and into the reign of Darius (completely skipping the reign of Cambyses). Most of this detail is not found in Ezra. Resumption of worship at the altar, suggests Myers (70), reflects the "zeal" of the returned community.

The Text in Contemporary Discussion

The exclusionary practices of the group from the Diaspora are particularly notable. The motivation for their opposition is not developed, leaving readers to presume that the locals were not serious in their original offer to help. But it is the Judean community whose members have planted the seeds of conflict here. This will lead directly to the mixed-marriage crisis, another form of the conflict over who is the "true Judean" in this context. Isaiah 56 and the story of Ruth both attest to the continued debates about who is an acceptable member of the "inner circle," the "legitimate community." Infighting among indigenous peoples is a sad legacy of imperial disappropriation.

1 Esdras 6:1-34: Darius Commands the Temple's Completion

The Text in Its Ancient Context

Although 1 Esdras usually follows the *Vorlage* of Ezra-Nehemiah closely, it is interesting that the differences tend to favor the Persian officials. Their inquiries about the building of the temple in Ezra seem gruff and official, whereas in 1 Esdras their questions are rendered a bit more gracious (see 6:5). Still, names are taken (another list), and inquiries are made. When the Judean leaders claim that they have royal permission from Cyrus, Darius not only confirms this but also adds additional threats to any who would further interfere.

The Text in the Interpretive Tradition

Talshir (2001) notes that Zerubbabel's name is added to the discussion with Persian officials, but further notes the awkward inconsistencies of following the Ezra material too closely. According the story of the three youths, it was Zerubbabel's cleverness that earned Darius's favor, and Zerubbabel then had full support for rebuilding Jerusalem and the temple. Here, however, Darius knows nothing of the building until a search is made in the archive. This seems to be further indication that the story of the three youths was rather roughly forced into place, and the editor then strangely does not correct the other textual problems created by aligning closely with the older Ezra-Nehemiah materials.

The Text in Contemporary Discussion

Is this apparent contradiction a real problem? Has Darius forgotten his clever Jewish advisor so quickly? If so, then there are dramatic parallels with the image of absentminded Ptolemy in 3 Maccabees, who constantly forgets his previous decisions with regard to the Jews in his realm, or even with the frequent *re*introductions of Daniel in Daniel 1–6. Are we to be reminded of the inconsistency, the untrustworthiness, and the sheer fickle nature of imperial rule?

1 Esdras 7:1-15: Passover and Purification

The Text in Its Ancient Context

After the successful completion of the temple, chapter 7 narrates a return to normal. The Passover is being celebrated again, precisely where we began the narrative of 1 Esdras. There is a sense, therefore, that the community has restored the righteousness (if not power) of Josiah. Although the hints of opposition to local peoples remain, the image suggests a community in restoration. The addition of the narratives about Ezra in chapters 8 and 9, however, suggests that this is a calm before another storm.

The Text in the Interpretive Tradition

Most commentators note the significance of the temple in later biblical texts, and here also "glorification" of the temple is "characteristic" of 1 Esdras (Myers, 78–79; Bird, 17). Further, R. J. Coggins notes that the total absence of Nehemiah glorifies Ezra himself (55). Temple personnel, and especially the high priest, of course, rise to a central role in Jewish life after the exile, well into the Roman period. Japhet, however, also notes the abbreviated nature of the celebrations in comparison to Ezra and Chronicles, particularly noting the absence of singing or music, which was a "hallmark of Second Temple ceremonies" (764). Bird notes the importance of referring to the twelve tribes in 7:1-9, implying the restoration of the whole of Israel, which is further emphasized by the otherwise odd reference to "Assyria"—that is, the restoration includes those carried away by Assyria in 722 BCE from the north (Bird, 226, 230).

The Text in Contemporary Discussion

The transformation here is notable. The Hebrew people are passing from a small nation (among many other "nations" and "peoples" in the immediate area) to a minority in a larger imperial context. Similar to many modern experiences of minorities, the changed status heightens tension over issues of identity, resources, and relations to other peoples.

1 Esdras 8:1-96: Under Persian Rule

The Text in Its Ancient Context

Once again, the text emphasizes an unusually positive relation with the Persian rulers (8:4) when compared to Ezra-Nehemiah (also Myers, 79), hinted at by small changes (e.g., not so many punishments threatened in 8:24, friendly relations with the king in 8:25-27). Indeed, in 8:80-81, the Persians give food and help, which is associated with the "favor" of the king, and not the steadfast love of God "before the King" (Ezra 7:28). Furthermore, there are not even threats from ambushes in 1 Esdras, suggesting limited Persian authority (cf. Ezra 8:31).

The Text in the Interpretive Tradition

The varied discussions about the heritage, descent, and thus status of the group accompanying Ezra back to Palestine is a matter of frequent analysis (Coggins, 60–65; Myers, 96–97; "his caravan . . . representative of the whole people," Japhet, 765). After a long, more positive introduction, the text turns on the issue of mixed marriage and Ezra's horrified response (Smith-Christopher). What is less often noted in the many discussions of these events, however, is the text's use of ancient ethnic markers to recall Joshua's conquests (8:69), implying previous rights to land as well as traditional hatreds (e.g., Perizzites, Jebusites, Canaanites; see Josh. 12:8).

The Text in Contemporary Discussion

Who is the "authentic" member of a community? Divisions created by apportionment of economic benefits is a tactic with a long legacy in colonialism. Communal tensions are exploited by foreign powers to "divide and conquer": tempers flare, attitudes harden, and communities divide into factions. The Maori of New Zealand were deftly divided into allies and opposition, as was India under British occupation, and Native American tribal groups of the eastern United States in the seventeenth and eighteenth centuries, and even the Japanese American internees during the Second World War.

1 Esdras 9:1-55: Restoring the People

The Text in Its Ancient Context

The final "purification" of the community involves the infamous dismissal of foreign wives. When Ezra is informed of the defilement of the "holy seed" (Ezra 9:2), he launches into one of the many examples of the postexilic prayer form typically identified as "the penitential prayer" (1 Kings 8; Daniel 9; Ezra 9; Nehemiah 9; Baruch; see Werline). This confessional prayer form emphasizes communal guilt from the past as well as the present, and pleads for God's help in the present. The placement of this episode as the final chapter of 1 Esdras tends to emphasize that the community is now fully prepared to face the future—its community rebuilt, at home, and purified. Bird comments that after rebuilding the shrine, rebuilding the people "must accordingly follow" (231).

The Text in the Interpretive Tradition

Coggins refers to chapter 9 as "a particularly lame conclusion" (70), but Myers and Bird have both tried to take the issue of mixed marriage seriously as a social and religious threat (Myers, 98; Bird, 257, who even refers to foreign "contamination" [!], 272). Similarly, Japhet (766) notes that the significance of the mixed-marriage crisis is magnified in comparison to Ezra-Nehemiah: "The implication is self-evident: the only way for Israel to atone for this sin is to purify themselves, to detach themselves completely . . . from the peoples of the land" (767). Much has been made of the notion that law is given the "last word" in 1 Esdras—a law given to the redeemed and purified, and not in order to redeem or purity them (Bird, 233).

The Text in Contemporary Discussion

First Esdras 9 ultimately shows a community unified by its own moral traditions, but at the horrific price of a rejection of "the other"—for example, minorities, different ethnicities, different people. "Unity" (like "patriotism") is too often achieved by vilifying minorities or outsiders (Bird, 256, even refers to "traditional enemies," a sobering phrase). The caution here, however, is that it is a moral law backed up by the authority of a state, and indeed the threat of violence from that state. Since Constantine's authorization of Christianity, the church has too often succumbed to the temptation of backing its authority with the use of power and violence. Indeed, both Islam and Judaism similarly face temptations of mixing religion and power. First Esdras is thus a cautionary tale for virtually all modern readers, and commentators have been altogether too sanguine about its portrayal of national and/or religious revival.

Works Cited

Bird, Michael F. 2012. *1 Esdras: Introduction and Commentary on the Greek Text in Codex Vaticanus*. Septuagint Commentary Series. Leiden: Brill.

Coggins, R. J. 1979. *The First and Second Books of Esdras*. CBC. Cambridge: Cambridge University Press.

Davis, Stacy. "1 Esdras." In *The People's Companion to the Bible*, edited by C. P. DeYoung, W. Gafney, L. A. Guardiola-Saenz, G. Tinker, and F. M. Yamada, 200–201. Minneapolis: Fortress Press.

Japhet, Sara. 2001. "1 Esdras." In *The Oxford Bible Commentary*, edited by John Barton and John Muddiman, 751–70. New York: Oxford University Press.

Klein, Ralph. 2003. "1 Esdras." In *The New Interpreter's Study Bible*, edited by Walter J. Harrelson, 1633–54. Nashville: Abingdon.

Myers, Jacob. 1974. *I and II Esdras: Introduction, Translation and Commentary*. AB. New York: Doubleday.

Schuller, Eileen. 1992. "The Apocrypha." In *The Women's Bible Commentary*, edited by Carol A. Newsom and Sharon H. Ringe, 234–43. Louisville: Westminster John Knox.

Smith-Christopher, Daniel. 1996. "Between Ezra and Isaiah: Exclusion, Transformation, and Inclusion of the 'Foreigner' in Post-Exilic Biblical Theology." In *Ethnicity and the Bible*, edited by Mark Brett, 117–42. Leiden: Brill.

Talshir, Zipora. 1999. *I Esdras: From Origin to Translation*. Atlanta: Society of Biblical Literature.

———. 2001. *1 Esdras: A Text Critical Commentary* [Septuagint and Cognate Studies 50]. Atlanta: Scholars Press.

Werline, Rodney A. 1998. *Penitential Prayer in Second Temple Judaism: The Development of a Religious Institution*. Atlanta: Scholars Press.

PRAYER OF MANASSEH

Christopher Frechette

Introduction

Manasseh ruled Judah from either 698 or 687 until 642 BCE, and the accounts of his reign in both 2 Kings 21 and in 2 Chronicles 33 condemn him for causing Israel to do more evil than any of the other nations had done. Of the two accounts, only the former cites his offenses as the cause of the destruction of Jerusalem by the Babylonians in 586 BCE, and only the latter tells of the king's repentance; it describes how God has Manasseh taken captive to Babylon by the Assyrians because of his idolatry; once there, the king humbles himself and entreats God, who hears his prayer and restores him to rule in Jerusalem, where he then corrects his prior idolatry by enacting cultic reforms. The narrative does not provide the wording of the king's prayer. Yet close parallels between the Prayer of Manasseh and the situation described in the narrative suggest that this text was understood to be that wording, and from its earliest attestations the prayer bears a superscription attributing it to Manasseh.

The earliest known versions of the Prayer of Manasseh are in Syriac and Greek, but it is uncertain whether either of these, or perhaps an unknown Hebrew or Aramaic version, represents the original. The earliest Hebrew version, preserved in a tenth-century manuscript from the Cairo Genizah document, is considered a translation (Davila). The prayer is included in the following ancient texts: the odes appended to the Psalter in versions of the LXX from as early as the fifth century CE; an appendix to some Syriac copies of Chronicles; and a conflation of the two biblical accounts of the reign of Manasseh found in two Christian handbooks from the third–fourth centuries CE: the *Didascalia* (ch. 7) and the *Apostolic Constitutions* (2.22). The prayer was likely composed between the second century BCE and the third century CE. Its central theme, that God allows grievous sinners to repent, is at home in both Christianity and Judaism, and although Jewish authorship of the prayer cannot be ruled out, it may provisionally be considered a Christian work (Davila).

Some evidence suggests that the prayer was composed for inclusion in the Christian handbooks (Nickelsburg). The prayer appears in the Eastern Orthodox canon and in modern editions of the LXX, but Jewish, Protestant, and Catholic canons do not include it.

The Text in Its Ancient Context

While sharing several elements with Psalm 51, which is the most elaborate treatment of repentance among biblical psalms of an individual, the Prayer of Manasseh presents God's capacity to forgive in even more emphatic terms. Both prayers are attributed to a king, but the contrast is dramatic: for Psalm 51, it is Israel's archetypal king, David; for the Prayer of Manasseh, it is the archvillain of Israel's kings. The Prayer of Manasseh begins by addressing God as "Lord almighty, God of our ancestors, of Abraham and Isaac and Jacob and of their righteous offspring," and as the Creator who has mastery over chaos, symbolized by "sea" and "abyss" (vv. 1-3). Assuming the ancient worldview that sees transgressions against God as violations of divinely established social harmony, the prayer describes God's capacity to restore that order by destroying those who commit such violations (vv. 4-5). Yet it affirms that God is merciful beyond measure and has established an alternative means of restoring order: repentance (vv. 6-7). Claiming access to that repentance, the speaker confesses being an unworthy sinner, whose sins are "more numerous than the sands of the sea," and who consequently is weighed down with "many an iron shackle" (vv. 8-12). The speaker then asks to be forgiven and preserved from eternal punishment by God, here named not as "God of the righteous" but as "God of those who repent" (v. 13). In support of this petition, the speaker declares that in God's forgiving the undeserving speaker, the goodness of God will become manifest in him, who will in turn praise God continually, as do all the heavenly host (vv. 14-15).

Like a number of so-called penitential prayers from early Judaism, for example, Ezra 9, the Prayer of Manasseh would have given those who prayed it a voice with which to appeal to God as one who receives and responds mercifully to those who repent. Moreover, its implied context in the narrative of 2 Chronicles affirms that God indeed responds mercifully to such prayers. Although in many "penitential prayers" the people speak as a corporate body linked to prior generations in their transgressions, it is an individual taking responsibility for personal guilt who speaks here; the significance of this difference deserves further investigation (Newman).

The Text in the Interpretive Tradition

The Prayer of Manasseh had considerable influence in early Christianity but is much less conspicuous in Jewish traditions. The ancient Christian handbooks cited above place it within an exhortation to bishops to enact well their ministry of healing and reconciling of the faithful. Thomas Aquinas quoted lines 6-7a of the prayer in arguing that the sacrament of penance could be repeated (*Summa Theologiae* 3 q. 84 a. 10). The prayer is cited by several patristic authors in exhortations to penitence, and there is abundant evidence for its liturgical usage during the patristic period from the fifth century onward; it is included, for instance, in the liturgy of Jerusalem and in the Coptic, Ethiopian, and Mozarabic Psalters (Rose). However, it was not included among the canticles in the Roman office (1911) or the Liturgy of the Hours (1971). Some of the earliest printed German Bibles include the prayer at the end of 2 Chronicles, and although Martin Luther considered it apocryphal in his Bible, he circulated it in a variety of contexts (Bream).

The Text in Contemporary Discussion

Perhaps the greatest challenges that the Prayer of Manasseh poses for modern readers concern its depictions of God's capacity to destroy sinners in anger and of the speaker's self-abasement. However, interpreting such portrayals within their cultural context and in light of the prayer as a whole can disabuse the reader of the assumption that this prayer addresses a misanthropic God who requires that sinful people abandon their dignity in order to gain forgiveness. Here, as in many biblical and other ancient Near Eastern texts, divine anger is portrayed as erupting in response to violations of the social harmony intended by God, which includes all aspects of human behavior. Since, in the biblical view, a key purpose for which God established that harmony is to provide a place in which people can thrive in relationship to God, portraying God as angry over violations of that harmony actually affirms God's fundamental care for humanity. At the same time, the prayer accents not the angry destruction of the sinner but repentance and forgiveness, as being the preferred means by which God allows order to be restored after it has been violated. The speaker's claims of unworthiness and hyperbolic confessions of sin need not be taken as reflections of the speaker's value in an objective sense. In their ancient Near Eastern context, such expressions constituted an affective mode of speaking understood to convey sincerity.

Works Cited

Bream, Howard N. 1986. "Manasseh and His Prayer." *Lutheran Theological Seminary Bulletin* 66 no. 4:5–47.

Charlesworth, James H. 1983–1985. "Prayer of Manasseh." In *The Old Testament Pseudepigrapha*, edited by James H. Charlesworth, 625–37. Garden City, NY: Doubleday.

Davila, James R. 2007. "Is the Prayer of Manasseh a Jewish Work?" In *Heavenly Tablets: Interpretation, Identity and Tradition in Ancient Judaism*, edited by Lynn. R. LiDonnici and Andrea Lieber, 75–85. Leiden: Brill.

Newman, Judith H. 2007. "Form and Function in the Prayer of Manasseh." In *Seeking the Favor of God*. Vol. 2, *The Development of Penitential Prayer in Second Temple Judaism*, edited by Mark J. Boda, Daniel K. Falk, and Rodney Alan Werline, 105–25. Atlanta: Society of Biblical Literature.

Nickelsburg, George W. E. 2001. "Prayer of Manasseh." In *The Oxford Bible Commentary*, edited by John Barton and John Muddiman, 770–73. New York: Oxford University Press.

Rose, Andre. 1988. "La prière d'Azarias (Dan 3.26–45) et le cantique de Manassé dans la tradition chrétienne et dans la liturgie." In *Liturgie, conversion et vie monastique: Conférences Saint-Serge, XXXVe semaine d'études liturgiques, Paris, 28 juin–1er juillet 1988*, edited by Achille M. Triacca and Alessandro Pistoia, 293–305. Rome: C.L.V. Edizioni liturgiche, 1989.

PSALM 151

Christopher Frechette

Introduction

Psalm 151 comes to us in shorter and longer versions, both of which divide into two parts, each narrating events of David's youth (1 Samuel 16–17). Part A celebrates David, who began by making music and tending flocks, but whom God anointed as ruler. Part B recounts the young David's legendary victory over the Philistine warrior. Among the ancient versions of this psalm, the longer is preserved only in the Hebrew text of the *Great Psalms Scroll* from Qumran, in which part B is separated from part A by a superscription. The LXX contains the shorter version, on which the Syriac, Latin, and Ethiopic are dependent. This version combines in a single unit part A, which is much shorter (twelve phrases) than the Hebrew (twenty-eight phrases), with part B (five phrases) in a single psalm. That the Hebrew manuscript of part B is missing about eight lines (each with a capacity for three or four phrases) after the initial two phrases indicates that this part would have consisted of much more text. Both versions were likely based on a prior Hebrew version dating to before 200 BCE. It seems probable that even though the LXX version may have left out some parts of that prior version, some significant portions of the Hebrew were likely expansions on it (Smith).

The Jewish, Protestant, and Roman Catholic canons do not include Psalm 151. Both the LXX and the *Great Psalms Scroll* position Psalm 151 at the very end of the collection of psalms, and its superscription in the LXX identifies it as "outside the enumeration" of the Psalter. With a more flexible understanding of canonicity than in the West (Pentiuc), Eastern Orthodox Bibles include it but with a lesser level of canonicity than the 150 psalms, following Athanasius's consideration that it is not *kanonizomenōn* ("canonized") but rather *anaginoskomenon* ("readable").

The Text in Its Ancient Context

The shorter version of Psalm 151 highlights the wonder of how God selected David, a youth of humble origins, to defeat the Philistine and thereby remove the shame experienced by Israel. Such an emphasis would have encouraged the Jewish people living under a succession of empires with a message that God can choose the humble to remove the shame brought about by foreign powers. The LXX superscription identifies this psalm as an "afterword" to the Psalter that serves to attribute the entire Psalter to the David, God's unlikely chosen warrior, and so to frame it as prayers of resistance (Zenger).

In the longer version, part A conveys the reciprocal character of the relationship between David and God. After describing David's making of pipe and lyre, the Hebrew includes eight phrases in which David honors God, none of which are present in the Greek. This section provides a counterpart to the subsequent section that tells of God's hearing David and then, in eight phrases, selecting and anointing him as ruler over God's people. Thus the longer version emphasizes that it is David's honoring of God, particularly through music, that provides the key to understanding God's honoring of David by selecting him to be Israel's archetypal king. Portraying God as taking notice of David's musical worship and responding favorably to it would have encouraged Jews living under empire to hold fast to their own liturgical practices under cultural pressures to abandon them. Furthermore, elaborating on the ideal king's honoring of God makes clear that the authority to rule remains fundamentally grounded in the ruler's subordination to God. Portraying the king exercising power as the humble and conscientious servant of the deity is well attested among ancient Near Eastern cultures; although we may see in such portrayals a device for legitimating rulers who presided over hegemonic institutions, such texts could also serve to bolster an expectation that rulers exercise authority justly.

The Text in the Interpretive Tradition

Psalm 151 has enjoyed a place in Coptic, Armenian, and Ethiopian liturgy. The Coptic liturgy employs it on the night of Holy Saturday; the Armenian liturgy, at Pentecost. In the Ethiopian liturgy, it is read on the night of Good Friday, and parts of it occur in the ritual for the enthronement of the king. Although Psalm 151 is printed in some Eastern Orthodox liturgical books, currently it is with the understanding that it not be read during liturgies.

The Text in Contemporary Discussion

The emphasis of the psalm's longer version on reciprocal relationship between God and ruler underscores the fundamental tenet that those who claim divine authority for the exercise of power must act within proper relationship to God. This version thus serves to confront tendencies among those who exercise such power to act unjustly or in self-interest. The prominence given to honoring God through music affirms the value of liturgical worship for cultivating such proper relationship with God.

Both versions emphasize David's restoring Israel's dignity by killing the Philistine, who had not only threatened violence against Israel but also further offended the people's dignity with his cursing. Two distinctions are helpful to assist contemporary readers in understanding the role of killing in this text. First, the central concern is God's care for the dignity of the people, and killing the offender is a means employed to restore it. The association between parts A and B, present in both versions, makes clear that the restoration of dignity results from God's empowering the humble David, who was committed to proper relationship with God. Second, it is important to distinguish between taking the account as a model for behavior and employing it for its capacity to convey symbolically and dramatically God's concern for the dignity of those who are violated (Frechette). David effectively confronts the offender by killing him, and according to the ancient worldview, killing in this situation was legitimate. However, modern psychology reveals that the ability of those who have been violated to reclaim their dignity does not depend on the fate of the perpetrator. Yet, being violated can cement within a person perceptions of lack of dignity and of abandonment by God in such an emotionally intense way that these perceptions can prove resistant to reinterpretation. As a phase in one's recovery process from such violation and without harming anyone, reading dramatic narratives such as Ps. 18:1-19, in which God confronts the offender, can be helpful as a symbolic means of asserting that God judges the violation to be wrong and upholds the victim's dignity. The present psalm can support such a symbolic confrontation of violations against human dignity.

Works Cited

Frechette, Christopher G. 2014. "Destroying the Internalized Perpetrator: A Healing Function of the Violent Language against Enemies in the Psalms." In *Trauma and Traumatization in Individual and Collective Dimensions: Insights from Biblical Studies and Beyond*, edited by Becker, Jan Dochhorn, and Else K. Holt. Studia Aarhusiana Neotestamentica 2. Göttingen: Vandenhoeck & Ruprecht.

"Introduction au psaume 151." 2011. No author cited. In *La Bible: Notes intégrale, traduction oecuménique, TOB*, 2065–66. 12th ed. Paris: Éditions du Cerf.

Pentiuc, Eugen J. 2014. *The Old Testament in Eastern Orthodox Tradition*. New York: Oxford University Press.

Smith, Mark S. 1997. "How to Write a Poem: The Case of Psalm 151A (11QPs[a] 28.3–12)." In *The Hebrew of the Dead Sea Scrolls and Ben Sira: Proceedings of a Symposium Held at Leiden University, 11–14 December 1995*, edited by T. Muraoka and J. Elwolde, 182–208. Leiden: Brill.

Zenger, Erich. 2011. "Excursus: Psalm 151 LXX as Afterword to the Septuagint Psalter." In Frank-Lothar Hossfeld and Erich Zenger, *Psalms 3: A Commentary on Psalms 101–150*, 665–69. Translated by Linda Maloney. Hermeneia. Minneapolis: Fortress Press.

3 Maccabees

Samuel I. Thomas

Introduction

The book 3 Maccabees is included as a canonical work in Orthodox and Armenian collections of Scripture, and is considered noncanonical in Protestant and Catholic traditions. Originally composed in Greek by an anonymous Jewish writer living in Alexandria sometime after the Battle of Raphia (217 BCE), and perhaps as late as the reign of the Roman emperor Caligula (37–41 CE), 3 Maccabees constitutes three main episodes involving the Ptolemy-Seleucid conflict and persecution of the Jews of Alexandria.

The title of the work is something of a misnomer, since the narrative of 3 Maccabees does not involve any members of the Hasmonean family and its historical setting is well before the Maccabean Revolt (167–164 BCE). Nevertheless, it was grouped with the books of 1 and 2 Maccabees in early manuscripts, and presents a plot line that is thematically similar to them. In genre, it can be compared to other Maccabean literature, the books of Esther and Daniel, and the *Letter of Aristeas*, especially in the way that it presents an account of royal conflict and Jewish persecution with a degree of historical verisimilitude.

The literary style of 3 Maccabees, which has been described as "bombastic" and "pretentious," fits within the range of Hellenistic Jewish writings of the period (Croy, xiii–xiv). While the author employs some conventions of Greek style in the composition, he appears less interested in style than in religious and nationalistic propagandizing.

Scholars generally agree that the beginning of the work is missing. The extant version of 3 Maccabees opens abruptly with an account of the Battle of Raphia between Antiochus III and Ptolemy IV Philopator, moves to a narrative about the latter's persecution of the Jews of Alexandria, and ends with a story about a gruesome plot to slaughter apostate Jews and purify those who have remained faithful to the covenant community. The work as a whole is intended to uphold the authority of torah and the sacredness of the Jerusalem temple—either in the face of an immediate persecution or in memory of one—and to affirm the status of Israel as the covenant people. The author's theology shows no apparent signs of interaction with the apocalyptic eschatology and messianic hope then current in Palestine (and, to a lesser extent, in the Diaspora), advocating instead for a traditionally Deuteronomic understanding of divine favor and retribution.

3 Maccabees 1:1—2:24: Historical Prologue

The Text in Its Ancient Context

Third Maccabees begins with a terse account of the Battle of Raphia, a confrontation between Ptolemy IV Philopator and Antiochus III ("the Great") in 217 BCE. This event is recorded also by Polybius (*Histories* 5), whose lengthier account accords with the general shape and details of 3 Macc. 1:1—2:24. The perspective of the author of 3 Maccabees differs from that of the ancient Roman historian; for the former, the historical details are the raw materials out of which he fashions a narrative that is not primarily a work of historiography, but one that is polemical and apologetic at its core, arguing that Jews should not trade their ancestral faith for acceptance in Greco-Roman societies.

The characters in this account are for the most part known from other sources: Philopator, Antiochus, Arsinoë, Dositheos son of Drimylus, and Theodotus—all of these figure into Polybius's rendering of the episode, and some are mentioned by Josephus. The author of 3 Maccabees, however, is interested in these characters primarily insofar as their roles can be manipulated to serve his purposes. The victory of Philopator over Antiochus, for example, provides the occasion for the Ptolemaic king to become "eager" to visit the Jews in Jerusalem and to worship their "faithful" God (see below). Dositheos (whose existence is also likely attested in *P. Hibeh* 90) is introduced as one of the "apostate" Jews who, as a group, are scorned and executed in the conclusion to the work.

The rest of the prologue is taken up by an account of Philopator's attempt to enter the Jerusalem temple. Here the author juxtaposes the pious and humble Jews with the arrogant, haughty king, deploying maudlin appeals to emotion in order to underline the importance of maintaining the covenant obligations. This episode may reflect a real event (it is recorded elsewhere that Philopator visited other sacred sites of Coele-Syria in his postvictory tours), though it is unlikely to have transpired in the way 3 Maccabees narrates it. The author is possibly drawing from a parallel story in 2 Maccabees, a story in which controversy arises out of a pagan king's desire to enter the temple (2 Macc. 3:1-40; cf. Josephus, *Ant.* 11.329–39; 2 Macc. 5:11-21; Josephus, *Ant.* 14.67–72; Philo, *Embassy* 203; Josephus, *Ant.* 18.252–309). This section concludes with a prayer by the high priest Simon II, who presided over Jerusalem during the last fifth of the third century BCE. Simon's prayer follows a series of dramatic escalations of suspense—young maidens rushing forth, mothers and nurses abandoning newborn children, and so on—serving thus as the climactic reversal of the plot's movement. Using language and structure reflecting "a type common in postexilic Judaism (Ezra 9; Nehemiah 9; Daniel 9; Bar. 1:15—3:8) that reviews salvation history and emphasizes the righteousness of God and sinfulness of Israel" (Collins, 1756), Simon's prayer brings about God's intervention in the story. According to the narrative, Philopator falls paralyzed and mute and then slinks away in defeat.

The Text in the Interpretive Tradition

Sara Raup Johnson aptly notes that scholarly interpretations of the date of 3 Maccabees fall into two main categories, each of them with consequences for how to understand the message of the work as a whole. Those who have viewed 3 Maccabees as a pre-Roman Hellenistic composition (prior to 30 BCE) have tended to "stress the possibilities for peaceful compromise found in the story," while those who ascribe it a date in the early Roman period "stress the elements in the story that depict the Jews as a persecuted minority" (Johnson, 2683). She writes that "both interpretations are possible, and ultimately readers must decide for themselves whether the text works more effectively as a model for life in a time of compromise, or life in a time of crisis and conflict." This view no doubt represents the various ways 3 Maccabees functioned for later readers attempting to navigate their own experiences of cultural difference, persecution, and assimilation, and may help to explain why this text was transmitted despite its questionable canonical status.

The Text in Contemporary Discussion

Third Maccabees reframes historical events in order to address questions of religious identity and piety. This is a tendency found in other biblical texts, and appears to be a perennial theme in religion more broadly. While this particular passage does not figure explicitly into contemporary discussions, it represents a continually relevant problem: How is the telling of history used to shape culture and self-understanding? Should history writing be about the politics of identity, or should it strive for some more objective truth about the nature of human affairs?

A more contemporary example might be the way the history of the United States is sometimes framed as a story of moral progress and of the instantiation of "Judeo-Christian values" in national life. History then becomes the theater for a series of ideological claims that serve to shore up the identity of certain contemporary groups—often at the expense of others. One thinks, for example, of the revisionist history of evangelical author David Barton, who draws on the reconstructionist and racist theology of R. J. Rushdoony in his glorifications of the American past. Whom does this kind of historiography serve? While the overall goals of Barton and the author of 3 Maccabees are clearly very different, they share the tendency to intermix history-telling with religious propaganda.

3 Maccabees 2:25—6:15: Ptolemy IV Philopator's Persecution of the Jews

The Text in Its Ancient Context

Philopator was apparently not adequately chastened by his experience entering the Jerusalem temple. According to 3 Maccabees, he went to Egypt and added to his nefarious deeds, most especially by setting out to restrict the Jews from worshiping at their religious sites, registering and "branding" them, and relegating them to the status of slaves (2:25-30). Alternatively, they could choose to participate in the "mysteries" of Dionysius and receive the same political rights as citizens of Greek descent. This moment in the narrative introduces the possibility that some Jews will become apostate and align themselves with the king—which is what the story as a whole attempts to circumvent (see below). These apostates thus serve as a counterexample to the kind of religious fidelity that 3 Maccabees advocates.

The registration (*laographia*) of the Jews was to include branding by fire with an image of the Dionysian ivy leaf—representing the family god of the Ptolemies—and, perhaps, the payment of a special tax (see 2 Macc. 6:7). It was not uncommon in the history of the Roman Empire for Jews to be subject to special laws and taxation (see especially the *fiscus Iudaicus* of the first century CE and following; see Josephus, *J.W.* 7.218; Suetonius, *Life of Domitian* 12.1–2; Cassius Dio, 65.7.2, 67.14.1–2), but this practice is otherwise unattested in pre-Roman Greek law.

Philopator's warning of servitude is reminiscent of the exodus story, perhaps deliberately invoking the paradigmatic account of liberation for a new time and place: Jews in Egypt threatened with slavery by a king whose aims are frustrated by divine intervention. As the narrative unfolds, the Jews are imprisoned and several chapters in this section recount the changing moods and designs of Philopator, who is presented alternately as a madman and as someone whose intentions can easily be undermined by the divine will.

This section as a whole emphasizes the various ways in which God (or "providence") frustrates the plans of Philopator to persecute the Egyptian Jews. First, the registration in the hippodrome fails for lack of time, paper, and pens. In response, Philopator issues the strange order to unleash a large number of intoxicated elephants on the Jews assembled in the hippodrome. Philopator then reverses his disposition—which, according to 3 Maccabees, is yet another instance of divine intervention—and castigates Hermon (whose name is reminiscent of Haman, who plays a similar role in the book of Esther) for seeking to carry out the elephant plan too diligently. Another reversal by Philopator then heightens the drama, as he charges Hermon once again to execute the genocide. Here the capricious and moody character of the king perhaps intentionally plays on a trope found elsewhere in early Jewish texts: that of the mad king (see Daniel 4; *Prayer of Nabonidus* [4QPrNab]).

The episode involving drunken elephants is unlikely to have transpired exactly as described (see Josephus, *Ag. Ap.* 2.52–55, in which there is a similar scene involving not Philopator but Ptolemy Physcon). Elephants were often used in war and in games and other public performances in the Greco-Roman world. While it is highly implausible that Philopator could have actually assembled five hundred elephants, and the number simply appears to have been symbolic for a very large quantity, "the rhetorical force of the number is unmistakable: the Jews faced a calamity of mind boggling proportions" (Croy, 84). If the number of elephants was exaggerated, other sources attest that their drunkenness remains an intriguing possibility (Josephus, *Ag. Ap.* 2.53–55; 1 Macc. 6:34).

With his plans to kill the Jews foiled several times, and with those in attendance at the banquet growing unruly, Philopator additionally resolves to invade Judea and destroy the temple in Jerusalem. While he never undertook such an attempt, this notice serves to heighten the drama of the narrative and connect the current episode with earlier parts of the work. Here the text refers to Philopator as a "Phalaris in every way," invoking the image of the sixth-century-BCE ruler of Acragas (Sicily) whose name was synonymous in antiquity with savage tyranny (Polybius, *Hist.* 12.25.1–5; Diodorus Siculus, *Bib. hist.* 9.19, 13.90, 19.108; Lucian, *Phal.* 1.11–12)

At the climax of suspense, this section of 3 Maccabees concludes with an intercessory prayer by Eleazar, in which that figure calls forth Daniel and Jonah as exemplars of Jewish redemption from death by beast and the three companions in Babylon as examples of fidelity in the face of persecution and death (Daniel 3; cf. the Prayer of Azariah and the Song of the Three Young Men). The identity of this Eleazar is unknown; in most manuscripts, he is described as a "priest," though elsewhere he is simply one of "the Jews." His supplication is structurally and thematically reminiscent of the prayer of Simon II at the end of chapter 1, referencing also Israel's salvation history and God's reputation among the gentiles as reasons for his saving mercies to work once again. It is worth noting that the beginning of his prayer calls to mind a standard Jewish daily prayer known as the *Amidah*, the opening of which also appeals to the God of Abraham, Isaac, and Jacob and recounts the saving acts of God in history. The themes of the prayer align with the basic Deuteronomic sin-punishment/repentance-deliverance theology found in some biblical texts.

The Text in the Interpretive Tradition

While some German biblical scholars aligned with the ideology of the National Socialist German Worker's Party and produced scholarship that exhibited antisemitic tendencies (see, for example, Kittel's *Theological Dictionary of the New Testament*), 3 Maccabees was not apparently used directly to support the Nazi program of Jewish extermination. Nevertheless, some of the most chilling lines from 3 Maccabees—lines that would be echoed more than two millennia later by leaders of the Nazi Party in the 1930s and 1940s—come in the decree issued by Philopator in chapter 3: "we have given an order that as soon as this letter reaches you [royal functionaries in the provinces], you are to send to us those who live among you, together with their wives and children, with abusive and harsh treatment, bound on all sides in iron chains, for an irremediable and ill-fated slaughter befitting enemies. For we have come to understand that, when these people have been punished together, the affairs of our state will be perfectly established for us in stability and the best order for time hereafter" (3 Macc. 3:25-26; translation from Croy, 13).

The Text in Contemporary Discussion

Perhaps the most salient aspect of this passage for contemporary reflection is the registration and marking of Jews—or any ethnic group—for "special" treatment. Third Maccabees thus represents perhaps the earliest source attesting to what will later become an enduring practice in Roman, European, and some Islamic societies, culminating in the yellow "Jude" badges of the German Third Reich in the twentieth century. This passage thus represents an opportunity for dominant groups to consider ways in which minority religious communities might be similarly "marked" and oppressed or marginalized (or perhaps the ways in which groups that "mark" themselves with outward signs of religious observance might receive different treatment from others in positions of power).

3 Maccabees 6:16—7:23: Reversal, "Conversion," Revenge, and Homecoming

The Text in Its Ancient Context

King Philopator finally arrives at the hippodrome to witness the spectacle he has ordered, and his appearance provokes an outcry of terror on the part of the captive Jews. But suddenly angels of the Lord intervene and the elephants "forget" their mission (because of their inebriation? or because of the terrifying angels?), thus mirroring the amnesiac mania of the king in all his earlier reversals. The angels represent a common theme in early Jewish—especially apocalyptic—literature of the Hellenistic era, namely, that God's redemptive plans are brought about by the work of heavenly intermediaries. The fact that these particular angels remain invisible to the assembled Jews is striking, leading at least one interpreter (Grotius) to suggest that "God did not want the Jews, who were already traumatized, to be further frightened by the angels" (Croy, 103). Here the story finds parallels in other early Jewish literature in which angels come to the rescue of Jews in heavy-hitting displays of supernatural power (see the parallel story in Josephus, *Ag. Ap.* 2.53–55; cf. 2 Macc. 3:25-29; Wis. 17:3; Herodotus, *Hist.* 6.117).

In 3 Maccabees, this reversal serves as the pivot point between Philopator's earlier forgetfulness and his present inability to remember that he himself was responsible for the situation now culminating before him. Both the king and the elephants turn on those executing the plan against the Jews, and the king is safeguarded, presumably, so that he can repent and then vindicate the Jews in their triumph. Perhaps not surprisingly—the theme is found elsewhere in biblical and early Jewish literature—the entire scenario provides the occasion for a "foreign" king to pay homage to the God of the Jews and to "confess" that he owes his own prosperity and authority to none other than Israel's God. While such a scenario is historically unlikely, it fits the propagandistic purposes of the story.

The feasting and celebrating then becomes the prerogative of the Jews, who, having barely escaped death (Hades), take the place of Philopator's previously favored guests. Only now, as if to emphasize that this is indeed a "festival of deliverance," the celebration takes place in the hippodrome itself (3 Macc. 6:31; cf. Luke 9:14). The author of 3 Maccabees apparently wishes also to commemorate the celebration of this deliverance in repeated ritual observance (cf, e.g., Esther 9:20-32; 1 Macc. 4:56; 2 Macc. 10:5-8), though there are no signs that this was ever instituted in early Jewish practice.

According to 3 Maccabees, Philopator issues a letter at this point for the Jews to take with them on their journeys home. Here the irony of the story reaches a climax: the king accuses his (former) companions of having designed the treachery against the Jews who had only ever shown "steadfast good will," and he grants the Jews safe passage on account of their standing as children of "the most high God." It is implausible that such a letter would have been written, and yet it represents an effort on the part of the author to lend verisimilitude to the story (cf., e.g., Ezra 1; 1 Macc. 8:23-30; 10:25-45; 2 Macc. 9:19-27; Gk. Esther 13:1-7). The presentation of a foreign king praising the God of Israel has parallels in other texts of the period, such as in Dan. 4:34-37.

In a dramatic denouement, the Jews who have been freed by Philopator do not depart until some final business is settled. The author of 3 Maccabees wishes to make another point—and perhaps, in the end, this is the central goal of the composition—namely, that those who previously converted or acquiesced to the king's demands ought to be put to death. In this way, the end of the work circles back toward its beginning, so that only those who steadfastly resisted the temptations of assimilation to Greek religion and society would live on to enjoy the deliverance from the hippodrome and the return to their homes. Here, then, is another dramatic irony: Philopator's "conversion" turns him against the very Jews who earlier had acquiesced to his demands. What is more, it is the faithful Jews who petition the king for the right to slaughter the apostates, and thus divine clemency is juxtaposed to human desire for retribution and purification.

The Text in the Interpretive Tradition

While 3 Maccabees does not appear to have much of an interpretive afterlife in Jewish and Christian traditions, it attests to a theme that is prominent in contemporary and later discourse: that of apostasy. Later Jewish traditions make examples out of apostates such as Elisha ben Abuyah (*y. Hag.* 2:1), and there is epigraphic evidence that the practice of Jewish defection was not uncommon around the Mediterranean world for a long period of time (Wilson, 44–65). Stephen Wilson aptly notes that defection and/or conversion are always two sides of the same coin, but that accounts of apostasy are "generally not interested in both sides at once" but seek to assure their audiences that "leaving the fold" is a poor option (Wilson, 134).

The Text in Contemporary Discussion

Perhaps especially in the Hellenistic Jewish Diaspora communities (such as in Egypt), assimilation was a social and religious problem that was negotiated in various ways by different individuals and groups. Some chose to embrace Greek culture, religion, and authority, and others to resist it. Thus the question of whether and how much to assimilate was a central fact of life for Jewish people in the Hellenistic age, and it gave rise to both external and internal conflicts. While the depiction of the released captives happily slaughtering three hundred of their apostate kinfolk is surely not historically factual, it is an apt literary expression of the inherent tensions of Jewish existence during this period.

Some contemporary scholars have suggested that the conditions inviting assimilation in Hellenistic settings may be compared to those of the modern period. Elias Bickerman, for example, draws a parallel between the enticements of Hellenistic "belonging" and those of nineteenth-century European societies in which Jews left or modified their traditional practices in favor of more modern ones (see Wilson, 25). In this way, the beginnings of Reform Judaism can be seen as a response to the conditions of contemporary Western life—an attempt to align Jewish life with the ethical, intellectual, and cultural values of modernity.

Works Cited

Croy, N. Clayton. 2005. *3 Maccabees*. Leiden: Brill.

Collins, John J. 1993. "3 Maccabees." In *HarperCollins Study Bible with the Apocryphal/Deuterocanonical Books*, edited by Wayne A. Meeks, 1752–67. New York: HarperCollins.

Johnson, Sara Raup. 2013. "3 Maccabees." In *Outside the Bible: Ancient Jewish Writings Related to Scripture*, volume 3, edited by Louis H. Feldman, James L. Kugel, and Lawrence H. Schiffman. Philadelphia: Jewish Publication Society, 2681–2707.

Wilson, Stephen G. 2004. *Leaving the Fold: Apostates and Defectors in Antiquity*. Minneapolis: Fortress Press.

2 ESDRAS (4, 5, AND 6 EZRA)

Robin Darling Young

Introduction

The early second-century Jewish apocalypse called Ezra (Greek and Latin, *Esdras*) records and interprets the distress of a Jewish community probably in Roman Judea three decades after the Roman general Titus conquered the country and destroyed Jerusalem in the war of 66–71 CE. Yet, like other apocalyptic books, it claims to have been written far earlier, under prophetic inspiration. Its purported author was the Ezra who returned from Babylon in 457 BCE to build a new city and temple and to enforce Jewish law among its inhabitants, just as the biblical books of Ezra and Nehemiah report. Although that earlier Ezra was not a prophet but a scribe and priest, the apocalyptic genre transformed an ancient leader into a visionary sage and a prophet of the later Roman destruction, showing how the scribe responsible for the rebuilding of Jerusalem in the 450s BCE actually knew two destructions and two reconstructions of the city and its temple: first, he witnessed the destruction under the Neo-Assyrians; and second, he foretold its destruction under the Romans with a reconstruction promised for the near future. Cyrus financed the first rebuilding; the second did not happen in antiquity.

No traces of a Hebrew text survive, and no later Jewish literature is known to have used it. The Greek text was not quoted after Clement of Alexandria (d. c. 220 CE). A Latin version was frequently copied and quoted, and a Syriac version survived in only one manuscript. Other ancient versions—Ethiopic, Georgian, Arabic, and Coptic—probably came from the lost Greek version, and the Armenian was probably translated from the Syriac (Stone 1990).

The standard name for the original Jewish Ezra apocalypse is 4 Ezra, so enumerated because two earlier scriptural books have the title "book of Ezra." In Bibles translated into English, 4 Ezra does not appear in its original form, remaining as the long, middle section of a larger book called 2 Esdras. Second Esdras, in turn, is the expanded version of 4 Ezra; translated from Latin, it appears in the Apocrypha section of English Bibles. The reason for this expansion of 4 Ezra is conjectural; at some point before 900 CE, an unknown copyist added two later oracular texts, each having a different origin; the copyist then put them on either side of the earlier 4 Ezra, giving the title of the new, expanded version, 2 Esdras.

The book of 2 Esdras appears in modern Bibles (Protestant and Catholic) because, beginning with Ambrose (340–397), bishop of Milan, the medieval Western church considered it inspired Scripture. Jerome disagreed, calling it a "book of dreams" and omitting it from the Vulgate, but biblical manuscripts retained the work until the sixteenth century. Columbus thought it predicted that New World voyages could lead to Jerusalem and a final triumphant Crusade to retake the Holy Land. Anabaptists and other dissenters were attracted to its apocalyptic eschatology. Spanish Catholic authors used the text to justify their New World colonies.

Such European interest lasted despite Renaissance textual scholars' doubts about its authenticity. Protestant Reformers rejected it because it was not part of the Hebrew Scriptures. Because the Church of England accepted 2 Esdras and the other apocryphal biblical works of the Vulgate, the King James Version includes 2 Esdras in the Apocrypha, as does the Revised Standard Version.

In editions of the Catholic Bible from the sixteenth century, 2 Esdras also remains apocryphal. The Council of Trent, responding to Protestant criticisms of church tradition, did not include 2 Esdras in its list of canonical Scriptures but did not remove it, along with other disputed books. After Catholic scholars' debates, 2 Esdras was removed from the Sixtine Vulgate of 1590, but restored in the Clementine Vulgate (1592); it appears in the Apocrypha of the Douay-Rheims English translation of the Vulgate. Only the Slavonic Bible of the Russian Orthodox Church still contains 2 Esdras in its canon, but calls it 3 Esdras. The smaller, Jewish text of 4 Ezra, however, has been retained in Ethiopian and Armenian Bibles; although it exists in the Syriac Peshitta in one manuscript, it has long been noncanonical in that tradition. It was not included in the Septuagint, and does not appear in Greek or Eastern Orthodox Bibles. For many readers of the Bible, then, 2 Esdras is unfamiliar.

Second Esdras combines three works. Its longest part is a core of fourteen chapters containing seven distinct discourses. The title 4 Ezra emphasizes its continuity with the Jewish traditions about Ezra, beginning with the canonical book of Ezra. Its seven episodes have four conversations between the putative author, Ezra/Shealtiel and the angel Uriel, and three are visions—apocalypses—granted to the visionary Ezra, revealing the future restoration of Jerusalem by a conquering Messiah, and the return of the dispersed tribes.

The bookends of 4 Ezra are Christian works composed to adapt the Jewish work for Christian use. The first, now called 5 Ezra, dates from the second century CE. It numbers two chapters, and functions as a preface. It recounts Ezra's genealogy, and an account of his prophetic call (1:4), lists God's spurned favors to Israel and subsequent rejection, and refers to Israel as a mother who then receives new children, the "nations that hear and understand" (2:34). The second bookend of 4 Ezra is usually called 6 Ezra, and it is an appendix concerning persecution and martyrdom. It envisions a cosmic battle, the protection of the people faithful to God, and the deliverance of God's elect at the end of time; it is now believed to date from the third century. In neither bookend is there a developed Christian teaching, but the use of typology and the theme of Israel's rejection, as well as the preservation of the book in Christian circles, point toward a Christian author who has cleverly reoriented the book to Christian polemic against the Jews.

Fourth Ezra thus has been interpreted against itself by the later addition of this preface and conclusion. As the last Jewish apocalypse of its era, it was the most explicitly messianic of any Second Temple Jewish text outside apocalyptic works in the New Testament. Yet Ezra's Messiah is not like Jesus; he is a militant conqueror who fights against the enemy and then dies. The remnant of Israel preserved by that Messiah turns for preservation to renewed and augmented Scriptures. The Jewish Christians who added to 4 Ezra the two later bookends of 5 and 6 Ezra forced the original Jewish text to serve their arguments against the Jews who did not accept Jesus. They thought that the Jews' alleged failures explicitly to obey God's law and in rejecting Jesus as Messiah made them subject not to God's rescue, but to rejection. Ironically, they turned 4 Ezra into 2 Esdras, one of the earliest anti-Jewish works in the Christian tradition, turning an apocalypse conveying hope for Jewish restoration into a condemnation of the Jews and an assertion of Christian triumph.

2 Esdras 3–14 (4 Ezra): An Apocalyptic and Prophetic Tapestry

The Text in Its Ancient Context

In its ancient context, chapters 3–14 of 2 Esdras form an elaborate work in the prophetic-apocalyptic tradition, intermingled with elements of the earlier wisdom tradition. It dates from after 71 CE, that is, from the Roman war against, and conquest of, Judea. Like other non-Christian Jewish apocalypses from the period, such as *2 Baruch*, the *Apocalypse of Abraham*, and parts of the *Sibylline Oracles*, it represents one Jewish reaction to the event. The disastrous rebellion against Roman rule led to a brutal imperial military campaign that led to the burning of the temple, the slaughter of thousands of Jewish subjects of Rome, and the exile and/or death of many of those who had survived the battles of the five-year war. The loss of the Jewish community—its people, books, holy sites, and rituals—gives the unknown author the occasion to assume the identity of an earlier Jew who was not a prophet, but a scribe and community leader. Ezra the scribe and hereditary member of the priesthood helped lead the Jewish community that had returned from Babylon in the late fifth century BCE; thus his restoration of the community around the Second Temple and the law gave him the status of a founder of Israel in succession to Abraham, Moses, and David/Solomon. As Shealtiel, he was son of Jehoiakin king of Judah (1 Chron. 3:17) and thus a successor to Israelite royalty.

This section (4 Ezra) is constructed as a prophecy from that older, historical Ezra, who reports in the prologue (2 Esd. 3:1) that he was "troubled" in Babylon "because I [fore]saw the desolation of Zion and the wealth of those who live in Babylon." Like the contemporary book of Revelation, it makes Babylon a symbol of Rome and its rule, thus contrasting God's faithful to their brutal oppressors. The author relied on his readers to understand that he was appropriating the identity of the earlier Ezra in order to issue prophetic denunciations, as well as consolation, to the Jewish people. Ezra speaks in the first person all the way through the text; in this, he resembles not only Paul but also the visionary of the book of Revelation.

Not only the prophetic mode appears in 4 Ezra; Lamentations also inspires a long complaint about human weakness, including the presence of an "evil heart" that is present in human beings from Adam, which makes it difficult to obey the divine law. In 4 Ezra, the "angel that had been sent to me, whose name was Uriel," becomes the *angelus interpres* questioning Ezra in return, illustrating his points with parables. Uriel resembles a heavenly messenger like the angels who converse with Ezekiel, Daniel, and Zechariah, in the noncanonical book of *Enoch*, and in later rabbinic and Christian works (such as the *Shepherd* of Hermas). As one of the priestly line, Ezra thus is an example of the association of angels with priests of the temple, a relationship having to do with the offering of sacrifice. In conversing with Uriel, Ezra gains in wisdom, and thus one recent interpreter has argued that the book is a combination of wisdom-traditions and apocalyptic discourse.

The final chapter of 4 Ezra is the commissioning of the prophet as a scribe. It takes an esoteric turn: first, Ezra receives divine instructions to withdraw for forty days and commit his own visions to writing with the aid of five well-trained scribes. Ezra dismisses the people of Israel whom he was commissioned to lead with instructions to "rule over your minds and discipline your hearts" (2 Esd. 14:34). For forty days, Ezra withdraws to a field. "A voice" calls Ezra to give him a special drink, in a cup containing a liquid like water, but with the color of fire. Then "my heart poured forth understanding, and wisdom increased in my breast" (14:40). Ezra's mouth is opened and his spirit retains its memory, and five scribes sit for forty days, taking down his dictation, in letters they do not understand; they "ate their bread at night" (14:42) but spend each day writing out what Ezra dictates. In the end, "the Most High" instructs Ezra to reveal twenty-four books he wrote first to both the worthy and unworthy, but to keep the seventy written last for "the wise among your people. For in them is the spring of understanding, the fountain of wisdom, and the river of knowledge" (14:46). The genuine apocalypse of Ezra (4 Ezra) thus ends with an endorsement of secret wisdom and Ezra's ascent (Hogan 2008).

Second Esdras 3–14 (4 Ezra) has much in common with the concerns of other Jewish authors of the first century—not only with the author of *2 Baruch* but also with those of the letters, Gospels, and apocalypse of the New Testament. The "evil heart" afflicting humanity since Adam has parallels in Paul (particularly in Romans); its insistence on following the law in continuity with Mosaic injunction recalls the Gospel of Matthew; its interest in the Messiah links it with all four Gospels; and its concern for the eschaton and the restoration of Jerusalem links it with Revelation (Longenecker 1991).

The Text in the Interpretive Tradition

Second Esdras, or for that matter 4 Ezra, had a long but limited influence on the interpretive tradition of European Christianity. Clearly related to the literary compositions of prior apocalypses, some of which are in the canonical Old Testament, it also participates in the wisdom tradition as exemplified in the book of Job, and it is most closely related to the works of first-century Judaism, including the New Testament. Ezra's instruction about the small number of the saved resembles Paul's views in Galatians and Romans. His seven apocalyptic visions mirror, or perhaps inspired, those in the book of Revelation. His conversations with the archangel Uriel resemble Enoch, a book still read in the first century; over all, *2 Baruch* mirrors it. Finally, his dependence on the judgment and combat scenes in Daniel echoes themes in the Gospel of Matthew, as does his recourse to the gathering of disciples to transmit esoteric teaching. Because 4 Ezra was not preserved in the post–Second Temple Jewish tradition, it seems to resemble more closely the trajectories of early Christianity; but in the first century, Jewish and Christian worlds of discourse overlapped; therefore, a full treatment of 4 Ezra should resemble studies of the New Testament texts as Jewish literature (Najman and Young).

The early Christian tradition shows interest in the text. Fourth Ezra (in a now-lost Greek version) has been quoted by Clement of Alexandria and called "the prophet." He also seems to be quoted by Cyprian and Tertullian from the Latin text, as well as from Commodian. Ambrose of Milan quoted 4 Ezra/2 Esdras frequently, and a tradition of respect for the text developed in Spain, where it was preserved and quoted as an authority. In particular, because it refers to the presence of lost tribes in a distant land, it was taken to indicate the existence of the New World. But although such a tradition is of interest to scholars of the text, it shows only that 2 Esdras had a durable but extremely narrow authority in the Latin West; originating in an apocalyptic literary tradition, its influence remained relegated to that current in the theological tradition of the West.

The Text in Contemporary Discussion

Although 2 Esdras holds great interest for scholars of first-century Judaism and Christianity and for those interested in medieval textual traditions and the reception of prophetic discourse in medieval and early modern Europe, it seems to have had little attraction initially for those contemporary communities that read the Old Testament. Hence, it is not often thoroughly compared with the contemporary Christian texts with which it shares so many theological points of view. This is especially true of its most thorough commentary to date (Stone 1990). Ironically, its esotericism seems to have worked to make it relatively inaccessible. Yet a consideration of 2 Esdras offers the opportunity to address the growing tradition, in the second and third centuries CE, of the hostile appropriation of Jewish Scriptures that marked the Christian community from Justin Martyr's *Dialogue with Trypho* forward. But 2 Esdras can be a resource for the appreciation of a first-century Jewish messianism centered not on Jesus of Nazareth but on the hope for the military defeat of Rome and that looked toward a renewed reverence for the Law, both as a set of books and as pattern for conduct. Thus readers of the New Testament could appreciate the text as a contemporary of and a contrast to the other first-century Jewish texts of that book.

In addition, 2 Esdras raises other questions fruitful for exploration: What is the ongoing role of prophecy and denunciation/consolation, as encouraged by the reading of this book? How is the doctrine of election received in the Christian tradition to which 2 Esdras has been joined? How does the text's conception of an "evil root" relate to the teaching of original sin, itself now as problematic as the doctrine of the end of the world articulated in the book's visions?

Following Michael Stone's massive commentary on the text, some interpreters have focused on a "psychological approach" (Hogan 2008) to Ezra 4—for instance, interpreting the woman/Zion as a symbol of the author's transformation from mourner to prophet and sage (Humphrey 1995);

or as a projection of the author's own dilemma (Daschke); a literary expression of the struggle for identity (Burkes); and the interpretation of dreams (Flannery-Dailes). Collins also emphasizes the psychological approach as an interpretation of apocalyptic (reassurance, not literal prophecy). But like Longenecker, Brandenburger, and Harnisch, Karina Martin Hogan reads 4 Ezra as a "literary representation of a theological debate external to the author, a debate between two schools of wisdom at around 100" (2012).

Second Esdras is a work of high drama containing many of the theological concerns of ancient Judaism and Christianity but posing many of the same problems to nonliteralist modern interpreters and readers, who must choose between allegorizing the texts or reducing them to curiosities.

2 Esdras 1–2; 15–16 (5–6 Ezra): Rethinking Israel's Restoration

The Text in Its Ancient Context

In reinterpreting the text of 4 Ezra, the additions of 5 and 6 Ezra reflect the teachings of two separate communities that had turned away from the idea of the literal, political restoration of Israel. Extant only in the Latin tradition, these are therefore Western additions. For the author of each text, the real Messiah sent to rescue the remnant was one whom not the gentiles, and not the Jews, followed. These additions represent a thorough repudiation of 4 Ezra's conviction that some—a remnant—of the Jewish community will continue to obey the law and be vindicated at the end of Ezra's revelatory experiences. In particular, the two chapters of 5 Ezra (2 Esdras 1–2) may represent the origins of the *Improperia*, a series of antiphons and responses formerly appearing in the Good Friday liturgy in Roman Catholic and other traditions, by which Christ mourns his rejection by Israel.

Second Esdras 1–2 (5 Ezra) commences with a fictive genealogy of the prophet Ezra, and an account of his prophetic commission. There follows a series of accusations against Israel (1:5-23) gathered from earlier prophetic utterances in the canonical prophets. The remainder of the chapter asserts the rejection of Israel and the substitution of the gentiles ("the people who is to come") for Israel as the recipients of both the covenant and the promises of God. Finally, the membership in the patriarchal religion ("of Abraham, Isaac, and Jacob . . .") is transferred to "a people who is coming from the East" (1:38). Here the text may recall traditions about the Persian *magoi* recorded in the Gospel of Matthew, where the Persians stand for the future faith of the gentile kingdoms.

The second chapter of 5 Ezra (2 Esdras 2) begins with a direct, traditionally prophetic statement, "Thus says the Lord," and records that Israel no longer deserves its inclusion in the kinship group loyal to God: "Let their names be blotted from the earth because they have despised my covenant" (2:7). The kingdom of Jerusalem will be prepared for the gentiles; the promises are transferred to the gentiles; and a new law will be given from them. Finally, the chapter makes of Ezra a second Moses, brought up to Mt. Horeb, where he has a vision of the Christian martyrs and the Son of God, and is commissioned to "go and tell" his vision more widely (2:33-48).

The original context of 5 Ezra, then, was probably a community of Jewish Christians that had separated from the synagogue only recently. Because it incorporated 4 Ezra, it cherished the traditions of Second Temple Judaism, but condemned those Jews who did not think that Jesus was the Messiah, and insisted that God had transferred his care to the gentiles who were ready to inherit Jewish Scripture, adjusted to point typologically to Jesus. Thus the text brings 4 Ezra closer to the views of the book of Revelation or the Gospel of John. There is no condemnation of scribes or Pharisees, but an implicit rejection of early rabbinic endorsement of the written and oral laws (Bergren 1990).

Because 6 Ezra (2 Esdras 15–16) was meant to modify and extend the conclusion of 4 Ezra, it reinforces the apocalyptic sections of the central and original text with a series of eschatological images. God commissions Ezra in the first verses to speak "in the ears of the people the word of the prophecy . . . and cause them to be written on paper, for they are faithful and true" (2 Esd. 15:1–2). The last clause may reflect Revelation 20, and its evocation of warring nations in very general terms—Egypt, Syria, Babylon, and Asia—also echoes earlier prophetic discourse in the canonical Old Testament prophets. The rest of 6 Ezra underlines the chaos and destruction coming in the last days, illustrating the chaos of the end of the world by recounting the calamities coming upon "my people." There next will be a respite from calamity; at the conclusion of this prophecy, the author recalls God's work of creation and predicts that the God who has made human beings will know how to judge them on the Day of Judgment. Finally, the text predicts persecution of a kind that points to the end of the second century: the wrath of "a great multitude" causes persecutors to "drag some of you away and force you to eat what was sacrificed to idols" (2 Esd. 16:68). This persecution tests which of the new people of God are faithful. The ones "who keep my commandments and precepts" will be rescued from the tribulation (Bergren 1998).

The Text in the Interpretive Tradition

The additions of 5 and 6 Ezra signal the implicit recognition of the text's origins, among the earliest Christians who received and used the text. Since 4 Ezra clearly differed from developing Christian teachings about Jesus and the church, it needed to be altered slightly to be used in community settings—thus the Christianizing adjustments that appear, and that make Ezra a prophet of Christianity, much like John the Baptist, or like Enoch in his Christian reception.

The Text in Contemporary Discussion

Recent scholarly discussions of 5 and 6 Ezra have shown their function in claiming the larger text for a Christian community and its scriptural tradition. They are treated as part of 4 Ezra in discussions of the ongoing use of the text in medieval and Renaissance Christianity, but their semicanonical status limits their interest largely to scholars of Christian rewritten Scriptures (Hogan, 2008).

Since 5 and 6 Ezra (2 Esdras 1–2, 15–16) together constitute a Christian addition to the original, Jewish work ascribed to Ezra the scribe, contemporary discussion could take two directions. The first direction would separate the two additions, since they are thought to come from different time periods; the second would treat them together as part of the Christian appropriation—and in this case a hostile appropriation—of an originally Jewish work.

In the first direction, it could be observed that the first addition (5 Ezra) seems to add Christian material to an originally Jewish chapter (1), to make up an apocalyptic prediction of persecution and triumph. This first addition, written in around 200 CE, comes from an era when apocalyptic prophecy had not been marginalized in early Christianity; but the second addition, possibly composed in the third century, marginalizes prophecy and anticipates heavenly reward for those suffering distress. This direction of discussion could ask about the ongoing production of prophecy in Christianity and would be concerned with matters of authority and legitimacy in Christian communities as eschatological anticipation became embarrassing or illegitimate.

In the second line of discussion, the text could be queried as to its anti-Jewish invective. How is a Christian community to handle such invective when it appears as canonical Scripture? This approach raises questions about inspiration and mutual reprobation that, while disturbing in the present, could be a fruitful subject of discussion in a period in which discussions between Jews and Christians have become more frequent.

Works Cited

Bergren, Theodore A. 1990. *Fifth Ezra: The Text, Origin and Early History*. Atlanta: Scholars Press.

———. 1998. *Sixth Ezra: The Text and Its Origin*. New York: Oxford University Press.

Coggins, R. J., and M. A. Knibb. 1979. *The First and Second Books of Esdras*. New York: Cambridge University Press.

Michael D. Coogan, ed. *Oxford Annotated Bible*. 3rd ed. Oxford: Oxford University Press.

Hamilton, Alastair. 1999. *The Apocryphal Apocalypse: The Reception of the Second Book of Esdras (4 Ezra) from the Renaissance to the Enlightenment*. Oxford: Clarendon.

Hogan, Karina Martin. 2008. *Theologies in Conflict in 4 Ezra: Wisdom Debate and Apocalyptic Solution*. Leiden: Brill.

———. 2012. "2 Esdras." In *The Women's Bible Commentary*, edited by Carol A. Newsom, Sharon H. Ringe, and Jacqueline E. Lapsley, 370–75. 3rd ed. Louisville: Westminster John Knox.

Humphrey, Edith M. 1995. *The Ladies and the Cities: Transformation and Apocalyptic Identitiy in Joseph and Aseneth, 4 Ezra, the Apocalypse and the Shepherd of Hermas* (Journal of the Pseudepigrapha Supplement Series). Continuum International Publishing Group.

Longenecker, Bruce. 1991. *Eschatology and the Covenant: A Comparison of 4 Ezra and Romans 1–11*. Sheffield: JOST Press.

———. 1995. *2 Esdras*. Sheffield: Sheffield Academic.

Myers, Jacob M. 1974. *1 and 2 Esdras*. AB 42. Garden City, NY: Doubleday.

Najman, Hindy. 2014. *Losing the Temple and Recovering the Future: An Analysis of 4 Ezra*. Cambridge: Cambridge University Press.

Najman, Hindy, and Robin Darling Young. Forthcoming. *Fourth Ezra: A Commentary on The Syriac Text*. Berlin: de Gruyter.

Stone, Michael E. 1979. *The Armenian Version of IV Ezra*. Armenian Texts and Studies 1. Philadelphia: University of Pennsylvania Press.

———. 1990. *Fourth Ezra: A Commentary on the Book of Fourth Ezra*. Minneapolis: Fortress Press.

Stone, Michael E., and Matthias Henze. 2013. *4 Ezra and 2 Baruch: Translations, Introductions, and Notes*. Minneapolis: Fortress Press.

Thompson, Alden Lloyd. 1977. *Responsibility for Evil in the Theodicy of 1V Ezra*. Missoula, MT: Scholars Press.

4 MACCABEES

Samuel I. Thomas

Introduction

Fourth Maccabees is an early Jewish composition written in Greek and included as an appendix in some manuscripts of the Septuagint, eventually becoming canonical in the Georgian Orthodox tradition. The composition was grouped with other books about the Maccabees (Hasmoneans) despite its lack of any explicit mention of the family of Mattathias and Judas Maccabaeus; this is probably because 4 Maccabees retells much of the martyr narrative of 2 Maccabees 6–7, recasting the language and purpose of the story for a new setting under Roman rule. Given its focus on martyrs, the text played an important role in early Christian theologies of martyrdom, perhaps early enough to have a direct influence on some New Testament compositions.

The author of 4 Maccabees seems principally concerned to present Jewish torah piety as a prime vehicle for the triumph of reason over the passions, thereby reflecting a theme common to Hellenistic philosophical ethics. For this reason, among others, commentators have often dated the composition to the mid- to late first century CE, during which time the literary style and philosophical outlook of the author would fit well within its context. While both Jerome and Eusebius attribute the work to Josephus, contemporary scholars argue that the author is an unknown Diaspora Jew writing from Antioch or Alexandria.

David deSilva characterizes the literary features of 4 Maccabees as "epideictic rhetoric including elements of different genres such as encomium, sermon, diatribe" (deSilva, xxi), and the philosophical perspective reflects a relatively sophisticated awareness of Greek structures of argumentation and oratorical topics. In particular, the author draws on the form of the funeral oration in his presentation of the lives of the martyrs—a presentation that constitutes the bulk of the narrative. Despite the author's immersion in Hellenistic intellectual trends and literary forms, he advocates a life guided by traditional observance of the torah.

Fourth Maccabees is not well attested in later (rabbinic) Jewish tradition, perhaps because of its popularity among Christians by the second century CE. The only Jewish text that may show familiarity with 4 Maccabees is *Lamentations Rabbah* 1:16, which refers to the martyrdom of Miriam bat Tanhum and her sons (see 4 Macc. 5:29). In contrast, 4 Maccabees was influential in the early church, with citations or allusions in the letters of Ignatius, the *Martyrdom of Polycarp*, Origen's *Exhortation to Martyrdom*, *Perpetua and Felicity* (Eusebius, *Hist. eccl.* 5.1), *Martyrdom of Montanus and Lucius*, Tertullian's *On Patience*, and the sermons of John Chrysostom, Gregory of Nazianzus, and Ambrose of Milan. The text is also included in the Sinaiticus and Alexandrinus codexes, which serve as the basis for most modern critical editions of the Septuagint.

4 Maccabees 1:1—3:18: Introduction

The Text in Its Ancient Context

The author of 4 Maccabees opens his exordium with an appeal to pious reason as the "absolute master of the passions." The author informs the audience in advance that in order to demonstrate the truth of this claim, it will be necessary to know his procedural method: first, he will expound the hypothesis, and then he will prove it by recourse to a story about the moral excellence of people who died in order to uphold their faith.

The framing of the work in this way reflects the literary conventions of the time, and with specific uses of language ("most philosophical," "passions," "reason," "self-mastery," etc.) the author invokes a set of concepts common to Greek virtue ethics. This author, however, wishes to reframe the discussion of rational virtue in terms of the Jewish scriptural tradition. He both draws on schools of thought represented by the Stoics, Peripatetics, and others, and at the same time cautions that Greek "philosophy" is itself not adequate without pious adherence to torah. The author of this work avoids specific references to Greek figures or stories, and instead draws all of his examples of virtue and reason from the Jewish tradition.

In its rather lengthy introduction, 4 Maccabees provides the interpretive lens by which to understand the examples of the martyrs, whose stories constitute the main body of the work. While the author purports to define the nature of the "passions" and of "reason" in this section, he does little more than provide a catalog of their common characteristics. In any case, for this author, reason is a faculty of the mind that, along with "right thinking," leads a person to wisdom. All this is made possible by the right kind of education (*paideia*, an important term in Greek philosophical discourse), a notion that will return later in the composition in relation to the torah.

It is fitting to the period that the author attempts to integrate Jewish wisdom with Greek traditions regarding the four cardinal virtues of prudence (*phronēsis*), justice (*dikaiosynē*), courage (*andreia*), and moderation (*sōphrosynē*), claiming that torah, as the embodiment of wisdom, is the way to foster each virtue in the life of the sage (see Wisd. of Sol. 8:7; Philo, *Leg.* 1.71). Indeed, wisdom in its cardinal forms is "knowledge of divine and human matters and the causes of these," and comes from "the instruction gained from the Law" (4 Macc. 1:15-18).

According to the introduction to the work, knowledge of the law leads primarily to prudence, which is ultimately a kind of ethical restraint. As an example of this virtue, the author has recourse to David's mastery of his thirst, by which he overcame the desires of the body with "the nobility and goodness of reason" (4 Macc. 3:18). Here we find a reflection of a well-attested theme in Hellenistic literature, namely, the "mind-body" dualism found also in Philo, the letters of Paul, and elsewhere. But here, too, the author of 4 Maccabees exceeds other accounts of David's thirst (for example Josephus, *Ant.* 7.12.4) in the way he embellishes and transforms the story to suit the purposes of his argument.

The Text in the Interpretive Tradition

It is difficult to know in many cases whether the introduction to 4 Maccabees has influenced other texts and traditions of early Judaism and Christianity. Perhaps because of its marginal status in scriptural collections, 4 Maccabees as a whole has not elicited much commentary beyond late antiquity.

The author of 4 Maccabees was indebted—and made his own contribution—to the Jewish wisdom tradition of the late Second Temple period. In the introduction to the work, one may discern the influence LXX Proverbs, Ben Sira, and the Wisdom of Solomon may have had on the concept of "pious reason" in 4 Maccabees. This is especially true with respect to the development of the association between wisdom and torah (Prov. 8:22-30; Sir. 1:26; 24:23; Wis. 6:17-20; 9:9; 4 Macc. 1:16-17; 2:21-23; cf. Collins, 23–61), a development that reaches full expression in the opening lines of *Genesis Rabbah* several centuries later. In this commentary on Genesis, the rabbis make explicit the association between wisdom and torah, and deduce therefore that the torah was the blueprint for all creation.

While the direction of influence is difficult to determine, there are close affinities between 4 Macc. 1:1—3:18 and several New Testament compositions (see deSilva, xxxii–xxxviii). This is particularly evident in the Pastoral Epistles, in which self-mastery is crucial to rightly order oneself to desires and achieve piety and faith (cf., e.g., 4 Macc. 1:1, 31-32; 2:1-6; 2 Tim. 2:22; 3:6; Titus 2:12; 3:3). The explicit uses of this text in later Christianity seem limited to the passages regarding martyrdom.

The Text in Contemporary Discussion

While the introduction to 4 Maccabees has not elicited extensive commentary in the contemporary world, it addresses certain themes that continue to be relevant today. What is the relationship between "faith" and "reason"? Is there such a thing as an appropriate demand to remain dedicated to a way of life even in the face of death? During a time of prosperity and consumerism, what might it mean to restrain "desires" in the service of wisdom and the ethically good life?

Fourth Maccabees also carries a challenge to the present age of borrowing, debts, and deficits. Drawing on LXX Deut. 15:2, 8-9, the author teaches the importance of reducing debts in order to avoid the accumulation of wealth and in favor of the well-being of the community. Fourth Maccabees thus offers "remedies against the human tendency toward greed" so that "mastery of the passions is part of the means by which justice in human relations can be secured" (deSilva, 98). In an era of a widening gulf between rich and poor—individuals and nations—it is appropriate to ask: What would the world be like if human communities took these admonitions to heart?

4 Maccabees 3:19—7:23: Antiochus IV and the Martyrdom of Eleazar the Priest

The Text in Its Ancient Context

The narratives of the martyrs occupy most of the rest of 4 Maccabees, and serve as the "narrative demonstration" (3:19) of the author's opening argument about reason, the passions, and the life of torah observance. After an introduction (3:19—4:26), this section recounts the martyrdom of Eleazar, a story based on the presentation of this figure in 2 Maccabees.

Fourth Maccabees 3:19—4:26 reflects an adapted and stylized version of a story known from other sources, beginning with an account of the idyllic and peaceful rule of the high priest Onias III (204?–175 BCE), who was the last of the Oniad family to inherit the high priestly office (VanderKam, 188). Second Maccabees also refers to the reign of Onias III as a time of "unbroken peace," when "the laws were strictly observed because of the piety of the high priest Onias and his hatred of wickedness" (2 Macc. 3:1-3). Beginning the episode of Eleazar's martyrdom in this way serves the dramatic purposes of the author by setting up the contrast with what is to follow—political intrigue, subterfuge, and persecution.

The story of Eleazar is set during the time of the Seleucid ruler Antiochus IV Epiphanes (here mistakenly called the son rather than the brother of Seleucus IV), whose reign is well known for its persecution of Jews in Jerusalem and for creating the conditions for the Maccabean revolt. The activities of Antiochus were despised and resisted by a number of early Jewish groups and writers, including the authors of 2 Maccabees and Daniel.

The account in this section of 4 Maccabees, however, differs from 2 Maccabees in some important details. For example, 2 Maccabees reports that it was one Heliodorus—and not Apollonius—who attempted to seize funds from the temple treasury (2 Macc. 3:7-8; cf. 3 Macc. 1:8—2:24), a discrepancy that may derive from the fact that 4 Maccabees is interested more in the mechanics of his "narrative demonstration" than in historically accurate details (deSilva, 116). In any case, a common theme in the "temple-robbing" narratives in early Jewish literature is the drubbing of the temple invader followed by his supplication according to standard Jewish forms of prayer.

This story revolves around a crucial question for Jews of the third and second centuries BCE: Embrace Hellenism or reject and resist it? Like other writers dealing with this period in Jewish history, the author of 4 Maccabees uses particular characters to represent, on the one hand, advocates of the appropriation of Greek culture into Judaism of the period (e.g., the Simon of 4 Macc. 4:1, Jason the High Priest, Antiochus IV) and, on the other, those who resisted the incursions of Hellenism for the sake of tradition and piety (e.g., Onias III, the Maccabees). The story of the martyrs is thus offered here as part of the author's commentary on this period, and as the main ideological vehicle of his "narrative demonstration."

In 4 Maccabees, Jason the high priest, who is portrayed as a usurper, is responsible for the decay of a more traditional way of Jewish life. But while Jason may have taken measures to remake Jerusalem into a Greek *polis*, it was in fact not Jason who undertook to abolish the temple cult but his successor Menelaus (2 Macc. 6:1-5; cf. 4 Macc. 4:20). The attribution of the latter action to Jason serves the author's larger aims, however: in the narrative logic of this episode, it is the suspension of the temple cult that makes necessary the "sacrifice" of the martyrs for the sake of the preservation of the covenant between God and Israel (deSilva, 121–22).

The work of the martyrs in 4 Maccabees serves as a "demonstration" of the basic Deuteronomic principle that collective infidelity to the covenant (i.e., in the form of Hellenization, worship of foreign gods, etc.) would result in punishment, and that corporate obedience leads to restoration. Thus Eleazar and the other martyrs provide the examples of fidelity that would prompt a renewed covenantal harmony should they be emulated by the rest of the community.

In what follows in this section, 4 Maccabees offers its own unique intervention in its presentation of the rhetorical contest between Antiochus IV and Eleazar—a scene that doubtless is not historical, however compellingly narrated it may be. Fourth Maccabees refers to Antiochus IV as a "tyrant" (e.g., 5:1; 14; 6:1), a term that is used deliberately to contrast him with Eleazar and to suggest that the confrontation between those two was a confrontation between tyranny and innocence; this term may also connect 4 Maccabees here with other "resistance literature," such as the early Christian martyrologies (see deSilva, 125).

One of the most distinctive aspects of Jewish identity in the Greco-Roman world was in the sphere of dietary practices. Non-Jewish commentators often took note of this distinction in a derogatory way in order to marginalize Jews and establish Judaism as a kind of superstition (in contrast with the "noble" and "lofty" religion and philosophy of the Greeks and Romans). Dietary and other religious practices served also to fuel a major controversy between the Antioch and Jerusalem factions of the earliest Christian church (Galatians 2–3; Acts 15).

Fourth Maccabees presents the violation of the Jewish food laws as the main vehicle for apostasy, especially since it is the wicked king Antiochus who seeks to persuade them (via Eleazar) to eat pork as a sign of their recognition of the superiority of the Greek way of life. The debate between Eleazar and Antiochus thus revolves around the question of the relationship between obedience to the Jewish law and the use of reason in pursuit of the "natural law" of the Greek philosophers.

To counter Antiochus's argument regarding the "necessity" of obeying his command, Eleazar argues—it seems for the sake of his audience—that the only "necessity" is to obey God by observing the torah. This rhetorical strategy (on the part of the author, who speaks here through Eleazar) connects with and animates a number of Greek philosophical virtues, most especially those of courage and piety, as well as the notion of the ultimate freedom of the ones who resist tyranny by remaining true to principle. This latter idea reflects a characteristically Stoic outlook in which the true sage renounces worldly comfort or success in favor of a life (or death, as it were) of integrity and honor.

The heady exchange between Antiochus and Eleazar on matters of religion and philosophy may seem strange in view of the gruesome scenes of torture and death that follow. Yet there is a connection between the two: the structure and logic of the debate seems to invite a ghastly display of piety insofar as this becomes necessary as a consequence of Eleazar's rhetorical victory. The greater the suffering of the martyrs, the greater their integrity; the more graphic the detail, the more compelling their witness—a witness that underscores Eleazar's greater embodiment of *both* Jewish and Greek virtues. In fact, here 4 Maccabees departs considerably from its base text in 2 Maccabees in its embellished account of the torture and death of the martyrs, causing some interpreters to become uncomfortable with its vivid description.

At the end of this section, the author returns to his main thesis by way of a narrative intermission. The martyrdom of Eleazar confirms the notion that pious reason—or the use of steadfast reason as the foundation for piety—allows one to overcome the passions (fear, pain, pleasure, etc.) in moments of trial. Eleazar is given an encomium in a manner consistent with Hellenistic conventions, and he is presented in this eulogy as the ideal sage—and as the model for those who would come after him.

The Text in the Interpretive Tradition

Fourth Maccabees—and in particular the account of Eleazar's martyrdom—seems to have been influential in the presentation of later Jewish and Christian martyr figures. While the question of whether 4 Maccabees had direct influence on writings in the New Testament is debated (and unlikely in most cases), 4 Maccabees does provide some important parallel material regarding certain first-century-CE ideas and themes. This is especially true with respect to attitudes about torah observance (Galatians 2–3; 5–6) and the "noble death" of those who suffer for the sake of others (e.g., Mark 10:45; Rom. 3:24-25; 1 Tim. 2:6; Heb. 9:1—10:18; Phil. 2:5-11), though other conceptual and linguistic parallels exist (see deSilva, xxxii–xxxiii).

The description of the death of Eleazar in 4 Maccabees evinces a theme found in other early Jewish and Christian texts: that of an obedient individual (or several individuals) whose voluntary suffering and death prompts the favor of God to the benefit of others (cf. the LXX interpretation of Isa. 52:13—53:12 and 39:5-7; 2 Macc. 8:5; Heb. 10:5-10; 1 Pet. 2:21-25). This idea—and surely the presentations of the martyrs in both 2 Maccabees and 4 Maccabees—also informs early Christian martyr accounts such as the letters of Ignatius of Antioch (*Eph.* 21.1; *Smyr.* 10.2) and the diaries of Perpetua and Felicitas, among others. It is also possible that the *Martyrdom of Habbib* relies on 4 Maccabees in the way Habbib "makes a claim for recognition before God for not fleeing the torments when he was able to do so" and insists on the just punishment of the tyrant (deSilva, xxvii; *Martyrdom of Habbib* 36; 4 Macc. 6:27).

The Text in Contemporary Discussion

The exchange between Eleazar and Antiochus represents the tension between the (then) dominant culture's view of Judaism and the case for the Jewish way of life from an insider perspective. This "debate" also attests to the fact that assumptions about identity are always and everywhere shaped by one's vantage point and by power and social position.

Fourth Maccabees deals with a problem that spans many ages and cultures. How should religious minorities deal adequately with the tension that arises between adherence to customary beliefs and practices and living in a dominant culture that emphasizes different values? What are the demands—and the limits—of conformity to imperial life? Fourth Maccabees argues that it is better and more reasonable to adhere to a traditional culture than to acquiesce to the pressures of assimilation. What forms might this kind of resistance take in contemporary life, especially when it comes to the kinds of pressures that religious minorities face? Conversely, what obligation do traditional, religious communities have to demonstrate the reasonableness and nobility—that is, the acceptability—of their traditions within the larger social and cultural systems?

The martyrdoms of Eleazar and others in 4 Maccabees have the effect (in the narrative) of destroying the power of the ruler through self-restraint and martyrdom coupled with the sophisticated political rhetoric of honor and shame. David deSilva puts it well: "The underlying question [in the debate between Eleazar and Antiochus]: is what truly is compelling. Is it the force of law or power and the concern for temporal well-being on which they depend in order to work, or concern for maintaining one's integrity in regard to the values one holds inviolable?" (deSilva, 133). Fourth Maccabees depicts an act of nonviolent resistance to oppression, serving thus as an ancient example of a perennial impulse that also finds expression in the contemporary world—Gandhi, Martin Luther King Jr., and the writings of Gene Sharp readily come to mind.

The martyrdom of Eleazar has also served in recent years as an example of the construction of masculinity in the ancient world. Drawing on gender studies and poststructuralist approaches, for example, Stephen Moore and Janice Anderson have argued that the classical virtue of courage—*andreia*, which can be translated as "manliness"—is the principal virtue that 4 Maccabees wishes to lift up for emulation. At the end of the encomium of Eleazar, the author of 4 Maccabees declares that "some persons appear to be dominated by their emotions because of the weakness of their reason," but that "only the wise and courageous [*ho sophos kai andreios*] is master of the passions" (4 Macc. 7:23). The text thus inverts the notion that manliness is related to physical or coercive power and roots it instead in self-mastery—a masculine ideal that applied also to women (see the martyrdom of the mother, 4 Macc. 15:23, 28-30; 16:3-4; see below for further discussion).

4 Maccabees 8:1—14:10: The Martyrdom of the Seven Brothers

The Text in Its Ancient Context

Both the torture and the rhetoric are heightened in the narrative about the seven brothers. While 2 Maccabees 7 once again serves as the point of departure for this martyrdom account, here the author of 4 Maccabees elaborates and embellishes the story to serve his own rhetorical purposes. It is not implausible that something like this episode may have occurred in antiquity, but in keeping with his grandiose style the author is not primarily concerned here with historicity.

In the ancient Greek world, youth was often associated with a certain brashness and lack of control over impulses and passions (see Aristotle, *Rhet.* 2.12). How much more significant, then, that these seven youths submit themselves to the pious reason shaped by their education in torah! This is rhetorically forceful for the added reason that the young men were offered enticements from Antiochus—positions, land, wealth—that may have been hard to come by for nonestablishment Jews of second-century-BCE Jerusalem.

Antiochus proceeds to torture each of the brothers one by one, and 4 Maccabees narrates the methods and implements used in gruesome detail (a rhetorical technique known as "vivid description," or *ekphrasis*) with the express aim to make the audience squirm with discomfort (4 Macc. 14:9). Some of the instruments of torture are known from other ancient Greek sources, while others are not. The text seems to assume that the audience would have been familiar with these contraptions, most of which were dedicated to inflicting acute pain at extremities and joints (see deSilva, 162–64, for a detailed discussion).

In keeping with the theme of 4 Maccabees generally, each brother embodies the triumph of pious reason over the temptations to acquiesce, appealing also to the reward that is greater than any Antiochus has to offer—that of an afterlife that honors their ancestors and vouchsafes immortality (e.g., 4 Macc. 9:1-9). This theme is reflected also in Plato's depiction of Socrates' last moments in the *Gorgias* (*Gorg.* 527A–B), and in Jewish Wisdom and apocalyptic literature of the age (Wisd. of Sol. 1:16-5:23; 6:17-20; *T. Mos.* 9:6-7). Fourth Maccabees also connects the theme of honoring ancestors to the example of Abraham, who preferred "sacrifice" over disobeying God (4 Macc. 9:21; 13:12; 14:20; 15:28; 16:20).

Toward the end of this section, 4 Maccabees strongly evinces the theme of "brotherly love," or *philadelphia*, which is a kind of virtuous friendship discussed also in Aristotle's *Nicomachean Ethics* and other classical sources. The ties that bind these brothers include their education in the Torah, their association with a larger community of the faithful, and their shared moral excellence. This fraternal bond helps to heighten the sense of sacrifice and lend it an aura of the paradoxical: their passionate, mutual affection became the very force that compelled them to obey "reason" and to resist the demands of the tyrant (13:19—14:1).

The Text in the Interpretive Tradition

The brutal treatment of the seven brothers in 4 Maccabees becomes a template for the presentation of later (Christian) martyrs. The *Martyrdom of Polycarp*, for example, contains a graphic depiction of the hero's torture and death (though in this case by burning, stabbing, and other bodily insults) and gives Polycarp a similar justification for choosing martyrdom: that he will be eternally rewarded while his persecutors will be forever caught in the fire of judgment (*Mart. Pol.* 11; cf. 4 Macc. 9:7-9; 10:11; 13:14-15).

Fourth Maccabees clearly influences subsequent Christian martyrologies. Some of the most interesting legacies of the narrative about the seven brothers and their mother include its concept of martyrs as "athletes" and "devotees" and even "contestants" of piety and virtue (Origen, *Exhortation to Martyrdom* 23; *Passion of Saints Perpetua and Felicity* 10.1–4; cf. 4 Macc. 12:11-14; 13:27; 17:15). The athletic metaphor here is apt, given the emphasis on endurance, victory, and the ultimate vanquishing of the heroes' foes.

The Text in Contemporary Discussion

The most striking aspect of this section of 4 Maccabees is its vivid portrayal of torture. While this may be understandable from a rhetorical point of view—the author wished to underscore the severity of the brutality so as to heighten the readers' respect for the self-sacrifice and religious integrity of the brothers—it is unsettling to imagine these torments actually taking place. This is especially the case when we recognize that the perpetrator in this text (Antiochus) was a functionary of the "rational" imperial regime and that the victims were among the persecuted and caricatured religious minorities of the time.

Torture has long been a staple in the official (or unofficial) treatment of enemies of any state. It is, in essence, treatment of the dominated body toward its coercive capitulation to the will of the dominator. Refusal to capitulate is the last refuge of the martyr—or the one who would become a martyr to the people he or she represents. In this way, "martyrdom" is always defined and narrated by those who experience their own reality to be one of persecution—and it can thus be a way to claim moral power for the otherwise powerless. Accounts like this—indeed, perhaps all martyrdom stories—call one to recognize that experience and perspective are important dimensions in the creation of martyrs, and that there is often a polemical edge to martyrdom discourses.

In an age of terrorism, school shootings, and waterboarding, it is fitting to ask: What are the conditions of "martyrdom" today? Is torture a necessary component, or is anyone who dies for a belief a martyr? From whose perspective is torture a legitimate exercise to induce compliance? And finally, whose martyrdom counts as martyrdom?

4 Maccabees 14:11—18:19: The Mother of the Seven

The Text in Its Ancient Context

The author of 4 Maccabees combines ancient Greek gender stereotypes with examples from nature in his presentation of the mother of the seven martyrs. This figure, whose depiction derives also from 2 Maccabees (7:20-41), provides the climactic example in the author's "narrative demonstration" of reason over the passions. While the mother is not named in any of the earliest sources, rabbinic traditions call her Hannah or Miriam bat Tanhum, later Greek sources name her Solomone, and Syriac texts refer to her as Mart Simouni (Young, 67).

It was generally assumed in ancient Greek contexts that there was a "natural" correspondence between men/reason and women/passion, and that the former held pride of place over the latter (for a classic formulation, see Aristotle, *Pol.* 1.13). If the (male) children were able to overcome the passions with reason, goes the argument in 4 Maccabees, how much more remarkable that a woman—and a mother—would do so (cf. Xenophon, *Oec.* 7.24). This, then, is the ultimate effect of torah piety: it allows even a woman to become "like Abraham" in faithfulness, bracing her also to experience the appalling deaths of her sons.

Fourth Maccabees contrasts the expected "this-worldly" and "fainthearted" response of a mother who has lost everything (16:5-11) with that of the mother of the seven martyrs, whose steadfast purpose was to "rebirth" them for an immortality accomplished by witnessing to the faith. Fourth Maccabees even draws on the Septuagint (Greek) translation of Deut. 33:3 to make the argument that the martyrs have found their eternal home with God.

In this section, 4 Maccabees uses the language of martyrdom ("witness") in an explicit way, while also adapting the imagery of athletic contests to the trial of the mother and sons (17:11-16). Here the heroes are "athletes of the divine legislation," a trope that has echoes in other early Jewish literature and that derives from ancient Greek ideas about the practice and endurance of the virtuous sage (see, e.g., Philo on the Essenes, *Prob.* 88–91; Josephus, *Ant.* 18; 20). Here, as in Greek and Roman athletic games, the "athletes" have spectators whose presence serves to heighten the drama and to provide additional energy and legendary status to the heroes.

Fourth Maccabees presents the mother's suicide as the only honorable way for her to meet her end (cf. Plutarch, *Mulier. virt.* 15 [*Mor.* 240C–263C]; and the depiction of Hecuba in Euripides' *Trojan Women* 1282–83). In this way, she avoids improper handling by the soldiers and accomplishes both the preservation of her womanly chastity and the expression of her manly courage—which, in the view of the author, is the highest possible attainment of virtue.

The final passages in this section (17:7—18:5) represent the author's closing perorations, written in a style reminiscent of Hellenistic honorary inscriptions and *epitaphios logos* (see deSilva, 242–44). The final exhortations use the self-sacrifices—the victories of pious reason—of the martyrs to encourage the audiences of 4 Maccabees to continue their witness to the integrity of the Jewish way of life.

The Text in the Interpretive Tradition

Traditions involving the mother of the seven are plentiful. She is first mentioned only briefly in 2 Maccabees, and thus the elaborations of her account in 4 Maccabees appear to serve as the primary basis for later interpretive presentations.

The only known Jewish tradition associated with the mother of the seven comes from *Lamentations Rabbah*, an early interpretive work on the biblical book of Lamentations. This midrash throughout juxtaposes Athens and Jerusalem, elevating the latter fallen city above the former in prestige and piety—and perhaps for this reason invokes motifs from 4 Maccabees. In a passage depicting the martyrdom of Miriam bat Tanhum and her seven sons under the rule of Roman emperor Hadrian (117–138 CE), *Lamentations Rabbah* adapts 4 Maccabees to a later persecution under a different ruler—one closer in time and cultural context to that of the early rabbis. This midrash, like 4 Maccabees, likens the mother to Abraham and even promotes her above him. The mother says, "You built one altar [for Isaac] and did not sacrifice your son, but I built seven altars and sacrificed my sons on them. And for that matter, yours was a trial, but mine was a fact" (*Lam. Rab.* 1.16 N; Henten and Avemarie, 150). The comparison with Abraham is found also in early Christian traditions (e.g., *Martyrdom of Montanus and Lucius* 16.3–4).

If 4 Maccabees asserts any influence on New Testament writings, the Epistle to the Hebrews seems the most likely candidate. Hebrews and 4 Maccabees share thematic emphasis upon the role of (self-)sacrifice as it relates to atonement, the centrality of faith, and the eternal rewards for the righteous. The two texts even evidence several verbal parallels that may indicate a direct relationship (e.g., 4 Macc. 17:4; Heb. 3:6, 14).

The Text in Contemporary Discussion

Depictions of gender and virtue in 4 Maccabees have special importance in contemporary discussions of this text. The most obvious point of contemporary controversy would be the way 4 Maccabees incorporates Greco-Roman assumptions about "the sexes"—namely, that women are associated with the body and the passions and men with reason and piety, and that the latter has higher status than the former. This dichotomy is also put to use, for example, by the *Gospel of Thomas* (114: "every woman who will make herself male will enter the kingdom of heaven") and Philo (e.g., *QE* 1.8; see Tobin, 32), and it has a long history in Western ideas about sex, gender, and their relation to language and social and economic life (Boyarin).

The point of view of 4 Maccabees is challenged by a modern feminist tradition that (arguably) begins with Elizabeth Cady Stanton's *The Woman's Bible* and, later, Simone de Beauvoir's *The Second Sex*, and continues through many different trajectories of feminist criticism. Beginning in the 1960s, feminist theologians such as Mary Daly and Rosemary Radford Ruether began to challenge patriarchal and paternalistic assumptions about sex and gender, proposing new and compelling ways to read the Bible that drew from the full scope of feminist theory.

Moore and Anderson argue that the theme of gender and virtue in 4 Maccabees "denigrates women's biology and constructs female gender negatively" (Moore and Anderson, 269), and they seek to offer a critical reading of the text that deconstructs its gender assumptions. They note, too, that not only is the mother's victory masculinized in 4 Maccabees, but also Antiochus's defeat is "feminized" insofar as he gives in to his passions and becomes a "failed man" (252–64). Mary Rose D'Angelo sees the sudden emergence of the father of the seven sons in 4 Macc. 18:9-19 as another sign of the author's worldview—he represents the "family values" of piety and reason, and thus takes his "rightful" place as the primary teacher of torah (D'Angelo, 156–57).

4 Maccabees 18:20-24: Conclusion

Fourth Maccabees concludes by rehearsing its main points and closes with a doxology reminiscent of other ancient texts (Heb. 13:21; 2 Tim. 4:18). In the Hebrew Bible generally, the phrase "to be gathered to one's fathers" conveys a notion of death that rests on the metaphor of burial—literally to be buried in the family tomb and deposited in Sheol, and to be remembered as one among the ancestors. In 4 Maccabees, the promise of gathering and memory is framed in terms of eternal life, reflecting the widespread Jewish adoption of Hellenistic ideas about immortality during the late Second Temple period. Thus the work closes on a note that reiterates its central idea: eternal life is preferable to temporary satisfactions, and it is made possible by steadfast commitment to pious reason—and to a life of honor and religious integrity.

Works Cited

Boyarin, Daniel. 1998. "Gender." In *Critical Terms for Religious Studies*, edited by Mark C. Taylor, 117–35. Chicago: University of Chicago Press.

Collins, John J. 1997. *Jewish Wisdom in the Hellenistic Age*. Louisville: Westminster John Knox.

D'Angelo, Mary Rose. 2003. "*Eusebeia*: Roman Imperial Family Values and the Sexual Politics of 4 Maccabees and the Pastorals." *BibInt* 11:139–65.

DeSilva, David. 2006. *4 Maccabees: Introduction and Commentary on the Greek Text in Codex Sinaiticus*. Leiden: Brill.

Henten, Jan Willem van, and Friedrich Avemarie. 2002. *Martyrdom and Noble Death: Selected Texts from Graeco-Roman, Jewish, and Christian Antiquity*. London: Routledge.

Moore, Stephen D., and Janice Capel Anderson. 1998. "Taking It Like a Man: Masculinity in 4 Maccabees." *JBL* 117:249–73.

Tobin, Thomas H. 1983. *The Creation of Man: Philo and the History of Interpretation*. CBQMS 14. Washington, DC: Catholic Biblical Association of America.

VanderKam, James. 2004. *From Joshua to Caiaphas: High Priests after the Exile*. Minneapolis: Fortress Press.

Young, Robin Darling. 1991. "The 'Woman with the Soul of Abraham': Traditions about the Mother of the Maccabean Martyrs." In *Women Like This: New Perspectives on Jewish Women in the Greco-Roman World*, edited by Amy-Jill Levine, 67–81. Atlanta: Scholars Press.